CREOLE INDIGENEITY

CREOLE INDIGENEITY

Between Myth and Nation in the Caribbean

SHONA N. JACKSON

FIRST PEOPLES
New Directions in Indigenous Studies

UNIVERSITY OF MINNESOTA PRESS

MINNEAPOLIS • LONDON

Publication of this book was made possible, in part,
with a grant from the Andrew W. Mellon Foundation.

Epigraph "Birds" was originally published in *A Tempest* by Aimé Césaire, translated
by Richard Miller. Copyright 1969 by Aimé Césaire. Copyright English translation 1985, 1992.
Published by Theatre Communications Group. Used by permission of
Theatre Communications Group.

Epigraph "Natural Ways" was originally published by The Hamburgh Register, 1998.
Copyright 1998 by Basil Rodrigues. Reprinted by permission of Basil Rodrigues.

Portions of chapter 3 were previously published as "Subjection and
Resistance in the Transformation of Guyana's Mytho-colonial Landscape," in
Caribbean Literature and the Environment: Between Nature and Culture, ed.
Elizabeth DeLoughrey et al., 85–98 (Charlottesville: University of Virginia Press, 2005).
Portions of chapter 4 were previously published as "Guyana, Cuba, Venezuela,
and the 'Routes' to Cultural Reconciliation between Latin America and the
Caribbean," *Small Axe: A Caribbean Journal of Criticism* 19 (2006): 28–58.
Portions of the Introduction and chapter 5 were previously published as
"On the 'Threshold of Nationhood': The Politics of Language and the
Contemporary Crisis in Guyanese National Identification," in *Ethnicity, Class,
and Nationalism: Caribbean and Extra Caribbean Dimensions,* ed.
Anton Allahar, 85–120 Lanham, Md. Lexington Books, 2005.

Every effort was made to obtain permission to reproduce material used in
this book. If any proper acknowledgment has not been made, we encourage
copyright holders to notify us.

Published by the University of Minnesota Press
111 Third Avenue South, Suite 290
Minneapolis, MN 55401-2520
http://www.upress.umn.edu

Library of Congress Cataloging-in-Publication Data

Jackson, Shona N.
Creole indigeneity : between myth and nation in the Caribbean / Shona N. Jackson.
(First peoples : new directions in indigenous studies)
Includes bibliographical references and index.
ISBN 978-0-8166-7775-7 (hardcover : acid-free paper)
ISBN 978-0-8166-7776-4 (pbk. : acid-free paper)
1. Creoles—Race identity—Guyana. 2. Creoles—Guyana—Social conditions.
3. Indigenous peoples—Guyana. 4. Myth—Social aspects—Guyana. 5. Nationalism—
Social aspects—Guyana. 6. Guyana—Colonial influence. 7. Guyana—Race relations.
8. Myth—Social aspects—Caribbean Area. 9. Nationalism—Social aspects—
Caribbean Area. 10. Caribbean Area—Colonial influence. I. Title.
F2391.A1J33 2012
305.8009881—dc23
2012030016

Printed in the United States of America on acid-free paper

The University of Minnesota is an equal-opportunity educator and employer.

20 19 18 17 16 15 14 13 12   10 9 8 7 6 5 4 3 2 1

For

CELESTINE WILLIAMS, JOYCELYN SQUIRES, JENNIFER JACKSON,

and

AYIRA

exile thus goes into the feeder made of stars
bearing clumsy grains to the birds born of time . . .

> —Aimé Césaire, "Birds"

Out for a long walk along the path I wandered.
What I once took for granted now I see.
Birds sang to me of the joy of being free
as they, the hawk and kiskidee.
Acushi ants and wasps worked united;
laden jamoon branches giving alms
to birds and flies and worms;
dark shadows, dreaded hawk flashes by.
Birds echo a warning cry,
"Escape your death—fly, now fly!"

> —Basil Rodrigues, "Natural Ways"

Contents

Preface

THIS WORK HAS ITS ORIGINS IN THE LATE 1970S AND EARLY 1980S, WHEN, growing up in Guyana, I experienced something that has stayed with me ever since. Every afternoon around four o'clock, sunlight would flood our family's living room, and our already hot house in South Ruimveldt became unbearable, especially when the curtains were open. At the same time, what was then and is still often dismissively referred to, in an undifferentiated way, as "East Indian" music would begin to play on the radio that had been on since morning.[1] My grandmother would call my brother and me from our favorite spot, the veranda, then close the shades and shut off the radio until the sun changed position. When I finally met my half–Indo-Guyanese grandfather, who lived in London and brought me English currency as a gift, I did not yet understand the significance of what my grandmother, who never spoke of him, had done. I did not yet understand why this family, which looked Afro-Guyanese, spoke in pejorative terms about Indo-Guyanese and could only refer to my maternal great-great-grandmother as "Lady Buck."[2]

While many Guyanese admit that they are mixed, we figuratively close the shades on other parts of our blood, ignoring the meeting of worlds within us in order to assert our identities as historical continuity and not as "limbo." After years of inarticulate longing dissolved into an English pound from my grandfather, whose migration to England by plane and by boat on the MV *Venezuela* preceded ours to U.S. territory by two decades, I began to understand how empire and the legacy of colonial domination continued to mediate our cultural relationships in Guyana, our concepts of self and place. I saw how Guyanese and other Caribbean peoples came to belong to the land to which so few could be considered "indigenous" by tacitly accepting the shared culture created while relying on fragments to assert a historical right to belong that could provide legitimacy for contemporary claims to power. They did this alongside genuine efforts to mobilize and reorganize labor and the historical relationship to work of Guyanese under colonialism, such as those of my great-uncle, the late Gordon Todd. More important, I saw how the Afro-Creole nationalism, to which my grandmother unconsciously responded, worked. Looking back, I do with this book what I longed to but could not as a child, dutifully outfitted in my "Burnham bedding"; I ask the sun to shine brightest in a different spot, to illuminate those interwoven histories beneath the surface, so that I could stay in mine. My ultimate hope is that so-called Third World societies, economically and culturally marginal (to the North and West), can fulfill the potential of their liminality, the potential to create true alternates and alternatives to European modernities that *do not* on any level require forms of subordination.

Creole Indigeneity: Between Myth and Nation in the Caribbean is fundamentally concerned with the conflicts of blood and history that can be transformed with the turn of a dial or drawing of a curtain into the antecedents of daily life. It is a sometimes formal, and sometimes informal, discussion with the humanist work of Sylvia Wynter and an attempt to take seriously her insistence that at base there needs to be awareness of the ways in which humanity is "rule governed" and beholden to the continuous "autoinstituting" of the "terms of our culture." The book is thus partly motivated by Wynter's generalized attempt to literally move us out of our present "ethnoclass" mode of producing global humanity and subjectivity by revealing just how this mode of being works or is enacted in the social and historical context of the modern Caribbean. By revealing the architecture of our collective being, the book seeks to empower us to become more self-critical participants in our cultures and ultimately from those positions of being and seeing, to change them.

Introduction

AJI AYA BOMBE!
("Better dead than a slave!")

—TAINO CHIEF GUARIONEX OF OTUAO

GUYANA EXTENDS VERTICALLY INTO SOUTH AMERICA. THE BULK OF its inhabitants, Indians and blacks, live in or near the capital on the Atlantic coast. Much of its indigenous population is spread out on reservations closest to the coast, such as the Moruca Reservation in the North-West District, down through the interior savannahs and forests to the southern border with Brazil.[1] In December 2006, a Cuban friend and I made the half-day trip over land and by motorboat from Paradise on the East Coast to Moruca in order to meet the Lokono/Arawak writer Basil Rodrigues. With only two solar-powered phones for all of Moruca, it took several days to reach Rodrigues, and upon arrival we still needed to obtain permission to enter the reservation, which must be granted by the Toshao or chief. On the trip itself, we watched the landscape change from Georgetown's overcrowded and busy streets to an abundance of vegetation dotted with homes mostly made of wood. In Moruca we saw small homes of concrete and wood, some set closely together, and one dry goods store. On the final leg of the trip, from the market at Charity on the Pomeroon River, where heaps of fresh palm fronds waited to be transported, there were only three nonindigenous passengers left: me, my friend, and a Portuguese priest returning to the small church in the Santa Rosa village.

The changes in the landscape that accompanied my visit to Rodrigues reflect a natural geography familiar to Guyanese. The changes in the indigenous status of those in the boat reflect another: the remapping of space with the economic and cultural geography of colonial and postcolonial modernity. A look at this geography reveals that the division between "interior" and "coast" that shaped my access to Rodrigues is neither natural nor a reflection of how indigenous or First Peoples viewed and used the land. During the colonial period in Guyana, which lasted from Dutch rule in the early seventeenth century until independence from Britain in the latter half of the twentieth century, the coast was converted into plantations worked by enslaved labor from Africa and indentured labor, the bulk of which came from India. Following the expropriation of their lands, Indigenous Peoples largely retreated and were forced from the Atlantic coast and essentially outside of the plantation economy and its regimes of coercive labor, though their existence continued to be profoundly shaped by it. The interior is today considerably underdeveloped in relation to Georgetown and surrounding areas, despite its mining, cattle, and other industries that employ indigenous labor as well as Indian (Indo-Creole) and black (Afro-Creole) workers. In other words, it persists as a space of underdevelopment in relation to those areas of Guyana that were more fully integrated into the colonial political economy and that remain the center of postcolonial political economy and governance.

Emerging within the "contact zone" of Europe and the Americas, the distinction between the "native" interior and the "Creole" coast in Guyana iterates a historical, economic, and philosophical division that shapes this book and its dual critique of early modern and Enlightenment humanism and the project of postcolonial nationalism in Guyana: between Europe and its others; between the execution and limits of the social contract; and between the Global North and the Global South. Within this context, I locate this exploration of how Creoles and Indigenous Peoples within the postcolonial state come to be subject to different narratives of belonging and forms of citizenship and sovereignty. This book scrutinizes the ways in which blacks and Indians established belonging and legitimacy in the New World as they transitioned from embeddedness in the myths that *preceded* the establishment of plantations and shaped European discovery to postcolonial nationhood. Between the myth of great wealth waiting to be discovered in the New World and the nation-states that eventually emerged as expressions or completions of rational capitalism, offering social rebirth from colonialism, Creoles come to belong, or indigenize. I argue that the resultant disarticulation of aboriginal and Creole identities reflects the way in which Creole material and metaphysical belonging (indigeneity) to the New World evolved through two intertwined and necessary phenomena.

The first is the real and figurative displacement of Indigenous Peoples. It is through their marginalization across the Caribbean that the colonial map was first drawn and that the postcolonial one has been redrawn as a reflection of settler-Creole social being and material right. Despite having been in the Caribbean islands for at least 6,000 years and in the mainland territories for twice that length of time, Indigenous Peoples have largely faced the substitution of cultural representation for political power.[2] In contrast, the descendants of enslaved and indentured peoples hold a greater degree of cultural and political power, with better access to capital. In this book, I demonstrate that displacement and objectification of Indigenous Peoples is a complex part of the new material and ontological relationship that blacks and Indians developed to the land under colonialism, and it cannot strictly be understood through the terms of white settler colonial paradigms such as those of North America. Nor can it be singularly figured through dominant binary approaches to Caribbean identities that see them either in terms of subaltern versus hegemonic European, especially prior to independence, or in terms of a struggle among majority racial or ethnic groups. It requires the difficult assessing of Creoles as themselves settlers because of the ways in which they maintain power within the postcolonial state. In dominant settler colonial paradigms, it is the white settler who holds power compared to minority groups. However, we must begin to address the ways in which, in the Caribbean and even within settler states like the United States that fit the dominant model, those brought in as forced labor (racialized capital) now contribute to the disenfranchisement of Indigenous Peoples. This work is happening for other settler contexts such as Canada and Hawai'i. In the latter, for instance, the edited volume *Asian Settler Colonialism* is devoted to examining how Asians brought to labor in Hawai'i starting in the late nineteenth century now function as settlers in relation to the indigenous Kānaka Maoli.[3] For Canada, Bonita Lawrence and Enakshi Dua claim that critical race theory and postcolonial theory neglect Indigenous Peoples because they do not recognize "the ways in which the entry of people of color into Canada put them in colonial relationships with Aboriginal peoples."[4] This perspectival shift in how we understand settler colonialism forces us to look beyond the (white) body of the settler and instead look at how within what Jodi Byrd calls "arrivant colonialism," even those ethnic groups coercively brought into a territory in which Indigenous Peoples exist now hold identities through which settler colonial power works affectively: whether deliberately or unwittingly, they extend the colonial subordination of Indigenous Peoples.[5] While Caribbean societies were largely envisioned as colonies of exploitation, and in the Anglophone Caribbean whites remained a minority that diminished with independence, I deliberately employ the loaded term *settler* to describe formerly enslaved and indentured peoples in order to recast the struggle among indigenous, black, and Indo-Caribbean peoples in the region. My goal is to illuminate the particular power dynamic of settler and native that continues to inform Caribbean social reality and identity formation.

The second phenomenon is the introduction of a new, more socially viable mode of being to which political and material right are attached: labor. The raison d'être for the introduction of enslaved and indentured workers into the Caribbean, labor becomes the dominant social discourse around which Creoles form new identities: the basis for their subaltern, settler modes of indigeneity and power. In the Taino declaration that it is "better" to be "dead" than enslaved, the choice then is not simply one of being or not being free, but of rejecting modes of belonging that are determined by modern, coercive labor.[6] The formation of identities that hinge on modern labor (even the development of a language of resistance within it) ultimately reflects an investment in an idea of time as progress (read development). It results in the supplanting of indigenous or pre-Columbian time, which is marked as "prior" and less legitimate when determining political and social rights. Labor thus becomes what I refer to in chapter 1 as the new "time of belonging" for Creole settler groups and societies. As the product of the labor of the enslaved and indentured in the Caribbean, the postcolonial state is perceived as an ethnic inheritance for Creoles, not for Indigenous Peoples. Thus we are left with two senses of indigeneity: Creole ones that are associated with material accumulation, and those of Indigenous Peoples, such as Rodrigues, that come to be associated with deprivation and underdevelopment.

To address the former in terms of its difference from and relation to the latter, I make the unconventional move in this book of first uncoupling "native," as an identity used by both Indigenous Peoples *and* Creoles in the Caribbean, from indigeneity. In doing this, I recognize "native" as first an objective identification of Indigenous Peoples that positions them with regard to European time and Renaissance through Enlightenment modes of determining humanity, and second as a term appropriated by Creoles to signal fixity with regard to belonging. In contrast to "native," indigeneity emerges as the practices and processes that constitute belonging for Creoles and Indigenous Peoples. I then develop and deploy the term "Creole indigeneity" as a conceptual lens or analytic. From Guyana's particularity, I introduce a theory of Creole indigeneity to suggest that modern Caribbean history and discourse are driven dialectically not *only* by external forms of conflict or even internal conflict between majority groups. They are also driven by the opposition between settler *practices* of belonging (in this case Creole) and indigenous ones and the ways in which they reproduce the conflict between labor and capital, and between idealist and materialist critical practices and cultural forms of expression.

This focus on indigeneity is meant to achieve a rewriting of the dominant modes of cultural historiography in the Caribbean through an elaboration of both why and how the continued subordination of Indigenous Peoples shapes postcolonial nationalism and social being for Creoles. While black subordination is often considered foundational for European modernity, I hope to demonstrate that it is more complexly intertwined with the subordination of Indigenous Peoples, requiring their marginalization during the colonial era and their continued marginalization under postcolonial governments, which—like Guyana's—see the right to rule and control state resources as belonging to their majority groups. In challenging the singular assertion by Paul Gilroy—son of Guyanese writer Beryl Gilroy—and others that slavery is foundational within modernity, Lawrence and Dua, for instance, "wonder about the claim that modernity began with slavery . . . rather than with the genocide and colonization of Indigenous peoples in the Americas that preceded it. . . ."[7] I agree with Lawrence and Dua but maintain that it is not a matter of either blacks *or* Indigenous Peoples, but it is the relationship into which they are placed under colonialism that is definitive for Caribbean modernity.

Creole Indigeneity is located within two broad intellectual trajectories in North American indigenous studies and in Caribbean studies. Examples of the former include Shari M. Huhndorf's *Going Native: Indians in the American Cultural Imagination* and Philip J. Deloria's *Playing Indian,* which look— as this book does for Caribbean Creole identity—at how native identity is used to define and maintain what it means to be American.[8] In Caribbean studies, the work sits in conversation with that of scholars such as Sylvia Wynter, Elizabeth Deloughrey, and Maximilian Forte, who have substantively dealt with Creole identity *and* indigeneity in the Caribbean. Wynter has usefully argued for creolization to be understood as an indigenizing process. In their work, Forte (anthropology) and DeLoughrey (literature) trace the significance of indigeneity within postcolonial society and culture. Collectively, these works reflect both a reconceptualization of indigeneity and, with Forte and DeLoughrey, an approach to Creole society that suggests the need to make indigeneity a central consideration in discussions of Caribbean society, theory, and cultural production. This book adds to these discussions by shifting our attention from white settler engagements with Indigenous Peoples to focus on the lingering coloniality of belonging in postcolonial

Creole societies. Its attention to indigeneity and creolization as intertwined and interdependent in the production of both material right and socio-political belonging in the postcolonial state is meant to contribute to the discussion on settler colonialism in the Americas through its rethinking of the relationship among subaltern, settler, and "native" populations in the Caribbean.

Creole Indigeneity is *not* a study of indigenous groups in the Caribbean and their modes of being and belonging or their own mobilization of labor for such purposes. It is *not* a cultural study of Indigenous Peoples (called Amerindians) in Guyana. It may frustrate some readers, but as much as possible this book rejects the ethnographic project as an essential component of work on Indigenous Peoples in the academy. The book is concerned, however, with the *concept* of indigeneity, its reinvention, and its deployment in the assertion of Creole belonging. Its primary focus is Guyana; the aim is to demonstrate how what appears natural in Guyana reflects divisions that, as indicated previously, have economic, philosophical, and historical consequences for it and for the region. The book can be divided into two sections. The first section, which includes the rest of this introduction and chapters 1 and 2, elucidates the concept of Creole indigeneity and addresses how early modern and Enlightenment modes of producing subjectivity inform postcolonial citizenship in Guyana, making necessary the displacement of Indigenous Peoples in the Creole's ability to sustain a sovereign existence within the parameters of European modernity. The second section, which contains chapters 3 to 5, addresses the displacement of Indigenous Peoples inside postcolonial nationalism as well as the transformation of Creoles into natives, although both of these critical impulses overlap throughout.

I begin by briefly laying out Guyana's political landscape, with a discussion of prominent national symbols. I also outline Guyana's role in the book through an elaboration of the divisions that inform this study.

The Politics of Symbols: Cuffy and the Umana Yana

Emancipation in the English-speaking Caribbean in the nineteenth century saw the introduction of Indian, Chinese, and Portuguese indentured laborers, among others, to work on the plantations that formerly enslaved blacks were leaving. Together, these groups came to form a culturally and racially mixed, or Creole, population and a complex social fabric. As most Anglophone countries surged toward independence in the 1960s, of paramount

importance was the struggle to guarantee control of limited economic resources and labor power as well as the political legitimacy of individual
ethnic groups. In Guyana, the struggle crystallized around the two leading
political figures: the Afro-Guyanese Linden Forbes Sampson Burnham and
the Indo-Guyanese Cheddi Bharat Jagan. The split of their shared political
party, the Peoples Progressive Party (PPP), in the 1950s, coupled with intervention by the United States and Britain to get rid of the "communist" threat
posed by Jagan, cemented a divisive and lasting cultural politics. At times,
this has led to widespread violence, prompting the writer Eusi Kwayana (formerly Sydney King) to call in the 1960s for the breakup of the country into
three zones: one for blacks, one for "East Indians," and a "free" zone.[9]

Kwayana's ethnic geography unintentionally recalls Dutch demarcation
of what would become independent Guyana into three administrative regions:
Berbice, Demerara, and Essequibo. His call—a return at least ideologically
to a division that is fundamentally colonial—is literally the writing over of
space with the ethnic and racial demarcations of colonialism. It reflects the
fact that since the late 1950s, Guyana has experienced the "fragmented
nationalism" by which Franklin W. Knight characterized the entire Caribbean. However, in Guyana, the split between the black lawyer Burnham and
the Indian dentist Jagan, who went on to form the two dominant ethnic
political parties, is less divisive concerning the country's indigenous population. Behind both their individual, labor-oriented, nationalist visions has
been the displacement of Indigenous Peoples.

In Guyana, where Indigenous Peoples today are 9.2 percent of the population, the Umana Yana provides one of the best examples of their relative
cultural embrace and simultaneous political marginalization.[10] The Umana
Yana is a 55-foot-tall, cone-shaped *benhab* (shelter), a large replica of the
ones used by Indigenous Peoples living in the interior or hinterland of the
country. Members of the indigenous Waiwai were brought from the southern
Rupununi to Georgetown, the center of social and political life in Guyana,
and commissioned to build the structure for the Non-Aligned Foreign Min-
isters Conference in August 1972.[11] The Umana Yana has continued to host
cultural events, some in celebration of indigenous culture. However, at a ceremony there in 2000 for the dedication of the work of the poet, essayist,
activist, and champion of political and cultural freedoms Martin Carter, I
asked Prime Minister Samuel Hinds's wife, Yvonne, about the use of the
facility by indigenous groups for their own events. Her response was, "No!
This is our national thing."[12]

The Umana Yana. Photograph by author.

Hinds's response at an event that depoliticizes Carter's own anticolonial agitation and eventual opposition to both Burnham and Jagan is illuminating. It reveals the conspicuous use of indigenous culture to represent the "national thing." Her articulation of a distinction between the nation as a Creole one and an indigenous cultural element subsumed within it echoes and serves as a solution to a problem identified by Wayne Jones in 1981. Jones is the author of a study written for the Ministry of Information about the development of the Guyanese interior, which is repeatedly framed as the "development of the natives." In the study, Jones addresses the 1969 Rupununi Rebellion, in which a group of ranchers and Indigenous Peoples backed by Venezuela—which in defiance of an 1899 Arbitral Award continues to maintain that two-thirds of modern Guyana belongs to it—revolted against the Guyana government. Jones surmises that the rebellion occurred in large part because "the natives have a vague sense of nationalism," fostering an "unawareness" of the border dispute with Venezuela, which "poses a threat to the defense of the territory."[13] While Jones is echoing the Burnham administration's plan to develop the interior and integrate Indigenous Peoples into

Guyanese cultural life, he also alerts us to the disarticulation of indigenous and national identity, demonstrating the way in which the postcolonial nation-state is not a reflection of the desire or sentiment of its most marginalized groups. Jones and Hinds reveal the fragility of the "national thing" and the peculiar tension around what it includes and what it excludes. Their claims show recognition that when Indigenous Peoples assert identity and belonging in *other* than national terms, they represent a threat. Yet, the appropriation of indigenous culture allows for the depiction of national roots that are precolonial, even if the borrowing itself is ultimately anti-indigenous and neocolonial. The Umana Yana thus emerges as a powerful political symbol for controlling indigenous difference and its disruptive potential. It also reveals that the Creole (settler) state has a double approach to indigenous groups: a cultural embrace alongside policies that maintain their economic and political marginalization.

Across town from the Umana Yana sits another national symbol that is no less problematic: the statue of the former slave, Cuffy, who led the most famous rebellion for black freedom in Guyana.[14] In the early 1960s, Jagan and Burnham shared the hope that the date of Guyanese independence from Britain could be the anniversary of the February 23, 1763, rebellion.[15] Cuffy at the time represented a broad symbol of anticolonial resistance rather than any specific ethnic group. However, independence was not granted until May 26, 1966, the anniversary of one of the most violent attacks against Indians (especially Indian women) by blacks two years prior in the predominantly black area of Wismar/Christianburg/MacKenzie, renamed Linden after independence and in honor of Burnham.[16] The anniversary of the Cuffy rebellion instead came to mark the Burnham administration's establishment a few years later of the Co-operative Republic of Guyana, envisioned as the "fulfillment" of Cuffy's bid for liberation.[17] In declaring Guyana a republic, Burnham said of the rebellion that "it is the contention of the Party in Government that the establishment of the Republic of Guyana should coincide with the celebration and/or anniversary of an event of peculiar Guyanese significance" because "a country without its own history, without its own heroes, without its own legends, I contend, would find it difficult to survive."[18] Thus, the making of Cuffy into a postcolonial national hero who represented both plantation labor and resistance to it became wedded to a black, pan-Africanist nationalism.

The erection of the statue symbolized the consolidation of Afro-Creole nationalism and political power in the country under the Burnham regime, which interpreted the right to rule Guyana as a cultural right for blacks. The Cuffy imagined by Jagan and Burnham in the early 1960s as a national symbol is not, therefore, the same that today stands across from the old presidential residence. The statue is a reminder of both the hoped-for vision of national unity and the evaporation of that vision when the PPP split along racial lines. That split continues to manifest itself in ethnic antagonism, such as the violence that occurred during the 1997 election.[19] Shortly after that election, the statue of Cuffy was routinely defaced by the dumping of trash at its base.[20] In the defacement we read one mode of query and possible rejection of black nationalism in Guyana. The eventual ascension of Jagan to the presidency aside, another is the success of the decades-long attempt to make a holiday, Indian Arrival Day, commemorating the start of Indian indentured servitude in the nineteenth century. The institutionalization of this holiday, to which I return in chapter 5, implicitly challenges the political rights blacks claim from having constructed themselves as more legitimate inheritors of the nation than both Indigenous Peoples and Indians.[21] Additionally, monuments such as Enmore Martyrs, which commemorates slain Indo-Guyanese workers, seek equal purchase on the national imaginary. While the Creole slave Cuffy may have been the "first" and most memorable national symbol, according to government and popular narratives that ignore early indigenous resistance to colonialism, Indian Arrival Day secures the narrative of having "rescued" the colony after emancipation.[22]

Cuffy thus stands as a black symbol for an entire nation that is not black and for a narrative of social, economic, and political progress that links the labor and resistance of enslaved peoples to the economy of the nation-state. Collectively, however, Cuffy, Enmore, and the Umana Yana represent the symbolic reification of two different modes of belonging within the state. The former represent belonging (again, read: indigeneity) and social being grounded in anticolonial resistance and labor resistance, while the latter represents a reduction to a largely culturally understood presence not tied to plantation labor. Rather, Indigenous Peoples are tied to the interior in the political and cultural imagination of the nation, regardless of the presence in Georgetown of, for example, the Amerindian Peoples Association (APA), a civil organization begun by Indigenous Peoples, and the government's Ministry of Amerindian Affairs. As a postcolonial national symbol, the Umana Yana renders their labor visible only as *cultural,* not the productive labor of economic development that allows the formerly enslaved and indentured to claim belonging and political right.

This mapping of Guyana's ethnopolitical situation in terms of its symbols reveals a relationship between labor and nation that brackets indigenous differences that are inscribed within the country's physical geography. Moreover, in the national symbols we see another inscription of the division of coast (Cuffy) and interior (Umana Yana) and its clear connection to politics. These symbols render natural the broad differences of Indigenous Peoples and Creoles, which leads in this book to a consideration of *both* Afro- and Indo-Creole subjectivities in later chapters. Not only do they naturalize these differences, but they obscure a way of relating to the actual and political landscape of the country in terms of its real mapping—the historical, economic, and philosophical divisions that extend into the postcolonial era the marginalization of Indigenous Peoples under colonialism.

First, the division is historical rather than "natural" because it makes sense within the West's conception of its own history as universal. In this conception, the Lockean social contract that informs the development of modern European social and political structures is applied to the New World during the colonial period, where it is transformed into what Carole Pateman calls a "settler contract" that renders native space *terra nullius*. Thus, the "state of nature" with which Indigenous Peoples have been overidentified is "replaced by civil societies" in one form of the contract, while in another, Pateman argues, aspects of indigenous society that do not conflict with the new contract are allowed to remain.[23] Pateman's is an attempt to deal separately with the issue of *terra nullius* as a key feature of the domination of Indigenous Peoples and space that Charles Mills discusses in *The Racial Contract*. Outside Europe, Mills argues, when the "social contract" takes effect it is transformed into a "racial contract" in which "both space and its inhabitants are alien."[24] Further, Mills argues, "since the Racial Contract links space with race and race with personhood, the white raced space of the polity is in a sense the geographical locus of the polity proper. Where indigenous peoples were permitted to survive, they were denied full or any membership in the political community. . . ."[25] Mills therefore claims that non-Europeans consequently are overidentified with the "state of nature," while whites are identified with "civil society." Of the former, Mill adds, "this raced space will also mark the geographic boundary of the state's full obligations. . . . Thus, one of the interesting consequences of the Racial Contract is that the *political space* of the polity is not coextensive with its *geographical space*."[26]

Following Mills and Pateman, I suggest that in Guyana the settler contract applies to the coastal area, while the interior exists at the limits of that contract, more broadly falling within a racial contract (for our purposes, a structure of feeling with real effects) that justifies differential treatment of its inhabitants. Thus while blacks, Indians, and Indigenous Peoples are fully raced subjects within European history, the former are identified thoroughly with civil society. The spaces Creoles inhabit (Georgetown and surrounding areas, some of which can be considered remote) are not "white" spaces but fall more completely within Eurowestern structures of governance. Indigenous Peoples, in contrast, come to be associated with an underdeveloped, wild, and raced space that is largely outside the plantation economy and society and that continued retellings of the myth of El Dorado, the subject of chapter 3, still manage. As Brackette F. Williams notes in her influential study of ethnicity and nationalism in Guyana, "The interior became the Natives' physical place and the symbolic source of their rights and privileges within the total sociocultural order."[27]

The position of Indigenous Peoples outside the colonial state is clearly documented. Mary Noel Menezes demonstrates in *British Policy towards the Amerindians in British Guiana, 1803–1873* that Amerindians were crucial for both colonial Dutch and British survival. Nonetheless, she observes that they were seen during British colonialism as outside the state and only marginally useful within it. Thus, while Menezes's book contains in its appendices copies of documents that clearly address indigenous labor, she also notes about the colony's governing body that ". . . the policy of the Combined Court was to have no policy towards the Indians, for they were outside the body politic and economic and were of negative value, good for nothing."[28] In Guyana, the interior is the last remaining space undeveloped by white colonials onto which blacks can shift the narrative of civilization. In the continued deployment of colonial logic within the postcolonial state, to leave it underdeveloped would be to prove black inferiority. The indigenous body, collapsed with this space, remains that which must be but cannot fully be integrated, civilized, or developed, forcing the state to maintain a contradictory approach to Indigenous Peoples and their lands, which simultaneously represent the limit and measure of black humanity within the modern state.

Second, the division is economic, because the postcolonial state in its historical relation to the colonial state maintains itself as that which moves forward in time and history toward greater accumulation of capital, with its interior remaining underdeveloped yet perceived as a source of potential material and cultural wealth for the coast and its largely Creole inhabitants. Consequently, the material reality, social identity, and well-being of

Indigenous and Creole Peoples are tied to two different economies within the postcolonial state. In spite of Guyana's location in the Global South as one of the poorest nations in the Western Hemisphere, the well-being of Creoles is more closely tied to the economies of the Global North, while that of Indigenous Peoples constitutes an *internal* South. The region's economies therefore reveal a remapping of global political economy: for instance, Immanuel Wallerstein's world-systems theory, in which he cites the decline of the indigenous population in the Canaries and in the Caribbean, due largely to the introduction of "monocultures," thus figuring native disappearance in the rise of capitalist modernity.[29] Within this modern globality the coast/interior division reflects the unevenness of the nation's economy regarding its Creole and indigenous citizens. Guyana's attempt to develop its interior through mining, which is similar to attempts by Suriname and French Guiana, necessitates the displacement of Indigenous Peoples who occupy those lands in search of wealth for the Creole economy. Guyana has leased to foreign mining companies an area that is roughly "the size of Portugal."[30] This is indigenous land, and on it the search for wealth through gold, bauxite, or logging occurs within a particular way of seeing the interior that arose with conquest and the myth of great wealth to be had not for those who are already there but for imperialist and now nationals that maintains the nation and national good as distinct from Amerindian good.

Third, the division is philosophical because the remapping of the entire territory in terms of colonial history and epistemology significantly shapes cultural and theoretical ways of knowing and existing, or being, in the Caribbean. Cuban intellectual Antonio Benítez-Rojo's influential book *The Repeating Island: The Caribbean and the Postmodern Perspective* offers an example of how theoretical production about the region that seeks to define it, however complexly, is informed by that North–South relationship. Through a postmodern framework that draws on continental, philosophical thinking, specifically the work of Deleuze and Guattari, *The Repeating Island,* restates the classic materialist arguments of former Trinidad Prime Minister Eric Williams and others about the role the region has played in the rise of capitalism. Williams's strict economic determinism, which holds that the development of finance capital in Europe and the first Industrial Revolution were fundamentally dependent upon and hence determined by enslaved labor, becomes the following: "Without deliveries from the Caribbean womb Western capital accumulation would not have been sufficient to effect a move . . . from the so-called Mercantilist Revolution to the Industrial Revolution."[31]

Benítez-Rojo's graphic image of a vaginal Caribbean "stretched between continental clamps" is more than just his novelist tendencies taking over. The feminized aesthetic—a reflection of the largely masculinist production of Creole identity as indigenous—is in fact the ultimate trope of productivity. The labor of the enslaved, indentured, and others is captured within an aesthetic economy that not only articulates the particular subordination of the South to the North but does so in such a way that that relationship remains reproductive for and hence gives meaning to his postmodern trope of it as "a Caribbean machine."[32] A Deleuzean metaphysics of repetition and difference thus works differently when brought to bear on the Caribbean because of the way in which Benítez-Rojo links it to its productive, material economy. The Caribbean emerges in his work as a totality: a metaphoric island in which the difference of mainland territories is not significant enough to be raised to a level of theoretical production outside the dominant theoretical and aesthetic economy. His brief attention to the way in which colonial epistemology still governs the relationship Guyanese have to the land as an El Dorado of sorts does not account for what this might mean apart from its role in the always-*already* of the Caribbean machine.[33] What Benítez-Rojo has done is pull a non-island space (to the extent that he discusses Guyana) into an island framework. Non-island territories like it are also similarly affected by or made invisible within the aesthetic doubling of island geographies and populations in Caribbean theory. It is this gesture that this book takes pains to point out and critique. Further, the subordination of the difference of mainland to island territories in the deployment of a regional trope is the condition of a theory of Caribbean postmodernity as a series of repetitions. These repetitions are the figurative effects of the plantation economy, which maintains both a material and cultural periphery. In other words, as the Guyanese interior is regarded as a necessary and potentially productive "excess" to plantation economy in its dependence on that economy to give meaning to his trope, Benítez-Rojo's theory also maintains an excess: the nonproductive cultural economy, the nonproductive trope of native difference. It is for this reason that the divisions noted must also be understood through another lens, the one that is most "productive" for this study: between Guyana as a non-island or mainland Caribbean territory and Guyana as a machine of difference *within* Antonio Benítez-Rojo's Caribbean machine, *la isla que se repite* ("repeating island"). Like Benítez-Rojo's work, many studies that emerge from the Caribbean privilege the history, society, and geography of islands as paradigmatic, ignoring how those territories on the margins, such as Guyana, French Guiana, Suriname, and Belize, offer places to possibly intervene in and shift archipelagic methodologies.[34]

The problem with these works is that throughout the Caribbean, Indigenous Peoples are largely considered extinct in the Greater and Lesser Antilles. They are most often depicted as having disappeared entirely from some islands in the colonial period, or as constituting too small and often too isolated a population as social and historical findings become the basis for literary and other cultural analyses. Thus, Christopher L. Miller can comfortably assert in his recent book *The French Atlantic Triangle: Literature and Culture of the Slave Trade* that "by 1656 the aboriginal people of Guadeloupe were eradicated and three thousand enslaved Africans worked on the island, in the presence of twelve thousand French people. . . ."[35] Miller's statement—which doesn't account for the "how" of this disappearance through extermination, migration, or intermixing—rings true with historians of both the Greater and Lesser Antilles and most other non-mainland territories. The most often cited exceptions include Trinidad and the so-called Black Caribs of St. Vincent and Dominica, the result of intermixing between runaway enslaved peoples (Maroons) and Indigenous Peoples (Carib).[36] More recently, DNA evidence has sought to account for survival beyond just culture, language, and "pure blood" by identifying indigenous genes in the larger population of islands such as Puerto Rico.[37] When the ways in which Indigenous Peoples self-identify and articulate historical continuity are taken into consideration, the indigenous presence is much greater and widespread.[38]

In circum-Caribbean mainland territories, there is a different story. In each of the mainland countries, there exists an indigenous population that interacts differently with Creole society, the nation, and the law. In Belize, there are several different Maya groups, some of which existed in the territory prior to British occupation in the seventeenth century and others who entered and remained in the area after fleeing from the Caste Wars of the Yucatan in the nineteenth century. In Belize, there are also Garifuna, the descendants of the so-called Black Carib groups who fought the British presence in St. Vincent. In the late eighteenth century, many eventually surrendered and were forcibly relocated from St. Vincent to coastal Honduras. Then, in the nineteenth century, large groups of Garifuna migrated from Honduras to Belize. There, the British sought to control Garifuna peoples by applying to them the same Alcalde system in use to administer rule over Maya peoples in the territory, whom the British saw as a potential labor force for the timber industry.[39] French Guiana has seven indigenous groups and three Maroon groups. Suriname has four indigenous and half a dozen Maroon groups. These indigenous and Maroon peoples largely occupy Suriname's interior, which, like Guyana's, is the majority of the country. Further, although not indigenous, the Maroon groups are generally viewed in the same manner as Indigenous Peoples within state and international law, a juridical identification that merits further study. Guyana boasts nine indigenous groups that continue to be displaced and largely occupy reservations and liminal geonational spaces. Like Belize, in each of the Guianas—which form part of an ecologically diverse area known as the "Guiana Shield"—indigenous and/or Maroon groups are at odds with the state, where international law has both recognized them and their rights to the land while each country is left to implement these laws on its own terms, and many often do not. In their excellent study of Suriname, Ellen-Rose Kambel and Fergus MacKay wrote in 1999 that "the state maintains that indigenous peoples and Maroons are merely permissive occupiers of privately owned state land without any effective rights thereto. . . ."[40] The Indigenous Peoples and Maroons of non-island territories are thus particularly positioned with regard to citizenship and sovereignty. Behind Georgetown's hugely symbolic Umana Yana are peoples fighting for rights *against* Afro- and Indo-Creole–led governments.

Guyana thus represents the objective liminality that fuels this book's intervention in Caribbean studies. I highlight Guyana as a continental history in terms not of its sameness to other mainland territories or its difference alone from island territories that are overrepresented in the most prominent theory such as Benítez-Rojo's work. What I am interested in is what happens if we take Guyana and the continuing *presence* of Indigenous Peoples there and throughout the Caribbean as a starting point for modern Caribbean history and political and cultural theory. Guyana's difference from other Caribbean territories as a space where a significant number of indigenous groups are visible is therefore crucial to my rethinking of indigeneity there and in the wider Caribbean. Its particularity, what its peoples and geography make visible, is the place from which I engage a range of discourses on the Caribbean in order to argue that the displacement of Indigenous Peoples is more than just historically or geographically significant, but that it is instrumental in producing Creole subjects and citizens and the Caribbean discourses that reflect and institute Creole subjectivity.

As such, this book's centering of Guyana's political and cultural discourse and history and its juxtaposition to regional cultural historiography is meant as an intervention. Positioning Guyana's difference as a non-island space as a reconcilable one allows me to ask and answer an "old" question quite differently. That question is, What is the source of the conflict among ethnic groups within territories such as Guyana? In the sociological literature, the interethnic conflict is largely viewed as a competition for resources and political power by Indo- and Afro-Creoles—collectively more than 70 percent of the Guyanese population—who effectively convert cultural nationalist discourse into political power. While I agree with this assessment of the conflict, in seeking my own answers I refashion the question that this research addresses to focus on the following: How have Creoles come to belong to the region and what does it mean to belong to the Caribbean (as a political, aesthetic, or intellectual project) both in the colonial era and in the present? Furthermore, why does this belonging produce a division that is visible, such as the competition for material and cultural capital that preoccupies political sociological approaches, and another that is relegated to demographic and epistemological excess but nonetheless still matters for material reality and social being, that is, the indigenous presence that has shaped plantation society and is still routinely marginalized? These questions necessarily move me away from sociological methods and answers to view the conflict among ethnic groups not just as a material or cultural struggle. Rather, I see these conflicts as the consequence of Indo- and Afro-Creole production of belonging (understood as both material and metaphysical) to the region. In this conceptual shift the definition, marginalization, and displacement of Indigenous Peoples within the Guyanese state must be examined. What specifically merits attention is the way in which the law (those sections of the Guyanese law meant to affirm their rights) fixes their identity within the state separately from Creoles in an extension and redeployment of colonial policies and attitudes.

"ACTS" OF DEFINITION:
AMERINDIAN IDENTITY BEFORE THE LAW

There is a growing body of scholarship on the relationships that Indigenous Peoples have with the law. In *The American Indian in Western Legal Thought*, Robert A. Williams Jr. traces the medieval, Christian origins of the Western legal discourse that were applied to Indigenous Peoples in the Americas. Williams definitively demonstrates how Western law in its application to the non-West is first and foremost an empirical tool. Today, however, it is this empirical tool of Western legal discourse that first redefined who they were and limited their rights that Indigenous Peoples must use to fight for self-determination within states, a dilemma that James Tully credits to a persistent "internal colonialism" of Indigenous Peoples.[41] Increasingly, international human rights law (which Gayatri Spivak cautions must not be misunderstood as singularly Eurocentric) has become central in determining who Indigenous Peoples are and their rights.[42] In his book, *The Origins of Indigenism: Human Rights and the Politics of Identity,* Ronald Niezen refers to indigenism as a "global" movement that is "grounded in international networks."[43] For Niezen, therefore, indigenous identity has a triparte expression: an identity, an analytic term, and a legal category.[44] This global, legal dimension to the rights struggle of Indigenous Peoples is thus central to defining who Indigenous Peoples are and is addressed by numerous studies, if not as an explicit focus. Two significant works on "self-determination" as a legal principle are S. James Anaya's *Indigenous Peoples in International Law* and Maivân Clech Lâm's *At the Edge of the State.* Both take issue with the instability of self-determination. Anaya, for instance, points out that the principle of "self-determination" in the Western legal tradition has in the past not applied to Indigenous Peoples; it also has different political and social meanings. Diane M. Nelson's *A Finger in the Wound,* Alison Brysk's *From Tribal Village to Global Village,* and Ellen Rose Kambel and Fergus MacKay's work are among the more detailed studies that provide examples of historical and contemporary struggles of Indigenous Peoples, especially their mobilization within states and their relation to local and international rights discourses, global markets, and so on in Latin America and the Caribbean, respectively.[45]

While international law and human rights discourses have been instrumental in the rights gains of Indigenous Peoples in the past three decades, rights struggles still (as we saw with Suriname) hinge upon the simultaneous granting and restricting of rights within states and the failure for claims recognized internationally to be fully executed within countries. The Inter-American Court of Human Rights (IACtHR), for instance, has decided repeatedly in favor of land claims by Indigenous Peoples in Suriname, Paraguay, and Nicaragua, but implementation has continued to be problematic, stuck in the courts for years.[46] In 1989, the International Labor Organization (ILO) adopted Convention 169 on the rights of indigenous and tribal peoples, but, to date, fewer than two dozen countries have ratified it.[47] Guyana is not one of them. In 2007, the UN General Assembly adopted the "Declaration on the Rights of Indigenous Peoples," which emerged out of its Working Group on Indigenous Populations. The declaration's forty-five articles assert the rights of indigenous groups to their traditional lands, development in their own national interests, cultural preservation, and "self-determination."[48] However, its enforcement is up to individual countries. In each of the mainland Caribbean territories mentioned in the preceding section, Indigenous Peoples, Maroon peoples, and Garifuna have fought for recognition of their land rights in state law as well as international law and through human rights institutions. Within the mainland territories, the failure to grant Indigenous Peoples rights to lands they occupy is directly tied to the desire to limit indigenous rights to the resources on those lands and what we see is the coloniality of contemporary claims.

Indigenous Peoples in Guyana have had their land rights recognized within the international community through participation of, for instance, the APA in the Amazon Alliance, the International Land Coalition, the Inter-American Commission on Human Rights Working Group, and appeals to the United Nations, which also has a Permanent Forum on the Rights of Indigenous Issues (UNPFII) that advises its Economic and Social Council. In Guyana itself, there is a tense relationship between civil organizations such as the APA (one of the strongest and most visible groups working on behalf of indigenous rights in Guyana), the National Toshaos Council (an organization of indigenous chiefs), the Amerindian Action Movement of Guyana, the Guyana Organization of Indigenous Peoples, and the government agency, the Ministry of Amerindian Affairs. In 2010, for instance, the ministry, under Pauline Sukhai, spearheaded a protest of Amerindians against the APA and its efforts to educate Amerindian Peoples about a Low Carbon Development Strategy (LCDS) being considered by the government that might affect Amerindian lands and rights to those lands.[49] Another former head, Carolyn Rodrigues, was often viewed as having sold out Indigenous Peoples. It was under Rodrigues, however, that in 2006 the Amerindian Act of 1976, which essentially formalized policies for the protection of Indigenous Peoples, instituted by the Dutch and later maintained by the British, was updated and expanded to offer even more protection.[50] Initially, according to Mary Noel Menezes, the Dutch respected indigenous rights to the land because of trade and defense. The Dutch established a practice of renumerating them for capturing runaway enslaved peoples which included payment of "20 fl. for the hand of a Negro killed while resisting capture."[51] In 1793, they made it illegal to enslave "free" Indigenous Peoples. After formally taking over the territory from the Dutch in 1814, the British eventually extended Dutch alliances. Indigenous Peoples became essential for British survival in the colony because of their knowledge of the land, from which they were increasingly being displaced, and because the British too used them to capture runaway slaves. It was not, however, until after the emancipation of enslaved blacks that a real debate about the protection of Indigenous Peoples took place.[52] Menezes documents the shifting, often ambiguous, nineteenth-century approaches to indigenous rights and well-being by the British colonial government and Christian missions, which range from protection through neglect. By the twentieth century, however, it seems as though these changing policies had congealed, and protection clearly meant integration. In a 1959 document created by British Information Services, which contains a "warm" recommendation of the books on its dependent territories by Winston Churchill, the brief section on Amerindian Policy refers to the new Amerindian Ordinance passed in 1951: "This set out a new Amerindian policy based on the principle that it is possible and generally desirable to adapt Amerindians to Western civilisation so that they are able to take their place in the general life of the colony."[53] As part of this effort at integration, in 1946, Amerindian lands were grouped into three large administrative districts—Mazaruni-Potaro, North-West, and Rupununi—that are still in effect today and are subdivided into regions (Moruca is in Region 1), reservations, and villages.[54] Thus, under British policy, Amerindian rights to their lands were approached through the ideological lens of incorporation.[55]

Despite its claims to the contrary, it is through this same ideological lens that the Burnham regime handled the rights of Indigenous Peoples in Guyana. A note appended to an origin story of the Warrau people published by the Ministry of Education in 1972 best sums up the regime's policies. In the note, we see continuity of British aims at integration: "Today's Amerindian is rapidly being absorbed into the Republic's mainstream, where, like all the other groups of Guyana, he rightly belongs."[56] The integration plan is also clearly laid out in 1970 by the Ministry of Information and Culture, which claimed that postindependence Guyana's relationship to its Indigenous Peoples is distinct from the British: "Unlike the Amerindians of the planter's era, the Amerindians of today's Guyana are an essential and highly regarded part of the body politic."[57] In a slightly contradictory manner, however, the ministry states that the question of Amerindian integration is moot because it was decided by colonization. In other words, while postindependence policies are supposedly different than colonial ones, they derive authority from and extend the logical result of colonization: increased and inevitable integration into Creole society.

Many of the provisions of the 1951 ordinance, the basis for what will become the 1976 Act, reflect the findings of the British colonial Aboriginal

Indian Committee. In an "Interim Report," the committee recommended the division of Amerindian lands into "Reservations," "Amerindian Areas," and "Open Areas," each of which offers various degrees of rights and protections to Indigenous Peoples.[58] The report, submitted by committee chairman and Commissioner of Lands and Mines F. Ray H. Green and based on inquiries by Amerindian Welfare Officer and committee member P. Storer Peberdy, also sought to define just who could be considered an "Aboriginal Indian" according to male blood, or patrilineal descent, and marriage. The 1976 act can thus be simplified and viewed in terms of the following: (1) provisions that regulate Amerindian lands, communities, and their governance; and (2) those provisions that deal with the person. I divide the following discussion into these areas.

With regard to the regulation of indigenous lands in the 1976 act, the Ministry of Amerindian Affairs retained the right to grant title to lands and to "revoke" such title or repossess Amerindian lands. The ministry also had the power to appoint Toshaos (a practice that harkens back to eighteenth-century Dutch policies of formally recognizing indigenous chiefs with whom they could liaise) and members of the District Council, one of the governing bodies responsible for indigenous villages and districts.[59] As part of the negotiations for independence from Britain, Indigenous Peoples in Guyana were supposed to receive titles to their lands, a job entrusted to the Amerindian Lands Commission. Despite gains since independence that, according to Janette Bulkan and Arif Bulkan, saw the increase of Amerindian land title from zero in the colonial period to 11.2 percent, the early Burnham administration did not fully keep its promise to many groups.[60] In 1969 (the year of the Rupununi Rebellion), the "Report of the Amerindian Lands Commission" that had been established two years prior stressed the need for such protections. In 1985, the human rights charity Survival International found that in three key regions, Indigenous Peoples were continually denied rights to land under the 1976 Amerindian Act.[61] According to the group, the most significant reason for denial was that the Guyana government considered "Indian land claims as obstacles to development. . . ."[62] Nearly a decade later, Janette Forte, with the Amerindian Research Unit—located at the University of Guyana—compiled a list of "Amerindian Concerns" collected from village councils that detailed grievances with regard to the 1976 act. In that document, indigenous groups assert the need for hospitals (as opposed to understaffed "health centres"), schools, teachers, mineral rights, public transportation, and so on.[63] Of the more than sixty grievances, the following serves as one of the best illustrations of the failure of the government to attend to basic needs:

> Transportation in Amerindian communities is a sore point. We call for its correction. No steamer, no mails, etc. Speaking for the Berbice River, there is no longer the weekly steamer or launch service up to Kwakwani. . . . The Ida-Sabina Dispenser and Hospital is non-existent. Years ago the Dispenser visited by boat all the riverain areas, at least once per week. We call for the return of this service and the establishment of radio sets in Amerindian communities. Many Amerindians die in cases of severe sickness due to the lack of early medical attention. Each riverain Amerindian village should also be equipped with ready boat and engine as well as a medical outpost.[64]

The grievances reflect a condition of dependence and economic neglect of Indigenous Peoples that is coextensive with land rights issues. They suggest that where land rights are granted, since Indigenous Peoples can't fully control mining on their lands or accesses those revenues, land title and sovereignty might mean what Lenin refers to as "juridical ownership" but not "real ownership." Nonetheless, the most significant difference between the 1976 ordinance and the 2006 version of the Amerindian Act is the greater power of Guyana's Indigenous Peoples under the latter to control their own lands and to argue for the expansion of those lands. Under the 2006 act, the Ministry of Amerindian Affairs has less say about what Amerindians do on their land and less power to repossess it. In a propaganda piece put out in 2005 by the Ministry of Amerindian Affairs and designed to essentially "sell" the act to indigenous groups prior to its ratification, the ministry claims that the new act "removes the Minister's authority over Amerindian titled land"; although, of course, the Ministry still grants titles.[65] According to the document, the new act provides greater rights and protections for Amerindians concerning mining on their lands (even the power to reject what are deemed "small-" and "medium-" scale mining projects) as well as forestry. However, while the ministry is keen to stress the fact that the act represents important gains for indigenous groups and that Guyana's Indigenous Peoples have more protection than others in South America, indigenous communities feel that it is insufficient, and the National Toshaos Council has challenged it. These challenges to the Amerindian Act around the issue of land rights and governance suggest not only that Amerindians are battling with the legacy of colonialism, but that their struggle within the postindependence state is in fact a continuing *anti*colonial one because the revised act of 2006 still has its origins in a particular colonial framework.

Equally as complicated as land and sovereignty issues are identity issues. Under the 1976 act, at age twelve all native persons had to "register" as Amerindian (as well as be prepared to show identification cards whenever asked). The ministry also had the peculiar ability to decide that those Amerindians who needed exemption from the laws of the ordinance could in fact no longer be considered Amerindian.[66] Finally, in one of the more notable provisions in the act with regard to labor—and one that probably best reflects its colonial origins—Amerindians could only be employed as "casual labor" for two weeks in any occupation. Any work in excess of this had to be approved by the district commission, a move that clearly fuels or supports the excision of Indigenous Peoples from discourses of rights and nation attached to plantation labor.[67] The act's provisions concerning identity reflect a shaping irony of Amerindian identity and freedom in Guyana—that of having to exist within the law in order to then be limited by that law. It is an irony best expressed by Ian Griffith Williams, identified as being from Paramakatoi, Region 8, in an excerpt from his poem "Revise 29:01."

1. All Guyana is an independent nation,
We cut ties from Mother England.
Yet they still have an Act for me,
Laws written for a colony.
On me heart I put me hand,
Brothers and sisters let us revise 29:01.
. . .
4. Guyana my beautiful native land,
We come and live here before any other man.
But for me to live in me own land,
I have to be registered to be an Amerindian.
On me heart I put me hand,
Brothers and sisters let us revise 29:01.[68]

Williams illuminates the way in which Amerindian self-definition is still limited by the coloniality of Guyanese law. His call to revise the Amerindian Act—which he refers to strictly in terms of its numerical position in Guyana's laws—articulates its colonial roots and the deep contradiction between indigenous identity and state citizenship in Guyana. It illustrates the way in which contemporary law controls Amerindian citizenship and cultural identity in a vastly different way from all other peoples. This conflict emerges in the ministry's decision not to replace "Amerindian" with "Indigenous Peoples" in the revised act—in other words, a decision not to let Indigenous Peoples self-define.

The ministry assures indigenous groups that under the revised act they will not be prevented from gaining rights and further international recognition by being called *Amerindian* as opposed to *indigenous,* a term prevalent in international human rights discourses.[69] In consultations with indigenous groups on the provisions of the new act, the name change was identified as a "common issue."[70] The government, however, argues that the term *Amerindian* must be retained in Guyana because other groups (who are not mentioned) can also be considered indigenous. It is only in this brief moment that the minister's office even gestures to the larger problems surrounding indigeneity in Guyana, which begins with the difficulty of saying who in fact are Indigenous Peoples. In the opening chapter of her book, Menezes attempts to identify the indigenous groups that are the object of her study and who are themselves descendants of earlier peoples. What becomes quickly apparent, however, is the discrepancy between how Indigenous Peoples self-define and how explorers such as Robert Schomburgk, who was commissioned to demarcate then British Guiana's boundaries in the nineteenth century, attempted to classify them. Relying at least partially on such early sources as Schomburgk's documents, Menezes identifies major groups: Arawaks, who refer to themselves as Lokono; Caribs, who, according to Menezes, can be further subdivided. To add to the complexity, Menezes identifies as early Carib kingdoms areas that are now largely Arawak, such as Pomeroon, Moruca, Waini, and Barima.[71] She notes that the Arawaks in the Moruca region today did not arrive until the nineteenth century, having fled north during the Bolivarian struggle in South America.[72] Additionally, Philip P. Boucher, in his study of the Carib presence in the Caribbean, notes that many Carib peoples actually speak Arawakan languages.

Menezes, nonetheless, retains the distinction between the aggressive and warlike Caribs and other groups found in colonial documentation. It is through this erroneous attitudinal distinction in Menezes's work that the Arawaks emerge as "the gentlest of all the tribes"—a colonial point of departure for defining indigenous groups that recent anthropology has sought to avoid.[73] In contrast, in his very detailed study of the Waiwai who live in the southern Rupununi, anthropologist George Mentore begins with a critique of how indigenous and nonindigenous identities are in fact "irreducible" to the way in which the nation-state records and naturalizes differences.[74] In identifying what are officially accepted as the nine indigenous groups in Guyana today, Mentore writes:

> In its official text the state presents the Akawaio, Arawak, Arecuna, Carib, Makushi, Patamona, Waiwai, Wapishana, and Warrau as its national Amerindian presence. Here the known Amerindian amounts to an anatomically determined individual belonging to a biologically fixed racial and ethnic totality. Only such an Amerindian can be recognized by the state and, for example, become eligible for access to its many modern services. . . . While being reassuring to the state and helping to constitute and facilitate its operations, the form of Waiwai identity with which the state works bears very little resemblance to those the Waiwai hold of themselves.[75]

Throughout *Of Passionate Curves and Desirable Cadences: Themes on Waiwai Social Being*, Mentore advances and reinforces the idea that the Waiwai in fact represent a different mode of being "human" that has largely been misread in acts of anthropological translation and government categorization. Mentore and Menezes, to a lesser degree, both point toward the difference between indigenous identities as they are understood for state citizenship, for academic study, and by Indigenous Peoples themselves.

The redefinition of Indigenous Peoples by the state allows for the management of an identity that threatens the state itself by continually gesturing toward its limits and illegitimacy. It is for this reason that the discourse of "prior rights," through which Amerindians seek to gain greater access to political power, is often dismissed as "racist" doctrine.[76] The continued identification of Indigenous Peoples in terms other than those in which they see themselves, and consequently relate to the land, represents their real and figurative displacement. It also reflects attempts to not necessarily disappear Indigenous Peoples but to subvert the radical difference they represent. Where this is not possible, as with Guyana, we saw their marginalization and disenfranchisement within the postcolonial state.

Following, I suggest that the introduction of new natives, or the extent to which Creoles are able to imagine and institute themselves *as* natives both politically and culturally, rests upon the management of this radical difference through discursive repetition of native extinction. It is a phenomenon that complexly reflects what Canadian-based anthropologist Maximilian

Forte has identified as a "historical trope of anti-indigeneity" in the bulk of wider Caribbean historiography.[77] Guyana's relation to its indigenous groups allows us to see that what Forte identifies as a regional, historiographic trope is central to discourse, political economy, and Creole subjectivity. In other words, the *idea* of native disappearance, either sociolinguistically or historically, emerges as central to a broad range of Caribbean discourse and to the introduction of new natives. While their disappearance from some territories in the Caribbean, such as Antigua and Jamaica, may be considered "fact," I suggest that prior disappearance in some territories is no less instrumental in the formation of Creole subjectivity than the presence of Indigenous Peoples in others, such as Guyana. The repetition of the "fact" of their extinction effects a second expropriation of Indigenous Peoples, especially to the extent that the repetition is taken for granted as regional reality, where archipelagic social and cultural history doubles for that of the entire Caribbean. The move of Indigenous Peoples away from the coast during colonialism in Guyana can be understood as the geographic representation of their excision from the space and economy of labor within the Anglophone Caribbean as a whole, where the *encomienda* did not take root and where it is presumed that Indigenous Peoples have mostly been killed off. It reflects the production of indigeneity through a teleological relation to labor intrinsic to understandings of New World humanity in which labor (via the plantation) is what indigenizes modern subjects.

Introduction of New Natives: Elaboration of a Method

In Caribbean studies, there has been a clear shift in attention to Indigenous Peoples. There has been notable work by Peter Hulme, who takes issue with how Indigenous Peoples are identified, provocatively arguing that the terms *Carib* and *Arawak* are not only colonial misreadings of indigenous groups but are inaccurate ways of labeling Indigenous Peoples today. There is both general and country-specific work by Philip P. Boucher, Irving Rouse, Andrew Sanders, Mary Noel Menezes, George Mentore, Ellen-Rose Kambel, Desrey Fox, and Peter Rivière, among others. The *General History of the Caribbean—UNESCO,* edited by Jalil Sued-Badillo, significantly treats the indigenous presence in the Caribbean in its first and second volumes. Contemporary works like B. W. Higman's excellent discourse on the "project" of writing Caribbean histories does lead to significant consideration of Indigenous Peoples but it has not substantively changed the location of them at the beginning of the historical project for most scholars.

There remains, therefore, the need for more work that does not either place Indigenous Peoples outside or only at the beginning of modern history and thus makes them irrelevant to contemporary analyses of society and culture.[78] Nearly every historical and political work on Guyana, with the exception of Maurice St. Pierre's *Anatomy of Resistance,* begins with the narrative of the replacement of Indigenous Peoples by enslaved Africans and then indentured Indian labor. In most histories of the colonial Caribbean, the reason given for the introduction of black labor is, with few exceptions, indigenous disappearance. Frank Pitman, for instance, surmises from readings of Richard Lignon and others that in the seventeenth century, where "Indians" were enslaved in "Barbadoes," theirs was not plantation field labor. He further notes that by the middle of the following century, "Barbadoes had no Indian slaves."[79] Thus, this disappearance, either through extinction or racial mixture, is a given in much of Caribbean cultural and theoretical writing, and it has even been significant in the early articulation of postcolonial criticism.[80] Cuban writer Roberto Retamar, for example, uncritically quotes a speech by Simón Bolívar in 1819 in which Bolívar claims, "The greater part of the native peoples has been annihilated."[81] For Maximilian Forte, such assertions of indigenous disappearance constitute "paper genocide" of Indigenous Peoples.[82]

Consequently, few works address the profound marginalization of Indigenous Peoples by the simple narrative framing of indigeneity within the language of disappearance or the introduction of black and Indian labor. Nor do they address the way in which the anticolonial and postcolonial nationalisms in the Caribbean failed to consider Indigenous Peoples. None to my knowledge discusses the marginalization of Indigenous Peoples in Guyana and in the wider Caribbean as a significant feature of the region's current political economy, cultural discourse, and identity formation. I am not arguing that there has not been significant work on Indigenous Peoples in the Caribbean. However, the bulk of scholarship in political sociology and anthropology that has explored the issues of political instability, class antagonism, and economic underdevelopment ensuing from the rise of ethnic nationalism fails to address Indigenous Peoples in a significant way, leaving them on the margins of history and academia. Notably, there is the work of Percy Hintzen, Clive Y. Thomas, and Brackette F. Williams on Guyana. Like the bulk of Caribbean historical and sociological analyses, these studies deal only marginally with Indigenous Peoples. While not intentional, they reflect moves such as Franklin Knight's *The Caribbean,* which places Indigenous

Peoples at the beginning of Caribbean history, *outside* of modern, nationalist processes. Thus, in its primary emphasis on color, caste, and class, which invariably leads to a misreading of ethnicity *for* race, the current critical field fails to significantly factor in Indigenous Peoples.[83]

Aboriginal or native disappearance, repeated in literary, social, and cultural criticism, emerges as a largely unquestioned feature of Creole subject formation and of the alternative modernities created by enslaved and indentured peoples, and thus of Caribbean modernity.[84] While most scholars are clear on how black subordination works as a key feature of modernity, a point most successfully elaborated by Paul Gilroy, its other feature, native subordination, is always dealt with either separately or ignored as an implicit or contingent logic. The difficulty in seeing how one subordination structures the other arises in large part because Indigenous Peoples were not established as other in the ways in which blacks were (through the *complete* denial of humanity), nor did blacks or Indigenous Peoples have real power or control over their engagement with each other.

I, however, suggest that native displacement and either real or figurative disappearance serves as the *necessary* or enabling condition of black being in the Caribbean, both epistemological and ontological, and is essential for constitution of that being through the rise of national consciousness and class consolidation. Throughout the book, the term *ontoepistemic* is used to signal the link between Creole being and the production of discourses that support social being by narratively instituting Creole subjectivity *as* indigenous. In these discourses, the repetition of indigenous disappearance emerges as a significant epistemological component. We therefore see the rerouting of indigeneity or instituting of new natives, Creoles, in both of the region's dominant critical or philosophical traditions—idealist and materialist—that Paget Henry beautifully outlines in *Caliban's Reason: Introducing Afro-Caribbean Philosophy*. The tension and distance between the two is in some senses false, as we saw for instance with Benítez-Rojo's figurative reworking of the materialist tradition. Both traditions underscore the plantation system's introduction of a new, more socially viable and integrating basis for belonging: labor; it is in positing a specific relationship to Western modes of labor as the ontologically necessary condition of social being and belonging that Creoles have been able to recast indigeneity.

While Benítez-Rojo's work serves as one example from the idealist tradition, it is the materialist tradition that I unpack next. My aim is to demonstrate that the materialist tradition in Caribbean discourse and the dominant framework of anticolonial struggle that pits a collective of subalterns inside modernity against the colonial power are limited. They obscure how resistance to colonialism by Afro- and later Indo-Creoles conflicts with the indigeneity (or ongoing indigenization) of First Peoples, for whom the dualism of resistance and labor is not similarly formative. In this light, the repetition of indigenous disappearance as history is factual to the extent that it rhetorically supports the political economy of the postcolonial state as an extension of the settler contract's need for the territory to be *terra nullius,* as Pateman reminds us. It reflects a new writing over or mythologizing of indigenous space in keeping with colonial epistemology and the settler/racial contract. This writing over ultimately has, as we saw with Benítez-Rojo, epistemological significance in which the "real" displacement of Indigenous Peoples that we witness, for instance, in Guyana is discursively repeated or reenacted.

An example of a strict materialist understanding of the Caribbean can be found in political scientist Jorge Heine's (former president of the Caribbean Studies Association [CSA]) response to a questionnaire for the CSA president's archive. Heine remarked:

> I tend to think that if there was some confusion as to what we meant by "Caribbean" in the mid-seventies, when CSA was founded, it was quickly cleared up. Most observers would now agree with the definition of the Caribbean based on a certain mode of production, that of plantation society. This definition, encompassing the island nations of the Caribbean Basin, plus those adjoining it that have shared in that mode of production, i.e., the Guyanas plus Belize, has served us well, and has organized our research and scholarly endeavors.[85]

Heine's emphasis on "a certain mode of production" as that which defines the Caribbean reveals the epistemological core of the materialist tradition that is either repeated or rejected by the idealist one in ways that are not always more positive. The materialist tradition in fact weds the economic thesis to indigenous disappearance in such a way that not only does the latter appear causative, but their imbrication appears natural. For the materialist tradition, the disappearance has epistemological weight and is actually the condition of the emergence of a proletarian subject in Marxist historicism, something we see, for instance, in C. L. R. James's work. James's classic study of the Haitian Revolution, *The Black Jacobins: Toussaint L'Ouverture and the San Domingo Revolution,* begins with a chapter titled "The Property," in reference to enslaved blacks who clearly evolve into a proletariat. In

James's Marxian framework, this transition from property to class does not include Indigenous Peoples. They literally are not there. They are outside, in other words, James's identification of "the sugar plantation and Negro slavery" as the twin elements that dictate "the *history* of the West Indies."[86] He writes:

> The West Indies has never been a traditional colonial territory with clearly distinguished economic and political relations between two different cultures. Native culture there was none. The aboriginal Amerindian civilisation had been destroyed. Every succeeding year, therefore, saw the labouring population, slave or free, incorporating into itself more and more of the language, custom, aims and outlook of its masters.[87]

This absence of Indigenous Peoples and their fundamental opposition to a thoroughly modern notion of labor is reiterated by Walter Rodney in 1981, when he identifies the "working people" in Guyana and marginalizes Amerindians.[88] Rodney's method and James's unquestioned assertion ("Native culture there was none"), which David Scott reads in *Conscripts of Modernity* as a reflection of his understanding or invocation of the Caribbean as a thoroughly "modern" space, leads to two observations.

First, despite the seeming veracity of James's statement, it is completely false. There is *always* a "native" to contend with, both in territories where there is a visible presence and in others where there is not: either as something that has been left behind (premodern and hence essential to understanding and articulating modernity, especially in regional historiography) or something that one is moving toward and that must be realized as modern through race—that is, the production of new natives. None of this is reflected in James's Marxist historicism or in the Haitian writer Jacques Roumain's Marxist aestheticism. In his novel, *Masters of the Dew*, for example, the "indigenous" black peasantry are made indigenous not only by their labor but by the position, much like in Césaire's long poem "Notebook of a Return to the Native Land," that they are placed in by the *return* of the protagonist. For both the subjects and the populations to which they return, this native status is stabilized along multiple points, including gender roles, language, nature, and so on. While this study is limited in that it does not offer a gender analysis of indigeneity or a discussion of sexuality and nationalism in settler societies, Creole Indigeneity's chapters clearly reveal that Creole indigeneity is a gendered phenomenon in which the sovereign Creole is masculinist and the Creole and native woman, in a heternormative gender economy, remains as other but essential to this process of becoming.[89]

Second, James's claim marks Creole subjectivity because we are not just talking about the Africans and Creoles who revolted but also about the I/we of James's narrative, as always-already modern; it is modern not just because the conditions of possibility are thus, as Scott claims, but by the discursive act of stabilizing the native presence with regard to time and underdeveloped land, or land upon which no (Western) labor has been performed. This epistemological dependence is apparent in *The Black Jacobins,* where native disappearance is a necessary justification not just for black labor but in general for the type of modern labor that is the core object of historical materialism. James's text further reveals how the Marxism that influenced so many attempts at socialist government allows for the continued writing of the Caribbean subject in terms of its specific ontoepistemic need.[90] In representing Caribbean subjectivity in this way, James is simultaneously writing the conditions of possibility for his own speech, which rests on the labor of slaves, on the fully modern transition from property to proletariat and on the discursive instituting of labor as a function of history. Since labor requires or signals would-be modern subjects, being modern is measured by the possibility of freedom and control of the colony (later the state), which becomes a reflection of that labor (recall Frantz Fanon's "whole body of efforts," often misread as being largely cultural).[91] In my next book I shall discuss the need for a thorough reevaluation of Marxist modes of Caribbean cultural subjectivity, both historical and novelistic; through *Creole Indigeneity* we can understand the way in which the Creole peasant-cum-proletariat (and in Guyana, labor union member and ethnopolitical citizen) as a historical subject and a discourse object, is essential to the representation of twentieth-century Creole subjectivity.[92] This has required the disappearance of the native person-body, who cannot be represented as a true Creole because he or she is *outside* labor, as defined by the plantation system. The literary and other sociocultural traditions reworked in the Caribbean novel (pastoral bildungsroman and others) are fundamentally antagonistic to native identity even as they usher in *new* native subjects. Indigenous Peoples are left out of the discussion—not because they were not there but because of our so-called modern modes of investigation, part of what Walter Mignolo refers to as an apparatus of the "coloniality of power." In this light, Marxist historicism and aestheticism must be viewed as a generalized consolidation of the initial narrative of displacement and a viable system and language for the representation of the

Creole as a valid, modern subject with the capacity for rationality and self-liberation or freedom. Through James, we can understand that native disappearance necessarily closes off alternative epistemic possibilities that would prevent the representation of the Creole subject as thoroughly modern and self-determining.

Materially, blacks became proletariats and middle class, but psychically, the validity of both class positions depended on a new relationship to the social and a viable indigeneity that would rest on two things: exile to the New World and the transformation of an identity *as* capital to one that allowed for the transfer of wealth. While Creole identity is not rigid, nor is the relation of sociohistorical subjects to labor fixed, there was nonetheless a futurity granted to labor that became the ontoepistemic condition of Creole social and cultural being and political subjectivity. For blacks and other Creoles, to become indigenous or native is to have greater access to capital, but for Indigenous Peoples their status as native continues to signal dispossession. Further, it is either indicative of greater creolization or an assertion against postcolonial Creole identity. Finally, their identity is only granted futurity within the postcolonial state, which requires they not be indigenous (on their own terms) in order to belong and have rights as full citizens.

Lakota activist Russell Means offers the most concrete example of what I am referring to as a split between Creole and indigenous identity around labor. In his 1980 "Black Hills Speech" he states that "the only manner in which American Indian people could participate in a Marxist revolution would be to join the industrial system, to become factory workers, or 'proletarians,' as Marx called them. [Marx] was very clear about the fact that his revolution could only occur through the struggle of the proletariat, that the existence of a massive industrial system is a precondition of a successful Marxist society."[93] In his critique of Marxism as an inadequate tool for indigenous liberation, Means notes that it fundamentally first sees Indigenous Peoples as economic identities. It transforms them within the modern economy—setting aside their own anti- and ante-capitalist modes of being human—so that they can be represented as human within capitalist modernity. While we are not speaking here of revolution, the socialist-inspired political programs that cropped up after independence throughout the Caribbean reflect the primary identification of citizen subjects as market-based identities defined by their access or lack of access to capital. It is this mode of belonging to the region with which Indigenous Peoples struggle and that reflects both a material and discursive transformation of indigeneity in terms of both space (hinterland versus Coast and indigenous versus Creole) and time (colonial, labor economy).

The Marxist or materialist approach offers a view of history and social organization that unavoidably locks Indigenous Peoples in the past. In contrast, the poeticist tradition often reduces them to trope. In both traditions, the conflict between labor and capital reproduces itself both socially and epistemologically. It is therefore in this space between disciplines that I hope to make the strongest case possible for the *centrality* of aboriginal presence in Caribbean culture and thought. I therefore situate this work methodologically between materialist critiques that see the plantation mode of production as paramount in the development of Caribbean societies, thereby privileging plantation-derived interpretive methodologies and social structures, and idealist or poeticist critiques to which they are often opposed. This allows me to critique the productive and (neo)colonialist ends to which labor, as a key element in Caribbean social formation and as a category of analysis, has been put in the development of Creole social and political subjectivity.

My own focus on plantation economy and culture does not mean that Creoles are only produced through plantation or plantation-organized labor, or that labor for them does not result in other forms of human value. By, however, insisting that relations among subalterns should be viewed in terms of the avenues through which they seek to satisfy the material *and* ontological requirements of being and belonging, it does mean that the indigenizing function of modern labor for political subjectivity needs to be addressed, as does its role (seen and unseen) in social and cultural subjectivity. Such a focus allows us to read a dimension to the conflict among ethnic groups that is far beyond a strictly materialist analysis, yet is just as essential for belonging and rights claims because of the way in which it can be articulated within capitalist modernity. That dimension is myth.

The labor (institutionally or narratively) performed first in history by the enslaved and second for the production of the Creole I/we achieves epistemic status only when secured by, as Sylvia Wynter would describe, an extrahuman (what she refers to as "divinely ordained" for Christian Europe) and thus always-already validated and validating element that is not determined by the plantation and the labor identities it supports.[94] For the Caribbean, this element is the myth of El Dorado. This myth must be understood as more than just imaginative discourse without material effect but as foundational as material culture. It is for this reason that, after the elaboration of the significance of labor through chapter 2, the book turns in chapter 3 to myth as an additional framework or lens for understanding Creole modes of belonging. I argue that myth must be read not apart from but *with* plantation analyses as constitutive of how Creoles become settlers and new natives. While it may seem logical to position myth as part of the idealist tradition in the Caribbean, I make the methodological and conceptual move of positioning it here as a component of the materialist one and its undergirding of Creole belonging.

Myth is fuel for the conquistadorial imagination and a foundational context for all settler groups. Myths such as El Dorado are the *first* imaginative discourses that emerged to reorder, remap, and write over the lands of First Peoples so that they could be productive for the material wealth of the Old World. The first economy, then, that comes out of the Western encounter is discursive. Therefore, those ethnic and racial groups that come into conflict do so within not only the social, cultural, and economic processes that give their identities concrete meaning, but also the related discursive and metaphysical processes that provide equally important "validating" elements. These elements require us to look beyond the plantation to understand the additional dimension to the recreation of Indians and Africans as Creoles whose transformation is fundamentally shaped by an attachment to the land that has become an *indigenous* attachment. This indigenous attachment is, for instance, demonstrated by the decision not to allow Amerindians to call themselves Indigenous Peoples in the updated Amerindian Act because others (presumably Creoles) can also be considered indigenous. Beyond, therefore, both culture and economy, Creole right to belong is secured by a discourse of indigenization that exceeds both.

It is in this way that the search for wealth and the emergence of the plantation must be understood as occurring fully within the symbolic structure or sign system of the myth and its role in *explaining* being in the New World and hence serving as a "founding myth" of Guyana, the South American region, and the modern-day Caribbean.[95] A combination of fact and fiction, the myth has become history at key moments in colonial and postcolonial cultural articulations. It is no longer a question of whose myth is being enacted, but of how the myth, crafted out of pre-Columbian native cultural tradition and existing European myths, heralded the development of the region and the displacement of its original inhabitants. We must also ask how the myth shaped the eventual transformation of territories into what Percy Hintzen calls a "colony of exploitation" and ultimately the transition to postcolonial society.[96]

The myth of El Dorado was central after Guyana's independence in facilitating a transition from colonial narratives of exploitation and domination to one of national destiny. Moreover, at independence, the myth was incorporated into the nationalist discourse of the nation's new subjects, its generative capacity transformed. The myth of El Dorado, therefore, continues, in the hands of Guyana's nation builders, to produce the landscape as a postcolonial national space. It also continues to produce the raced and gendered subjects that simultaneously try to rewrite their roles in this shifting narrative. Consequently, the myth can be understood as constitutive of Guyanese culture and politics, and in chapter 3, I deploy it as an investigative framework that restores to plantation-based analyses the structuring absences created by the plantation itself.

The tension between the Guyanese coast and interior, with which this introduction began, is in many ways the framing tension of this book and its conceptual yoking of creolization and indigeneity, as well as the two dominant critical traditions—materialist and idealist—as a method. It is a method that produces a study that is narrowly focused on Guyana but more broadly engages the Caribbean. As such, the chapters in this book reflect a movement between Guyanese specificity and Caribbean social and cultural discourse in general as they develop and extend the book's major arguments about Creole belonging.

To advance arguments about indigeneity and labor, each chapter of *Creole Indigeneity* considers a range of core texts meant to suggest a more integrative approach. They bring together cultural and political documents such as government propaganda, speeches, interviews, biography, philosophy, and drama. While the texts represent vastly different genres, their choice has been determined by the interdisciplinary nature of the book and the attempt to let its primary object, Guyana, come into focus outside of fixed disciplinary lenses. Further, I situate these texts alongside each other throughout the chapters to suggest a new strategy of reading Caribbean discourse.

Chapter 1, "Creole Indigeneity," serves as both a literature review of some of the salient arguments about creolization and an elaboration of the titular term as an expression of a settler/native dynamic in the Caribbean. I draw on the body of critical work on creolization in the Caribbean, including that of Sylvia Wynter, Richard Burton, Kamau Brathwaite, and others. My specific focus is on how and where in the critical literature being and becoming Creole is elaborated as an indigenizing process. The chapter is therefore concerned with the conceptual imbrications of creolization and indigeneity. Drawing upon existing discussion of settler colonialism and the settler/native dynamic, it introduces the concept of Creole indigeneity and argues that the disarticulation of Creole modes of indigenizing and those of Indigenous Peoples occurs along a fundamental axis: time.

Chapter 2, "Labor *for* Being: Making Caliban Work," continues my elaboration of a theory of Creole indigeneity with discussion of the literary figure of Caliban—emblematic of the dialectic of struggle with colonial power and ideology in the Caribbean. The chapter takes as its object primary texts such as Shakespeare's *The Tempest* and Césaire's *A Tempest*, as well as critical engagements with them. In arguing about the relationship between the two, I do not collapse the admitted temporal and epistemic differences that are responsible for their articulations. Several scholars, most recently Vanita Seth, have argued for the need to pay attention to the ways in which difference is not singularly but rather diversely constituted across the Renaissance, classical, and nineteenth-century epistemes.[97] I therefore focus on the breaks and continuities between these Calibans and their modes of production. Specifically, I argue that as the paramount symbol of the resisting Creole subject, Caliban performs labor for Creole subjectivity in an extension of the labor performed for Western subjectivity in the early modern period. Creole subjectivity thus works in a profoundly Hegelian or "Calibanesque" fashion in which Indigenous Peoples move into the dialectic in the place formerly occupied by blacks in order to work for black being within modernity. Postcolonial creative and critical engagements with the figure of Caliban reveal its narrative reinscription of material labor as the key value in Creole social legitimacy and hence nationalism. This turn to Caliban is not an effort to explain social or sociological phenomenon through philosophical concepts. It is, however, meant to indicate that the social and political subjectivities of blacks and Indians are informed by and emerge through the anticolonial consolidation of early modern and Enlightenment articulations of what it meant to be human and what it meant to be a citizen. We cannot escape, for instance, the link between the Hegelian dialectic of history and self-consciousness and the reemergence of this dialectic in anticolonial explanations of black humanity that grapple with and reinscribe labor as paramount in the social, ideological, and ontological transformation of blacks in the New World. It is for this reason that Indigenous Peoples emerge as the ontologically necessary other in the production of Creole identity as both fully human and sovereign.

Chapter 3, "'God's Golden City': Myth, Paradox, and the *Propter Nos*," represents a turning point in this book from the elaboration of the dialectic of being in which Creoles and Indigenous Peoples are involved to an examination of how the postcolonial, nationalist project institutes and epistemologizes their marginalization. It therefore takes up El Dorado as a "founding myth" for social formation in the Caribbean region and as part of the discursive framework for cultural and political articulations of Caribbean modernity. The chapter traces colonial and contemporary reinscriptions of the myth in order to understand how Caribbean subjects are represented within plantation social hierarchy while simultaneously being fitted into and refashioning the discursive structure of the myth to suit their own needs, making it central to the Creole cultural imaginary. The chapter finds that the myth of El Dorado works by encoding conquistadorial attitudes that first managed the difference of Indigenous Peoples in a way that remains productive for postcoloniality. For Guyana, I demonstrate that the myth enabled Guyanese at independence to figuratively represent the country's landscape as the gold that was once lost but is now found in the realization of the postcolonial nation as a specifically Creole patrimony or gift of Christian providential destiny: "God's golden city." It allows for representation of the land as no longer existing for the sake of God or for the colonizer, but, in conversation with Wynter, *propter nos* ("for our sake") for the sake of the Creole. Postcolonial retellings of the myth of El Dorado can be thought of as part of the deployment of a postcolonial settler contract by Creoles who see the hinterland as the last space onto which the myth of innate colonial right can be realized for former colonials at independence.

In chapter 4, "From Myth to Market: Burnham's *Co-operative Republic*," I focus on Afro-Creole subjectivity in Guyana and the ways in which black postcolonials set the terms for an articulation of citizenship by themselves and Indo-Creoles that would constrain Indigenous Peoples. I center my discussion on a piece of cultural propaganda commissioned and disseminated by the Burnham government, *Co-operative Republic, Guyana 1970*, a deeply self-conscious transformation of a colonial historical narrative by the regime. With *Co-operative Republic*, we witness the attempt to transform the figurative wealth of "God's golden city" into material bounty through the socialist program of economic egalitarianism put forward by the first postindependence government and centered on the interior and on its Indigenous Peoples. Thus, the document reveals the emergence of a political consciousness of the need to integrate Indigenous Peoples into the nation-state as a cultural object ("our Amerindians") that was also a necessary marker of the new status of Afro-Creole identity as *interior* belonging. I argue that *Co-operative Republic* mobilizes not the myth of El Dorado itself but the poetics of the myth to produce Guyanese nationalism as an inherited right of Afro-Creoles and at the same time create a social template to which all groups seeking power would have to subscribe. The chapter proves that despite the achievement of postcolonial status, the myth continues to produce a reality for politics in the region with which all groups seeking power negotiate. Finally, the chapter explores the two senses of indigeneity that, I argue, operate in Guyana.

One of the best examples of the way in which Indo-Creoles have articulated belonging on the model of blacks is the renaming of Guyana's Timheri airport for the first Indo-Guyanese president, the late Cheddi Jagan. *Timheri* is a native word that described early, pictorial images on rocks. The airport was renamed amid barely documented protest by Indigenous Peoples in order to create a legacy for Jagan. With the renaming as a point of departure, chapter 5, "The Baptism of Soil: Indian Belonging in Guyana," explores Indo-Creole subjectivity in Guyana and essentially argues for the links between *kala pani* (Indian Diaspora) and black Atlantic (African Diaspora) trajectories of modernity with regard to labor and native displacement. It explores these links by focusing on social, cultural, and historical writings by Indo-Guyanese, including Jagan. *Creole Indigeneity* concludes with a discussion of the work of Basil Rodrigues and what it would mean to shift from the Calibanesque mode of producing Creole political and cultural subjectivity that I trace throughout.

From myth to politics, *Creole Indigeneity* strives to illuminate the dynamic of social and cultural being and belonging in the Caribbean that sees North–South and colonizer–colonized relationships repeat among ethnics within capital. Whether the conditions of arrival for blacks and Indians make them "involuntary colonials," Creoles are now, collectively, in positions of power over Indigenous Peoples on whose land they have built homes of wood, concrete, culture, and nation.[98] In other words, between founding myths and concrete nation-states we find not just Creoles (racial/ethnic groups) but new indigenous subjects whose belonging is secured by material and cultural capital and an historically constructed excess. This book is meant to be a step toward unpacking these difficult relationships without recourse to a politics of blame. To recognize one's own role in the oppression of others is not about blame but about opening our eyes to how power works and how we can redirect it so that it doesn't diminish us all. I begin in chapter 1 by elaborating the work's framing concept, Creole indigeneity. As a term and a theory, Creole indigeneity is, I argue, a way of recovering the excess or remainder of history and identity that shapes both social formations in the postcolonial state and Caribbean intellectual production. While it might seem to represent a "contradiction," as a colleague said upon hearing it, it is this contradiction between "settler" Creole and "native," as well as the various attempts to reconcile it, that shapes Caribbean history and society.

1 Creole Indigeneity

O N THE EVE OF THE HAITIAN REVOLUTION IN 1791, MOST OF THE
half-million enslaved peoples in the most profitable of all the French
colonies had been brought directly from Africa. It is this character of the Haitian population that is often thought to have been fundamental in its ability
to turn a slave rebellion into an ultimately successful bid for liberation in
1804. Just three years after Haiti became a free nation, Britain declared an end
to the slave trade in its territories, sharply reducing the number of African
blacks coming into the New World. Thus the population that faced emancipation in the Anglophone Caribbean in 1834 and the early end of appren-
ticeship four years later was markedly different than the population of Haiti
at the start of its revolution. It was already, as Richard Burton argues, Creole.
Writing specifically about Jamaica, Burton states in *Afro-Creole: Power,
Opposition, and Play in the Caribbean* that "by 1838, as Jamaican society
stood on the brink of the most revolutionary change in its history, a culture
had been forged that was certainly no longer 'African' (though it retained
many more African elements than are commonly allowed) but had become
Creole, or more precisely, Afro-Creole."[1]

This move from African to Creole preoccupies this chapter's attempt to
offer a theory of Creole belonging. Its specific focus is on how and where in
the critical literature being and becoming Creole is elaborated as an indigenizing process. The chapter is therefore concerned with the conceptual imbrications of creolization and indigeneity as processes distinct from concrete
racial and ethnic identities.[2] It demonstrates that creolization as a process of
indigenization—to the extent that it is based on difference and resistance—
reflects a dialectic of being. While it may be easiest to understand this dialectic

in terms of a formal settler–colonial or master–slave relationship, I instead argue that the dialectic is also one between Creoles and Indigenous Peoples in their presumed "absence" from the land. In other words, while the colonizer represents a formative, external figure in the articulation of a Creole belonging or new indigeneity, Indigenous Peoples are maintained as the internal and largely invisible other.

The imbrications of creolization and indigeneity are probed in Carolyn Allen's essay "Creole: The Problem of Definition." Allen is interested in defining what she terms "functional principles" for the term *Creole* that allow it to be understood as a "genus" despite the proliferation of racial, linguistic, geographic, and other differences it signals. She therefore moves through several meanings, the most significant of which for this work is her illustration of the way the term has been used to designate some kind of native or indigenous status. Allen notes that its purchase for "nationalistic movements" derives in part from "the importance of nativity within the concept, a role closely associated with the adaptation which made of the Creole a distinctive type."[3] She then elaborates on Franklin Knight's use of the term: "Perhaps more important than race, then, is the Creole's affinity to place," an affinity that she articulates as "identification between inhabitant and land. . . ."[4] These two definitions gesture toward the ability of Creole to function not just as a cultural or racial marker of difference, but as a term with significance for political rights attached to a specific place or land. They reveal that what is at stake is articulating and defining creolization. More illuminating, however, is Allen's highlighting of Sylvia Wynter's 1972 definition in which she argues for the uncoupling of creolization and indigenization, whereby the former refers to the element of force involved in black adaptations or adoptions of European culture and the latter refers to the element of resistance within these adaptations.[5] Allen explains Wynter's understanding of creolization and indigenization as separate processes, saying, "She depicts [indigenization] as secretive, a kind of maroon activity, by which the dominated culture resists and survives."[6] Wynter's definition is often, however, ignored by those who collapse the terms and simply read creolization *as* indigenization. I return to Wynter's specificity in her even earlier articulation of indigenization as the resistant element of African (not European) belonging to the New World that cannot be subsumed within creolization. This earlier elaboration serves as the point of departure for my deployment of Creole indigeneity.

In her 1970 essay for *Jamaica Journal,* "Jonkonnu in Jamaica: Towards the Interpretation of Folk Dance as a Cultural Process," Wynter argues that cultural performance in the New World by blacks was representative of the "parallel" and overlapping processes of "acculturation" (creolization) *and* "rooting" ("indigenization" or cultural survival and retention, which was also an anticolonial resistance).[7] In short, for Wynter, black indigeneity is the result of the modes of resistance—read, in Burton, as the ability to preserve "many more African elements than are commonly allowed"—to colonialism enacted by the formerly enslaved. She writes:

> Alienated from Africa, their movement of "negritude" was a spiritual return to Africa. . . . But Price-Mars represented . . . a *negritude* that was *indigenist*. For the more total alienation of the New World Negro had occasioned a cultural response, which had transformed that New World Negro into the indigenous inhabitant of his new land. His cultural resistance to colonialism in this new land was an *indigenous* resistance. The history of the Caribbean islands is, in large part, the history of the *indigenization* of the black man. And this history is a cultural history—not in "writing," but of those *"homunculi"* who humanize the landscape by peopling it with gods and spirits, with demons and duppies, with all the rich panoply of man's imagination.[8]

In the indigenist movement (*Indigénisme*) in Haiti, spearheaded by those such as the intellectual Jean Price-Mars, Wynter finds a way of making sense of cultural production by blacks in Jamaica (and North America) under colonialism. She borrows from Price-Mars precisely because of the work he does in texts such as *So Spoke the Uncle* [*Ainsi Parla l'Oncle* 1928] to affirm the transformation of African culture in the New World against the rejection of such culture and its crucible—the peasant—by the Francophile middle class and political elites in early twentieth-century Haiti. In Price-Mars's discussion of Haitian folklore, Wynter identifies an anticolonial assertion of black identity—negritude—that is indigenizing in a manner similar to the Jonkonnu dances in Jamaica. Her borrowing from Price-Mars and her insistence that "resistance to colonialism . . . was an indigenous resistance" allows her to claim, for example, that "elements of Christianity would become an indigenous rather than a *merely* Creole part of Jamaican folklore."[9] For Wynter it is an indigenous resistance because nowhere else would it have occurred in this manner, and it reflects a relationship to the land that, though shaped by the material, exceeds both (recall her reference to the metaphysical: "Gods and spirits"). After Price-Mars, calling the process whereby blacks come to belong "indigeneity" rather than "creolization" is Wynter's way of foregrounding resistance to European culture and power rather than the assimilation of such, as enslaved peoples came to belong.

Wynter's suggestion that resistance is what grounds blacks' remaking of themselves as what she terms "new natives" alerts us to three crucial elements of Creole belonging. The first, which is substantively dealt with in chapter 2, is resistance as *a* mode of black becoming. Crucially, resistance to colonial oppression for Wynter emerges as the "how" of transformation. What preoccupy this chapter are the second and third elements of Wynter's elaboration: indigenous belonging as a *dimension* of black being in the New World and the way in which this indigeneity depends on difference, specifically that of the colonial exterior or outside. This becomes an orienting point for identity in the period of anticolonial, national resistance.

The chapter begins by tracing the discourse of creolization in the field of Creole studies, largely through the work of Kamau Brathwaite. The aim here is to situate the book's concern with Creole subjectivity in the existing discussions of creoleness and indigeneity. The next section of the chapter elaborates the relationship among labor, discourse, and becoming that informs the discussion of Creole subjectivity throughout the book. It outlines two orientations of Creole indigenous belonging: a material and a discursive. This lays the groundwork for the introduction and definition of the concept of "Creole indigeneity" in the third section, briefly framing it within both the existing conversation on settler colonialism and, more specifically, the arguments about the settler/native dynamic in work such as that of Frantz Fanon and Mahmood Mamdani as well as scholarship on indigeneity in the Caribbean. The chapter concludes by focusing on what is fundamentally at stake in this ongoing dialectic of being between Creoles and Indigenous Peoples, between settler and native: the ability to turn labor into time.

Creole Studies

Richard Burton's work is part of a body of research on Caribbean culture and society that has looked at being Creole as a process (creolization) by which African culture is retained in every sociocultural area, from linguistics to performance to religion, among others. Burton's work reflects one of two major tendencies in discussions of creolization as a distinct cultural process that produces belonging to the region. There is the tendency either to see creolization as a loss of African culture or as retentive.[10]

According to Maureen Warner-Lewis, the view of creolization in terms of African cultural retention represents a perspectival shift in the social sciences from earlier work that either focused on loss or placed cultural retention squarely in the past of West Indian societies.[11] The most significant theoretical intervention in the discussion of creolization as cultural retention is Kamau Brathwaite's, when he describes it as

> a cultural process . . . which . . . may be divided into two aspects of itself: ac/culturation, which is the yoking (by force and example, deriving from power/prestige) of one culture to another (in this case the enslaved/African to the European); and inter/culturation, which is an unplanned, unstructured but osmotic relationship proceeding from this yoke. The creolisation which results (and it is a process not a product) becomes the tentative cultural norm of the society.[12]

In Brathwaite's view, the shift in Caribbean societies from being more African in character to being more Creole is one in which Africa was *adapted* to the New World through regimes of labor and social organization rather than excised or lost. He thus rejects the more negative implications of creolization as corruption. He also does not endorse Elsa Goveia's claim, although he is influenced by her historical work, that what really links Caribbean societies is the inferiority of blacks.[13] Brathwaite's intervention is substantively dealt with in *Questioning Creole: Creolisation Discourses in Caribbean Culture, In Honour of Kamau Brathwaite*, which contains essays that critique and extend his concept and its limits.

The volume dedicated to Brathwaite, in which Carolyn Allen's piece appears, does important work in demonstrating the complexity of the concept's socio-cultural and sociological development and trajectories. It also reveals how problematic the term can be. Its "slipperiness" is foregrounded by Veronica Gregg at the start of her essay in the volume when she states, "It is impossible to read or write the term creolisation without warnings, caveats, proviso, explanations, reworkings and even scare quotes."[14] The reason for this is a lingering definitional instability within and across time. In his essay, political sociologist Percy Hintzen, for instance, points to "blackness" as a cultural dimension that *conflicts* with creolization, and indeed in an essay by Jean Rahier in the book *The African Diaspora,* blackness is made visible within and against creolization.[15] As a term then that describes change both through culture and, more problematically, race, *creolization* is demonstrably irreducible to a single process and begins well before the intellectual enters into and begins to shape either the process or our understanding of it. It also has a significant number of sociocultural and literary trajectories as well as linguistic and semantic iterations: *creole, créole, criollo, creolized, créolite, creoleness, creolisation,* to name a few. Even more complex, the noun *Creole* does not function to designate blacks and Indians in the Caribbean equally, and their individual creolization processes differ.

This is most clear in the anthropological literature. In their studies of ethnicity and nationalism in Guyana and Trinidad, Brackette F. Williams and Viranjini Munasinghe, respectively, offer detailed accounts of how racialized groups such as blacks and Indians become "ethnic" and how they imagine the nation. In an earlier essay, Williams clearly outlines how ethnic comes to signify nation. She begins "A Class Act: Anthropology and the Race to Nation across Ethnic Terrain" by examining existing anthropological literature on ethnicity to argue that most of this work has not successfully accounted for the role played by civil society, the state, and specific "power relations" in defining ethnicity and the self-definition of groups: in other words between the "empirical" and the subjective. One area of concern for Williams is the failure of existing work to sufficiently account for how ethnic identity can designate subordinate identities within both a state *and* majority groups. Williams suggests that it is a particular "state-backed race/class conflation that becomes the ideologically defined 'real producer' of the nation's patrimony" against which "ethnic," "minority," or other marginal groups struggle.[16] Earlier, she notes that in ethnically stratified societies, race reflects the reification of nonbiological properties so that "the *right* blood becomes a euphemism for inheritance of the state, and of control over a set of criteria on the basis of which rights in the state will be distributed to marginalized citizens."[17] What this means is that although blacks and Indians in Guyana are considered ethnic groups, their ethnic identities were not always equally associated with a right to rule the state. In her work, for instance, Munasinghe, who draws on Williams, points to the disarticulation of Creole and "ethnic" Indian identity. It is clear that Creole, as a cultural term, applies not to Indians but to Africans or blacks who then imagine the nation as (Afro)Creole, based on both prior arrival to Indians and earlier and greater cultural integration, positioning Indians as marginal ethnics. Further, as my discussion in chapter 5 demonstrates, marking themselves as Indian and *not* Creole was especially crucial to Indians during the indenture period when the goal was not to integrate but to return to India.

While I am aware of this distinction, and in this chapter I focus explicitly on the creolization processes of blacks, I do collectively refer to blacks and Indians as Creoles in order to make clear the way in which their processes of becoming and belonging in the Caribbean allow them to signify on the nation in ways that maintain Indigenous Peoples as culturally and economically marginal. In other words, while *Creole* may be a noun used primarily to refer to blacks, and an adjective when applied to Indians in the post-Indenture twentieth century, I use the term to indicate the way in which both their identities now are collectively woven through with state power. Indigenous Peoples' own creolization processes do not allow them to signify on the nation in ways that grant them the same citizenship status of blacks and Indians, largely because of the ways in which their labor was constructed in the colonial and postcolonial state. Anthropologist Aisha Khan has remarked that Indigenous Peoples are "the elided or marginalized figure . . . in creolization discourses, which typically commemorate post-Columbian peoples."[18] What I hope to underscore is that to the extent that labor plays a role in becoming Creole, both Indians and blacks are able to tap into this language of becoming to the exclusion of Indigenous Peoples. Thus Indians, in laying claim to the nation and remaking it, mobilize discourses around labor in much the same way that Afro-Creoles do, grounding legitimacy and power in Indo-Creole identity. Unlike, therefore, the Williams and Munasinghe studies, I focus only briefly on ethnic identity, because as ethnics, blacks' and Indians' identities are tied to and legitimated by the state, which affirms the racialization of their differences and the articulation of those differences with power. In contrast, to the extent that Indigenous Peoples claim self-determination by tapping into, as Ronald Niezen indicates, transnational networks, they refuse the close articulation of their identities in state terms. Referring to Indigenous Peoples as "false *irredentas,*" Niezen writes, "Indigenism . . . is commonly placed in the same category as ethnicity or ethnonationalism. Indigenous peoples, however, do not as a rule aspire toward independent statehood."[19] I am therefore interested in the processes of creolization and indigeneity, primarily with regard to blacks, in order to show the ways in which creolization becomes a process of belonging that, although it might maintain blacks and Indians as separate ethnic groups, produces Indigenous Peoples as minority or marginal ethnics.

To illustrate the understandings of creolization that shape black and later Indian belonging, it is necessary to engage Brathwaite's foundational work, specifically its negotiation of the past of Creole identity and the writer's role in shaping it. For want of space and time, I do not detail the development of Brathwaite's theory from earlier debates on Caribbean sociocultural organization, as the contributors to *Questioning Creole* have so excellently done.

Instead, I focus on his defense in a 1970 essay of the principle that informs his theory that creolization does not mean a loss or move away from Africa. Published a year before the work that put him on the map for Creole theory, the essay "Timehri"—the former name of the Guyana airport and a native word for centuries-old rock paintings said to be put there by the god Amalivacar—is especially useful here because of its consideration of the "native" Caribbean *alongside* Afro-Creole culture. Brathwaite and later Burton provide twin points of departure for my discussion of Creole indigeneity, allowing me to situate a brief discussion of the evolution of the Creole as a sociohistorical and discursive subject.

Brathwaite begins "Timehri" with a definitive rejection of the idea that creolization in the Caribbean is about "rootlessness, of not belonging to the landscape; dissociation, in fact, of art from the act of living."[20] He claims that such an attitude is the product of the "intellectual elite" in its failure to develop and retain an African consciousness. [21] It is thus a product of class division. Brathwaite therefore argues that the artist must acknowledge the African presence (with which he himself reconnects after living in Africa) and reject the kind of creolization that embraces white European culture and power. In defining creolization, he draws on the work of Richard N. Adams, stating, "'Creolization' is a socio-cultural description and explanation of the way the four main culture carriers of the region—Amerindian, European, African, and East Indian—interacted with each other and with their environment to create the new societies of the New World."[22] His definition of creolization in terms of regional types ("mulatto" and "mestizo") is anticipatory of the trajectories that will develop from his work. With it, however, he is able to acknowledge that for intellectuals and artists such as Guyanese painter Aubrey Williams and novelist Wilson Harris, who do not claim that creolization is "rootlessness," their rooting is in fact different and finds its source not in Africa (via Caribbean blacks) but in the "Amerindian." Brathwaite says of Williams and Harris that, "coming from mainland South America, they found themselves involved not with the problem of mulatto-creolization, but with mestizo-creolization. Their starting point was not the Negro in the Caribbean but the ancient Amerindian." In contrast, he writes, "Most of us, coming from islands, where there was no evident lost civilization—where in fact there was an 'absence of ruins,' faced a real artistic difficulty in our search for origins."[23] By the end of the essay, Brathwaite argues that their work is a "medium" for recognition in the rest of the Caribbean of the "Maya who were already us" and disavows any fundamental distance or antagonisms between Amerindian and African cultures in the New World.[24] Indeed, he even comes close, we can suggest, to Harris's own view of creoleness as one form of the "complex revisionary bridges" needed to link creoleness with its limits.[25] Brathwaite writes:

> But what Williams' work has revealed . . . is that the distinction between African and Amerindian in this context is for the most part *irrelevant*. What is important is the *primordial* nature of the two cultures and the potent spiritual and artistic connections between them and the present. In the Caribbean, whether it be African or Amerindian, the recognition of an ancestral relationship with the folk or aboriginal culture involves the artist and participant in a journey into the past and hinterland which is at the same time a movement of possession into present and future. Through this movement of possession we become ourselves, truly our own creators, discovering word for object, image for the Word.[26]

While Brathwaite largely focuses on the African presence, in the preceding quotation there is a sustained engagement with other non-European cultural aspects as "origins," funneled under the signifier Timehri. Brathwaite's signified, however, is not necessarily the *specificity* of Guyanese indigenous culture but the "primordial" culture (again, Maya) that cannot be readily recognized *throughout* the region, except by artists in countries where it exists. The ability of this culture to be collapsed under Timehri becomes significant for politicized appropriation and writing over of indigenous culture. Here, Brathwaite carves out a special relationship for the artist as a cultural medium and a means of allowing what is "primordial" to be made visible in the present. Thus, despite his years-long stay in Africa and the presence of Indigenous Peoples in Guyana, the difference between these cultures is negligible within creolization. Both African and indigenous cultures are in a past or are associated with a past, and it is the artist's job to continuously make these cultures present in the creation of the postcolonial Caribbean subject: "truly our own creators." Thus, the artist's cultural work or labor is to provide a bridge between African and Amerindian cultures as a simultaneous "journey into the past and hinterland" and "a movement of possession into present and future." The "our" of Brathwaite's creation, however, the "I/we" or subject it invokes, is one that does not exist only in the realm of culture. Brathwaite ignores the land rights issues that, in Harris's Guyana, relegate indigenous cultures to a true hinterland. We must therefore ask how these "pasts," which

I do not read as a metaphor of difference, differ. In other terms, for Indigenous Peoples in the Caribbean, are their "source" cultures located in the past in the same way that they are for the Creole? In "Timehri," indigenous culture must be mediated by the intellectual, who makes it visible in the "Word" (in essence, through its rewriting) with his intellectual labor. In foregrounding the necessary cultural work of the intellectual—of the same class responsible for "rootlessness"—Brathwaite reinforces the division of labor instituted by the colonial plantation and that initially produced these cultures as something from the past. Although Brathwaite rejects a teleology of culture in suggesting that African and Amerindian similarly serve as origins, creolization emerges as cultural belonging that is equally rooted by indigenous or African culture precisely because of the ability to make these cultures subject to intellectual labor, which secures Creole being in the postcolony.

This connection between African and Amerindian pasts is absent from Burton's work, which, according to Verene A. Sheppard and Glen L. Richards in their introduction to *Questioning Creole,* is a return, via Brathwaite's influence, to earlier theories of plural society. While I don't endorse plural society models, Burton's work is especially useful here because of his systematic—albeit more teleological—"attempt to chart, stage by stage," the transition from African to Creole.[27] Although Burton is more broadly concerned with culture and power, he begins by tracing how Jamaica, which like other Anglophone territories had a large influx of blacks, transformed itself in four more or less distinct stages from a colonial society with individual racial and cultural groups into a Creole society.[28] Burton carefully maps the shift from being culturally and cosmogonically African to ethnically Creole. This transformation is marked first by a "loss," in this case of "Guinea," and the process of transformation, which includes the "narrowing" of the distance among blacks, whites, and others. While we may debate whether or not what Burton frames as loss is cultural erasure or more in keeping with Brathwaite and other Afrocentric views of creolization, what interests me is how his sociocultural stages map a cultural shift from the development of plantations and the introduction of slaves from 1655 to 1700, through what he terms "consolidation and expansion" from 1700 to 1750, in which both the African and the Afro-Creole population grew together; and between 1750 and 1780, which Burton calls "the fulcrum." In this third stage, the population balance between Africans and Afro-Creoles "shifted" in favor of the latter, and in the final stage between 1780 and 1838 there was, Burton claims, an "acceleration" that led to Afro-Creole "synthesis."[29] Ultimately, for Burton, being Afro-Creole represented different stages of social, cultural, and economic participation and integration (in culture, language, dress, and class) into society.

For my focus on subjectivity, I amend Burton's initial stages—with Brathwaithe in mind—and articulate the transition from African to Afro-Creole as follows. Rather than Burton's strict sociocultural categories, I instead see five temporal, cultural, and material moments or shifts in a dialecticial operation:

1. The shift from being a geographic (and ontological) resident of continental Africa to African/enslaved New World resident or settler
2. The shift from being African/enslaved to Creole (understood in terms of different processes of creolization within African culture and between African and European and Indigenous cultures)/enslaved
3. The shift from Creole/enslaved to Creole/free/racialized with both the rise of race in the nineteenth century and in distinction to new, racialized indentured labor that was not *yet* Creole)
4. A new creolization with regard to indentured peoples (undergoing their own complex patterns of creolization) in territories where they were brought in large numbers, and
5. The shift from Creole/colonial subject to Creole/postcolonial citizen *and* native.

While all of these moments are essential to any discussion of Creole subjectivity, I focus on the final, often unmarked, moment of becoming that is often collapsed with/in creolization, so that to be creolized is to belong, to be native. In separating them, I call attention to the problems with their conflation, and I elaborate two orientations or modes of creolization as an indigenizing process, both of which remain integrative of the requirements and modes of Western humanity: a material orientation and a discursive one.

BEING AND BECOMING CREOLE

The material orientation of creolization involves a greater emphasis on the state and places the Creole in more solid social (and ethnic) class divisions that were not those of slavery or after, at least through the early twentieth century. It also involves the twentieth-century processes of decolonization that were not tied to independence in every case. However, independence, where it does occur, becomes a definitive consolidation of ethno-Creole identity in its difference from the nation's internal (Chinese, Indigenous Peoples, and so on) and external others. The reason for this is that in the New World, blacks have done two things that Indigenous Peoples did not and could not do. They have sought to become both native *and* national subjects, and *within* the economy of these positions, they have also claimed their humanity. They have recast this new native identity away from its paradoxical opposition to the colonial state (and association with deprivation when it designates Indigenous Peoples as native), making it contemporaneous with the formation of the postcolonial state.

Writing of enslaved blacks, specifically Creoles, José Luis González has argued in *Puerto Rico: The Four Storyed Country [Puerto Rico: el país de los cuatro pisos]* that they were the first Puerto Ricans because, having "the greatest difficulty in imagining any other place to live," they were the first to have to *make* the island a home.[30] In some sense, González echoes Walter Rodney's claim that the labor of blacks and indentured laborers is what transformed and "humanized" the land.[31] Both reflect a core Marxian value (Marx, Engels, Gramsci) that labor is not only the basis of social being but that it literally makes us hu/man.[32] Hungarian Marxist György Lukács, himself preoccupied with the subject–object relationship that develops uniquely to human labor, writes that labor is "the motor of man's humanization," largely because it is teleological and involves choice, or what he terms "alternatives," for attaining the goals of labor. More important, he finds that labor is instrumental in the development of human consciousness.[33] In short, man, as a physical being capable of cognition, does not exist without labor, and while there is, in Lukács's understanding, always some kind of goal, the human (society and imagination) is nonetheless also an outcome, a by-product of the "teleological positing" that inheres in the labor process.[34] For Lukács, labor does not simply effect outward change on objects but works to transform and produce human subjects in the process.[35] Thus, the subject literally performs his or her labor *for* being (the focus of chapter 2). Munasinghe notes that "the term *Creole* in popular Caribbean usage 'refers to a local product which is the result of a mixture or blending of various ingredients that originated in the Old World.'"[36] It is a definition of who the Creole is within society and for academic discussion that reveals the Creole as a *product* of a kind of sociocultural labor that is originary, if not native. What is problematic is that this labor necessitates an understanding of Indigenous Peoples as not fully human—in the context of postcolonial governments that fail to grant them rights—because their humanity is not teleological, having not been based on this modern concept of labor.

Gonzalez and Rodney, however, emphasize not just physical plantation labor but a more abstract notion: that work transforms the land, the self, and both the lived and imagined relationship to it, thereby creating a concept of "home" that was not necessarily posited as a goal of that work. In part, the desire to belong to the land as home (crucial in bridging the gap between the material and cultural forms of labor) is what led blacks to reject postemancipation indenture schemes that threatened this metaphysical ownership or possession where a material one had not been realized.[37] As the literal *house* of the subject, the colony as a home emerges as the latent goal of labor and demonstrates that what was once a desire or need to belong is now teleological. This is also the means by which an identity as enslaved laborers was transformed into what Percy Hintzen identifies as the "cultural capital" of blacks. In other words, the cultural capital that secured black political power was validated by a particular method of creating belonging in labor or social validity as new natives. Although Lukács has argued that Hegelian idealism essentially exploited "the teleological character of labor" and mistakenly "made teleology into the motor of history," it is nonetheless the Hegelian model of history that allows Creoles to complete or realize the product of their labor, where it could not be done materially, and to posit social being in *Western* modes of labor as the ontologically necessary condition of social being and belonging.[38]

At the moment they exited the plantation, blacks were subject to nineteenth-century economic humanism, which required labor for emerging (colonial) capitalist markets. In other words, they were subject to a new, capitalist globality that was in the process of redefining the modern laboring subject. Their identity as ex-slave labor was bound up with allowing them to claim that, following Guyanese historian Vere T. Daly, they were the first to "make" the country a home. This method of producing home as an object of capitalist labor is of course articulated within economic theory by Eric Williams in *Capitalism and Slavery* and later by Walter Rodney. Rodney's previously noted claim that humanization of the land required labor is essentially the same as the validation of the "human" required for Creoleness/ Caribbeanness. In this alternative way of reading the region's economic discourse, as a repetition of the new value of identity in labor, we can make the following observations. While Indigenous Peoples may in fact be quintessentially modern (to the extent that the category *native* is an invention of colonialism), blacks seeking a new identity inside a modernity that already shifted the terms of its participation, became not vassals—as in the sixteenth century—but free labor. They did so in a modern, colonial state that rede-fined its humanism away from the native, which it cast as premodern and illegitimate subjects who must remain so in the subsequent transformation of the state.

The key in this predicament, in the new mode of validating or guarantee-ing modern identity, was labor—both material and discursive. Both forms of labor were required and gained meaning under the new episteme or order of knowledge that Michel Foucault claims took hold in the nineteenth cen-tury. By the time blacks began leaving the plantations, labor was already abstracted and represented in or through other objects as their value. Value, in Foucault's definition, now rests in labor, both as the time it takes to com-plete work and its opposition, the tangible commodity produced from that expenditure. Labor, he claims, comes to mean the "'source of all value'" and thus it has a direct relationship to (Western) history, which Foucault defines as "labor, production, accumulation, and the growth of real costs."[39] An "end" to history, which Foucault discusses, can only occur through an end to labor and its current epistemic configuration: the much decried end of modernity. Black leaders in the Caribbean understood this. Thus we can construe Forbes Burnham's and Cheddi Jagan's early socialist vision as an attempt to recon-cile labor (as time) with the commodity. However, since black *belonging* is now contingent upon and validated by the social and epistemic status of labor, where blacks seek socialism or even a true communist society, their ontol-ogy seeks capitalism (in the embrace of modernization theory) as the guar-antor of an ontoepistemology based in its mode of labor. Socialism also does not undo the value placed in modern labor. Consequently, Indigenous Peoples, who throughout the Americas form a large peasant population, must also function as surplus labor, lest a new socialism (for example, Bolivia under Evo Morales) or episteme grant them equality.

The second orientation, the discursive, has to do with the ability of Cre-oles, largely after 1838 but certainly during the independence struggles of the twentieth century, to "see" themselves in discourse as distinct from the colonizer-settler, but in such a way that what was once a mark of inhumanity now becomes a sign of black humanity. The rise of literary subjectivity marks this phase. While the initial "cultural process" may have been extraliterary (recall Jonkonnu), by the time of the anticolonial moment, it has been trans-formed by ethnography, fiction, and exegesis. Douglas Midgett captures the significance of literary output when he states that "the very act of writing in societies that are as profoundly colonial as those in the West Indies is initially an assertion of identity."[40] More than just an assertion of identity, the writing of the Creole self is also, and intimately, a writing of resistance that marries cultural and political resistance. Thus resistance becomes essential to Creole identity, as illustrated by Wynter's work. Denise da Silva's writing on the subject—defined as "the thing that actualizes reason and freedom"—sheds more light on the role of resistance and its relation to the assertion of humanity for the subaltern.[41] She writes that "the racial subaltern is always already inscribed as a historical subject who finally comes into representation as a *transparent 'I'* when articulating an emancipatory project."[42] Emancipatory projects, in this case real and cultural (read Caliban from Shakespeare's *The Tempest*), become essential for overcoming what Silva calls the state of "affectability"— the "condition of being subjected to . . . power"—and moving into the state of "transparency" that represents a state of sovereignty in reason.[43] For Silva, "raciality" is significant in "the writing of the national subject as a *transparent 'I,'*" or as a version of such.[44] Thus, that state of transparency achieved by the former subaltern hinges on an identity based in race, something that has huge consequences, as we see in the following section, for the representation of Indigenous Peoples as ethnic/racial others who are not productive as market identities-cum-sovereign citizen-subjects.

What I hope to demonstrate in chapter 2 is that as a troping device, Caliban comes to represent and make possible the subject's understanding of *himself* as engaged in the dialectic, in the project and process of liberation that leads to transparency. Thus, while in the material emancipatory struggle the state is the outcome (telos), in discourse the struggle is, to recall Lukács, the human. What I suggest here is that Caribbean literary, cultural, and critical discourse become essential for the "self-troping" or "autoinstituting" of the Creole subject, where that belonging also establishes the emotive "rights" that the Native American writer Vine Deloria Jr. claims all settlers lack. According to Deloria, "There is a profound difference between American Indians and all of these other groups. The Indian is indigenous and therefore does not have the psychological burden of establishing his or her right to he land in the deep emotional sense of knowing that he or she belongs there."[45] Deloria's claim opens the way for thinking about the labor of formerly enslaved and indentured peoples not only as a material labor ultimately captured by the state but also as a labor *for* being. It is a labor that has produced the two senses of "right" (emotive-psychic and material) that require a poetics of indigeneity through which the Creole can emerge as simultaneously a subject in discourse and a native subject. In other words, it requires a poetics that can support Creole modes of being that are both real and emotive.

I develop this reading of the function of cultural and critical discourse from Sylvia Wynter's claims about the function of literary discourse in two of her essays. In "The Ceremony Must Be Found: After Humanism," Wynter writes that "far from 'literature having no function,' as it is assumed, it is we who are the function. It is as specific modes of imagining subjects of the aesthetic orders which literature's figuration-Word weaves in great feats of rhetorical engineering that we come to imagine/experience ourselves, our modes of being."[46] In other words, our discourse is essential to guaranteeing our modes of being and specifically for my reading of Creole subjectivity, the mode of being in and through labor. I couple Wynter's articulation of the role of literature with her reading of ideology as outlined in "Columbus and the Poetics of the *Propter Nos*." There she articulates a theory of human action and thought that involves ideology and truth, subjectivity and language, cognition and biology (primate). She uses Paul Ricoeur's work on ideology to define it not in Althusserian terms as "false consciousness" but instead to suggest that ideology is a self-justifying discourse that works through our own discursive-cultural self inscription or "autoinstituting" and consists of "the symbolic systems which orient behaviors and which, as [Clifford] Geertz says, 'provide a template or blueprint for the organization of social and psychological processes. . . .'"[47] She then links this definition to Richard Rorty's notion of truth and defines ideology as "what 'it is good for us to believe' within the logic of our culture's self-conception."[48] Following Wynter, I suggest that Caribbean cultural and critical discourses function to achieve both the autoinstituting of the subject and specifically the ideological function of the dominant class. The works of George Lamming and Aimé Césaire (a former mayor of Fort-de-France, Martinique), which have marked significant achievements in the depiction of a black literary subjectivity, provide an example of the working of the discursive orientation. In them, we see the function of literature in general and in terms of the ideology of the middle class in their achievement of a subject that reflects an excavation from within colonial ways of knowing and the assertion of a black Creole subjectivity that is or becomes native in its resistance to these ways of knowing.

Lamming, in *The Pleasures of Exile*, one of the most important collections of essays on Caribbean culture, explores the psychological condition of colonialism in the West Indies and its effects on Caribbean literary production. Key in his argument about the special colonial attitude held by black West

Indians is the difference from both the black African and African American experiences. What sets a West Indian apart from an African, Lamming claims, is that the latter "in spite of his modernity, has never been wholly severed from the cradle of a continuous culture and tradition."[49] Lamming thus imagines an enduring and unbroken African civilization in the Caribbean. In contrast, what distinguishes black Americans from West Indians is not just the way in which they have been differently severed and affected by the loss of culture, but, essentially, demographics or their numerical relationship to whites. In a long section in his essay "The Occasion for Speaking," Lamming reads in James Baldwin's *Notes of a Native Son* an echo of Hegel's devastating assessment of black history in *The Philosophy of History*. Baldwin's opinions of black, especially African, "backwardness" are the result, Lamming concludes, of a minority position that the West Indian in a predominantly black environment would never have to experience. What this means for Lamming is that even though he will go on to claim that "colonialism is the very base and structure of the West Indian's cultural awareness," he finds that "no black West Indian, in his *own* native environment, would have this highly oppressive sense of being Negro."[50]

Despite the problematic nature of his invocation of a modernizing Africa as the repository of two opposed chronologies, I am not interested in a criticism of Lamming at this point. Rather, I am interested in his framing of the West Indian subject with an English cultural surrogacy that, while formative, needs to also be rejected. For Lamming, this socially felt surrogacy (as distinguished from its institutional reality) does not seem to require either the individual's conscious or concretized articulation (as evidenced by a girl in British Guiana who Lamming notes in 1956 "does not yet understand what it means to be colonial") and thus constitutes, after Raymond Williams, a contemporary structure of feeling.[51] What Lamming demonstrates with *Pleasures* and with his seminal literary work, *In the Castle of My Skin,* is the economic, social, and cultural ground of colonialism that forms the basis for a psychological experience of *belonging* that is uniquely black, uniquely West Indian. He also does it in such a way that *native* is not adjectival, but in this articulation functions to denote a belonging that is about ownership. It is this unique sense of place that is invoked to a certain extent in Césaire's long poem, "Notebook of a Return to the Native Land," which presents the speaker as a subject whose return to a still-colonial Martinique is already being made within the context of a belonging to the land that is an indigenous one. Read another way, in telling us what it means to be black in the Anglophone and Francophone Caribbean, Lamming and Césaire are also articulating contingent native positions based on a particular experience of culture in place. It is this discursive position that found social expression in the Belizean writer John Watler.

In 2006, Watler, in a conversation about that country's border dispute with Guatemala, referred to himself as a "native," invoking a common Belizean identity for Creoles and Indigenous Peoples alike.[52] For Watler, Maya peoples appear within the state literally rescripted from the margins of political life. Lamming and Césaire articulate a twentieth-century native identity that names itself in comparison to the relationship to colonial power. While Lamming and Césaire seem to express a Creole identity that is synonymous with and can be invoked interchangeably as a native identity (regardless, one should note, of the political situation) shared by Caribbean blacks, Watler reveals the anchor of these other articulations, their objective character. However, what serves as the condition of possibility for these positions is not articulated as such. It is presumptive and unstated: it is that black, New World identity (this native identity) is based both on material and discursive labor. The Creole, as a thoroughly colonial and masculinized subject in Lamming's view, has managed to establish a claim to the land through a rejection of this surrogacy, an operation that allows him to see himself not simply as black but as a native grounded by a renewable temporality.

Lamming's, Césaire's, and even Watler's, however, is a new native identity that does not evenly or equally incorporate the three cultural, historical, geographic, and other differences that Stuart Hall has argued are at the basis of an "always-already" diasporic Caribbean cultural identity, especially for Watler's Belizean native. In "Cultural Identity and Diaspora," Hall suggests that the Caribbean model of ethnicity that developed through the crucible of migration, displacement, and difference is neither singular nor hegemonic. Rather, it is constituted by overlapping cultures of difference and similarity underlined by three "presences": *Présence Africaine, Présence Européenne,* and *Présence Americaine.* While the first two are largely cultural presences that have persisted, the final, which he refers to as the "Third, New World presence," is marked as "Terra Incognita" or "the beginning of diaspora, of diversity, of hybridity, and difference" that underlies Caribbean identity.[53] Hall reduces this third presence, after African and European, to land (not labor or necessarily culture); to a difference that only materializes as the ground of Creole cultural enactment. In Hall, there is no consideration of the over- and misidentification of Indigenous Peoples with land, alongside the expropriation of their lands and the recreation of their relationship to land through the reservation. Nor does Hall consider that the discourses of displacement and loss applied to African or European culture may not smoothly articulate and may in fact limit the possibility for an "enunciation" of native culture, identity, and sovereignty.

Lamming and Césaire effectively rewrite Hall's material ground as a cultural terra incognita, a palimpsest for their articulation of black identity as native. They therefore offer an I/we that continues to marginalize Indigenous Peoples and hinges upon the labor of resistance, performed for instance by Caliban, as *the* Creole subject. The *I* of Césaire's black subject is necessary for the dialectical relationship that allows blacks to position themselves as native as opposed to others, and it is also at this moment that displacement of Indigenous Peoples becomes central or necessary for black reinvention. What is more interesting is that the model for becoming native, in Césaire's anticolonial poetics, comes from both Haiti, where the revolution made blacks native, and Martinique, where the returning native is black.[54] One model is "post" colonial, the other is anticolonial; a further example of the renewable temporality (read Brathwaite's pasts for futures) for Creole indigeneity that secures representations of *being* here, not in the "past," as we saw with Brathwaite, which is now designated as the time-space-place of Indigenous Peoples and the mode of indigeneity as dispossession to which they were relegated within the colonial state and now the postcolonial state. The deployment of the material goal within the discursive tradition is most clear in examination of the Forbes Burnham regime in chapter 4, which reveals how the link is articulated by the educated poets, writers, and cultural producers whom Burnham tapped to represent his vision for the country. In that vision, Indigenous Peoples become collapsed with the lands they inhabit in the development plan for the country's interior, thereby treating both as *terra incognita* in the articulation and deployment of an indigenous Afro-Creole identity.

CREOLE INDIGENEITY

The key terms that emerge in this reconceptualization of Creole modes of producing belonging and identity are *settler* and *native*. This section draws on work on settler colonialism and thinking about the settler/native dynamic in the extra-Caribbean contexts of Australia and Africa. Beginning with Patrick Wolfe's *Settler Colonialism and the Transformation of Anthropology: The Politics and Poetics of an Ethnographic Event* in 1999, there has been an explosion in settler colonialism studies and vigorous debate that explores the term's usefulness as an analytic and paradigm for a broad range of political and geographic contexts with their own specific histories of imperialism and colonialism. More recently, the debate on the term *settler colonialism* entered the blogosphere through "Tequila Sovereign," to which Wolfe himself has contributed, and the "settler colonial studies blog."[55] Apart from the growing number of studies that fall within the heading of settler colonialism studies, there is thus a simultaneous rethinking of the term, not unlike that undergone by postcolonial studies, which seeks to both assert its relevance for describing contemporary settler relationships in, for instance, North America and its limits when thinking beyond the traditional white settler colonial context. In a 2008 special issue of *South Atlantic Quarterly (SAQ)*, these engagements with the term were played out, the former nominally represented by Alyosha Goldstein's essay on U.S. settler colonialism and the latter by María Josefina Saldaña-Portillo's on the limits of the term's applicability for Latin America.[56]

While *Creole Indigeneity* sees itself as contributing to that discussion, I do not reiterate the definitions and debates since Wolfe. More work needs to be done on the applicability of the term as an analytic for contemporary nation-states (subordinated politically and economically to First World capital and neoliberalism) that developed out of the forcible transportation of laborers who, now majorities, have settled. The complications of easy application to the Caribbean can be probed through Wolfe's seminal work in which he distinguishes between settler colonialism in Africa and elsewhere (largely but not exclusively about the object of his study, Australia). Wolfe claims that the objective of settler colonialism is not "to extract surplus value from indigenous labour," but that it is more or less to get rid of the native and supplant his and her cultural and political systems with those of the settler.[57] This statement is useful for thinking about what has happened in the Caribbean, where Anglophone colonies that were not necessarily envisioned as settler colonies, but as colonies for the singular extraction of wealth from black labor, eventually left black bodies as surplus. Wolfe's definition underscores both the applicability of the term to the Caribbean and its failure to work there. While the desire to assimilate Indigenous Peoples by the British can be seen as a general attempt to remove the native presence for potential settlement, the ultimate settlers were those they sought to extract labor from, and they are the ones who eventually rearticulated this assimilationist position in their anticolonial struggle.

My application of *settler* to designate Creole relationships to the indigenous population, a move that will undoubtedly be controversial, is neither uncritical nor static. It does not rest on whether or not the Caribbean can be considered a settler colonial space and what its differences are or are not from others more easily defined, such as Canada, the United States, Australia, and so on, or less well defined such as Fiji. Rather, it derives from a consideration of the techniques of settler belonging and their ability to be refashioned and redeployed. To that end, the most relevant essay in that *SAQ* issue is Grant Farred's "The Unsettler," in which, discussing Darfur primarily, he defines the *unsettler* as the contemporary outcome of the settler but one whose motive is, using military force, to exterminate the native.[58] So defined, the term *unsettler* is not applicable to the Caribbean. Nonetheless, Farred usefully characterizes the settler in four key ways: first, as a "political force that makes publicly evident the subjugation of the colonized"; second, as having a need to be rooted, although this is continuously deferred; third, through a need to "deracinate" rather than exterminate the native; and fourth, as preoccupied with "temporality," more specifically the need for the time of autochthonous people to be "surpassed" by "the modernity of colonialism."[59] According to Farred, "The settler is a figure of contradiction rather than uninterrupted colonial hegemony."[60] I draw on Farred's definition of the settler because it is illuminating for our understanding of how Creoles indigenize and how they relate to Indigenous Peoples where even what can be construed of as disappearance, or a narrative of such, represents a tension that maintains the native as present or immanent and hence always part of the Creole's dialectic of being and becoming. Farred's recognition of the dis/continuity of settler identity and power is what we see following in Frantz Fanon's and Mahmood Mamdani's discussions of settler and native not as concrete identities but as both fixed within particular historical moments and configurations of modern power and fluid across the shifts and changes in that power, such as Caribbean independence.

In *The Wretched of the Earth*, Fanon discusses "settler" and "native," in this case French colonials and Algerians, in stark terms. His writing evinces the dualism of the anticolonial movement later critiqued and rejected by poststructuralist methodologies in postcolonial studies. For Fanon, the settler clearly represents a position and identity of power during the colonial period to which the native is diametrically opposed. However, in a gesture that seems to anticipate complications of the settler/native dichotomy by later theorists, Fanon writes that "it is the settler who has brought the native into existence and who perpetuates his existence. The settler owes the fact of his very existence ... his property, to the colonial system."[61] Although he almost exclusively identifies the settler with access to and accumulation of capital, Fanon defines both settler and native as mutually constitutive products of the colonial system. Settler and native, for Fanon, reflect the conflict between labor and capital that produces, maintains, and transforms social classes. Equally important, for our purposes, Fanon sees a mutual dependence of settler and native in that their identities derive from each other and are in fact maintained by each other. While the anticolonial position had focused on the struggle to get rid of the "settler," a process that is arguably and disastrously still ongoing in Zimbabwe, for instance, Fanon hints at a much more complicated and even dialectical relationship between the two whereby neither category can function without the other.

Mahmood Mamdani teases out some of this complication in his essay on violence among groups in contemporary Africa, "Beyond Settler and Native as Political Identities: Overcoming the Political Legacy of Colonialism." He argues that the political-economic model of underdevelopment theorists, which perceives groups as "market-based identities," cannot explain violence. Mamdani also rejects dominant cultural models that fail to see that race and ethnicity are "political identities" produced through the colonial state and reproduced in the postcolonial state. He therefore maintains that the positions of settler (dominance) and native (subordination) were problematic during the colonial period and remain so in postcolonial African states. Consequently, Mamdani asserts the need to recognize that although postcolonial states have passed through independence, the designations of *native* and *settler* still continue to determine identity and rights as they intersect with culture and political economy. During the colonial period, he writes, Indigenous Peoples were regarded as ethnic groups and hence were excluded from civil society, and nonnatives or settlers (though this group could include natives) were regarded in terms of race and hence subject to the laws of civil society. In postcolonial, nationalist ideology, however, Mamdani identifies a shift in what he identifies as the "native-settler dialectic" where rights are now conferred according to indigenous status, and nonnatives or settlers, such as those who migrated for work, are denied rights. *Settler*, Mamdani claims, no longer refers to white colonials—as it does for Fanon—but to "all immigrants," with problematic and confusing results. He cites, for instance, the example of Nigeria, where those who belong to different ethnic groups are considered indigenous only within the territory of their "ancestral homes." Once outside that territory, even though they remain within the borders of the Nigerian state, they are considered nonindigenous. In identifying settler and native as embattled political identities, Mamdani suggests that in the African context not only do we now have "postcolonial settlers" and "postcolonial natives," but he recommends that for African states, indigeneity should be rejected as a basis for rights claims.[62]

Although Mamdani's recommendation that indigeneity be abandoned as a "litmus test for rights" is problematic, his work intervenes in the settler/native dichotomy in useful ways.[63] Not only does he assert that they are political identities, which is the essence of the problem, but he makes an important distinction when arguing that "the process of state formation generates political identities that are distinct . . . from market based identities" and "from cultural identities."[64] Mamdani upends static understandings of settler and native by illustrating how different groups slip in and out of these identities and the ways in which they inform political reality in the postcolony. For instance, according to Mamdani, "yesterday's immigrants" have essentially "become indigenous" or do so when they struggle to remain.[65] He thus alerts us to the fact that in the postcolonial period, the terms can be applied to racialized groups with vastly different access to power and with the potential to be coupled and uncoupled from economic identities. This latter fact is significant in the Guyanese context, where Indigenous Peoples are understood as largely failed market identities and, as such, are denied "prior arrival" rights and political power stemming from a more integrated relationship to the current political economy. Although they are considered a racial group, it is an ethnicized racial group, to borrow from Mamdani, that reinforces their failure to be productive racialized market groups. Indigenous Peoples thus emerge in Guyana as ethnic identities who do not have market power: a distinction that is critical when a national identity as Guyanese, for instance, erases their difference from Creoles.

Mamdani's work alerts us, again, to the danger of homogenizing the racial subject. More important, it reinforces the complicated way in which settler and native, as identities that are invested with power, do not vanish with independence. This is especially so when, as Daiva Stasiulis and Nira Yuval-Davis note in their discussion of the problems of traditional scholarship on settler societies, migrant laborers were "constructed . . . as settlers" rather than as "'guest workers.'"[66] While these analyses do not speak of the Caribbean, they help me to demonstrate the ways in which the "dialectic" of settler and native continues to operate in the region. Mamdani and Fanon in particular offer a conceptual frame for my examination of settler and native in the Caribbean, which I recast as a dialectic between being native and (an indigenizing) Créolité. The titular term *Creole Indigeneity* is introduced as a way of coming to terms with the specificity of this power dynamic in the Caribbean situation.

Creole indigeneity refers to the practices of belonging and becoming that have provided a new material, symbolic, and discursive relationship to the land for blacks, Indo-Guyanese, *and* Indigenous Peoples. The term captures the unique tensions between settler and native—where *native* refers to a fixed identity of Indigenous Peoples and the inhabiting of that term by Creoles via their indigenizing and creolization processes—that still operate in Guyana and throughout the Caribbean. It rivets our attention to the evolution of Creole and native as interdependent yet oppositional identities that reproduce colonial geography and epistemology as natural. Thus, *Creole indigeneity is meant to capture the cultural, ethnic dimension of indigenous and nonindigenous identities where it intersects with and departs from their politicization as market identities.* Creole indigeneity should be understood as a reflection of the labor/capital dynamic within the Caribbean and between the Caribbean and the First World. It also reflects the materialist tradition in its opposition to the idealist tradition in Caribbean discourse. I deploy the term *Creole indigeneity,* rather than *postcolonial indigeneity* (to recall Mamdani's postcolonial natives) because the latter cannot account for the problems faced by Indigenous Peoples in the New World, nor can it address their own complex creolized modes of indigeneity. More important, Creole indigeneity captures what I see as the rerouting of indigeneity in the Caribbean as both a material and ontoepistemic phenomenon that produces the postcolonial economy and imaginary. In its attempt to capture this mutuality, the term is admittedly a destabilizing one, meant to reflect Fanon's intervention that these terms and political positions do not make sense without each other and, significantly, that they enact each other. In this regard we should remember that the term *native* or *Indian,* was not only a mistake—what Gayatri Spivak refers to as a "hegemonic false category"—but never existed in any Native American language, just as *black* never initially existed to describe a group of people, and in the Caribbean, *East Indian* had to be invented for another.[67] Despite, for instance, the acceptance of and even preference for the term by many Indigenous Peoples, including radical groups, the word *Indian* speaks to the long reinvention of autochthonous peoples in the Americas in languages, cultures, and juridical systems that socially and culturally produced them and maintained their subordination as Indian, as native, as other to (European) man.

Paying attention to this invention of the native (after Fanon's and Mamdani's intervention), my deployment of the term *indigeneity* reflects a strategic uncoupling from *native*. While being native has always been a construction of power within European modernity based on time, place, and alterity, indigeneity gestures to the practices of belonging that produce ontological viability and social validity for both indigenous *and* nonindigenous groups. As should be clear throughout this book, the expansion of the concept is not meant to in any way undermine the cultures or rights of First Peoples in the Americas. It is, however, meant to make a distinction between the fixed category "native" and the more fluid processes of belonging (indigeneity) that Indigenous Peoples *and* Creoles have. Next, I explore the ways social and anthropological theory have attempted to deal with indigenization in the Caribbean before further clarifying my own position.

In *Ethnic Identity in the Caribbean: Decentering a Myth,* Ralph Premdas writes that "creolisation is a cultural mode of indigenisation and for some serves as the litmus test of loyalty and entitlement to the patrimony of the land."[68] Premdas's claim speaks directly to the way in which greater or lesser identification with largely Afro-Creole culture determines both Caribbean cultural authenticity and positions Afro-Creoles against Indians, Chinese, Indigenous Peoples, and others in the region who are considered less authentically Creole and therefore less deserving of both political power and material wealth. What he identifies as "indigenisation," however, does not fully capture the material, cultural, and metaphysical aspects of belonging because it suggests that culture by itself is what determines the native status of Creoles. While I agree with Premdas, who echoes Sylvia Wynter's claim about cultural indigenization in her essay on Jonkonnu, the process of cultural becoming captured here with indigenization does not address how what it means to be indigenous has been redefined for Guyana and the entire region. It also continues to reserve a fixed definition of native belonging that ignores indigenous modes of creolization and indigenization. In contrast to the Creole indigenization Premdas discusses, which renders indigenous identity static against Creole cultural processes, there is anthropologist Maximilian Forte's intervention. Forte is founding editor of the online *Journal of Caribbean Amerindian History and Anthropology,* a publication of the Web-based "Caribbean Amerindian Centrelink," which compiles information about Indigenous Peoples in the Caribbean. His work is an approach to native indigeneity that seeks to account for an ongoing dynamic within Indigenous Peoples' identity in the Americas.[69]

Building upon contemporary questions in the social sciences and humanities on indigeneity, Forte argues in *Ruins of Absence, Presence of Caribs: (Post)Colonial Representations of Aboriginality in Trinidad and Tobago* that "indigeneity is not ontologically absolute, permanent, or inflexible in content, form, and meaning."[70] What he therefore does throughout his study of Carib indigeneity in Trinidad is distinguish between two forms of indigeneity for Trinidad. Forte acknowledges "the indigeneity associated with those identifying with an Amerindian heritage" and a "national indigeneity," which he suggests broadly incorporates an association or identification of the indigenous with the modern state, something usually done by cultural and political "elites" (recall Hind's evocation of the Umana Yana as a "national thing").[71] A large part of Forte's work is in fact concerned with the "re-engineering" of Carib indigeneity. Therefore, in discussing these two senses of indigeneity, Forte breaks the concept itself into the discursive, performative, and theoretical practices used to represent Indigenous Peoples, and indigeneity as it is conferred by "birth, national citizenship" or prior arrival.[72] Forte's articulation of indigeneity usefully gets beyond the thorny issues of cultural authenticity often identified in articulations and criticism of aboriginal identity. However, its distinction from my use is that for Forte, indigeneity as either a social concept or node of analysis still refers *only* to identity, however constructed. Thus, what he identifies as "national indigeneity" is just the process that describes the symbolic appropriation in the postcolonial period of that which is already native despite the ways in which this has changed for the indigenous groups he identifies. Further, what is already native and subject to new indigenization (reflecting a creolization) is thus in opposition to that which is fixed as Creole: for Guyana, we can understand it as the difference between the Umana Yana and Cuffy (see introduction to this book). My work, however, points to indigeneity as a process in which both subaltern-settler groups and Indigenous Peoples are engaged. Elsewhere, Forte argues that the presumed extinction of Indigenous Peoples having emerged as the justification for black introduction should be regarded as a "narrative component" of Caribbean sociohistorical discourse.[73] Departing from Forte, I argue that as more than just a narrative feature, Caribbean discourse, and consequently Creole identity, cannot sustain itself without the reiteration of this dual basis for black sociocultural identity: displacement of Indigenous Peoples and, through the plantation, the introduction of a new, more socially viable and integrating basis for belonging or being native: labor. Further, the narrative of extinction forecloses the possibility of a singularly laboring identity for

Indigenous Peoples that Europeans tried to establish with the *encomienda* and *repartimiento* systems.[74]

While Forte usefully rivets our attention to how Indigenous Peoples have gone through their own creolization, I suggest that indigeneity itself needs to be rethought in terms of its refashioning by both nonindigenous and Indigenous Peoples. The distinction, therefore, is between the modes of indigeneity associated with First Peoples and the modes of indigeneity (both prior to and after colonization) associated with Creoles, particularly because the latter is being deployed as a category of social being with consequences for political rights. It further renders ongoing indigenization by Indigenous Peoples either as a sign of their creolization and, hence, lack of rights from any prior presence in the region, or of Creole indigenizing and its ability to confer rights. While it might be confusing to use *Creole indigeneity* to refer to both processes that involve all ethnics (including Indigenous Peoples) and, especially in chapter 4, to designate black and Indian belonging as distinct from Indigenous Peoples' *native indigeneity,* it is important in this work to keep the term somewhat open-ended. By not fixing indigeneity, I make visible the active modes of indigenization that inform the historic and quotidian constructions and articulations of the identity of Indigenous Peoples in the Caribbean and of Creole cultural and political identity. Creole indigeneity is representative of the tension first between Indigenous Peoples and Creoles and second between the state of being native and indigeneity; in other words, between identity (especially for citizenship) and the processes of belonging. The term conceptually ties the destabilization of native to the reinvention of Creole as native through a relationship to labor that has a regionwide, ontoepistemic function to support modern belonging and the institution of the Creole as a new native.

Becoming native, however, or forming an indigenous identity out of or from a position of objecthood or non-personhood (the slave) is not just a performative act. The attempts to limit creolization to cultural processes, even when they assert that Creole culture is tied to labor, miss the fact that creolization as a process of indigenizing is conceived within the time, geography, and discourse of the Western encounter and as such requires negation.[75] With identity conceived as temporal and cultural progress, what for Deloria would be the Western choice of time (historicity) over space, displacement of Indigenous Peoples thus becomes the central feature of the reinvention of the formerly enslaved and formerly indentured laborers as postcolonial subjects in contemporary Caribbean states.[76] Becoming native, as a cultural and material phenomenon for Creoles, therefore, preserves Indigenous Peoples in the past of postcolonial time while "descent" from the plantation secures the Creole's present. The method in which each group was established as a laboring population, or failed to be fully identified with teleologically oriented labor, has specific consequences for later social rejection or integration. The plantation and its mode of being *in* labor, which saw its ultimate value in the onset of the Industrial Revolution, if one again follows Eric Williams's argument about the role of black slavery in the rise of capitalism, is now the condition of indigeneity for Africans *and* Indigenous Peoples.[77] Blacks recognize, exploit, and make this the new episteme for all other groups. In other words, material labor and intellectual or creative articulation of this labor constitute the dual basis of humanity for blacks in the New World and is by extension a core element of social and political subjectivity. A literary example occurs with Aimé Césaire's play about the aftermath of the Haitian Revolution, when his fictionalized Henri Christophe remarks in what can be seen as a regional, self-conscious assessment of the triumph and failure of Haiti: "I won't have the world so much as suspect, that ten years of black freedom, ten years of black slovenliness and indifference, have sufficed to squander the patrimony that our martyred people has amassed in a hundred years of labor under the whip."[78] Prior to Christophe's ascension to power, Jean-Jacques Dessalines had decreed that only blacks could own land in Haiti. For blacks, as Christophe imagined it, having rights to the New World and more specifically, black freedom, thus depends fundamentally upon labor, which was coercive both during slavery and after. It is upon labor that the spiritual, ethical, and structural claims of U.S. civil rights rested. Although Deloria claimed that Indigenous Peoples rejected the Christian ideology and institutional orientation of the struggle, it is more pointedly the role that labor plays as the epistemic ground or truth of black claims. Current calls by African Americans, for example, for reparations based on having worked for the nation or for human rights based in large part on labor, stand against those based on prior sovereignty and land rights that are both *anti-* and *ante-* (Western) labor. For labor to work for native claims of sovereignty and human rights, Indigenous Peoples would have to accept social and political being as workers for the modern nation. When we look at the anticolonial negotiation of Creole subjectivity and at postcolonial political discourse, we see that to be Creole is to literally rewrite what Wynter calls the "governing codes" for humanity in a way that does not oppose the Western conception of what it means to be human for non-whites. This mode of being is again, through labor, despite labor's function in marking degrees of in/humanity. Further, becoming Creole is both indigenist and indigenizing, because of the way in which it is validated as historically prior. The organization of labor in the plantation serves as the epistemic ground for articulations of Creole subjectivity. Thus, the Creole subject is always already grounded by, made possible by, the material structure of the plantation and its role in producing blacks as modern subjects.

NEGROS DA TERRA AND NEGROS DA GUINÉ: THE CONFLICTING MODES AND TIMES OF INDIGENEITY

The disarticulations of Creole modes of indigenizing and those of Indigenous Peoples charted in the introduction and this chapter occur along a fundamental axis: time. It is to this final issue that I now turn in order to underscore the ontoepistemic significance of modern labor. I argue that labor by formerly enslaved and indentured peoples is precisely what they are able to make into and reify as the new *prior* time of their belonging and with which they supplant the prior time of Indigenous Peoples. It is a time that guarantees their state-based identities and modes of sovereignty within the postcolonial state.

In the colonial period, we can chart the engineering of new relationships to time and identity. According to Jack D. Forbes, in their early interaction in the Americas, Indigenous Peoples (referred to as *Americans* in his work) and blacks once shared the same identity categories. In *Black Africans and Native Americans: Color, Race, and Caste in the Evolution of Red-Black Peoples,* Forbes writes of Indigenous Peoples in Brazil being referred to as both *indios* and *negros* well before enslaved blacks were a significant part of the population there. However, such early ambiguity eventually led to a sharper distinction within and stabilization of once-fluid identity categories. Thus, he writes that "when Africans are referred to in the Jesuit letters they are always called *negros da Guiné* (Blacks of Guinea) to distinguish them from *negros da terra* (Blacks of the land or Americans)."[79] Forbes cites a clause in a 1755 Portuguese law that freed the Indigenous Peoples of a particular area of Brazil, except those with enslaved mothers of "African descent." The clause states that they have been abused by "the unjustifiable and scandalous practice of calling them negroes. Perhaps by so doing the intent was no other than to induce in them the belief that by their origins they had been destined to be slaves of whites, as is generally conceded to be the case of Blacks from the coast of Africa. . . ."[80] Another 1750s Portuguese law eventually made illegal the substitution of *negro* for *indio*.[81] For Forbes, examples such as these illustrate the unstable nature of the ill-defined categories still in use, and they reflect the fact that *negro* originally referred to color, not race, biology, or geography. With these laws, the Portuguese in essence caught up with the Spanish, who had, two centuries prior, instituted this distinction theologically.

In the Spanish colonies, we know through the writing of the Dominican priest Bartolomé de Las Casas that Indigenous Peoples were placed under the protection of the Spanish crown after the hideous abuses of the *encomienda* system in Latin America. In his "defense" of Indigenous Peoples, Las Casas rejected the Aristotelian logic of natural slavery being used to subordinate them and essentially redefined natives not as the purely secular others that blacks would become, but as "gentiles."[82] Las Casas was, therefore, able to argue for black enslavement and in the sixteenth century, blacks were introduced to the New World as slaves. What is significant about Portuguese law and Spanish theology (and eventual law) is that in all, being native by the eighteenth century comes to mean not being black, not being essentially born to be a slave (property or capital).[83] More important, the distinction in the Jesuit letters suggests that what *indio* (in its distinction from *negro*) eventually comes to mean is a relationship to the land that blacks do not have. Black identity, in contrast, would always point to an alternative or external *terra* that conflicts with the geography of the New World. In the New World, this alternative geography signaled by and with black flesh (and, eventually, supposed differences in reason, physiognomy, and blood) became inextricably bound with an identity in labor, not the land (Africa) that was literally displaced in their skin.

The affective difference signaled by *da terra* versus *da Guiné* as modifiers of a single category—black—works to displace Africa as a prior time for black identity in the New World, which ultimately, as we see in chapter 2, becomes a condition of their humanity within modernity. The "time" of black indigenous identity in Africa is eventually replaced with the "time" of black identity—not in the land, but in modern labor and its ability to change both the self and the land. It is a time that contrasts sharply with Indigenous Peoples' embodied relationships to time, as discussed, for instance, by George Mentore.[84]

The initial legal and theological distinctions made by the Portuguese and the Spanish would set the stage for the evolution of two distinct social groups in Latin America and the Caribbean, one a laboring population primarily associated with a dying *encomienda,* and later, *repartimiento,* system and the reservation as a space of non-labor or unproductive labor by particular standards. The other would be associated with the rise of a thriving plantation system, the hallmark of Caribbean society. As eighteenth-century law gave way to nineteenth-century science and scientific racism, black and native became two separate categories that signified different juridical, social, and economic techniques for exploitation and displacement. They also came to manage different degrees of social and cultural integration in colonial society and integration in the national economy of the postcolony, according to different axes of time.

Césaire's poem "Birds," which, along with Basil Rodrigues's "Natural Ways," serves as the epigraph to this book, concretizes the relationship of Creoles to time. In "Birds," the cosmogonies of *indigenous* African peoples are made subject to and transformed by the confrontation with and immersion in European time. The painful and dehumanizing condition of uprootedness or "exile," for Césaire, must become the new spiritual food ("clumsy grains") of blacks transported across the Atlantic. Thus, in the opposition of "stars" to "time," or of African cosmogony to Western historicity, Césaire depicts the remaking of the African subject through engagement with postdiscovery, European subjecthood, economy, and society. In contrast, "Natural Ways" presents us with an aesthetic that is differently grounded in both labor and nature and stands apart from the production of the new grains, the new subject, the new aesthetic of the Creole seeking his or her freedom to the exclusion of the native subject, requiring his literal and figurative death, or at the very least, disappearance. It is against this requirement that Rodrigues writes and against which indigenous subjectivity, having gone through its own creolization with regard to coastal Creole culture, Spanish and Portuguese culture, and other indigenous cultures, is now affirmed. Although they are not considered Creole, Indigenous Peoples today *are* creolized to various degrees with regard to plantation society, and this creolization is part of their own reindigenizing in a territory to which they have always belonged. However, that belonging became in essence an unbelonging with the execution of the settler–racial contract. Further, Rodrigues's metaphorical subject, which cannot stand in as or for *the* native subject reflecting the particular creolization and indigeneity of some groups, is understood only through the time of Creole belonging (technically the time it took within the capitalist economy to transform raw materials and make them valuable and hence produce capitalist globality) and its aesthetics. It is not necessarily understood in terms of its own alternatively creolized aesthetic, which relates to but is not embedded within or delimited by "exile" within transformations of modern labor. The juxtaposition of Rodrigues's "Natural Ways" with Aimé Césaire's "Birds" is thus meant to signal the ways that Creole modes of indigeneity—in which the labor of the formerly enslaved and proletarians constructs the postcolonial state—abut and conflict with indigenous modes of being, which historically are not defined through modern labor.[85] It also reveals that in pursuit of the human, what feeds one body and spirit is not what feeds another. We must therefore understand that Césaire's "birds" *as* subject only make sense through the misreading of Rodrigues's "birds" in "Natural Ways," *for* subjectivity.

The poems point to the disarticulation of indigenous and black histories and cultures with the greater immersion of blacks and Indians within the European economy and the relegation of Indigenous Peoples to spaces largely outside the Caribbean plantation economy. Deloria again alerts us to the contemporary political consequences of this disarticulation when he argues that the civil rights struggle in the United States could not equally represent both blacks and Indigenous Peoples. He claims that few Native Americans participated in the civil rights struggle, largely because of its orientation toward institutional forms of justice that necessarily excluded Indigenous Peoples and because, as he sees it, it rested heavily on Christian ideology, which they necessarily had to reject.[86] Judy Rohrer reinforces Deloria's point in her examination of how U.S. mainland civil rights discourse hurts Kanaka Maoli attempts to maintain Kamehameha schools as spaces dedicated to preserving Hawai'i's Indigenous Peoples and cultures.[87] The failure of the black civil rights struggle to address the needs of Indigenous Peoples because of greater integration of blacks into white society in the United States suggests that we are encountering a model of black belonging in the Americas that might conflict (especially to the extent that it is based on resistance, as Wynter's work suggests) with but is not antagonistic to Euro-American modes of humanity, both materially and spiritually. Rodrigues points to a problem similar to the one Deloria identifies when, in an interview I conducted with him, he remarked that although independence—which in Anglophone territories such as Barbados, Trinidad, and Guyana was precipitated by labor agitation by black and Indian workers—was a hugely significant moment for Guyana as a whole, it did not mean that much for indigenous communities. In other words, it changed their reality very little. Both Deloria and Rodrigues remind us of how the postcolonial state emerges to capture and privilege those citizen-subjects whose identities are tied to modern labor and notions of progress, due to their linearly understood transitions from unfree to free labor to national subject and state citizen. Moreover, Deloria and Rodrigues point to the shared structure of native displacements (blacks from Africa; Indians from India; Indigenous Peoples in the New World; all of whom we must remember were indigenous or became so at the moment of each European encounter) that produce two Creole aesthetics, two indigenizing poetics (arguably collapsed in black Carib identity and Garifuna; see introduction) that are not equally validated by labor and the political economy of the postcolonial state.

With independence, Creoles then sought to transform identities based *in* labor and *as* capital to ones based more solidly on access to capital, thus resolving that fundamental "contradiction between capital and labour" that has been central to understandings of New World humanity.[88] This conflict, which resulted in African and Indian subordination under slavery and indenture, respectively, has produced the modern Creole subject's ontological dependence on labor, requiring the subordination of Indigenous Peoples as both the material and figurative other to the Creole *I*. Furthermore, it reflects how Creoles have had to ground their right to political power in the epistemological terrain of 1492 and successive waves of imperial power, which necessarily conflicts with native, subaltern populations who must reject the validity of 1492 and the social and political systems to which it gave rise and in which Creoles have sought power. Identities forged over time and within their own concepts of time, such as the concept of "time immemorial" deployed by Indigenous Peoples in Guyana to describe the occupation of land, are challenged by those others formed through a profound temporal break and shift (Creole).[89]

In her essay, "1492: A New World View," Sylvia Wynter argues that with the "discovery," America was brought into the new worldview that had been emerging with the humanists of the fourteenth century. This was marked by a shift from Judeo-Christianity to secular humanism based on a concept of "rational man" and his relationship not to the church but to the state, of which the church became the "spiritual arm." Discussing Suzan Shown Harjo's position and the possibility of a new history of the human, Wynter writes:

> Such a view . . . also begins, as Harjo also insists, with today's empirical situation of the ongoing subjugation, marginalization, and displacement of the indigenous peoples. Such displacement is perpetuated not only by the whites of North America and the mestizos of Latin America, but also by new waves of external immigrants of all races, cultures, religions, from all parts of the world—all in search of the higher standards of living. . . .[90]

That gap and the effort to satisfy two different displacements or exiles, to draw upon Césaire's phrasing, continue to shape our present as a particular relationship to time. In Guyana, those who had been formerly enslaved and indentured transitioned to greater social freedom and collective political and economic power, while Indigenous Peoples were forced to remain in the past, to serve in Guyana as an internal other that allows the new *time* of Creole society and identity, again understood in terms of transformations within modern labor, to be continually marked as progress. More specifically, it is Guyana that allows us to understand just how material labor, for Indo- and Afro-Creoles, in fact serves as the new *time* of belonging and how it is reinforced through processes of symbolic reification or the labor of being, or what Sylvia Wynter describes as the "autoinstitution" of our subjectivity in which the human is both biology and the logocentric writing over of our biology.

CONCLUSION

As a process through which belonging to the post–1492 "New World" is achieved, creolization must be understood not singularly as a dialectic between those who came but *among* those who came and *between* those who were always here. A clearer articulation of how creolization processes function to indigenize populations is essential for Creole studies' broader negotiation of both patterns. If the first significant intellectual leap in understanding such processes has been to transform the negative connotations of Creole as loss to Creole as cultural retention for blacks and also Indians, the next leap must be in understanding how creolization processes literally and figuratively clear the ground upon which they place new, indigenous subjects. Further, this ground clearing is not achieved once in the past with the annihilation of the native other or later with the taking of power from the colonizer. It remains active and formative in the ongoing production of belonging. Indigenous Peoples in the Caribbean today are thus continually positioned outside the sweeping five hundred-year-plus time span of creolization without an attention to how Creole indigenous becoming or Creole indigeneity is a process in which they are fundamentally caught and through which their own continuous belonging to the New World is being negotiated.

2 Labor *for* Being: Making Caliban Work

> I say I'm going to spit you out. . . .
>
> —AIMÉ CÉSAIRE, *A Tempest*

CHAPTER 1 ADVANCED A THEORETICAL FRAMEWORK FOR UNDER-standing Creole belonging that addressed both its materialist and ideal-ist underpinnings, thus laying the groundwork for the exploration in this and subsequent chapters of the rescripting of indigeneity as a socio-discursive and politico-economic phenomenon. That chapter identified critical argu-ments that represented Creole belonging in two dominant terms, both of which engaged regimes of labor that necessarily displace Indigenous Peoples: first in terms of not or no longer being African (Burton) and second in terms of a relationship to the New World that is an indigenous one (Wynter). Chap-ter 2 continues to elaborate a theory of Creole indigeneity by focusing on how the Creole as a new native subject is narratively instituted so that these two senses of belonging collapse under a single discursive sign: Caliban.

As I suggested in the book's introduction, Caliban represents the "I" of possibility for the inscription of Creole subjectivity as indigenous within the terms established by the myth of El Dorado, the plantation, and the nation-state. Through a discussion of Caliban's appearance in Shakespeare's *The Tem-pest* and subsequent adaptations of the play, we can chart the movement from being Creole to becoming native as an ontoepistemic phenomenon in which Caliban serves as a device or trope for Creole subjectivity. More specif-ically, not only does Caliban perform a certain kind of work for the early modern European subject in Shakespeare's play, but he also performs a cer-tain kind of labor for Creole subjectivity in twentieth-century adaptations of it. Those versions are in fact dependent upon and therefore do not make sense without Caliban's raison d'être in the Shakespearean version. Caliban's work is to perform "material" labor as Prospero's subject and, both before

and after the arrival of other Europeans, he must labor for Prospero's being
by serving as the largely illegible or not fully knowable other that represents
the threshold of Prospero's threatened humanity. This chapter's subtitle is
thus meant to indicate the ways in which Creole subjectivity literally depends
upon the ability to make Caliban *continue* to work for modern being, even
if in anti- and postcolonial writing that work rejects his initial othering. The
subtitle also implicates postcolonial critical attempts to address Caliban by
suggesting that they too find their value in his labor, even where labor is not
the focus of their criticism. Such is the case in works like Margaret Paul
Joseph's *Caliban in Exile: The Outsider in Caribbean Fiction,* in which she
not only reads Caliban *as* West Indian and representative of both author and
subject but suggests that Caribbean literature is a continuous "maturation"
of the Caliban figure from enslaved to self-sovereignty.[1] In fact, postcolonial
criticism affirms the particular relationship to labor (the master–slave dialectic at the heart of the production of Afro-Creole subjectivity) that Caliban
enacts. Such criticism reinforces the split between theory and practice that
reflects and is inscribed within what Terry Eagleton has described as the
intellectual division of labor.[2] In postcolonial literature and criticism, Caliban thus indigenizes the Creole and two, not always distinct, class interests:
that of the Caribbean cultural elite and that of the postcolonial critic. Further,
the appropriation of Caliban for Creole subjectivity obscures land rights
issues between Indigenous Peoples and Creoles in the contemporary postcolonial state.

    In its attempt to lay out just how Caliban works, this chapter locates his
labor as the figurative bridge between early modern "racial" ambiguity and
post-Enlightenment racial subjectivity, as well as between the material labor
of the formerly enslaved and the cultural and discursive labor of the anticolonial and postcolonial writer. This bridge is crucial. It is because of it that
any real move away from labor by Creoles (such as the transition from slavery to freedom or from peasant work to the civil service) does not result in
the loss of the ultimate product of labor: the colony or nation-state. Aimé
Césaire's adaptation, *A Tempest,* best captures Caliban's function as a material and cultural bridge because of the way in which it takes up and extends
his resistance *as* the other *for* the establishment of European humanity in the
Shakespearean version. In *A Tempest* Prospero does not return to the Old
World as he does at the end of *The Tempest* but remains engaged with Caliban. In *A Tempest,* resistance does not mean taking Prospero's place but
continuing to reject what Prospero represents. In the final act of the play,

freedom emerges as something that is not political, not concrete or objective, but a rather subjective revolution, as we read in the following lines:

CALIBAN: I'm not interested in defending myself. My only regret is that I've failed.

PROSPERO: What were you hoping for?

CALIBAN: To get back my island and regain my freedom.

PROSPERO: And what would you do all alone here on this island, haunted by the devil, tempest tossed?

CALIBAN: First of all, I'd get rid of you! I'd spit you out, all your works and pomps! Your "white" magic!

PROSPERO: That's a fairly negative program. . . .

CALIBAN: You don't understand it. . . . I say I'm going to spit you out, and that's very positive. . . .

PROSPERO: Well, the world is really upside down. . . . We've seen everything now: Caliban as a dialectician! However, in spite of everything I'm fond of you, Caliban. Come, let's make peace. We've lived together for ten years and worked side by side! Ten years count for something after all! We've ended up by becoming compatriots![3]

As Rob Nixon has pointed out, the play is clearly a rejection of Césaire's former teacher Octave Mannoni's claim that the enslaved is psychologically dependent upon the colonizer.[4] While early in the play Césaire emphasizes the dependence of the colonizer on the colonized and the former's role in producing the dependence of the latter as an effect of colonization, by its end the work of the formerly enslaved does not require recognition by the colonizer, but self-recognition. This attempt to reject the internalized social and political architecture of black subordination and self-hatred is Césaire's own "profit" from Caliban's resistance to Prospero in the Shakespearean version, in which Caliban famously says, "You taught me language, and my profit on 't/Is I know how to curse. . . ."[5] Césaire's Caliban's "spitting out" is thus the writer's labor (read cultural work) and doubling (that is, trope) of the labor of the formerly enslaved, in which it is the Creole subject, not the material world, that becomes the product of an operation that ultimately reconciles the contradiction between Creole and native within a single subjectivity. In other words, it is through this dialectic of exchange, through this resistance and utterance of "I" as a subject of linguistic and cultural opposition, grounded in a modern notion of labor, that Caliban (read again the Creole in twentieth-century adaptations) in fact becomes native. It is in fact the inscription of Caliban as a resisting subject within anti- and postcolonial discourse that functions as the first of three critical elements of black becoming as identified in Sylvia Wynter's writing in chapter 1. Thus, Caliban's assertion in Césaire's version represents an "I" of possibility for the inscription of the Creole as a "native" subject within a poetics of resistance based on two operations (that is, the doubling of labor): an "I say," or a declaration of *being,* and an "I'm going," or a ceaseless dialectic of exchange based on immanence or *becoming.* The Creole subject thus emerges through a grammar of being that excludes the modes of resistance or postcontact grammars of Indigenous Peoples. This chapter, therefore, addresses indigeneity as an ontoepistemic problem through Caliban, because he works to inscribe Creole being as a unique expression of Hegelian difference by relying on the master–slave dialectic. In a reworked dialectic, Indigenous Peoples represent a necessary other who are both excised from labor history and its outcomes, while at the same time they are brought into the regime of labor in which they must now work for Creole being or the establishment of "true" Creole subjectivity. The chapter begins by demonstrating, through a discussion of Caliban, the narratively instituted process of movement from being Creole to becoming native, in which the critic or intellectual plays the most prominent role. It then turns to a critique of Caliban's legacy in Caribbean philosophy—largely through Paget Henry's work—and later for black studies—through Michelle Wright's work. With both intellectual and critical traditions, I am interested in the a priori conditions for articulation of their subjects through the labor of resistance required to come into being against colonialism and both within and against Eurowestern modes of being human. This section demonstrates how the Calibanesque tradition remains Hegelian.

THE ONTOPOETICS OF CREOLE INDIGENEITY

The list of characters for Aimé Césaire's "black adaptation" of Shakespeare's *The Tempest* reads:

As in Shakespeare, with:
Two alterations:
ARIEL, a mulatto slave
CALIBAN, a black slave
An Addition:
ESHU, a black devil-god.[6]

With these changes, Césaire's *A Tempest* gives Shakespeare's "savage and deformed slave" form and recreates three of the major (or more visible) racialized class groups in the evolution of New World plantation society: the enslaved black, the colonizer, and the mulatto. Césaire's is one of many reworkings that uses the play to establish what Rob Nixon calls an "oppositional lineage" and to achieve both an aesthetic and ideological "liberation" from colonial culture.[7] Nixon points out that the play, and specifically Caliban's figure, has served a particular function in (black) diasporic revolutionary thinking, especially in the Caribbean. He argues that "the play was mobilized in defense of Caliban's right to the land and to cultural autonomy" and that George Lamming's appropriation in *The Pleasures of Exile* "can be read as an effort to redeem from the past, as well as to stimulate, an *indigenous* Antillean line of creativity to rival the European traditions. . . ."[8] In that work, Lamming in fact asserts that the linguistic struggle between Prospero and Caliban in *The Tempest* has the same generalized meaning for the entire Caribbean.[9] While "the nationalist struggle provides a shaping context" in this endeavor, Nixon writes that for anticolonial intellectuals, Lamming specifically, Caliban represents the "colonized writer-intellectual."[10] Thus, Nixon claims that "replacing" colonialist thinking with a native or "endemic line of thought and action" is what is "at stake" in these reinscriptions of Shakespeare's *The Tempest*.[11]

Nixon's well-known work reveals both the promise and limit of Caliban as an anticolonial figure who secures, as the bridge between material and cultural forms of labor, the patrimony that Henri Christophe could not. This again is the specific labor that Caliban performs for Creole subjectivity and for critics of the Calibanesque tradition: wedding subjectivity to sovereignty and land rights for Creoles. As I go on to demonstrate, Caliban works to inscribe Creole being as a function of Hegelian difference, but specifically as a relation *among* subalterns, not just in terms of mobilizations of the master–slave, self–other dialectic as it relates to whites and Europeans. The Calibanesque tradition consolidates this method of being and becoming Creole—being and becoming human in Creole terms—that is extended even in critical attempts to subvert it. Whether "he" is an anticolonial figure or a symbol of the postcolonial writer or person, discourse around Caliban constitutes an indigenizing poetics for the black experience in general and the Creole experience specifically. This poetics represents the ontology of the human for non-Europeans, postcontact (recall Silva's state of affectability) and largely rests on Caliban's illegibility and negation in his first appearance in Shakespeare.

Caliban's illegibility is clearly addressed in an essay by Steve Almquist. In "Not Quite the Gabbling of 'A Thing Most Brutish,'" Almquist critiques Aimé Césaire's *A Tempest*. Primarily concerned with language in the play, Almquist rejects the long-standing assumption that Césaire's play relocates to the Caribbean the fictional island of the Shakespearean version, which was thought to be somewhere between Europe, the characters' destination, and Africa, their point of origin.[12] Almquist instead claims that with the play, Césaire's "allusions to African flora and fauna contest these presumptions and locate the island somewhere neither in the Caribbean nor in Africa. This geographical negation provides a metaphorical space in which Césaire can pursue his construction of an African Diasporic text."[13] In addition to this denial of fixed territoriality to places mentioned in the play, such as Macaya, a mountain range in Haiti, Almquist also claims that there is still a certain degree of racial uncertainty or instability retained for Caliban's character when he is mistaken by the drunken Trinculo as a "Nindian."[14] Césaire's Caliban is a "destabilized 'Nindian'/black slave," Almquist argues, and the play "almost entirely elides the fact that Caliban is *not* in fact native to the island and, therefore, his claim to have inherited the island from his mother, Sycorax, implies a displacement of native peoples."[15]

Almquist echoes Peter Hulme's observations in *Colonial Encounters* in which he notes that Caliban is Mediterranean and Atlantic because of his New World-derived name and his African mother. This leads Hulme to conclude that "Caliban, as a compromise formation, can exist only within discourse: he is fundamentally and essentially beyond the bounds of representation."[16] For Almquist, Caliban's illegibility "suggests that on some level the total Africanization of Caliban is impossible, that there always remains the *(sub)conscious presence* of the displaced native, so that as much as Césaire is creating a diasporic Caliban, his own construction forbids complete elision."[17] In Almquist's rendering, in other words, Césaire's Caliban appears as an anticolonial other who elides both the spatial and racial-historical markers that govern this anticolonial characterization. Caliban is also denied a fixed presence because of a consciousness of a now discursively (re)enacted displacement. Here the implications for the relationship between space (real and metaphoric) and historicity are useful. What Almquist reads in Césaire is the problem surrounding the space *and* time of the subject necessary for the anticolonial position: the anticolonial subject's relationship to Western historicity and its implicit reliance on conceptions of space. For Césaire, the lack of fixed geographic space is necessary to achieve both the rejection of the coordinates of

Western time that structure the anticolonial critique and to create a place for the subject, narratively instituted as a function of that criticism. Anticolonial subjectivity in Césaire must therefore remain open ended when attempting to represent the Creole as a cultural and temporal hybrid. In postcoloniality, this positioning is foreclosed, and the play reveals the tensions that surround indigeneity *and* belonging, which in the anticolonial period is not mitigated by the state in the same manner as it is in the so-called postcolonial one. These tensions are revealed in Almquist's work through his engagement with Jodi Byrd's writing and its foregrounding of the issue of when Caliban is native and when Caliban is black.

In his discussion, Almquist cites Byrd's 2002 dissertation, which offers a reconsideration of postcolonial theoretical discourse in favor of its "absent/present" natives and the interactions that Indigenous Peoples had with blacks and other groups.[18] Byrd, in a truly excellent analysis of postcolonial literature, offers a theory of cacophony. With "cacophony," she addresses the failure of both postcolonial theory and literature to address the situation of Indigenous Peoples or to provide a way of rethinking the place of Indigenous Peoples and indigenous thought in postcolonial theory, away from the margins. Almquist's recourse to Byrd, however, introduces a set of concerns that speak directly to illegibility. According to Almquist, in cautioning against "over determined" interpretations of the figure of Caliban, Byrd's argument does not "discount" his claim "that Césaire's representation of Caliban produces an Africanized figure that embodies the complexity of the African diaspora in the middle of the twentieth century."[19] Byrd herself writes that in Shakespeare's play, Caliban is a "liminal" figure, somewhere, it seems, between beast and man.[20] (For Hulme, he is a "discursive monster."[21]) However, for black adaptations, Byrd writes, "When Caliban is claimed as primarily representative of African/New World slaveries, that act of delineating Caliban in exclusion to other histories serves the function of indigenizing that experience to the Americas, and makes individual slaves and their descendants the new new world native, a slippage which bears resonance today as African-Caribbean identity is said to be the 'native' identity."[22] Byrd here extends an argument of Spivak's that cautions against stabilizing representations of Caliban at the cost of native representation.[23]

I agree with Byrd that the play discursively institutes black indigeneity; through the figure of Caliban in Lamming and Césaire, for example, blacks become native. Byrd also does not preclude or foreclose Almquist's argument, as he rightly observes. However, Almquist does not formally deal with

Byrd's charge regarding native displacement and both seem to be arguing two different things. The first is that Caliban is, or represents, a new native (black), thereby obscuring the true or original natives; in other words, there is a stable and extratextual or residual New World native identity (an external referent before the sign). The second, Almquist's position, is that Caliban is *not* a native, though he is haunted by the "displaced" or again, true, native (his "subconscious presence"), which is either continental African or New World aboriginal, making his character always somewhat illegible and his "Africanization" incomplete.[24] Almquist's argument for a diasporic subject also suggests an "extra" when insinuating that Caliban in Césaire's play and blacks outside of Africa, by extension, are always subject to a reordering of time and geography to which "true" natives are not.[25] Despite what appear to be different arguments, what both critics read as displacement is actually the autoinscription (epistemic condition) of becoming native in the New World. In other words, black becoming in the Americas is predicated on its own *and* on New World aboriginal displacement, and it is the nation-state and the creation of an identity within it that will ultimately govern this new native status as a "historical (interior) determination" as opposed to exterior, structural markers of difference.[26]

We can suggest that although Césaire's Caliban represents anticolonial struggle (anticolonial nationalism), the postcolonial state emerges to capture and stabilize this figure, which is why I argue that the postindependence state consolidates Creole indigeneity. A historical and dually enacted native displacement is the core of all New World identity, but both are a function of Western time and narrative. Thus, the extratextual presences for Byrd and Almquist (blacks in Africa and Indigenous Peoples in the New World) are rewritten to work within colonial and anticolonial narratives. They cease to be objective. Without this reinscription, identity cannot be managed by the state. The even larger problem is that in Shakespeare's play, and attempts to contain the now discursive objects, Caliban emerges as a complex of negation—a *converging negation*—as a figure who is not a man, nor human (the distinction here is important), nor native, nor black. Failure to acknowledge this creates confusion among being native, becoming native, and the practices of belonging (indigeneity), which include the consolidation of those practices within the subject-sign that ultimately represent one's humanization. This structuring negation is instrumental in Caliban's ability to represent anticolonial struggle.

In *The Tempest*, Caliban asserts his right to the island through his mother, who was a prior inhabitant, to Prospero. The play makes clear that Caliban was in fact born on the island, and the text notes Sycorax's pregnancy at the time of her exile to the island, despite the suggestion that she has coupled with the New World devil, Setebos. Prospero also remarks, "Then was this island—save for the son that [Sycorax] did litter here. . . ."[27] This demonstrates Shakespeare's possible conformity with individual rights under monarchic rule. The island, in spite of Prospero's presence, is outside the bounds of monarchic laws regarding citizenship. It is a failed attempt by Prospero to recreate a European power structure and the basis for a European kingdom. Citizenship or state-determined rights are not what interests Byrd or Almquist, although it is essential for the Creole subject. The question that engages both Byrd and Almquist is Caliban's indigeneity, but they ignore the multiply negated foundation for it, which is the source of problems surrounding his representation and which Césaire, at least, must feed into the dialectic of resistance. Césaire's problem is that he must create a subject (re)presentable both within any future, politically independent state (recognizing with Africa the failure of these states) and as continually resistant to any present, colonial one.[28]

In Shakespeare's version, Caliban represents the still-abstract limit of Renaissance humanity within the early modern period, before consolidation as a racial other through European Enlightenment thought and nineteenth-century science. The slave, however, that Césaire uses to give him discursive form, is black. He is *already* the product or outcome of nineteenth-century scientific rationalizations and is seeking his indigeneity and humanity as their object: this is true in spite of Césaire's reference within the play to both Renaissance (the inquisition's rejection of Prospero's "knowledge") and the late seventeenth- and eighteenth-century (Gonzalo's desire to see the New World as representative of a perfect state of nature) ways of understanding difference. It is not until the end of the play that Caliban, in speaking to Prospero, engages the terms of his humanity (read *belonging*) and begins to represent the Creole black. In her recourse to Spivak, Byrd is acknowledging that the play does not mark what kind of native Caliban is, tied as it is to space. However, what it fails to confer on Caliban is native status of *any* kind. Byrd is again right that Caliban in the Césairean version represents the "new New World native," but she and Almquist confuse indigeneity (for them it isn't actively being engaged or constituted) with being native. Additionally, when we speak of the humanity as opposed to the nonhumanity of others, we are confusing being human with processes of becoming that contain and produce the human as a thing that can be (re)presentable as a citizen-subject.

Being native (as conceived through imperial discursivity, that is, Christopher Columbus's letters and log of his first voyage across the Atlantic) thus represents fixity in place and space and is not identical to indigeneity, which is always articulated within specific cultural and cosmogonic terms and processes. It is to this later identity that Vine Deloria Jr. refers when he notes that "the Indian . . . does not have the psychological burden of establishing his or her right to the land in the deep emotional sense of knowing that he or she belongs there."[29] I therefore argue that we, provisionally, at least, engage, uncouple, and slightly redefine the two terms (*native* and *indigeneity*) when dealing with Indigenous Peoples, Creoles, and all immigrant groups. The latter groups are forced to make indigeniety (a complex cultural process that is not static but involves the productive reworking of difference and exile) a function of belonging. They do so as they discursively (and here I mean cultural enactments and writing) institute and then (re)spatialize their belonging as indigeneity in order to *become* native. The slippage between being native and indigeneity, as a complex process, becomes the context for Caliban's appropriation.

The crisis of Caliban's belonging is clear. While Caliban in Shakespeare's version is referred to as "an islander" by Trinculo, he does not belong to it. He belongs to Prospero, as one of the play's most famous lines acknowledges: "This thing of darkness I acknowledge *mine*."[30] The play ends without a discussion of what will happen to Caliban, who can either be taken back to the Old World and exhibited or remain not as owner, but perhaps as native, meaning outside the state and still different from Prospero as European subject, not as someone with his or her own ontology. At that point the play does not acknowledge him as a native nor does it acknowledge his indigeneity, his own belonging. It is precisely the failure to do this that facilitates the Césairean appropriation. In New World discourse, a native identity designates some kind of belonging (performatively enacted) to the land, and that belonging is tied to a certain degree of humanity that rests above black humanity. *The Tempest* is written after New World Indigenous Peoples are made vassals of the Spanish Crown, according them a degree of humanity that is not entirely vested in labor but in the redemptive potential of the Spirit. However, Shakespeare's "degodded" (Wynter) text does not accord his islander that status of semihumanity and so cannot acknowledge its indigeneity. Further, Prospero's is a kingdom (an illegitimate one) and not a state. While Almquist writes that making Caliban black is a displacement of the native and Byrd argues that it also makes the black experience native, what Césaire appropriates from

Shakespeare is the ontic condition of blacks in the New World, that state of discursive unbelonging and condition of being owned that ultimately seeks a state to contain it. While Caliban in the Shakespearean text might be "inescapably . . . Shakespeare's version of Native Americans," to the extent that Caliban as an anagram for cannibal comes to designate the supposedly aggressive Carib, as several critics have noted, his ontology is *already* black.[31] The play, in other words, although it does not necessarily specify what kind of native Caliban is, outlines the condition for being native and simultaneously black in the New World: illegibility and displacement. The anticolonial Creole, as subject, is based on this. Shakespeare's Caliban, by not claiming indigeneity for himself, can thus come to represent the Creole who must discursively enact his indigeneity or belonging, thereby reproducing the labor that is at the heart of Caliban's ability to be represented in Shakespeare's play.

In *The Tempest,* Caliban is a displaced nonnative because in "giving" him language, Prospero has failed to accord him the status of native in that language. The final lines spoken in *The Tempest* with regard to Caliban are suggestive of his actual and cultural colonization and do not afford him an identity outside of that colonization, only as an other and as property (read slaves as capital, that is, primitive accumulation). He is only compared by a subordinate, Stephano, to "men of Ind" or "(West) Indian natives" as the text indicates.[32] In his twentieth-century rewriting of the play to address the colonial situation in the Americas, and specifically the black condition, Césaire stabilizes the seventeenth-century references to disposition, rather than fixed racial categories. The reference to "darkness" in *The Tempest* refers only to Caliban's spiritual, intellectual, and bodily subordination. In *A Tempest,* both Trinculo and Stephano "recognize" Caliban, but not as black. As Almquist rightly suggests, they recognize and confirm his status as a failed native, as a "nindian." However, the task of the anticolonial Creole is to articulate belonging (discursively) and in so doing, find a way to assert native status in the now borrowed and transformed language of the colonizers: an indigenous status that, again, can support not just belonging but the right to belong and to possess the land and eventual nation-state rather than allow for expropriation of land as with Indigenous Peoples.

An example of the attempt to institute belonging in *A Tempest* is the addition of the devil-god Eshu. Césaire inserts a god of the Yoruba pantheon rather than the New World Setebos mentioned in the Shakespearean version. This displaced native has brought his own gods with him, not the fictive ones of the European imagination. What Wynter reads as cultural retention in the

Jonkonnu dance is the work of cultural and psychic belonging that allows Césaire to do what Shakespeare's Prospero could not: accord his Caliban a native status with consequences for whether or not Prospero goes or stays, with consequences for Prospero's consciousness, and with marked consequences for what will become post-Enlightenment subjectivity. Césaire's Caliban thus moves from the requirements of a strictly black (in the negated sense), colonialist ontology to a New World native one and recreates its problematic foundation: conquest as a founding ontological moment that must be repeated physically (for example, the postcolonial conquest of Guyana's interior discussed in the following chapter), discursively, and within capital in order to support privileged places in globalized subjectivity. Césaire's Nindian is this ontological hybrid that is inserted into the dialectical exchange as "I," as a singular and codependent consciousness that in truly Hegelian fashion is bound up with that of the colonizer. Next to his gods, indicative of the African cosmogonies blacks brought with them to the New World, Caliban is a native, more native than they are, through his relationship to the land. A new native status is a way to respatialize these cosmogonies to make *them,* not necessarily the black slave, indigenous.[33] In other words, the ontic need dictates the form of indigeneity. It is not simply that Caliban represents the "new New World native" but that Caliban as a native is fundamentally different from any previously historicized native. With this understanding ("these tricky races"), Césaire makes room for it not in order to stabilize his Caliban but precisely to show that his Caliban is a hybrid (Almquist black or Indian) and is subject to a hybrid ontology. However, Afro-Creole ontology cannot sustain this hybrid status as it moves toward integration. Neonative status is problematic because it does not record the clans or diverse organizations of peoples, but it records their discursive substitution inside European discourse, as, for example, the tribe.[34] The poetics of this neoindigeneity (the mode of discursively instituting belonging either through a politics of resistance, retention, or liberation) is reaffirmed in Caribbean cultural and philosophical thought as it seeks to recover the humanity of the enslaved and recreate the initial material (laboring) relationship to space as a function of postcolonial ontoepistemolgy. In others words, in finding value in the figure of Caliban for anti- and postcolonial being, critics continue to make Caliban work. I now address the role that Caliban plays in the development of Caribbean philosophical thought and Creole understandings of what it means to be human. What emerges most clearly from the analysis is the *dependence* on the difference and otherness of Indigenous Peoples.

LABOR, CREOLE HUMANITY, AND THE
BURDEN OF CARIBBEAN PHILOSOPHICAL THOUGHT

The way in which Caribbean society and identity formation depend upon Indigenous Peoples—as a fixed native presence—even as they continue to be marginalized and mythified can be difficult to assess. The argument that the indigenous presence in the Caribbean is essential to Caribbean thought and being runs counter to prevailing views by several scholars. Writing on Caribbean literature, Jodi Byrd argues that it is still possible to claim that the Amerindian has been eradicated.[35] She rejects the following claim by Antonio Benítez-Rojo that although "it's always possible to try to wipe the Indian out . . . nothing of this kind could be the theme of a Caribbean novel" because the culture always gestures toward "integration" in order to "compensate for the fragmentation and provisionality of the collective Being."[36]

We can, however, suggest that Benítez-Rojo is correct because this already poeticized native exists as a central aspect of Caribbean thought, one that is crucial to its genesis and with which it seeks reconciliation as part of Creole ontology. This aspect is not, however, just a "subconscious presence" and reconciliation. The native, therefore, represented within Creole poetics, is not an ameliorative aspect of Caribbean thought because this representation has been achieved by the elision, displacement, substitution, and "fossilization" of actual Indigenous Peoples, primarily because Creole culture and thought have inherited the ontolinguistic structure and meaning of the word *Creole.*

Since, however, political discourse does in fact require "native" subjects, their displacement becomes problematic. Indigenous Peoples were the only ones with a viable ontological system that reflected the experience of already belonging in the New World, which Creoles recognized and even, as I discuss in chapter 4, borrowed. Being Creole, however, in the anticolonial period meant not only resisting colonial domination, but it also meant rejecting native status, the only other nonslave subject position available in the postemancipation colonies. What "saved" blacks and allowed them to inhabit a native identity connected with the future of the postcolonial state rather than its past is both their greater integration into colonial culture, and through the plantation, their primary identity as workers.

A number of critics have focused on Caliban's labor for Prospero in Shakespeare's text and on his linguistic labor. However, in making Caliban work in literary and cultural criticism (and as a socially liminal figure multiply reinvented), critics have not addressed labor and the value it holds and that they uphold in order for their criticisms to be viable. In other words, there is labor as value and then there is the value of labor. Together they work to delegitimize native status even at the level of the secondary, critical discourse that seeks to restore it. While some critics have argued that Caliban can equally represent blacks and Indigenous Peoples, blacks specifically affirm Caliban's labor for being that which institutes, in their borrowing, the displacement of Indigenous Peoples.[37]

As critics, our understanding of the significance of labor, physical or intellectual, is what allows us to proceed. In *The Tempest,* Caliban's role as a worker becomes the basis upon which he tries to manipulate Prospero, although without much success. Those who write on the plays in a postcolonial context can therefore, legitimately, focus a great deal on the forms of labor in the play and the transformative potential of labor and language and language as labor—its ability to create subjectivity and redeem Caliban. Poet Derek Walcott, for instance, cites the "beauty of his speech" as something to celebrate.[38] Critic Joan Dayan focuses on the linguistic work that Césaire undertakes in *A Tempest* as part of the anticolonial effort to represent the Creole as an agential, linguistic subjectivity.[39] "To see the formerly colonized as agents of knowledge," she claims, "remains the goal of Césaire's hybrid labour."[40] More important, she says of the figure of Caliban, "Labor is the fact of Caliban's existence."[41] Dayan makes recourse here to the Marxian reworking of Hegel, which "seizes labor as essence, as what proves good the essence of man."[42] Her turn to Hegel allows her to argue that Césaire's Caliban, singularly identified with labor in a way that Ariel is not proves the dialectic in which the slave "makes history."[43] In its conclusion, Césaire's play demonstrates Prospero's "defeat by the material world that Caliban's labor had commanded, shaped, and controlled."[44] Another critic of Césaire, A. James Arnold, has noted that "for Ferdinand labor is occasional and nonessential; for Caliban it is the principle which defines his existence."[45] He has also claimed that in Césaire's play, "the language of Caliban is proletarian as befits his station, and it possesses its own nobility," whereas Ariel's language is allied with Prospero. Stephano's and Trinculo's language is also "proletarian."[46]

Both Dayan's and Arnold's work reveal the critical emphasis on the dual forms of labor, though represented discursively. They demonstrate the value that labor has for the subject *and* those charged with excavating, reiterating, and in some ways reinscribing the subjectivity granted in the text. Afro-Creole subjectivity is based on the codification of labor as value inside capital. In order to reinscribe it, the value of that kind of labor becomes the epistemic basis for criticism. It thus matters (1) what Caliban is (Prospero's property and in reinscriptions as a Creole, the slave as capital); (2) what Caliban does (labor for Prospero); and (3) that he does it, in twentieth-century criticism, within the logic of a nineteenth-century episteme that we continually enact or invoke in order for the work to have meaning as a text and as a text undergoing critical excavation or archaeology. The real problem arises when we realize that this value placed on labor, and the division of labor it engenders and reinforces, is a requirement of social being for blacks and of black thought and it is the basis for its philosophical tradition. The choice between the traditional and organic intellectual, made by Roberto Retamar through Caliban, is thus much more than that. Labor and the class distinctions it produces structure the transition from slave or proletarian to peasant, bourgeois, nationalist, or native, forming the social and epistemic basis for Caribbean philosophical thought. In sociologist Paget Henry's work, where Caliban's labor is essential to the identification of the philosophical thought of the New World, we see how indigenous displacement is instrumental.

In *Caliban's Reason: Introducing Afro-Caribbean Philosophy,* Henry uses the work of C. L. R. James, Frantz Fanon, and Sylvia Wynter, among others, to examine the Afro-Caribbean philosophical tradition (Nixon's "endemic line of thought") as a "discursive field" with two major tendencies, materialist and poeticist, both of which have been shaped by colonial history and the failure to truly engage African philosophical systems.[47] For Henry, "Caliban's reason" refers to the attempt within the black philosophical tradition to conceive of itself and its inherited colonialist binaries ("colonizer/colonized, colony/nation, or black/white") in typical philosophical discourse ("being/nonbeing, spirit/matter"), in everyday practice (art, dance), and in literature.[48] In other words, on the ground, where philosophy is lived and from which its questions are derived.[49] In constructing a Caliban figure as a speaking voice for this philosophical tradition, the lineage Henry posits for this figure is a complex negotiation of African and New World aboriginal indigeneity. Eschewing the ambiguity we find in Byrd, Almquist, and other scholars, he identifies Shakespeare's Caliban as a "native Caliban (the Carib)" and then suggests that with New World slavery, "Caliban became African."[50] Of note are Henry's claims that unlike other "Afro-Caribbean cultural forms . . . Afro-Caribbean philosophy is the least creolized" and that "the African, European, and Indian elements in it are the least integrated."[51]

Henry argues for a new Africanization of Caribbean intellectual thought, one that reiterates the ontoepistemic displacement of Indigenous Peoples because of the way in which the turn to Africa would occur through the state and society and because of its recourse to exile and fragmentation. In *Caliban's Reason* and in his essay "Philosophy and the Caribbean Intellectual Tradition," Henry seems to suggest that nationalism and sovereignty are still the prime contexts for the new Caribbean philosophical orientation he argues for, even as he decries the need for Caribbean philosophy to "break" with ideology.[52] Through recourse to Wynter's idea of "origin narratives" and their importance for the development of the ego in African cosmogonic systems, Henry notes that Caribbean philosophy rejects this formative spiritual dimension under a system that has "turned Africans into Blacks, Indians into browns, and Europeans into whites."[53] In arguing, however, for the importance of African cosmogony, Henry proceeds from an idea of cultural fragmentation when he identifies the tendencies that emerge in the region for dealing with the "shattered Amerindian, Indian, and African worldviews."[54] The idea of cultural fragmentation that we see in Henry's and in other works supports the inscription of exile as the ontogenic basis for black belonging. Additionally, Henry marginalizes both Indian and Amerindian, or native cosmogonies and philosophical systems, and thus ignores the way in which all of these remain a cohesive, structuring bias of the region's sociopolitical discourse.[55]

In establishing the shift from native as Carib—the placeholder in European thought for New World peoples—to black slave, Henry references George Lamming's own extensive dialogue in the Caliban tradition, *The Pleasures of Exile,* in which Lamming seems to suggest an aesthetic integration of the two (as do Harris and others who seek "reconciliation" through the Creole subject). This integration is revealed in a passage quoted by Henry in which Lamming links African and Amerindian revolutionary lineages, saying, "The slave whose skin suggests the savaged deformity of his nature becomes *identical* with the Carib Indian who feeds on human flesh. Carib Indian and African slave, both seen as the wild fruits of Nature, share equally that spirit of revolt which Prospero by sword or language is determined to conquer."[56] This is the philosophical iteration of the displacement that Byrd and Almquist identify in literature. However, its reification occurs with a difference, a substitution (not a strict displacement). Proceeding from this discursive or poeticist conflation of the black and the native, Henry identifies a binary in these cosmogonic origin narratives that affects the formation of the ego: an opposition between "spirit" and "nonspirit." He writes that "this binary can be usefully compared to the Platonic binary between the world of being and that of becoming. The former is a spiritual world of eternal ideas, a world that always is. The latter is a world of changing forms that is always becoming but never really is."[57] He goes on to write that when the ego loses touch with the spiritual realm, loses touch with Okra (or soul in Akan tradition), the Platonic equivalent would be an "unawareness" caused by "the ego turning the soul toward the everyday world of becoming and away from the higher world of being."[58] Since Henry is interested in how the two different philosophical schools he identifies in the Caribbean handle this question of being and consciousness, he moves away from the Platonic concern with being and becoming that haunts Afro-Creole philosophical thought at the very level of Henry's substitution or reinvention of the Carib as enslaved black or African. Thus, in his assessment of the philosophic tradition, he replaces the trope of displacement (Indigenous Peoples) with fragmentation and exile that frames the experiences of all groups, ignoring the continuity of indigenous belonging in the Americas. In *Caliban's Reason,* Indigenous Peoples and blacks seem to become, equally, anticolonial or resistant figures, but in doing the work of human self-transformation, they are not equally linguistic laborers or equally human within the postcolonial nation-state. Therefore, Indigenous Peoples and blacks are affected differently by the state and its role as the backdrop for the enactment of belonging.

A look at Henry's positioning of the material and the spiritual in his discussion is essential in understanding the role the state plays. He argues that "onto-historicist" Caribbean philosophy, specifically in the writing of James, retained a European derived anti-African bias that negated this spiritual dimension of premodern African philosophy. For James, Henry argues, the emphasis was on the remaking of the self through a set of historical conditions or choices that were more formative than any spiritual dimension. He writes that "historicism has been the discourse through which our consciousness has established itself in the materialism and secular rationalism of the modern period" because of "the radical historicization of our existence that accompanied colonization."[59] For Henry, colonization represents an "expulsion from myth into history," and, through capitalism, "we have come to see ourselves as creatures of history."[60] For Henry, "history exists inside cosmology."[61] It is in this rejection of the spiritual dimension of premodern African philosophical thought that, Henry writes, James understood the transformation of African peoples into "negroes" in the New World.[62] The problem for blacks in the New World, as the poeticists deal with it, is the ontological function of cosmogony and the fact that African cosmogonic systems underwent radical shifts in the trans-Atlantic crossing. As a result of this loss,

Henry claims that the colonial state essentially came to provide the back-drop for the reinvention of the self, saying that "the institutional framework in which the Caribbean intellectual tradition developed was a very statist one. . . ."[63]

On its face, this assertion by Henry parallels Rob Nixon's claim that the backdrop for the reinvention of Caliban is the national struggle. Both suggest that first the colonial state, then the anticolonial national struggle for what would become the nation-state, are the context for Afro-Creole New World political ideology and ontology. In other words, blacks become blacks within a set of circumstances that are the product of a Western imperative: the rise of capital and the modern colonial state. The rise of the modern state is coex-tensive with the teleology of black labor and being in the New World. Black native identity in the New World is thus always mediated by the state and the modes of national becoming the state can support either in the pre- or post-colonial period. The transformation, within capital and of capital, by the Afro-Creole subject is significant because of the fact that it has occurred with both the colonial state and the postcolonial state as a backdrop and with their identification as proletarians. Apart from the disavowal of certain philosoph-ical traditions, the state has its own requirements for citizen-subject identity. Indigenous Peoples have been defined at or as the limit of the state, as a moral, rational, or spiritual form and as such, when present within the state cannot become citizens in the way blacks or even Indo-Caribbean peoples eventu-ally can. Although blacks were conceived of as inhuman, their identities were always more allied with the state because of its configuration of labor. In other words, their inhumanity was always conceived *within* the state, which sought to recreate the European state in the Americas, while the subhuman-ity of Indigenous Peoples was always conceived as existing *without* the state or rather as an antithetical element. This is also the trick of Shakespeare's Caliban, where Prospero's is a small, parallel state, illegitimate because it dis-regards the sovereignty and spiritual dimension of the monarchic—albeit changing—European state, which at their inception New World colonies also had to regard. Shakespeare's Caliban exists within the bounds of the state, the very one that will eventually define itself in later centuries against monar-chic "states." Again, his ontology is black. Further, black and Indo-Caribbean governments continue to enact this inside/outside role for Indigenous Peoples and Creoles through their commitment to the state, which requires them to pull Indigenous Peoples in to serve as new others within it. Both positions perform the function of enabling the state, much as Prospero's "sub-plot" and the recreation of Caliban in it, according to Peter Hulme, allowed him to achieve the "revenge" and restoration of place in the Old World that he sought.[64]

The problem remains that Henry sees the material as antithetical to the spiritual. Additionally, he does not address just how the material tradition reinvents itself with *myth,* as opposed to the "expulsion" he notes, and through the state. He does not entertain the idea that black human transformation in the New World, occurring materially through labor, forces a restructuring of the soul that does not necessarily have to be read as an anti-African bias. It can also be read as a rejection of modes that do not conform to indigeneity in or through labor. Further, the restoration of an African dimension to Caribbean philosophical thought is not the restoration of the lost soul or spiritual dimension, because it is being made within modernist epistemology.

In Henry's work, creolization thus emerges as a process of indigenization, which is in fact a process of belonging upon which multiple diasporas in and out of the Caribbean rest. For Henry, Caribbean philosophy has failed to achieve the "discursive indigenization" represented in other areas like the arts, which have become creolized.[65] It did not "break" with European philosophy or reject its anti-African bias. "Creolization," he writes, "is an active project that would indigenize Afro-Caribbean philosophy and end its state of Calibanization and limited activation."[66] This forces the continued enactment or repetition of these anti-African biases in the material composition and cultural constructedness of, for example, the black Caribbean and Indo-Caribbean diasporas that are found in the region and in North America and Europe. Throughout *Caliban's Reason,* Henry continually stresses, as Wynter does, that blacks were the "zero point on the scale of human rational capability" and in the Caribbean have experienced the "ego collapse" that Fanon chronicles in *Black Skin, White Masks.*[67] Henry moves on to talk about the poeticist tradition, which rejects the material-social determinism of the historicist in favor of the conscious (Harris) and unconscious (Wynter), partly because of their ego-critical function (like premodern African philosophy). He does so through discussion of Wilson Harris, who he says offers a more original and therefore creolized Caribbean brand of philosophy than the historicists. Of the poeticists, he says they "make the recovery of the postcolonial self an important precondition for institutional recovery, while the historicists tend to see recovery of self as following institutional recovery."[68] According to Henry, the historicists fail to distinguish among the different forms of consciousness (conscious or unconscious) that the poeticists do.

He writes of colonized societies, much in the vein of what Fanon says about ontology being unattainable in a colonized society, that "these societies do not have the option of covering up their nonresolution of ontological problems with imperial activity, excessive capital accumulation, or compensatory consumption."[69]

How then do we think about the state that Henry and Nixon have identified as a precondition? If Harris put consciousness first, what happens if we restore the state as a ground for consciousness? While this may seem historicist, and Harris would say that consciousness produces the state, the state does force a particular resolution of the ego in favor of politico-citizen-subjects whose ego production is bound to forms of capital accumulation or the arrangement of capital. One can argue that in both the historicist and poeticist traditions, the recovery of the precolonial self happens within the state. Further, this opposition in Henry between the poeticist and materialist is to some degree a false one. An example can be found in Wynter's emphasis on the role of the plantation as producing certain identities and categories. In other words, the state in its component parts, based on the division of labor, always mitigates both traditions. If according to Gramsci,[70] history is not divorced from philosophy, then the anti-Indian (native) bias is a poeticist or philosophic enactment of the racial contract mode of historicity.[71] Further, if in the platonic sense, invoked by Henry, becoming represents a state of nonspirit, then it also represents a material boundedness in which "change" must be read as shifts in the mode of production. Being Creole thus represents a particular (though not permanent or even closed) ontological state, and as part of a larger process of becoming, blacks necessarily experience indigeneity, however sought after, as alienation through capitalist labor processes and a material epistemology. Henry's desire for a Creole indigeneity can thus only repeat its structuring bias as part of this process of becoming. I turn now to explore this bias or paradox of being and becoming, specifically, as a problem for attempts to move within and beyond the Calibanesque tradition in black diaspora studies.

BLACK STUDIES AND CALIBAN'S LEGACY

The problem for any discussion of black being is, as Sylvia Wynter asserts, "We do *not* know about something called ontological sovereignty." In an interview with David Scott, Wynter continues, "And I'm being so bold as to say that in order to *speak* the conception of ontological sovereignty, we would have to move completely outside our present conception of what it is to be human, and therefore outside the ground of the orthodox body of knowledge which institutes and reproduces such a conception."[72]

Interpreted through the Fanonian claim that "every ontology is made unattainable in a colonized and civilized society," Wynter's statement speaks of a general colonial condition that substantively shapes our humanity.[73] Our understanding of ourselves as human is profoundly dependent, profoundly colonial. Thus critics, artists, and their subjects are all part of a generalized paradox in which, much like Forbes Burnham and other political leaders at independence, they seek one thing but, in acting out the conditions of their epistemology, inscribe another. Such is the case with recent trends in black diaspora scholarship. Influenced by work in the late 1980s and '90s in cultural studies and in anthropology that looked at globalization and the production of globalized ethnicities (ethnic localities) through late capital, black cultural and diaspora studies have embraced models of fluidity. African American and black studies have become less U.S.-Africa oriented and more diasporic. Africana studies programs have cropped up at universities, just as the temporally, geographically, or methodologically bounded fields of more and more literature programs are giving way to an emphasis on world literature. This shift away from the nation and from national identity as a disciplinary or methodological structure is all part of that attempt to move beyond Caliban, where as a diasporic figure his utterances are often nationalistic or essentialist.

Two things have emerged with this shift in black diaspora studies that are relevant for this project. The first is a concern with creating a single framework for black thought that, while allowing it to exist enough to constitute disciplines and literary or cultural projects, is not also essentialist or reductive. The second is the relationship this scholarship and relevant new theories have to European thought, either being brought into a single framework and thus simultaneously requiring the rethinking or framing of European philosophical and literary discourses, or rejecting European thought as foundational in favor of "indigenous" African or newly rooted black knowledge as the generative epistemological launching ground. These concerns have led to the development of land- versus sea-based epistemologies (to borrow Elizabeth DeLoughrey's clever framing of the problems of diaspora studies scholarship), which in so many ways continue to reduce ontology to subjectivity, those representations that make theory possible.[74]

Such challenges to early 1990s models for black diasporic work reflect the attempt to move beyond the Calibanization of black critical thought. While

Caliban has been most profoundly an anticolonial figure, the deployment of the Caliban figure, especially within criticism and theory, has often come to represent a sometimes geographic, racial, gender, or otherwise theoretical and conceptual limit. One attempt, as I read it, to move beyond the limits of this tradition is Brent Hayes Edwards's rejection of Paul Gilroy's concept of black modernity. In his essay "The Uses of Diaspora," Edwards makes a now-common claim that Gilroy's "black Atlantic" imposes a geographic limit for belonging in the black diaspora.[75] It is problematic in terms of time as well, in establishing a limit or locus for modernity. Edwards prefers *diaspora* to "ocean frames" like black Atlantic, "black Mediterranean," or "black Pacific" because they reinforce an "obsession with origins" even when they are looked at together. Paget Henry's work also attempts to move beyond the limits of the Caliban tradition in criticism in his attempt to reconcile idealist and materialist critiques. However, the problem that scholarship has today is that while some artistic and critical projects are trying to embrace more fluid models and reject any form of historical determinism, we are left with particularly limiting dualisms. Beginning with a discussion of Patricia Fox's work, I suggest that our criticism is indeed rooted in a paradox, leaving "ontological sovereignty" as that which is indefinitely deferred, while black being remains a function of some kind of dialectical operation, stuck in a general paradox of *being* and *becoming.*

Recent work by Fox offers a rejection of epistemological and geographic boundedness in favor of "improvisation" for plantation-defined peoples. In *Being and Blackness in Latin America: Uprootedness and Improvisation,* Fox argues that the underlying condition of blacks in the New World is one of "uprootedness," from both Africa and after emancipation, against which "territoriality" emerges as a coping strategy. Fox writes, "Neither founders, nor conquerors, Blacks were always, already poignantly out of place, especially in the immediate postslavery era."[76] These seem, for her, to be the only available positions for New World blacks, albeit ones they are denied, with native status completely unreachable. This being "out of place" by blacks (that is, their lack of existing native or settler status) has led to the yoking of identity and land for colonizer and colonized alike.[77] She continues with regard to territoriality, "The experience of peoples of African descent in the Americas attests to a tenuous and at the same time tenacious relation to territory in which they work a land not their own, fight for the independence of a nation in which they are not free, and occupy a space at the whim of systems disinterested in their well-being. Therefore to 'refashion territory' is to refashion both identity and one's relations to power."[78] In describing how this manifests itself in the plot of the novel *Juyungo,* by the late Ecuadorian writer Adalberto Ortiz, Fox cleverly points to the inability of "sweat equity" on the part of blacks to provide a valid legal claim, and she writes that for black peoples, much like their "fictional counterparts" in the novel, they are considered "squatters." For Fox, improvisation then emerges as a primarily cultural response to uprootedness and the need to solidify or "root" an identity, to become citizens and national subjects.

Fox is essentially describing the process by which Wynter suggests Jon-konnu can be regarded as indigenous. Rather than focus on how the land changes, as Rodney does when he claims that it was "humanized" by labor, Fox suggests a unidirectional *affect* of labor that is predetermined by the condition of not already belonging to the land. It is the failure to be already rooted, with rootedness serving as a kind of telos or goal for identity, and simultaneously being that which gives power. This last bit is particularly telling because the implication is that by rooting or being rooted one gains power. I quote again her claim that "to 'refashion territory' is to refashion both identity and one's relation to power." Fox ultimately leaves us stuck with a preoccupation with origins and rootedness that is in fact not fluid and works to support particular forms of identity, such as those of the nation-state. Thus, although Fox is interested in fluidity in identity formation, her work sits squarely in opposition to the sea-based epistemologies that, for instance, Elizabeth DeLoughrey explores in her work, *Routes and Roots: Navigating Caribbean and Pacific Island Literatures,* which I discuss in this book's conclusion. Fox's work does not address how racialized labor and nonlabor (as wealth, not waste) continues to govern both blacks and Indigenous Peoples, or how the plantation works as a governing epistemology whether or not one was on it. Her work thus misses the ways in which blacks in fact become new colonizers and seek to bind Indigenous Peoples to a laboring epistemology that they control, so that the appropriation of the native by the state, which I discuss in chapter 4, is fundamentally anti-indigenous because the new basis for the appropriation is labor. Next, I turn to a discussion of Michelle Wright's work as another in the tradition of black diaspora scholarship that grapples with this dilemma.

In Wright's work, the focus is on the dialectic of becoming. In her argument for a black diasporic subjectivity, Wright claims, "There is a twentieth-century intellectual tradition of African diasporic counter discourses of Black subjectivity" that defines "Black subjectivity *as that which must be negotiated*

between the abstract and the real or, in theoretical terms, between the ideal
and the material."[79] Wright's work thus bears some relation to that of Henry's.
Like Brent Hayes Edwards, Wright rejects the idea of a single shared historical or cultural moment or trope that indigenizes or homogenizes the black
experience and thus faults Henry Louis Gates's claim that for blacks there are
"indigenous" critical methodologies.[80] Within this framework, Wright argues
in her book *Becoming Black: Creating Identity in the African Diaspora,* that
her phrasing "becoming Black" is meant to signal "the fluidity of Black identity in the West, and our ever-evolving understanding of it."[81] She is thus
focused on critiquing the production of the black as other through dialectical processes in Eurowestern philosophy and the engagement of male anti-
colonialist (Fanon, Césaire, and so on) and later black women (Lorde and so
on) with this method of producing black subjectivity.

Key for Wright is what she sees as a "paradox" in Hegel's representation of
blacks as both "outside" history and, through the dialectical process, the necessary "antithesis" of white subjectivity. Further, Wright argues, it is this paradox
that black intellectuals engage when seeking to establish black subjectivity
through idealist or materialist dialectics.[82] This paradox within Hegel's work—
identified by Wright—is similar, in many ways, to the one identified by Susan
Buck-Morss in her essay "Hegel and Haiti." Buck-Morss reveals black ahis-
toricity and otherness as a generalized paradox in Enlightenment thought;
slavery, she finds, was both contrary to Enlightenment humanist ideals and
also central in advancing them.[83] My interests in Wright are twofold. The first
is simply her recourse to dialectics as a necessary point of engagement for
the most prominent black anticolonialists and, from her discussion of Fanon
and Du Bois, the suggestion that the more radical, materialist attempts to construct black subjectivity necessarily rely on *Aufhebung,* and also *Sehnsucht,* as
the dialectical means of approaching black subjectivity.[84] Second, there are the
implications that stem from her assertion that a true black subjectivity that
can encompass blacks in the Diaspora *cannot* come about through the nation,
which allows for representation of the black male subject as a heteronormative and masculinist function of its time, forcing black women to serve as their
"internal" others.[85] To make this claim about the nation and black subjectivity, Wright first turns to Hegel, offering a truly excellent analysis of his writing,
in what has become a familiar trajectory of black studies and its engagement with his work, primarily in *The Philosophy of History* where he negates
Africa and "negroes," and in *The Phenomenology of Spirit.* Following, I have
chosen to offer my own reading before returning to a discussion of Wright.

For Hegel, being is a function of geography, historical time, and reason. In *Philosophy,* he conceives of the world's history in stages with an "ante-historical" period to which he relegates African civilizations and peoples. In probably the most quoted series of lines from that text, Hegel writes:

> Africa proper, as far as History goes back, has remained—for all purposes of connection with the rest of the world—shut up; it is the Gold-land compressed within itself—the land of childhood, which lying beyond the day of self-conscious history, is enveloped in the dark mantle of Night. Its isolated character originates, not merely in its tropical nature, but essentially in its geographical condition. . . . In Negro life, the characteristic point is the fact that consciousness has not yet attained to the realization of any substantial objective existence—as for example, God, or Law—in which the interest of man's volition is involved and in which he realizes his own being. . . . The Negroes indulge, therefore, that perfect *contempt* for humanity, which in its bearing on Justice and Morality is the fundamental characteristic of the race. . . . Another characteristic fact in reference to the Negroes is Slavery. Negroes are enslaved by Europeans and sold to America. Bad as this may be, their lot in their own land is even worse, since there a slavery quite as absolute exists; for it is the essential principle of slavery, that man has not yet attained a consciousness of his freedom, and consequently sinks down a mere Thing—an object of no value. . . . At this point we leave Africa, not to mention it again. For it is no historical part of the World; it has no movement or development to exhibit. Historical movements in it—that is in its northern part—belong to the Asiatic or European World. . . . What we properly understand by Africa, is the Unhistorical, Undeveloped Spirit, still involved in the conditions of mere nature, and which had to be presented here only as on the threshold of the World's History.[86]

Throughout *Philosophy,* Hegel establishes that world historical development occurs in a line that begins and ends in Europe as the locus of reason, with North America just an "echo" of Europe. Hegel dismisses phenomena that characterize many societies, even the Greeks, such as oral narratives. He then suggests that rational thought is the only path to the spirit or salvation. Reason, in Hegel, brings us closer to God, and he argues that "universal divine reason" "in its most concrete form, is God."[87] He associates history with reason ("sovereign of the world") and after the classicists, aspiration to an inviolable object, God. He thus argues that nature is subordinated to spirit and reason. More important, the spirit in Hegel means freedom and is embodied by the state.[88] For Hegel, the state, then, is the instrument for achieving world historical progress and it also contains self-worth: "All the worth which the human being possesses—all spiritual reality, he possess only through the State."[89] Further down, he writes that "man is free by *nature*" but the state limits this "natural freedom" and "society and the State are the very conditions in which Freedom is realized."[90] Slavery thus serves the function of the state, but although he argues for the former's gradual ease, he does not suggest that we abandon the state as a structure that will ultimately be a necessary orienting point for European and black humanity. While Hegel's idealist historiography advances through dialectics, it does, as Wright suggests, produce in the black other that which it tries to negate, but it is now a crucial measure of European subjectivity as a function of time, geography, and climate. It, however, produces something else; a vanishing native subject in discourse that it positions in *relation* to blacks. What I suggest next is that we must look at and beyond the structuring paradox Wright identifies.

Hegel claims that "aborigines," whom he also says were intellectually and physically weak, "gradually vanished at the breath of European activity," and that in the New World, "negroes are far more susceptible of [sic] European culture than the Indians. . . ."[91] While the focus in anthropology and postcolonial criticism is on blacks as the ultimate, secular other after having taken the place of and exceeded the New World native (see, for example, Wynter's "Columbus and the Poetics of the *Propter Nos*" and Paget Henry), Hegel's dialectic in fact produces two others: one that it negates entirely through disappearance (although the dialectic of otherness does not work without them), and the other, blacks, that is maintained through a greater susceptibility to European culture despite the overwhelming identification of blacks with an irrational state of nature so corruptible that it must be excised from his own discourse. Enslaved blacks can remain through influence, creolization, or better yet, through the place they will come to serve in the materialist dialectic, as a necessary element in primitive accumulation. In Hegel, we have the different methods of subordination of blacks and natives. The latter are presumed vanished, as much in fact as they are in his substitution of aborigines for Indians; the former are conceived of as a blank slate that he suggests has been brought in because the former perished. Dialectics in the idealist tradition thus makes blacks and natives into objects, but it simultaneously makes native disappearance essential for conceiving the black subject in terms of its worth or value *for* white subjectivity; it thus holds them in dialectical tension within discourse as absent and present. However, native disappearance is represented in and by the dialectic as tension. Although disappearance is required, it must always be enacted or reenacted, hence the absent/present phenomenon that structures Maximilian Forte's reading of the native Caribbean. Hegel in some ways anticipates the position Indigenous Peoples will hold for black, Marxist historiography of the Caribbean (recall C. L. R. James) when he offers labor as the starting point for black history in the West. Marxist historiography repeats Hegel's claim of disappearance when defining its subjects in terms of their labor and through that labor, the possibility of no longer being, as Wright notes, the "exact antithesis of the citizen."[92]

Indigenous being, where it is not an oxymoron for the historical (versus ontological) Hegel, is tied to disappearance in a particular place (the New World), while black being (again approaching oxymoronic status in Hegel) is based on the disconnection from a place (Africa) that must disappear. What Hegel effectively does is replace indigenous status for blacks with creolization as a state of disconnection, based on European conquest through the sea and with their labor as slaves. Blacks cannot retain African native status in Hegel because when blacks *are* native they are not contributing to the world economy and (European) world historical development. They can only do so as culturally and geographically displaced subjects. On this ground, black indigeneity in the New World—Creole indigeneity—is differentiated from other modes of being indigenous. This affects not only Creole ontology but is instructive about what dialectics come to mean for Creole subjectivity, where the Calibanesque tradition inherits this particular epistemology of displacement.

When Shakespeare is representing Caliban in the early seventeenth century, blacks had already been laboring for nearly a century in the New World in what can be considered a still inaugural phase of the mechanization of plantation work. However, by the following century, and certainly by the time of Hegel's writing in the eighteenth century, if one observes Eric Williams's argument,[93] enslaved blacks cannot just be considered as representatives of an early stage of capital to be surpassed: they are the past *and* future of capital at the same time, and they help to bring about its industrial (and postindustrial) phase.[94] This is the real problem that Caliban poses and the reason for his transformation in the anticolonial discourses that clearly identify him not with primitive accumulation but as a classed individual intrinsic to and necessary for capitalist development.[95] Indeed, and to reiterate my earlier point about the false opposition between materialist and idealist dialectics, the often uninterrogated notion of primitive accumulation in Marxism owes a certain indebtedness to Hegel's own idealist positioning of the slave as worker and as someone who is humanized through work.[96] Marx's claim that peripheral societies must pass through capitalism is a similar ascription of Hegelian historical determinism.[97] When scholars like Wynter, Henry, Fanon, and others claim that blacks are the most other, they are referencing this type of Hegelian maneuver. Yet, they ignore that in Hegel it is predicated on native disappearance and that this is always already a *new* native identity that encodes their productivity. When blacks become native or come to see themselves as native, it signals a shift in their relationship to labor, but one they try to manage not as disappearance but as a claim to capital and the land as resource. The land as gold, like El Dorado in Guyanese historiography, is a recovery of the "gold" land of Africa that was so important to early trade. In this manner, within and through capital and myth, blacks are able to recuperate a particular relation to the land, one that emerged with European and early trade routes placing them in a global economic relationship, but one that existed prior to slavery and in which they were also central, in what is both a subversion and ascription of Hegelian logic.

Since the Hegelian dialectic produces two others, the materialist dialectic is stuck with this same problem of the residual, disappearing other that on the one hand could generally correspond to the *lumpenproletariat,* but on the other and with regard to race refers to aboriginals. The consolidation of blacks as the "zero" sum of humanity occurs in the idealist and materialist modes and also through the production of Indigenous Peoples as a vanishing other that exists outside the state and yet for the state. This method of European subjectivity for Indigenous Peoples is slightly different than it is for blacks in Wright's conception of an inside-black man versus an outside-black woman. Wright's work, in suggesting that in coming into being black subjectivity is literally filtered through dialectics (that it comes into being in no other way) thus points to the continued requirement of an other that is not simply female but is also necessarily native, with different consequences for Antillean or Algerian modern black subjectivity, for example. The position of blacks in anticolonial criticism and postcolonial studies, in which their humanity is necessarily a product of European Enlightenment, is dependent upon the Hegelian production of that being concomitantly with Indigenous Peoples as the necessary antithesis (the disappearing other). Thus, Caribbean subjectivity, or the "I" of possibility represented by Caliban, cannot exist without the representation (rather than disappearance) of Indigenous Peoples in a manner that suggests a slight reworking of the Hegelian dialectic of history for the Caribbean. Further, theories of creolization and mixture come face to face with the Hegelian notion of "susceptibility" as the locus of historicity and freedom.

Blacks as settlers, while more abased yet somehow more "susceptible" to European humanism, can't entirely wipe out Indigenous Peoples in the Americas and thus resort to the recuperative methods identified, for example, by DeLoughrey in her discussion of how Caribbean writers use Indigenous Peoples (in other words make them work) to "root." The infrahumanity of Indigenous Peoples is preserved because it is necessary for black humanity to be achieved within the dialectic that offers the last revolutionary potential for *Aufhebung*. Represented in terms of Fanon's own intervention in *Black Skin, White Masks,* the dialectic in which Indigenous Peoples and blacks are involved would look something like the graph on the following page.

In charting the evolution of becoming in European and black discourses, Michelle Wright's argument seems to suggest that black subjectivity as a function of post-Enlightenment, and more specifically, anticolonial intellectualism, proceeds *only* from this excavation of the Hegelian other. Even the alternative she identifies in Bakhtinian dialogics does not offer ontological sovereignty but is also involved in a similar project of excavation from a particular dialectical mode. Wright thus reveals the limits of focusing on the black subject as an intellectual or narrative aesthetic project; for her this is reflected in the tropes of masking and ventriloquism used by Fanon and Césaire, respectively, to make blacks speak from a negated position.[98] I use Wright here to demonstrate my claim in the opening of this section: that our criticism mirrors the political conundrum. As Maximilian Forte says, it is not just that natives are defined as pre- or antimodern, but in a state that is defined by degrees of progress (where salvation is economic), Indigenous Peoples are essential. In Caribbean history, which is not structured through the state, they come to serve in the place formerly designated for blacks, in this case, the beginning of Caribbean history. Read in this way, the continued dialogue with Hegel in the articulation of black subjectivity, with particular emphasis on labor and subjection, means that Amerindian subjectivity is fundamentally not Hegelian. However, and this is the "trick" of Hegel's logic, it is already subject to it. Black subjectivity ends up reassigning natives to prehistory. In other words, and ironically, Caribbean history does not exist without Indigenous Peoples, but precisely because as a modern history they are its antithesis. I argue that blacks recreate this condition with Indigenous Peoples and this is how their premodern, antiprogress status (Forte) should be interpreted.

Lord/Master

- Creole Black (already the subject of a dialectical operation meant to recover the self from a position as Other/Colonized/Enslaved)

Bondsman/Slave

- Native (consolidation of diverse individual peoples—Wapishana, Lokono, Waiwai, and others)

Native

- Creole Citizen-subject (produced by yoking of material and linguistic labor)

Rethinking Hegel's dialectic of history: The sublation of native to black New World becoming.

This is especially true to the extent that the postcolonial state has both a political and ontic function in guaranteeing the new freedom and salvic function of capitalism and the reinvention of "Negroes" (outside capital) into black proletarians (inside capital), and the fact that the colonial state is based on this opposition of pre- and outside history. What we read, therefore, at the start of this chapter as eradication and fossilization is the need for the settler, as Vera Palmer argues, to be desired in Hegelian fashion by the native other, in order to truly be or become native.[99] This tension that maintains the native other as a necessary limit in the production of blackness within modernity is simultaneously the desire for Hegelian or Calibanesque recognition in the achievement of native status as a future orientation for Creole identity.

So if there is a particular method of producing black subjectivity, then what is becoming? According to Wright, traditional arguments about Hegel's work claim that the dialectic positively advances to "becoming." However, for blacks, she claims that this is not the case because it "obliterates" them.[100] This obliteration must be understood as excluding blacks from becoming, as the Hegelian mode of producing subjectivity positions blacks as fixed and excluded from being. Now, although Wright points out that this fails in Hegel because of the already discussed paradox, it does indicate that becoming is reserved for certain subjects and is tied to a particular state of historical being that he does not grant to blacks or native, New World peoples. To be other is to exist in a paradoxical state of nonbeing. Hegelian becoming is about the establishment of the other: one vanishing (Indigenous Peoples), one potentially integrated (blacks); for formerly enslaved peoples it is already oriented toward indigeneity as the condition of their citizen status or as a condition of their participation in the nation-state. Becoming for Creoles then must be understood as an epistemic *and* social ontic process, and it is the latter Wright does not explore. Concerned with epistemology and subjectivity, Wright focuses on anticolonialists' writings and differentiates among the invocations of dialectics. However, in examining anticolonial poetics in addition to, for example, labor practices and the constructedness of historical narratives tied to them, we find that labor both produces the epistemological conditions for black subjectivity and also structures the social process necessary to claim becoming for blacks.

Hegel's "A. Independence and Dependence of Self-Consciousness: Lordship and Bondage" bears out the importance of labor for establishing this form of subjectivity (albeit dependent) when it claims that it is only through work that the bondsman attains consciousness: "Through this rediscovery of himself by himself, the bondsman realizes that it is precisely in his work wherein he seemed to have only an alienated existence that he acquires a mind of his own."[101] Not only does it make some form of slavery necessary for freedom, thereby establishing the two dialectically (see, for instance, Orlando Patterson's *Freedom in the Making of Western Culture*), but it makes labor—from which natives are excluded in *Philosophy*—necessary as well. The materialist dialectic thus works as a completion of an already begun Hegelian process of historicity and subjectivity. Susan Buck-Morss makes a somewhat different although related point when she rejects the materialist abstraction of the dialectic established in "Lordship and Bondage" as simply having to do with class struggle.[102] In her essay, Buck-Morss forcefully argues, through Hegel's readings of the journal *Minerva,* for an influence that grounds his dialectic in relations between black slaves and their masters. She writes:

> We are left with only two alternatives. Either Hegel was the blindest of all the blind philosophers of freedom in Enlightenment Europe, surpassing Locke and Rousseau by far in his ability to block out reality right in front of his nose (the *print* right in front of his nose at the breakfast table); or Hegel knew— knew about real slaves revolting successfully against real masters, and he elaborated his dialectic of lordship and bondage deliberately within this contemporary context.[103]

However, it is the master–slave dialectic that makes it difficult to conceive of the relationship between blacks and later subaltern settler groups in the New World to Indigenous Peoples. After resistance during slavery and during captivity on ships, the labor strikes by Afro-Creoles throughout the Caribbean in the early twentieth century can be read as social *Aufhebung,* where blacks were able to reinstitute becoming through the state as a positive outcome. Indian resistance under indenture was a different kind of resistance than that of blacks under slavery. However, their early resistance, as well as their participation in generalized labor strikes with blacks, was also oriented toward the state. The narrative they have produced of having "saved" the colony (Guyana) through rice cultivation reflects a labor ontology that is patterned after that of blacks. In our critical attempts to privilege notions of fluidity that allow for recovery of either a more popularly defined black, Indian, or Native American subjectivity, what we still fail to understand is how poverty and scarcity govern the relationships of so many to the land. We forget that Caliban, in his multiple manifestations, is a subaltern subject transitioning within an imposed poverty when we focus more on his word play. We must remember that vassalage, slavery, and indenture are all in fact about transitioning into *and* within an imposed social and world-systemic condition of poverty.[104] Becoming is part of this transition. Therefore, Vine Deloria Jr.'s claim that Indigenous Peoples do not have the "psychological burden" of settlers needs to be read somewhat differently. Indigenous Peoples have had to establish their native status within a shifting economic nationalism, an example being the current struggle faced in North America by the Lumbee.[105] Blacks, Indo-Caribbean peoples, and Indigenous Peoples are continually remaking themselves through or in land and sea epistemologies, but they are fundamentally remaking themselves as always-already citizens, in other words, as always-already competing for various degrees of humanity as defined by political and economic systems, the same systems to which our literary and other critical practices are subject. Further, their mode of indigeneity is one that must encapsulate the dispersal that resulted in a laboring ontology and the historical rootedness that is younger than aboriginal claims. It thus forces Indigenous Peoples to redefine their nativity as one *of* place, in spite of a history of movement within and between islands and continents, in order to maintain claims of prior right.

CONCLUSION

This chapter has focused on the indigenizing function of literary figure Caliban. This, I argued, is Caliban's labor for black or Creole being in the New World. It is a labor that we see elaborated as an ontopoetics of indigeneity across the various "insurgent" adaptations of Shakespeare's *The Tempest*. These adaptations and the repetition or representation of Caliban allow for the self-troping of the Creole as a sovereign and native subject. Throughout the chapter, I have sought also to demonstrate particular flaws of the critical tradition in postcolonial studies around Caliban and their consequences for both Caribbean philosophical thought and black diaspora studies. In Paget Henry's work we witnessed the attempt to resituate black critical epistemologies away from current binaries: material versus idealistic. However, different tendencies emerge with this trend: some argue for an indigenous black epistemology or at the very least a rerooting in Africa (Gates and Henry), while others reject that idea entirely (Wright). What I have sought to demonstrate is that the inside/outside paradox that Michelle Wright identifies from Hegel and its inscription in the hugely productive master–slave dialectic is also the limit of the Calibanesque tradition. Not only have we reached the productive limit of the dialectical tradition, but in the present moment it continues to reproduce the conditions of bourgeois humanism inside postcolonial critical discourse and with regard to Creole subjectivity. Ultimately, both black diaspora studies and Caribbean philosophy share a similar concern about their relationship to European thought. Like Caliban at the end of Césaire's *A Tempest,* they are stuck in an exchange or dialogue that is dialectical. However, we are left arguing for different positions within the same exchange without fundamentally undoing the method by which Caliban's productivity is retained, without undoing the profoundly colonialist tendencies inherent in these critical methodologies that mirror the colonialist practices in the production of social and political being. Hence, we fail to move beyond Caliban into ontological sovereignty. What the ontopoetics of indigeneity reveal is that it is not only the Creole that is indigenizing but that there is a way in which our critical and philosophical traditions indigenize a particular methodology.

While Indigenous Peoples were the first to belong to the New World and the first initial source of labor after the appearance of Europeans, and while they continue to constitute a large peasant class in Latin America, they have refused (at least in the Caribbean) a social being based on modern labor but nonetheless rooted in the land. They therefore refuse the grounds of Creole legitimacy, even in its attempts to represent or integrate them into anticolonial practice. Their resistance is thus beyond Caliban's opposition and against the foundation of his articulation when he is identified as black and as an "I"—as an affectable subject. Native American anticolonial resistance is therefore opposed to both neocolonial power and to Creole subjectivity's reinvention of humanity as modern belonging, in order to return blacks to an identity grounded in the past, an autochthonous status for Du Bois's "native peoples of the dark continent."[106] This is what we must recognize and read back into attempts to reconcile African and New World indigenous identities.

What this chapter did not address was gender and the specific question of whether or not Caliban functions to indigenize men and women Creoles in the same manner. Regrettably, the elisions of the Shakespearean and Césairean versions are the elisions of this work. In the Shakespearean version, there is no "mate" for Caliban, who supposedly desires Miranda. In "Beyond Miranda's Meanings," Sylvia Wynter reads this failure to have a mate for Caliban as reflective of the fact that Caliban is not supposed to reproduce his bodily difference, what will later become his racial difference. She also argues that Caliban's own bodily irrationality becomes the condition for Miranda's ability to speak in the play. In other words, both the disappearance of the black woman and the coding of the black body and mind as illegible and irrational are essential for (later) white women's racialized gains within patriarchy. Miriam Rosser has claimed in her critique of Glissant's and Bernabe et al.'s work that "*créolité* turns out to be a category that sublimates differences—of ethnicity as well as of gender and of class—in order to promote an organic vision of a whole, harmonious community."[107] Rosser largely takes issue with what she sees as a decidedly masculinist expression of subjectivity. The authors fail, as she points out, to consider depictions of Creole identity and culture by women writers and unlike later, woman-voiced theories of Creole subjectivity, such as Carole Boyce Davies's theory of migratory subjectivity, in fact close off possibilities for the subject. In her essay, "Figuring Caribbeanness," Rosser ultimately goes on to read the work of Simon Schwartz-Barth and Maryse Condé as alternatives to dominant masculinist representations. Others have envisioned Caribbean woman's literature in terms of a writing into the structuring absences of subjectivity, as suggested by the edited volume, *Daughters of Caliban*. The collection, however, simply "appropriates" the Caliban figure, and in the introduction the editors focus on Caliban's speech and its function as what they are drawing upon. The writing of the Caribbean women subject apart from the male-dominated literary tradition points to the way in which, as Michelle Wright observes, the black woman is produced as the other to the black man in these processes of becoming. However, when looking at what *Daughters of Caliban* borrows or how it inserts women into the Calibanesque tradition, it reveals that it is misleading to identify women, on the basis of gender difference alone, as constructing another narrative that is automatically not masculinist or does not rest on the same biases or elisions that inform black male subjectivity. Further, positioning or critiquing women's narratives in this way can also be a repetition of their discursive status as other. Pointing to the absence of a mate for Caliban is also an unwitting reinscription of a patriarchal, heteronormative gender economy in which women's value is reproductive. Admittedly, a discussion of gender and of women's labor in particular is beyond the scope of this work. However, as I suggested in the introduction to this volume, it is both women and Indigenous Peoples, the Indigenous woman doubly so, who are placed in a position of otherness with regard to the writing of the sovereign, Creole subject in literature. Beyond, therefore, intersectional approaches to identity, writing about ongoing processes of being and becoming requires a focus not on a singular dialectic but on the coterminous dialectical relationships in which modern subjects achieve or fail to achieve sovereignty.

3

"God's Golden City": Myth, Paradox, and the *Propter Nos*

Born in the land of the mighty Roraima,
Land of great rivers and far-stretching sea;
So like the mountain, the sea and the river
Great, wide and deep in our lives would we be;

. . .

Born in the land where men sought El Dorado,
Land of the diamond and bright shining gold,
We would build up by our faith, love and labour,
God's golden city which never grows old.

Thus to the land which to us God has given
May our young lives bring a gift rich and rare,
Thus, as we grow, may the worth of Guyana
Shine with a glory beyond all compare.

—W. HAWLEY-BRYANT, "The Song of Guyana's Children"

CHAPTER 2 CENTERED ON THE CALIBANESQUE TRADITION. IT ADDRESSED appropriation of the figure of Caliban by anticolonial and postcolonial writers who saw the discursive figure in terms of the conditions of speech for the black subaltern inside the West who seeks voice within the politics of cultural decolonization and a struggle for sovereignty. The chapter argued that these writers and critics seized upon the labor Caliban performed for being in the early modern period; in deploying it for twentieth century liberation projects, they used it to effect a bridge between the material labor of the formerly enslaved and the cultural labor of the intellectual. This figurative bridge came to serve as the basis for the articulation of Creole subjectivity in epistemological terms that reproduce class divisions within capitalism and further make the displacement of indigenous subjectivity necessary for the production of Creole subjectivity.

This chapter focuses on another aspect in the production of Caribbean subjectivity in this manner, specifically political subjectivity, and that is myth. While the choice of myth may seem strange as an entrée into the discussions of political discourse in the following chapters, in order to better understand how displacement of Indigenous Peoples works within the state, we cannot begin with the colonial plantation that has, of course, shaped so much of the cultural, social, and political structures of Caribbean societies. We must begin instead with what in fact precedes the plantation in the New World, what I referred to in the introduction as the first economy: the myth of enormous gold wealth that, as the poet Hawley-Bryant's song indicates, continues to inform the contemporary relationship of Guyanese to the land. The myth provides an image of the land as wealth that in turn legitimates the real and symbolic labor that, as I demonstrated with Caliban, is the ontoepistemic condition for Creole being. Myth persists as a way of inscribing Creole ontology in the time that would first produce it as difference and negation.

The myth of El Dorado led to the exploration of much of South America, including Guyana. From the initial encounter with Caribbean geography and peoples, myth was instrumental in producing an image of the Caribbean as a place for the extraction rather than development of economic and social wealth. Christopher Columbus initially abducted Indigenous Peoples in order to display them before the Catholic monarchs Ferdinand and Isabella as a sign of the abundant riches he failed to find.[1] Eventually, the cultural narratives of Indigenous Peoples became fuel for European myths of wealth, and after their own enslavement and the exploitation of their labor, blacks were brought from Africa to literally turn myth into material reality in the form of cotton, sugar, and other crops. Thus, El Dorado comes to inform Caribbean modernity and, as the chapter demonstrates, is in fact *no less* a crucial element of Caribbean political economy than the plantation or the postcolonial nation-state.

My recourse to myth as that which precedes the plantation should not be read as a view of myth as origin or prehistory. Instead, this approach is informed by a rejection of the opposition of myth to history and recognition of the social construction of the foundational elements within any culture. The chapter therefore focuses on the capacity in which the myth of El Dorado is engaged, refashioned, and deployed by individual actors and larger social forces and as such continues to inform Caribbean society and economy because it rhetorically supports the yoking of Creole identity with wealth. The myth is a core epistemological component of the writing or poetics of

Creole ontology and social being in the postcolonial state. It is through retellings of the myth that Guyana is continuously envisioned not just as an inheritance for Creoles but *propter nos,* for the sake of Creole being. It is this function of El Dorado that causes me to argue, after literary critic Richard Waswo, that the myth is a foundational one not just for Guyana, where there is concrete evidence of its continued enactment, but for the region. Ultimately, the chapter demonstrates that the role of myth in the Caribbean needs to be reexamined for its significance to political economy and for the way in which it is mobilized by Creoles within the postcolony as a way of managing the difference and continued subordination of Indigenous Peoples in order to make its economies productive within modernity. While the myth of El Dorado is not necessarily a myth of origin, it does work as a "founding myth" both in the initial imperial stage and in the postcolonial one.

For Latin America and the Caribbean, two of the most prominent discussions of myth occur in the work of Uruguayan writer Eduardo Galeano and Guyanese writer Wilson Harris. For Galeano, myths, especially the creation myths of Indigenous Peoples, reflect a "collective" consciousness. In an interview in 2005, Galeano states that myth is a kind of corrective to the elisions or silences of history.[2] Myths in many cases are therefore presented instead of what is typically considered history in Galeano's work. Wilson Harris too sees myth as a corrective to history, but his approach sits closer to critic and writer Édouard Glissant's claim that "myth is the first state of a still-naïve historical consciousness, and the raw material for the project of a literature."[3] In his work, Harris uses the term *myth* interchangeably with *imagination* and *fable.* Rather than colonial time, which places Caribbean cultures as backward and derivative, Harris sees myth or imagination as presenting an "inner time" that gets beyond the "fixity" of identity. Both Galeano and Harris are interested in myth, within the imagination of the writer-intellectual, as an alternative to history and rigid hierarchal social organization. I reference them both here because readers will expect to see them in any engagement with the myth in the Caribbean, but the impulse of their work has not been writ large in Latin America or the Caribbean. Neither work serves as a point of departure for my own, and, as I suggest elsewhere, Harris's own use of Amerindian myths remains problematic. Though their recuperative efforts are important, I am concerned with how the imbrications of colonial and pre-Columbian myths work in postcolonial society to manage the subordination of Indigenous Peoples. For this, the work of Waswo and Roland Barthes are more useful.

In his essay "The History That Literature Makes," Waswo writes of the significance of the meeting of myth and history. Waswo claims, ". . . The founding legend of Western civilization—the descent from Troy—in its literary retellings from Virgil to the sixteenth century shaped the actual behavior of Europeans and Americans in their subsequent contact with other, newly 'discovered' cultures."[4] He goes on to argue that the myth has had literary and scientific reenactments that validate or reify its telling, a phenomenon he attributes to the "constitutive power of any discourse."[5] Given this, Waswo claims, history is determined by myth and that literature, like myth, is an "integral, functioning part of an entire cultural system."[6] As an example, he points to the murder of Captain Cook, which essentially occurred, Waswo claims, because Cook "sailed into" a Hawaiian myth.[7] One can suggest that, much like Captain Cook, Western imperialists "sailed into" Amerindian sociohistorical narratives of El Dorado, mistook their ontoepistemic function within indigenous cultural discourse and society, and took them *literally*. However, the truth is that in taking them "literally," in setting them down, conquistadors and subsequent narrators in fact mythologized social history by rearticulating fragments of it in terms of the *propter nos* of the first humanists and redeployed it within the new episteme and structuring poetics for their presence in the New World. Quite differently from Waswo, Roland Barthes argues in his discussion of the role of myth in bourgeois culture that myth does not precede history. Rather, in his elaboration of myth as a sign system, Barthes suggests that myth possesses "an historical foundation."[8] It works, however, precisely because in its rearrangement of signs, it is able to create "distance" between that historical content and its new "signification." Barthes elaborates, "It is this constant game of hide-and-seek between the meaning and the form which defines myth."[9] Continuing, he writes that "however paradoxical it may seem, *myth hides nothing*: its function is to distort, not to make disappear."[10] It is precisely through distortion—what I simplify here as the collapse of one sign system within another, or in Barthes's words the transformation of "meaning into form"—that myth "transforms history into nature."[11] Barthes's and Waswo's writings on myth both shape my own approach and argument that myth for the Caribbean must be understood in terms of paradox. After Barthes, my use of the term *paradox* in this chapter is meant to signal the way in which the term preserves a tension rather than signals an elision.

In the remainder of this chapter, I make a strategic *return* to the El Dorado myth to illustrate the way in which in the twentieth century, for the

Caribbean, it has been kept viable precisely through its seeming "loss" and its endless ability to be reimagined or reinvented.[12] The chapter is divided into four sections. It begins by explicating the significance and workings of myth for Caribbean modernity and arguing for a new way of reading or approaching the retellings of El Dorado. The second section illustrates how the myth has remained current and how it works in neocolonial discourse such as tourist literature. It therefore examines the myth through some significant retellings or articulations of it in narratives that ultimately reveal how it continues to reinscribe the Caribbean and Latin America as the treasure itself and, in so doing, codes their representation as productive for First World territories within capitalism. More specifically, it covers two works that significantly articulate it in terms of First World history and economy to illustrate the neocolonial ends to which the myth is put. Throughout, I avoid lengthy discussion of what are considered definitive early works by clergy or explorers such as Walter Ralegh.[13] I also do not provide an exhaustive or chronological account of the retellings of the myth, which has not been retold, unimpeded in an unbroken line from the past to the present. Instead, this section of the chapter concentrates on the way in which those initial narratives are kept current and made socially relevant in the most seemingly benign ways. Thus, a children's book about the myth serves as a crucial point of departure. With it we see how a colonial myth so wedded to the abuse of Indigenous Peoples and the expropriation of their lands has been turned into regional children's literature: in other words, how the myth can both retain contemporary value and be emptied of its historical thrust. Better than most other texts, the recourse to children's literature provides one of the best examples of the myth's malleability. Eventually, children's literature is juxtaposed to a historical text and tourist literature to suggest that despite the bracketing of some texts as story or fantasy and others as history, they all reflect a deployment of the poetics of myth as that which validates their discourse.

The third section concentrates on a single work, Matthew French Young's autobiography, to address the ways in which the myth has been transformed from a colonial one into one that articulates for the postcolonial nation-state. In Young's work, we see how the myth becomes integral to the transformation of Guyana from colonial dependency to a postcolonial state. The analysis of the myth concludes in the final section's look at postindependence engagements with El Dorado. The discussion here centers on postcolonial applications of the myth such as Hawley-Bryant's "The Song of Guyana's Children"

to underscore how the myth informs political reality within the newly independent Guyanese state. [14]

MYTH, HISTORY, AND THE PARADOX
OF CARIBBEAN MODERNITY

Our understanding of myth and the role it plays in the Caribbean has largely
fallen into the split between what is considered idealist or imaginative, and
therefore potentially false, and what is considered socially concrete or real.
Thus, the real purchase of myth on society and economy remains relegated
to the imagination, to the domain of culture, without real attention to its
continued material effects. Yet, myth provides the poetic structure that both
precedes and encodes the plantation's material and sociocultural modes of
being. As such, the logic by which myth operates is in fact intrinsic to postcolonial society, economy, and cultural discourse—even where the latter pur-
ports to challenge the narrative of myths as false or overdetermining. In this
section, three points guide the discussion of how myth, specifically El Dorado,
works in the Caribbean. The first is that the myth is always fundamentally
about material and cultural displacement effected by semantic deferral or loss
of the object to which it refers. The second is that although the myth of El
Dorado is a so-called Western myth that predates capitalist modernity, its
origins are in fact always outside the West in what it seeks to imagine and
manage through prophetic discourse. The third, which I move to unpack
first, is that the myth remains relevant for the Caribbean because it manages
a structuring paradox or contradiction.

That paradox, ignored as such because of its definitive articulation as historical fact, is that the Americas began to liberate themselves at the *end*
of two empires: first at the end or decline of the European empire(s) they
helped create, and then at the *end* of the American empire, to the extent
that North America literally ends at the Caribbean and Latin America, and
forcibly incorporates their economies (North American Free Trade Agreement [NAFTA] for instance) much as earlier empires did. The problem is
that both the retreating European empires and the looming North American
empire retain a colonial attitude toward the Caribbean that is enacted by
its middle class and business elite and is cloaked, as Doug Henwood points
out, in the discourse of democratization. [15] The Caribbean is therefore caught
between these two imperial attitudes (those of Columbus and James Monroe
and Theodore Roosevelt) and three moments: the rise and decline of European imperialism; the rise (and dare we hint at the decline) of American

imperialism; and the transformation of global wealth in the economic order of empire, as conceptualized by Michael Hardt and Antonio Negri. This paradox of coloniality that ties the Caribbean to empire consequently forces the Caribbean to "repeat"—to recall Benítez-Rojo—itself and its history for the First World. By *repetition,* I refer to such twentieth-century colonial invasions, euphemized as either interventions or regime changes, of Grenada, Haiti, and the Dominican Republic, which repeat imperial incursions of the fifteenth and sixteenth centuries; the reenactments in the Virgin Islands of the Danish transfer of power to the United States that repeat the denial of political sovereignty under colonial rule; the annual recreation of Columbus's landfall on Trinidad and other such repetitions or reenactments of imperial power, real and symbolic. What's more is that these repetitions are considered ahistorical, occurring within the new universal time and culture of empire, which has surpassed that of European modernity and emerged to devour the history that produced it. As Hardt and Negri famously decry, "Empire exhausts historical time, suspends history, and summons the past and future within its own ethical order."[16] Even the first African American president of the United States draws on the now-abstracted notion of the end of history, a logic produced by empire itself, situating it alongside the discourse of market deregulation in the 1990s.[17] Consequently, fifty years after the emergence of viable, independent Caribbean and African states from European control, the nation-state and the political sovereignty it guaranteed ceases to matter, in part because of how the racialist logic of capitalism requires it to be an underdeveloped receptor for First World goods and a contributor to the wealth of First World nations. The repetition of imperial history thus becomes instrumental in the production of Caribbean and Latin American states as underdeveloped, poor populations whose own wealth would contradict the structuring "classificatory schema" of the present economic order.[18]

Hardt and Negri's work on empire frames a particular relationship between empire and history that must be brought to bear on the discussion of myth in this chapter, namely, What role does myth play in the face of the new ethical order of empire and in the face of historical death? If, as Edouard Glissant argues, myth is a "producer of history," it stands to reason that with the end of history—which Glissant famously refers to as a "highly functional fantasy of the West" that crumbles in the face of the self-articulation (read the role of the writer-intellectual-politician) of postcolonial societies—do we not also face the end of myth and its relevance for contemporary societies?[19]

The answer to this last question, I suggest, is no. The opposition between past and present that, according to Michel de Certeau, marks the beginning of history or between the event and its narration, according to Michel Rolph Trouillot, is encoded in myth because of the way in which this opposition or contradiction makes it the function of a single historico-ethical frame of global capitalism.[20] The consequence for Caribbean discourse is that rejections of history and even myth continue to enact the epistemological conditions that necessitate such a rejection.

Critic Michael Dash in *The Other America: Caribbean Literature in a New World Context* offers an example of how this unfolds. In his discussion, Dash attempts to avoid an extension of a Western worldview represented by myths and the continued articulation of a mythologized and false Caribbean that is the product of a semiotics of power that exists in "repetition" and "remythification."[21] To do this he opposes myth to history; indeed, he suggests that myth is in fact outside of history. For Dash, myths—such as Manifest Destiny—seem to be fundamentally preoccupied with origins, and he therefore looks toward postmodern aesthetics as a way out of an etiological modernism in the Caribbean.[22] Yet, in Dash's own work, we encounter the importance of myth within history when he claims that the view of the Caribbean produced by imperialists is the result of a "psychological urge."[23] Another way of understanding this urge would indeed be to refer to it as desire. Desire at least is the clearest motivation for exploration, as depicted, for example, in films such as the somewhat nostalgic documentary *The Magnificent Voyage of Columbus* and in Walter Ralegh's effort to offer his version of El Dorado as "*a way found to answere every mans longing. . . .*"[24] More specifically, it was a desire for wealth. As I explore in Sylvia Wynter's work, however, it was wealth that could transform the fifteenth-century social class position of those who were not royalty, clergy, or gentry, hence Columbus's own desire to be rewarded with a title (Admiral of the Ocean Sea) that he could pass on to his children. Dash's "psychological urge" is therefore rooted in a particular reality, in a particular identity, and the desire either to change or preserve it. While, therefore, the myths to which Europeans have been beholden may have been "false," they stem from both a material and ontological need and the way in which that need, not necessarily just the myths themselves, produced history as action or discourse. Dash and other critics who reject the role of myth in this manner, by securing it to the past and to origins, in fact miss the real role that myth plays in human and social needs. They also reiterate or reaffirm the structuring paradox that allows myth to continue producing the Caribbean: its opposition to history. However, myth cannot be dismissed as just a feature of literary (post)modernity, a lie, or false consciousness.[25] It is essential for the production of our "real," and within capitalism it functions, rather paradoxically, as concretely as history. Sylvia Wynter's work is significant in helping us to understand the function of myth.

In her 1997 essay "'A Different Kind of Creature': Caribbean Literature, The Cyclops Factor and the Second Poetics of the *Propter Nos,*" Wynter critiques the theory of Caribbean identity, *créolité*, offered by Francophone writers Jean Bernabé, Patrick Chamoiseau, and Raphaël Confiant in *In Praise of Creoleness*. First published in English in the African American literary journal *Callaloo* in 1990, *In Praise of Creoleness* is an artistic statement, war cry, and ontological experiment all in one. The Martiniquan writers call themselves "Césaire's sons," and while they only figuratively castrate the father, like Kronos they nonetheless take his place. On the first page of this treatise on Creole identity, culture, and being, the writers boldly state that theirs is not a dry anthropological exercise or sociological dictum but the most authoritative form of articulation, experience or "testimony." In short, as the subject and object of their own discourse, the Creole in this instance is not that of Burton's *Afro-Creole* or any number of academic studies. In a relatively short number of pages, Bernabé et al. eschew the prevailing racial, ethnic, and national identity categories of sociological study and replace "raciological distinctions" with the "interior vision" of Creole being. The authors align themselves with the anticolonial emphasis on cultural decolonization, in direct rejection of the notion of Caribbean cultural dependency, especially for territories like Martinique that did not achieve political independence; they attack the so-called monsters of exteriority—European and African cultural thought and identity—". . . one monopolizing our *minds* submitted to its torture, the other living in our *flesh* ridden by its scars. . . ."[26] A gesture to Césairean dialectics, in the first and most famous statement of the treatise, they declare, "Neither Europeans, nor Africans, nor Asians, we proclaim ourselves Creole."[27]

In this bold self-determination that repeatedly calls attention to the language and history that serve as its epistemological terrain, the authors seek to mark Creole identity as integrative, open ended, and "authentic." They share a similar desire with other writers of the Anglophone Caribbean, such as the novelist and essayist Wilson Harris, and of the Francophone Caribbean for a new self-consciousness and cultural expression that is not determined by the dominant culture, the political structure of the colonial state, or the narrow nationalism of the postcolonial one. Edouard Glissant, for example, whose version of cross-cultural, regional expression, *antillanité*, they reject in favor of Creoleness (*créolité*), despite similarities, also tries to imagine just such a way of being. Nonetheless, these approaches are collectively motivated by the failure of an economic and political structure, such as the West Indian Federation, and a cohesive, pan-Caribbean sociocultural identification to emerge (see Premdas), both of which create alternate ways of belonging to the state and suggest the possibility of a truly localized American culture and aesthetic as the house of the Creole subject. It is an attempt to move beyond objective social status, beyond the often limited way in which Creole fails to encompass all Caribbean identities, having been initially associated with the formerly enslaved and their descendants and is often seen as less authentic than those it leaves out.

Wynter argues, however, that their declaration is executed within the "biocentric" terms that produced nonwhites as the "other" to European man. She thus observes that *créolité* does not reflect real cultural difference from what defines Western humanity but is in fact limited to identification with, or "sameness." For Wynter, the theory then does not extend what she sees as the first poetics of the human, that first writing of man by the Renaissance humanists outside the requirements of Christian humanism, which held that the earth existed for God, not man, and onto which the social order was mapped, placing all those who were not royalty or clergy, including the humanists, at the bottom of the social pyramid. As Wynter demonstrates, they therefore began to imagine the earth as existing not for God but for the "sake" of man himself (*propter nos*).[28] The notion of ethnicity proffered by the writers of *Praise* instead reinscribes a notion of humanity that reflects that which emerged, in Denise da Silva's work, through the collusion of nineteenth-century science and Hegelian idealism. Within this concept of the human, I argue, they raise Indigenous Peoples' disappearance from political economy to theoretical production when they claim that the term *Creole* denotes all "human races" but could also never refer to Indigenous Peoples because of both place and time.[29] In doing so, they reveal the fundamental way in which indigenous identity marks the sociolinguistic edge or margin of Creole identity, a position that is reflective of their economic, physical, and political marginalization in the Guyanese state. Since the native presence in Martinique is not embodied in the way in which it is in Guyana, the reiteration of this absence may seem to constitute a truth in their work. However, what we witness with a claim that is not determined strictly by history is the attempt to reconcile the Creole through elision and negation; by *reconcile*, I mean that in the process of being or becoming truly Creole that they elaborate (créolité), the native is represented within *as* difference and limit. Indigenous Peoples as historical excess and epistemological a priori determined by the constitutive break of 1492 thus come to mark the limit of the Creole as human, where what we saw in the Guyanese landscape is repeated in the cultural landscape or discourse. *Creole* therefore is not just a renaming but a remaking that shows the link among labor, time, and discourse that produces it as different and distinct from indigenous identity. Bernabé et al. reveal the ontoepistemic embeddedness of the term *Creole*, which has always functioned to denote a particular difference from the established citizen-subject, where citizenship in some ways connotes cultural belonging as opposed to racial difference. Thus, Creole subjectivity and identity, in its new legitimacy, is solely a function of post–1492 geography and space, and the new ontoepistemic requirements of that historically and temporally bounded geography. Their claims also reveal the very way in which aboriginal displacement becomes the precondition (and as such a structuring and integrative element) for Creole identity formation. It becomes so at the level of language and historicity, which reduce aboriginal representation to a split subjectivity, irreconcilable within the "state" and the modes of representation it provides, but necessary to mark its boundaries and the difference from neoindigeneity now defined as "human."

In rejecting the Créolistes' ethnic notion of Caribbean difference as a reinscription of Western modes of humanity, Wynter states:

> If we see today's Caribbean as having its source, then, in the intellectual revolution of humanism and its poetics of propter nos which revalued the "sinful being" of the *Christian* by reinventing it as the "rational being" of *Man*, and therefore in the *mode of history* to which its hybridly religio-secular transumption of the matrix Judeo-Christian culture Narrative would then give rise, then it was not, as the Créolistes propose, the "yoke of history" which determined the terms of the coexistence of the peoples of the Caribbean. Rather it was *the yoke of a specific culture*, conception of being, and mode of the Imaginary that were to function as the hegemonic "ground" of this history in its actual unfolding.[30]

Wynter goes on to argue that by rejecting Aimé Césaire's "negritude"— which he coined by valorizing *negre* rather than the more palatable and assimilationist term for blacks in French, *noir*—the Créolistes reject "radical alterity"; they refuse a difference that she argues, like Columbus's challenge, questions the entire system of knowledge on which its articulation is based, just as the first humanist revolution rejected the system of knowledge out of which it emerged.[31] Wynter defines this alterity imagistically, by opposing it to what she sees as myths of cultural assimilation such as El Dorado, and instead envisions it in terms of a myth of difference which she refers to as "the Cyclops factor."[32] Important to her understanding of the relationship between imagination and reality, and certainly beyond the power of one to explain the other, is the ability to see the way in which individual culture is recast as historical, beholden to its techniques of deployment or enactment. Thus, she writes at the outset of the essay, "I also suppose that it is this Imaginary that in all cases institutes the modes of Carpentier's 'marvelous reality' (*lo real maravilloso*), and so of the modes of the Real that are specific to all human cultures, up to and including that of our contemporary Western and Westernized own. . . ."[33] In other words, with regard to the structuring opposition of myth to history that I earlier outlined, what is considered real, what is marked off from fiction, is both culturally determined and is in fact an effect of culture. It is constructed.

I quote extensively from Wynter for several reasons, the least of which is that it is always better to encounter Wynter in her own words. More important, and when read through Dash's claim that "New World writing" is "remythification" and Benítez-Rojo's articulation of Caribbean modernity as dynamically proliferative but nonetheless based on the plantation machine, we begin to see more clearly not just *that* the Caribbean "repeats" but *what* it repeats. It repeats the epistemological and ontological conditions of its inception—the paradox that subordinates and enslaves the world that emerged at the end of Columbus's voyage to *liberate* man from Christian humanism. Further, this repetition, which has led to breaks such as Césaire's négritude, continuously reinscribes a limit or "ground" for Caribbean reality. Moreover, Wynter helps us to realize that myth, in general, does not disappear in the divide between imagination and reality. Imagination and reality are in fact mutually constitutive, which is why I explore in chapter 4 how the myth of El Dorado is central to Forbes Burnham's understanding of Guyanese political economy and nationalism. The imbrication of the imagined and the real, of myth and history, is most clearly expressed by Césaire himself in his defense of poetry. In it he does not advocate rejecting myth but suggests that "the true manifestation of civilization is myth. . . . Civilization is dying all around the world because myths are dead or dying or being born. We must wait for the powdery frost of outdated or emaciated myths to blow apart. We are awaiting the debacle." He continues, "We have lost the meaning of the symbol. The literal has devoured our world. Scandalously."[34] While, according to Wynter, Césaire's negritude constitutes a new humanism (a "second poetics of the propter nos"), negritude's challenge to the existing racialist order became subsumed by postcolonial rewriting. It comes to depend upon, as we saw with Caliban in chapter 2, the displacement of Indigenous Peoples. Moreover, although the cycloptic eye—the eye that sees in terms of difference, not sameness—engages a search based on interior epistemologies, the myth of El Dorado continues to be mobilized in the region because its founding premise is that there is something to be found; it concretizes interior desire in some kind of object whether it is gold or a lost utopian past, something Fernando Ainsa makes clear in his discussion of the myth and the tension it represents between "object" and "objective."[35] Myth thus allows the human today (what Wynter refers to as "economic man") to be written in terms of a relationship to objects. Following, I use Ainsa to demonstrate this and its intertwined consequences for Indigenous Peoples.

In his essay "From the Golden Age to El Dorado: (Metamorphosis of a Myth)," Ainsa traces the development of the myth of El Dorado back to Greek mythology. He argues that the value of El Dorado, like other myths, is both real and symbolic, and must be understood as the product of a paradox of sorts: between what has necessarily already been lost to the past and what can be found in the future.[36] Ainsa writes that the myth of El Dorado, prior to its appearance in the narratives of the New World conquistadors in which it was imagined as both gold and the location of such, had already undergone a change from an earlier myth of place and era (the golden age) to object (the golden fleece).[37] According to Ainsa, with the discovery, Columbus realizes Seneca's prophesy of a new universe thus, he writes, "From October 12, 1492 on we are faced with the historical verification of a literary predetermination."[38] So, while the discovery or discoveries in general represent "a fall from a previous paradisiacal state in which man lived," or chaos, about the way in which navigation was understood, Ainsa claims it is the only means of recovering or reencountering such a state.[39] Yet, Ainsa's discussion of the myth and the continuity he demonstrates between Greek narratives and those who wrote of a New World El Dorado constitute more than just a transubstantiation from a golden era or place to gold itself and later back to place or location. It points to a paradoxical element in and of the humanist challenge, which is in fact where the Caribbean repeats itself. Despite the break that Columbian humanism represents (the fundamental reinvention of "sinful being" for "rational being" according to Wynter), there is a continuity inscribed within it that manifests itself *as* paradox, where myth holds in tension the object through its endless deferral, hence the repeated attempts to locate El Dorado throughout South America and even in Trinidad. This paradox of seeking something that is semantically deferred or differed ultimately makes sense of a continuous reality of being "fallen," where Wynter's sinner-cum-poor person or person of color (see note 18) represents the threshold or deferral of being or humanity necessary for capitalist globality. The myth works to maintain a particular mode of being that will always depend on an other, outside, or limit. It is thus fundamentally tied to bourgeois humanism and the expression of that humanism (within capitalism) through relationship to and acquisition of objects, where consumption reflects an endless deferral through its institution and repetition of a difference between the haves and have nots. The rearticulation and appropriation of the myth by Creoles in the postcolonial period comes to be a way of bridging the gap between those who labor and those who acquire, thus linking the object or product with the "Creole" labor through which it is produced or deferred.[40]

Thus we come to the myth's facilitation of the displacement of Indigenous Peoples by confining them in the modern period to an identity outside of modern, plantation-based labor and to a status as objects. Ainsa, for instance, who writes definitively that "the Golden Age cannot be disassociated from El Dorado" notes the following about labor:

> For some, the signs of the survival in America of the Golden Age increased. The Indians of the Antilles where Columbus landed rarely worked: they had their crops in common and found all they needed in the very place in which they lived. In the pre-Columbian myths and legends that missionaries and chroniclers collected references also appear to the epoch in which humanity lived in a "fortunate condition," an age in which "there was no price put on food supplies, our sustenance" as the Nahuatl songs tell about the days of the ancient Toltec heroes. . . .[41]

Indeed, in Columbus's first letters to the Catholic monarchs, there is no mention of labor or work by Indigenous Peoples, which is crucial to their representation as being in need of religion and civilization and of course having no real ownership of their lands.[42] Further, when Columbus sends them to

Spain in chains so that their labor will supplant the gold he cannot find, Isabella of Spain orders them to be freed. While the absence of organized work is subordinate to their status as idolaters, it is nonetheless preserved in the desire of colonials that mythologizes their real or material relationships to the land. As I demonstrated in the preceding chapters, for Creoles to become indigenous, Indigenous Peoples must be represented, as they are by C. L. R. James and Walter Rodney, not as laborers. Identity in labor is the new ground for citizenship and social subjectivity as established by Creoles; Indigenous Peoples are thus denied full citizenship in part because of their failure to be *able* to be represented as laborers and appropriation of their culture and lands as objects to be transformed by Creole labor. Ainsa's work allows me to demonstrate that this identification of them outside of labor, for modern history and Creole indigeneity, stems *not* from the plantation in the Caribbean, which is predominantly identified with black slave and Indian indentured labor, but from the myth itself (the notion of utopia it encodes) and even from attempts by Bartolomé de Las Casas to defend Indigenous Peoples. Ainsa's study indicates the way in which Indigenous Peoples are always already *not* conceived of as laborers, and this becomes a structuring element of Caribbean modernity, history, and subjectivity. The myth continues to support the paradox that governs and validates Creole indigeneity when it is called upon to represent postcolonial Creole cultural nationalism and indigenous belonging or indigeneity. The continued identification of Indigenous Peoples as being outside modern labor is what the myth both makes possible and requires as the ontoepistemic condition of modernity in the region. It is for this reason that neocolonialists and the Caribbean cultural and political elite continuously rearticulated it in twentieth-century historical and economic discourse. The true limit or failure of Césaire's work as a second poetics, for which Wynter argues, lies in the fact that the *difference* of Indigenous Peoples cannot be represented within Césairean radical alterity because of the way in which their displacement remains foundational for subsequent cultural articulations, including black anticolonial struggle and later postcolonial belonging for Creoles within nationalism.

What I hope to have demonstrated is that Caribbean (post)modernity is beholden to the syntax of myth as much as it is to that of capital. A. James Arnold has quoted Césaire on the "superiority of myth" as he challenges "the law of noncontradiction" in Western cognition. Césaire writes, "Only myth satisfies man completely; his heart, his reason, his taste for detail and wholeness, his taste for the false and the true, since myth is all that at once. . . ."[43]

Césaire here points directly to the way in which myth, again, does not fall into the split between the real and the symbolic, as he says "the false and the true," but ultimately manages the tension of this opposition. Myth reinscribes an opposition that has calcified on either side into history and the real versus the imagination, and as Césaire iterates in the anticolonial moment, is an instrumental expression of man's need or desire. Thus, myth continues to displace Césaire's second poetics of alterity articulated within an anticolonial discourse that hinges upon a notion of being in and through labor that is not native. El Dorado is thus not just a narrative feature that can be dismissed as overdetermining Caribbean reality, but in its articulation with the structures of modern, capitalist empire, it has a particular epistemological purchase for postcoloniality and Third World nationalism. It is through the myth and its continued deployment or retellings that the "racial contract" continues to be executed and updated in the postcolonial period.

Finding What Is Lost: Excess, Exclusion, and the Neocolonial Legacy of El Dorado

In the children's book *The Legend of El Dorado: A Latin American Tale*, illustrator Beatriz Vidal has written that "there came to be as many El Dorados as there were versions of the tale."[44] There are in fact several versions that appropriate indigenous cultural narratives. They invariably include a native *cacique*, or chief (El Dorado, the Golden Man), thought to be from the Chibcha (Muisca) people; a gold dust ritual; a lake filled with gold (Lake Guatavita); and later, a city of gold (Manoa).[45] One of the earliest sources for the myth of El Dorado, and the one that Vidal relies on, lies in the 1541 chronicles of explorer Sebastián de Benalcázar. Benalcázar claims to have been told by an "itinerant" Indian that Bogota was loaded with emeralds and gold. He also claims to have been told of a king who covered his body with resin and then gold before going out on a raft to make "oblations" in a lake. Benalcázar held that there were continual offerings of gold and emeralds made in and to this lake.[46] In Vidal's adaptation, the wife and daughter of the Chibcha's ruler were seduced by a serpent that rose from a lake into which they eventually dove and vanished. In a yearly ceremony, the mourning ruler covered himself in gold dust and offered jewels to the serpent so that the serpent would keep its promise and one day reunite him with his wife and daughter. In another primary version belonging to Gonzalo Fernández de Oviedo, the naked cacique was covered with gold dust every day.[47] Still another version holds that a goddess and her son rose from the lake and helped the Chibcha people, who in turn paid tribute with a ceremony that involved the chief covering himself in gold once each year and returning to the lake. In the opening to the story, Vidal's dedication to her father reads, "A mi padre, que me contó cuentos y me indicó el camino de El Dorado."[48] The story she now tells is a legacy of her father's made clear by her affirmation that "although the exotic flavor of those myths remained with me, it wasn't until much later that I came across the original source. Having *found* El Dorado once again, I realized I had uncovered a rich and fascinating treasure . . . ," one that exists only in the "inner city of the spirit."[49] "Paradoxically," she continues, "the mysterious El Dorado was indeed found . . . but the Spaniards never knew it. It was found in the enormous amounts of gold that the Indians extracted from the earth and shaped with the most admirable sense of aesthetics. It was found in the beliefs and the sacredness of the Indian's way of life."[50]

Vidal illustrates that in stories about the myth, the central idea is of passing on a cultural heritage and, moreover, that the thing at the heart of that heritage, the city of gold itself, can in fact be "found." The stories about the myth are themselves the treasure, and it is these that can be claimed, here by Vidal for Latin America, by Forbes Burnham and the Peoples National Congress (PNC) for Guyana in the late 1960s and early 1970s, and in 1596 for England, by Sir Walter Ralegh, despite the fact that his accounts were initially discredited.[51] The narrative of the myth, in this highly malleable and portable form, has been transported across cultures and regions with relative ease. Despite the fact that no real treasure was ever found and what ornaments were found only served to fuel the search, the myth and the treasure can still be located in and rescued from the narratives of the early conquistadors by neo- and postcolonials.[52] Author Norma Gaffron, in another text for young readers, writes, "I am fascinated by the sheer persistence of the conquistadors who pursued El Dorado, and by the fact that there are golden treasures still hidden in secret places somewhere in the land called El Dorado."[53] Yet, in a somewhat ironic manner, she says, "[El Dorado] may be a symbol for something that can never be found. . . . Will they ever find El Dorado?"[54] Gaffron's El Dorado is both lost and always awaiting potential discovery. Gaffron's and Vidal's work engages the poetics of displacement and deferral that allows the myth to be continually productive. It is this same poetics that John Hemming accesses in his own search for El Dorado, in which he attempts to trace the search by early explorers. In his work, he also shows how a Latin American myth arrives in Guyana. Although physical searches by the Germans, Spaniards, British, and others for the city of gold continued without success, the mythical land *could* be found in writing and became fertile ground for Hemming himself and those prior who stumbled upon Benalcázar's account of the Indian's (read native informant) description of a land filled with treasures.

In *The Search for El Dorado*, Hemming documents the attempts made to explore the South American interior in the search for the fabled El Dorado. He writes, "The legend of the Golden Man inspired more sustained exploration, of some of the wildest parts of South America, than any comparable idea, anywhere else in the world."[55] While working on the book, Hemming physically traced the journey of the early conquistadors and includes pictures of places they visited and of the descendants of the people they encountered, today's Indigenous Peoples. His title therefore collapses his search with earlier ones, which code and provide interpretation for his own, and the work firmly locates modern-day Indigenous Peoples in the past of the myth. Hemming gives accounts of the failed attempts, from 1562 to 1965, to drain Lake Guatavita, located to the northeast of Bogotá, in order to find the lost treasure of the Chibcha people. In the quest to find treasure, fertile land, and a sea route to the "Orient" that would rival the Islamic trans-Saharan trade in gold and spices, the South American interior became a place of exploration and exploitation. In conveying the religious justification for the search, Hemming cites Jesuit naturalist José de Acosta, who wrote, "'God placed the greatest abundance of mines . . . [in such remote places] so that this would invite men to seek those lands and hold them, and in this way to communicate their religion of the true God to those who did not know them. . . .'"[56] In this reasoning, the very distance (read deferral) of South America from the known world at the time lends credibility to the myth and the realization of the quest for it in the shifting religious-monarchical conception of the world into which the "New World" moved.

A host of explorers and historians, including Fernández de Oviedo, Pedro de Cieza de León, Gonzalo Jiménez de Quesada (who claimed to have conquered the Muisca), and Juan de Castellanos (who believed that the city was located in Bogotá), claimed to have either found the city of gold or to know where it was located. It is these men, according to Hemming, who produced all of the initial known variations on the original story.[57] However, Hemming says, Fray Pedro Simón's (b. 1565) account, in his *Noticias Historias de las Conquistas de Tierra Firme en las Indias Occidentales*, was where the myth really "took shape," even though it was a rewriting of Castellanos's version.[58]

The story continued to "evolve" with Juan Rodriguez Fresle and Bishop Lucas Fernandez Piedrahita until the "final version" in the eighteenth century by Basilio Vicente de Oviedo, which placed the myth further away from its Ecuadorian origin, nearer the Orinoco, on the Ariari River. This version claimed that, in one ritual, a young man from a local group of Indigenous Peoples was sacrificed. As part of the sacrifice he was "salted with gold dust" and therefore known as El Dorado.[59] Banned from the English court, Walter Ralegh adopted the story at this point and went, according to Hemming, in search of the "empire of Guiana," El Dorado (Manoa), following explorer Antonio de Berrio's path. Ralegh believed Domingo de Vera's account, which placed the mythical city further away from Ecuador and in the region of then Guiana. Ralegh's *Discoverie of the Large, Rich and Bewtiful Empyre of Guiana*, which was originally published in 1596, combined the previous stories of the myth and literally brought El Dorado to then-colonial Guyana's hinterland in the British imperial imagination. Thus, both the search for and the "loss" of El Dorado in Guyana begin to be narrated by Ralegh.[60] Without naming them specifically, Ralegh himself writes about the failures that led to his expedition, saying "I did therefore even in the winter of my life, undertake these travels, fitter for bodies lesse blasted with misfortunes, for men of greater abilitie, and for mindes of better incouragement, that thereby if it were possible I might recover but the moderation of excesse, and the least tast of the greatest plentie formerly possessed."[61]

Ralegh's colonial search for "the greatest plentie" reinscribes the region in terms of a wealth it is thought to possess and a search or deferral through which he hopes to make such wealth concrete. This tension between the imagined and the concrete is the precise way in which the poetics of the myth works, and it is this that the following twentieth-century texts use to undergird their own neocolonial engagements. John Crocker's *The Centaur Guide to the Caribbean and El Dorado* and David Hollet's *Passage from India to El Dorado*, an economic history of the Booker Brothers, a British-owned group of companies, both illustrate how this productive, poetic tension makes sense of the Caribbean for neocolonial economies and the management of its relation of subordination with regard to the North.

Crocker's book is a companion to his other work, *The Centaur Guide to Bermuda, the Bahamas, Hispaniola, Puerto Rico and the Virgin Islands*. Published in the late 1960s, it contains a description of several Caribbean territories, including Jamaica, the Caymans, the Leeward and Windward Islands, Barbados, Trinidad and Tobago, and the Guianas. It is strictly geared to the

tourist market of the late 1960s and early 1970s. Crocker begins with some
history, identifying the role the United States occupies as Big Brother in the
Caribbean. Despite American economic involvement and cultural influence,
with which he is preoccupied, he adds that the islands still "retain an essentially British flavour." He also notes that the political changes of the 1950s
and 1960s "have made the Caribbean a far more interesting and attractive
vacation-land."[62] Crocker provides information not only about the history of
each territory and its current political situation but offers information about
hotels and tourist activities. He includes scenic pictures and, in the section on
Guyana, pictures of Indigenous Peoples. In his introduction, he states that the
book is designed to give the tourist "something of the background, thoughts,
and aspirations" of the "inhabitants." His book aims to "describe what makes
the Caribbean tick in the second half of the twentieth century."[63] Next, I turn
to historical treatments of the myth in order to read tourist literature such as
Crocker's in tandem with this work. Such a conjunctive reading is not meant
to dismiss historical work but to suggest that both these genres rely on the
same poetics.

In his preface to *Passage from India to El Dorado: Guyana and the Great
Migration*, maritime historian David Hollett firmly locates Guyana's origin
and significance in myth and European desire when he confirms for his readers that "this country, commonly known as Demerara in the nineteenth century, was *in fact* Sir Walter Ralegh's fabled land of El Dorado."[64] Hollett's is a
history of the now-defunct Booker Brothers, McConnell & Company (here-
after Bookers)—the origin of the Man Booker Prize for Fiction—and the
Booker Line (shipping) in Guyana.[65] It is also a history of, he says, the 430,000
immigrants transported to the colonies after emancipation, mostly by the
Bookers shipping concern, to work in the sugar industry. For Hollett, the
histories of both are "inextricably bound." The first chapter, which covers
Guyana's early history, opens with a section titled "The Land of El Dorado,"
followed by the section on history that for Hollett begins with Columbus. He
claims that "this rich and varied land has an exceptionally long and interesting history, which *from the European perspective* started with the arrival of
that noted son of Domenico Columbo of Genoa—Christopher Columbus."[66]
In effect, Hollett starts by naming the Eurocentric bias from which his discussion proceeds. In his discussion of Bookers, in the chapter "The Land of
Sugar, Rum, and Gold," he mentions "disturbances" by Indians on sugar plantations and pictures of them in full ethnic dress, the women wearing a good
deal of jewelry, as a way of affirming visually the gold of El Dorado. The

book ends with a discussion of Bookers and a section on "Guyana today," which covers, briefly, its *improved* economic and social condition.

Crocker's tourist literature and Hollett's history are narratives that locate the twentieth-century El Dorado for us. In his work, Hollett delimits his sphere of interest, not by simply identifying the ships and indentured laborers, but by saying that the rise of Bookers is the "most significant" aspect of Guyana's history. Barring Bookers's considerable influence on the region's economy, especially in transporting Indians to the colony, the reader is instructed to view the colony's history from the orienting point of excessive accumulation of wealth and power by Bookers. Bookers's success or wealth, as well as the myth, confirms Hollett's point of view that today's Guyana, and nowhere else in South America, is or was an El Dorado. In other words, without Bookers, the region has no history, only myth: "The most significant aspect of British colonial rule in Guyana was the phenomenal rise of the shipping, trading, and plantation enterprises established by Josias and George Booker. . . . The history of these companies is consequently inseparable from the history of modern-day Guyana."[67] Further, the accumulation of capital is what changes myth into history. In Crocker's book, the myth is portrayed in the service of neocolonial economic exploitation of Caribbean lands and people in the continuous reflection of the Caribbean as a consumable geography.[68] The myth and the search it encodes are more than just the perfect marketing tool; as the commonwealth territories shifted from colonial to independent status, they maintain continuity in their economic function coextensive with their depiction, continuity essentially in the poetics of empire, that keeps the entire region as a productive organ for Western capitalist expansion. Thus, Crocker draws our attention to the struggle between postcolonial government (which effectively signals the end of one form of empire) and the extension of Western imperialism (neocolonialism) when he laments that "the government of Guyana has not yet had time to make full use of the fact that the interior of the country contains a lot of places which should be visited by the traveler who wants to make a name for himself 'back home.'"[69] At the end of his own account of El Dorado and the exploration in the Caribbean that the myth produced, Timothy Severin, an Englishman born in colonial India, wrote in 1970 of "the swarms of tourists migrating southward in response to the brochures and travel posters, with which a new generation of promoters was reviving the legend of the Golden Antilles."[70] Severin, who has written several books within the genre of exploration, suggests that the production of sugar, rum, cotton, and molasses "vindicated" earlier narratives like Ralegh's because these products made the Antilles golden in spite of the fact that the prophesied treasures were never found.[71] In other words, the products of enslaved and bound labor confirm the initial identity of the land as treasure. Scholars have noted that one of the major concerns of Western nations like Britain was that the new, postcolonial leadership in the territories would be "sympathetic" to their continued economic interest and would in fact safeguard businesses still in the region that produced wealth for a dwindling empire. The use of the myth here reveals a great deal about the (discursive) mechanism that facilitated the neoimperial expansion, spearheaded by the United States, into the region.[72] The retelling of the mytho-historiography of the Caribbean at this historical juncture is now used to recode centuries of exploitation, slavery, and indenture, bringing them into a postcolonial politico-economic rationality that makes the Caribbean a place where its wealth (people, nature, minerals, and so on) can be converted into the gold that was never found. Clearly neoimperial, Crocker presents to tourists a version of El Dorado as both the myth and the land, narrating it again for new, colonialist, capitalist consumption. The myth here, in the service of First World capitalism, places the Caribbean within the history (read economic rationalism of capitalist markets) of empire. It is not that tourism did not exist prior to this point. It was in fact thriving. However, Crocker's work and others like it reassured the tourist that, despite independence, the market was still there and that it had not grown a conscience that was antagonistic to hedonism as the new focal point or consumptive end of foreign wealth. The 1960s and 1970s ushered in a new wave of tourism that many former colonies are now wholly dependent upon for their survival.[73] Further, tourism is a profitable economy precisely because it affirms a nonthreatening image of the Caribbean that stems from the myth, an image of having wealth that *must* be either extracted or consumed. Both Crocker's and Hollett's texts leave intact the idea of "discovery."

In its academic life, the myth is central in preserving for Europeans and North Americans the discourse of 1492 that allows the Caribbean to remain a productive body for First World economies and historians of the West. However, it is also central, as I've been suggesting, for postcolonial political economy and Creole subjectivity. Following, I demonstrate the way in which Matthew French Young's posthumously published *Guyana, the Lost El Dorado: A Report on My Work and Life Experiences in Guyana, 1925–1980 (My Fifty Years in the Guyana Wilds)*, an autobiography of his explorations and work in Guyana's interior, records a key moment in which the myth is taken out of the hands of British explorers and Spanish conquistadors by a native, white colonial and handed intact, with minor changes—*you* (postcolonials) must now think differently of this treasure than *we* (colonialists) did—to a black and brown postcolonial governing elite.[74] In Young's work, we see how what was once a colonial myth becomes useful for new national narratives of progress and development as he both literally and figuratively helps to construct the road to El Dorado. Young's work reveals that the road between the coast to the interior that the Forbes Burnham government hoped to build around the time of independence (chapter 4), could not bridge these spaces or the conflicting modes of indigeneity they represent. Instead, that road, paradoxically, functioned to extend the gulf between Creoles and Indigenous Peoples.

The Road to El Dorado

Matthew French Young was a white colonial subject in British Guiana who then came to serve Burnham-led independent Guyana. According to his autobiography, Young was born in Guyana and spent his life working a variety of jobs, which included leading work gangs on sugar plantations, farming, and hydropower surveying, in addition to searching for mineral wealth. The back cover of *Guyana, the Lost El Dorado* describes it as "an engrossing account of one of the last untouched tropical rain forests in the world. . . . It is an indispensable guidebook for the intrepid armchair traveler, gold prospector and diamond panner!" In his introduction to the book, Brigadier Joseph G. Singh, then chief of staff of the Guyana Defense Force created by Burnham for defense and interior projects, claims that former President Desmond Hoyte and Guyanese novelist and critic David Dabydeen were among the notable figures who helped get the book published. In the book, Young, who is described on the back cover as a "surveyor of the uncharted bush," narrates his life in the interior, chronicling everything from historic events such as the Jonestown massacre to the Indian girl he "ruined" and the stillborn child that resulted. In qualifying his insider-outsider status, Young lets the reader know that because he was so well respected by Indian workers on the plantation where the latter incident occurred, it was not reported to officials because these workers did not want him to lose his job.

Young includes material on the culture of both Indo-Guyanese and Indigenous Peoples, such as the making of Casiri (wine made from cassava) and the practice of Mashramani (Guyana's annual carnival), respectively. Throughout the text, there are continual references to his father, a Scotsman who

settled in Guyana in the late 1800s and eventually sold his rubber plantations to the British Consolidated Rubber Company.[75] Young also worked for
Bookers for twelve years. Yet, he recounts very little of the politics of the
region. Of significance is the fact that after retiring, in 1970, he returned to
work for the new cooperative government of Guyana, then seeking to build
roads in the interior from Mahdia-Potaro to the Brazil border. Young claims
to have been recruited for his expertise, having, he says, originally carved a
trail along this route in his various explorations of the interior. He also worked
on a road from Wismar to Kurupukari, and from Wismar on Demerara to
Mabura Mountain, the latter in order to "enable the Forestry Department to
penetrate to the greenheart forests."[76] At the end of the narrative, Young tells
the story of reciting the poem "IF" by Rudyard Kipling—himself a colonial
born in British India—to graduates of Burnham's Agricultural Institute. At
a later address to the annual intercompany athletic championships, he says,
"Guyana has 83,000 square miles of land, most of which is virgin forest. There
are thousands of acres of agricultural lands waiting to be farmed, plus all the
diamonds and gold that there is in our country."[77]

In teasing out the significance of Young's text, I want to focus on his work
building roads to the interior for the newly independent nation. The road
project, which served to connect and open up parts of the interior for subsequent development schemes by the Burnham government, must be seen
as both a project of the postcolonial nation to develop Guyana's infrastructure and facilitate commerce *and* (in its narration) as a metaphor for the transfer of power at independence, as the myth and its promise of wealth shifted
from European imperialists and white colonials to black and brown postcolonials. In *Co-operative Republic, Guyana 1970*, which I discuss substantively in
chapter 4, an essay by the Hon. H. O. Jack, a minister in the Burnham administration, includes a picture of three University of Guyana (UG) students
working on the interior road. The legend beneath the picture tells readers
that the road has "caught the *imagination* of Guyanese and West Indians at
home and overseas. . . ."[78] However, it must be viewed in terms of what the
Burnham administration represented for the United States and Britain. It
was considered less of a threat to their Western-style nationalism and to their
own future economic interests in the region. Burnham's socialist reforms,
indeed his presidency, were sanctioned precisely because of the lack of a
threat it posed to First World economy, as the ouster of Cheddi Bharat Jagan
proves. As it appears in Young's text, therefore, the road is a symbolic bridge
of both narratives (colonial and postcolonial) that demonstrates how the

colonial source of wealth can become the postcolonial source of power for a new nation that needs to make its own claims on history, without challenging the late twentieth-century economic imperialism of the United States and Europe. It is a bridge built or crossed with the service of Young's skin, which allows him to move between colonial and postcolonial status with relative ease, unlike those who came to employ him and who have, on occasion, paid with their lives to bring the shift into being.[79] Young, whose status as a white colonial gets him many of the positions he held, narrates this transition as an explorer, as someone conducting his own search for something, tangible or not, that has now changed hands. His place in the race/class hierarchy allows him to hold economic and social positions that only his color can access. Young writes, "In time, what I came to see was that it was not the gold which should be the true subject of the search for El Dorado but what was incidental to the original myth: the lakes. . . . Here, for the Guyana of the future, lies a source of power and of vast acres of irrigated and fertile farming lands in the interior."[80]

In working on the road project, Young, who is able to tell his story, is figuratively helping to build the road to El Dorado while simultaneously effecting its transformation. His autobiography performs the continuity of *the* narrative of the search for wealth. More important, it reveals how the myth beyond its representation in "external" tourist literature comes to manage Indigenous Peoples in the postcolony at Guyana's independence as excess. The cultural practices of Indo-Guyanese and most especially Indigenous Peoples that Young includes are incidental to the stories of his life; they are narrative excesses that serve the function of giving credibility to his story, to his quest for minerals, to his being a native of Guyana. Though they are crucial to the original story of the myth, the culture and lives of Indigenous Peoples are portrayed as an "excess" in these narratives, from Benalcázar to Hemming, which have been concerned not with their lives but with the *life* of the myth. Further, to the inheritors of Guyana—the black- and Indo-Guyanese–led governments—the cultural surplus of the past is newly problematic because individual cultures and modes of being cannot be swept into a singular narrative of belonging. There are the rights claims of Indigenous Peoples, for instance, that will not be silenced by the celebrations of indigenous cultures (for example, Amerindian Heritage Month) that nationalize those cultures.

The continued renewal of the myth of El Dorado and its consequent deployment of the ethics of empire cannot support the claims of Indigenous Peoples who want their land rights upheld. The myth has not been discussed in the "culture-centric terms" of Indigenous Peoples but instead remains firmly in the ambit of Western culture and thought.[81] That generative myth has displaced the creation myths of Indigenous Peoples and has become the founding myth of today's Guyana and of its first inhabitants. It is therefore important, at this point, to try to understand the trajectory of the myth's development, which, as a discourse of progress, has and continues to produce a national ethos. Its embodiment in the land, as Young instructs, allows the new nation to measure itself and to continually exercise a narrative of development even though the country's economic prosperity has been shattered by mismanagement and remains illusory in the face of successive loans from the International Monetary Fund and World Bank. The myth is central to Guyana's conception of itself at independence, to its narratives of progress, which facilitate the subjection of indigenous Guyanese today. It continues to have new endings, such as Norma Gaffron's placement at the end of her young adult book, or the words to the theme song for the 1966 movie with John Wayne, *El Dorado*.[82] These new tellings continually script the subjection of the land and the people with which it is most identified in order to realize a historical continuity between empire and postcolony. In so many ways, retellings of the myth allow for the continued mythologizing of the past of the Americas with regard to the history of capitalist forces.

Postcolonial Adaptations

In Guyana, the subjection and displacement of Indigenous Peoples is facilitated by the ways in which Creoles have entered the "myth" and now narrate it. The problem for Guyana is that, following Waswo, the myth of El Dorado continues to be "elaborated as history."[83] It is an integral part of the country's national history. As with the "legend of descent from Troy," the myth continues to produce not only economic reality but political and social reality as well, and it must be considered alongside the plantation system as a composite part of Benítez-Rojo's "Caribbean machine."[84] Benítez-Rojo himself suggests that the myth has made the Caribbean region, that it is a key part of its history written when he writes the following: "The Antilles are an island bridge connecting, 'in a certain way,' South and North America, that is, a machine of spume that links the narrative of the search for El Dorado with the narrative of the finding of El Dorado; or . . . the discourse of myth with the discourse of history; or . . . the discourse of resistance with the language of power."[85]

Similarly to Benítez-Rojo's Caribbean "womb" that continually births supplies for metropolitan centers, the myth produces the racialized and feminized space of Guyana's interior landscape to which the semantic deferral of the treasure confines Indigenous Peoples. It is a space that no one can reach, except through the language of desire on the symbolic road to wealth, but one that must continually be lived out. In living it out, the possibility of transformation emerged and the old fiction became the truth of a new nation in 1966. That truth is that the nation has gold and other mineral wealth in its mines that is symbolically reflected by the yellow on its flag (known as the Golden Arrowhead). Blacks and Indians who were formerly integral to the myth's enactment as colonial subjects, as laborers, suddenly inherited the myth as their own narrative of progress. Thus, following Waswo, we can argue that we are still caught in the fictionalizing power of European historical discourse, and we must look at how that power reconstitutes itself and its subjects in postcolonial Guyana. Following, I discuss two texts from the independence era in order to demonstrate how postcolonial discourse not only continues to engage the myth's poetics but how the transition Young and others affected is now managed.

In the "Guyana Independence Issue" of the journal *New World*, edited by George Lamming and Martin Carter, the myth of El Dorado is brought into poetic arrangement, almost as a silent witness to this transfer of power in which Afro-Guyanese and Indo-Guyanese are becoming postcolonial. The poem titled "Gold," written by the late Trinidadian social scientist Lloyd (L. E.) Braithwaite and dedicated to the author Wilson Harris, bears mention here for its engagement with the myth. The poem, indeed the entire "Guyana Independence Issue," is a clear moment when the historical and cultural legacy of Guyana is being reimagined for Guyanese in a reinvention of the British, colonial aesthetic.

Girls wear on their wrists the gold
That Raleigh dreamed of:
El Dorado glints in your eyes:
. . . The Gold remains hidden:
The vision of guilt driven deep into under-
Ground silts.
. . . butterfly's wing hidden
Under sudden rushes of sound, there comes the whisper
Of footsteps, eyes of the past watching
Our journey over the soft fallen bone
. . . babel

Of leaves cry their warnings the tribe dies
Whose faith of green crumples; love
Of the good soil humbled by its gold.[86]

L. E. Braithwaite's poem is one of loss and of what has been found. It is replete with images of the landscape's beauty as that which remains, unchanged, as witness to centuries of history. The significance of Braitwaithe's poem, for this study, lies in its location in this journal, as the opening piece in this re-thinking of the culture and history of the New World (writing itself), which heralds the creation of a cultural-national aesthetic and historical narrative at independence. Framed by its tribute to Harris, who himself has returned to the myth in his novels in order to find a psychic origin or interior consciousness in which all Guyanese can locate themselves, the poem offers an image of a land relation that has been shaped and marred by this search for wealth.

Ralegh's gold is alluded to in the opening lines of the poem and in the issue there are quoted passages by Walter Ralegh, extolling Guyana's beauty. However, by the poem's close, there is a very different image of the gold and its (destructive) power, of the cost of searching for and finding it, for the land and its inheritors.[87] The poem's tone is thus one of humility and caution. In its confrontation with history, however, the gold of the search is both lost to the past and visible in the poem's structure that re-embeds it in the landscape, which by the end cannot escape its representation in and through myth: "love/Of the good soil humbled by its gold." Further, the historical consciousness in the poem that at some moments seems to reject the imperial search that led to exploration is not one that reflects the holistic interior consciousness Harris tries to create because it is achieved through death of indigenous consciousness: "The tribe dies." The poem, and this issue as a whole, reflects the tension between articulating a national culture and the imbrications of this culture with British colonialism. Thus, while Braithwaite hopes to offer a critical view of imperial history, that very history is appropriated in order to lend credibility to the new nation. This is reflected in the quoted passages by Ralegh and by the inclusion in the "Guyana Independence Issue" of a passage by Richard Schomburgk, the man who gave Guyana its modern boundaries, which it continues to dispute with Venezuela and Suriname. His inclusion authenticates the consolidation of the national body around the physical shape of the state, by allowing imperial and colonial cartography to be reproduced and validated in the outline of the now independent state—the state that was first guaranteed by myth, then literature, and finally by the history being made at the moment of independence.

While the tribute to Harris can be considered disruptive, it lays bare the land and its contents as a new tablet that others, including Burnham, can write on. Additionally, it is at this point that aesthetics begin to dovetail with national designs of inheritance, right, and progress. At independence, the Afro-Creole and Indo-Creole postcolonial subjects of the nation were given the chance to do what the imperialist and colonists could not: civilize the interior. It is not just the physical development of the interior, but the endlessly deferred civilizing of it and the Indigenous Peoples, through cooperative development programs, that allow the myth to continuously be reenacted. The Indigenous Peoples' subjugation and subjection provide the narrative currency for the myth's continual function. Beyond their subjection, their erasure from the coast is central because it coincided with the appearance of several peoples—Europeans, Africans, Indians, and others.[88] Further, this civilizing (again, through Amerindian subjection and the development of the interior) is not simply occurring on a physical level, as Benítez-Rojo suggests at the end of his (literary) analysis, but at the level of narrative, at the level of the myth itself. However, it is incomplete. Waswo has argued in regard to the legend of descent from Troy that it "presents civilization as that which comes from somewhere else" with the "indigenous population" either being integrated or destroyed.[89] Yet, in the case of Indigenous Peoples, neither has happened, making them a recalcitrant historical subject or other, with elements of their cultural being ultimately unrecognizable with the new telling of the myth.

The second and final example of postcolonial engagements with the myth in the independence era is Hawley-Bryant's "Song of Guyana's Children." A colonial era piece, sung by Guyanese schoolchildren growing up in the 1960s, and recorded (without the final verse) by Rudolph Shaw on his CD *Guyana Seawall Talk*, Hawley-Bryant's song invokes an almost prelapsarian image of the variegated landscape of Guyana, which includes savannah, jungle, rivers, waterfalls, and the coastal area. In the song, there is, noticeably, no mention of the sugar plantations, rice paddies, gold and bauxite mines, cattle ranches, and rubber industry, labored in by Indigenous Peoples, enslaved Africans, indentured Indians, Chinese, Portuguese, and other immigrants. In their place stand only the products of both Providence and labor such as the river, the mountain, diamonds, and gold: "Born in the land of Kaieteur's shining splendor/Land of the palm tree, the croton and fern/We would possess all the virtues and graces/We all the glory of goodness would learn." Not only does there appear to be an elision of the sites of labor for slavery, indenture, and other forms of forced and "free" labor, but it is precisely because of this that the somewhat naked landscape can already be imbued with the immaterial bounties of civilization—goodness and virtue. In the second to last verse of the song, there is deliberate reference to the mythical El Dorado and the European search for gold that began in earnest in the South American region in the late sixteenth and early seventeenth centuries. An independent 1960s Guyana literally and figuratively emerges from that search as a gift of Christian providential destiny, as "God's golden city."

In this and other national songs, Guyana is often identified as an El Dorado, albeit one that must be imagined or invented by those who now inhabit it. In the colonial period, the myth essentially captured the then-European relationship to the land as an uncivilized space, redeemed by its productive potential. In the postcolonial period, the myth has become instrumental for narratives of wealth, progress, origin, and nation. The viability of the myth also depended upon the way in which it could be successfully seen as capturing and thereby recoding elements of native history and culture to establish the region as a blank space for European narratives of conquest.[90] At independence in Guyana, postcolonial nationalist discourse consolidated Creole identity as a "native" identity, through the land, sealing a new ontological narrative for blacks that was deployed as Guyanese nationalism. This narrative was contingent upon the displacement of Indigenous Peoples, whose historical presence in the new nation was reduced to a cultural one by the continued reliance on myth. This mythohistorical Afro-Creole assertion of belonging and right in the land has been the template for other ethnonationalist claims to power, even those that do not seem to formally engage the myth.

Hawley-Bryant's song uses El Dorado to recast colonial underdevelopment as the *potential* for wealth of the postcolonial state by presenting an image of the land as virginal, rich, and endlessly yielding. It further gestures to the labor of the postcolonial state as that which can always be enacted upon the prelapsarian Earth. More important, it is the invocation of place through the myth that manages this image, again one of productivity and deferred labor, and thereby inscribes Creole origins ("born in the land of") as rebirth and renewal. In many ways the utopian image of the land or place as gold itself marks a particular historical continuity with ancient Greek narratives. However, the repetition here collapses secular and Christian ideology, in a sense offering a poetics that draws on aspects of each and collapses the immaterial and material riches of the land as an edenic space that has passed through empire and is recaptured by postcolonial territory and history. The song ultimately reveals that Guyanese national subjecthood is *propter nos*, here for the sake of the Creole, not Braithwaite's dead "tribe" founded through Christian humanism (what is outside the poem is that which can't be redeemed by God's grace or by the nation) and secular humanism (ultimately the notion of humanity that surpassed it and allowed the nonwhite body to serve as a source of labor into the twenty-first century) in a reflection of Wynterian "sameness."

Today, the Guyanese interior is a place of mineral exploitation and tourist excursions. It holds a place of both cultural significance and material promise in the postindependence national imaginary. The socialist program enacted by the Burnham government in 1969, to which I turn in the next chapter, sought to achieve agrarian reform in the hinterland through the redistribution of land and the vocational training of its Amerindian inhabitants. Despite its shift from being represented in white settler colonialist narratives to postcolonial nationalist narratives, Guyana's interior continues to be endlessly yielding and stimulating in the national imaginary. The myth of El Dorado, which "produced" the landscape and its subjects, continues to hold Indigenous Peoples hostage by extending both their representation as nonlaboring beings and as being located fundamentally in the past, to the extent that the underdeveloped hinterland represents the past of the postcolonial state by its ability to be endlessly explored, following Benítez-Rojo's claim that "the search for El Dorado continues . . . carried out by present-day Guyanese society beneath the slogan of 'repossessing the interior'. . . ."[91] The myth has not produced a new beginning for itself or for its subjects, only infinite endings that dovetail with nationalist design, hypercapitalist interest, postmodern illusions, and postcolonial realities and discourses. The myth not only codes colonial exploitation as postcolonial development, but it continues to facilitate Amerindian ethnographic subordination as people who are both literally and figuratively "bound" to the hinterland, their humanity reduced to their role as cultural capital and their *potential* as human capital. The Guyanese interior, in its over identification with Indigenous Peoples, represents the potential for continuous discovery and transformations of the myth, but simultaneously it represents the absolute limit of modern humanity and the ability to make a break with hierarchical notions of what it means to be human in the modern world. As I've tried to demonstrate, even attempts to challenge this mode of being human, such as Césaire's, are conditioned by this limit where the "real" interior serves a symbolic function within Caribbean anticolonial and postcolonial discourse as a place to manage and maintain the difference that structures the Creole "I."

CONCLUSION

A fundamental crisis of Guyana, the Caribbean as a whole, and its diasporas is representation: political, economic, cultural, and historical. Postcoloniality has been achieved through a deeply flawed concept of nationalism that, moored to a *Western-rational* base, has been insufficiently altered to suit the needs of those who have "passed through" colonialism but have still not "exited."[92] Whether it is at home or abroad, the nation is continually beckoning, forcing its reality on a disenchanted citizenry that is not seeking to overthrow it but to control it. Although there is no way to return to the origins of this Creole nation for solutions to its current crisis, groups often seek to do so because those "origins" today are now wholly intertwined with the nation-state that they have produced and the particular positions of power the state guarantees. The implicit argument here is that histories are narratives of origin that seek to return to moments that guarantee or provide justification for contemporary social status and political power. Thus, returns continue to be made within the ambit of neocolonial, economic reason in historical, political, and cultural discourse as groups struggle to control the nation on a variety of fronts. This struggle needs to be read through the "myth" of El Dorado and the waves of imperialism and colonial development that recreated the myth and allowed it to be refashioned as historical narrative and essentially remain embedded in the discourse of national identity and belonging.

In chapter 2, I sought to show the way in which labor has been rescripted for Creole being and postcolonial subjectivity; in this chapter, I have sought to show how myth, like labor, is in fact a structuring element and, with regard to Indigenous Peoples, it retains what can be considered a founding relationship to labor upon which Creole indigeneity is now articulated. In Guyana, at independence and at other historical moments, there have been shifts in the discourse as the myth was made to articulate with "new" cultural and political ideologies. This shift marks its potential to be subverted. However, it would be wrong to say, in an effort to check the myth's influence on Caribbean reality, that there has been some fundamental rupture.

I therefore argued that for the Caribbean and South American regions, the myth of El Dorado retains more than just a significant place within cultural discourse. The myth remains relevant for several reasons: first, in the break between Christian humanism and secular humanism, it maintained a particular objective relationship between humanism and material being; second, it maintains this relationship, which eventually became a key feature of Caribbean modernity and master–slave subjectivity, at the transfer from colonial territory to independent states by stabilizing the Caribbean's relationship to labor and wealth within globalization and in relation to Western nations. In other words, the relationship that imperial centers like France and Britain maintain to the goods and finances of their former colonies through, for instance, the installment of salutary political actors and the continuation of their bureaucratic and financial systems, is precisely what the myth functions within social and cultural discourse to protect. Finally, as that which fundamentally marks wealth and underdevelopment, the myth encodes a structuring paradox that is essential to Caribbean modernity and through which it is in fact extended into the cultural discourse and criticism of the region. This continues to be essential in managing a particular reality of the Caribbean as a consumable geography. While the myth is often dismissively referred to as fiction, it is precisely its epistemological expulsion from history that allows it to function as in fact a governing "fiction" in the way in which it conditions the production of a particular and cultural "real" of the Caribbean. As part of the writing of this real in order for the nation to fulfill its narrative of progress, Indigenous Peoples are continuously displaced in the interior and disenfranchised. In this *real,* their displacement under colonialism is now reimagined as the *place* the postcolonial nation-state allows them to have.

In recent decades, there has been a surge in material written about Amerindian myths from children's narratives to serious literary criticism. In spite of these attempts to "reclaim" the myths from religio-colonial narratives, such as the Rev. W. H. Brett's *Legends and Myths of the Aboriginal Indians of British Guiana*, published in the late nineteenth century, retellings of the myth continue to manage the subordination of indigenous groups rather than record their resistance, such as the 1512 and 1519 slaughters of Spanish settlers on the mainland, noted by explorers in their quest for gold.[93]

The transformations or retellings of the myth suggest that black and Indo-Caribbean humanity is still bound to neoimperial discursive mechanisms. There is no question that the global subordination of peoples of color is at the core of First World capital accumulation. Specifically for the Caribbean, however, native subordination was necessary for the realization of the "desire" of Europeans as a broad social ethic and raison d'être and so became a structuring logic in the importance of black slaves; recourse to myth is what allows us to read these things together rather than continually subordinate indigenous colonization to the primacy of slavery for Caribbean modernity. It is also true that in the postcolonial period, the continued subordination of Indigenous Peoples is what makes possible Creole subaltern–settler social and political being as a change with regard to labor and access to capital. In Guyana, Burnham manipulated the inherited model of the Western state and its inherent cultural and racial bias to produce a legacy for black rule in Guyana, while simultaneously securing the conditions of subaltern–settler indigeneity. Thus, the Caribbean has yet to achieve a generalized "second poetics of the *propter nos*" precisely because in its endless articulation, the myth of El Dorado—upon which Burnham's postcolonial nationalism consciously and unconsciously relied—maintains the structuring and paradoxical conditions upon which Caribbean modernity was inaugurated and within which blacks, Indo-Caribbean peoples, and others seek and achieve their humanity.

4

From Myth to Market: Burnham's *Co-operative Republic*

CHAPTER 3 SOUGHT TO DEMONSTRATE THE ROLE MYTH PLAYS IN Caribbean modernity. It argued that the rearticulation in neo- and postcolonial discourses of the myth of El Dorado, in particular, allows its imagistic and ideological structures to continually inform modern, Caribbean socioculture. The chapter ended by demonstrating how the myth is kept current in postcolonial Guyana. This chapter returns to the myth's role in postcolonial Guyana to look at how, in the decade after independence, the myth emerged as a generalized poetics of colonialism that informed Linden Forbes Sampson Burnham's and the Peoples National Congress (PNC) ethnonationalism. More specifically, I argue that while not all Burnham's and PNC engagements with the myth were formalized or direct, its mythopoetics of conquest and extractable wealth became instrumental in the postcolonial transformation and rebirth of the Creole as a sovereign subject of the modern nation-state whose identity is consolidated within the state as a new indigenous identity that is historically determined. The phrase "from myth to market" is therefore meant to signal the way in which the initial relationship to the region that the myth produced and sustains is extended into the new cultural nationalism and poetics of postcolonial economy. *Market* in this sense refers to the economy under Burnham, whose nationalization plans did not change the country's dependence on foreign capital and global market forces.

This discussion is centered on a key piece of propaganda produced by the Forbes Burnham administration and through which the administration offered a revised narrative of postcolonial Guyanese historiography, *Co-operative Republic, Guyana 1970: A Study of Aspects of Our Way of Life.*

Commissioned by the administration, *Co-operative Republic* is a collection of essays about Guyanese culture and economics that attempts to justify the ideology of cooperativism that Burnham sought to embrace in the early 1970s and the new direction in which he hoped it would take the country. *Co-operative Republic* contains a collection of carefully selected works by those recognized or identified as the nation's cultural and intellectual elites. The publication is sponsored by the Guyanese government and government-owned businesses that endorse the cooperative endeavor in full-page ads at the end of the book. In many ways, *Co-operative Republic* is designed to identify for Guyanese the sources of culture within the country and to connect them to this latest socialist experiment for the economic growth of the former colony.[1]

That experiment centers on the physical interior of the country and concomitantly required the rescripting or reenvisioning of the hinterland not as an indigenous space where the land rights of Indigenous Peoples attach but as a national/Creole space. Indeed, the Burnham regime even found a way to suggest that when Indigenous Peoples sought land titles, they were effectively expressing a *Creole* desire. In 1970, the Ministry of Information and Culture, for instance, simultaneously argued that the so-called traditional ways of Amerindians are still being practiced and that most Indigenous Peoples are in no way different than coast-dwelling Creoles. In a complex way, Amerindian cultural retention, then, is no different from black or Indian cultural retentions and the ability of those to make the latter Creoles. The ministry underscores this ethics of integration and assimilation by saying that Indigenous Peoples "want air-strips, Co-operative societies, transistor radios, sophisticated clothing, easier access to the Capital, titles to the land [sic] they live on, and greater recognition as the original inhabitants of Guyana."[2] Yet it affirms that the rate at which Amerindians integrate reflects their continuing difference with regard to Guyanese citizenship, their "freedom."[3] What we see here is the ambiguity of a policy that frames Amerindian desire for land titles as a Creole desire. It further maintains, without acknowledging colonial efforts to extract wealth from the interior, that the Amerindian, unlike the United States, Canada, and Brazil, "still has his *lebensraum,*" protected by post-planter government policies and lack of interest in settling the interior. Ignoring the mining in the interior by the British, which clearly showed an interest in the interior that is similar to Burnham's, the document goes on to cite a 1969 speech by Burnham in which he essentially represents postindependence, cooperative policies as correctives to the colonial attitudes and policies that kept Amerindians in a state of nature. In this speech and else-where in the document, Amerindian desire for land rights is a desire to have the same citizenship rights and benefits of Creoles and therefore do not run counter to the government policies of integration or interior development on their lands. What I demonstrate is that this reenvisioning of the interior and the profound tension between Amerindians as potential Creoles or citizens versus Amerindians as implacably other is the simultaneous deployment of the discursive mechanisms of the indigenous belonging of Creoles in labor. Thus, despite invocation of Indigenous Peoples, appropriation of the native by the state is anti-indigenous precisely because it occurs within the new basis for articulation, a teleology of modern labor.

The criticism of *Co-operative Republic* builds on prevailing arguments about Burnham's Afro-Creole nationalism. Specifically, I engage the work of political sociologist Percy Hintzen, who has published a good deal about both Burnham's regime and Afro-Creole nationalism in the Caribbean. Hintzen outlines the way in which, after the split between Jagan and Burnham, racial-ist politics were deployed by Burnham and the predominantly black PNC to legitimize its claims to power.[4] Hinzten argues that the middle class in the Commonwealth Caribbean allied itself with Afro-Creole nationalism, using race as "symbolic capital" to secure state economic resources and power and to legitimize continued dependence on international capital.[5] The conse-quence, according to Hintzen, is that "those whose identities were not embed-ded in images of an African diasporic community were *excluded* from the community of the nation."[6] Hintzen points to the way in which Afro-Creole ethnonationalism coupled with development discourse essentially produced the nation-state as a black inheritance in which only blacks could locate a cultural self that was linked to political and material right. His argument is one way of making sense of the exclusion of Indo-Caribbean and Indige-nous Peoples. Although I agree with Hintzen, instead of arguing that the gov-ernment was strictly legitimized by Afro-Creole nationalism, I focus on the mythohistorical dimension of the nationalist discourse that accompanied the Burnham regime's program of development. I thus identify consequences that are not apparent in dominant sociological analyses of how race (and racial and ethnic antagonism) operates.

What I suggest is that Burnham's Afro-Creole nationalism was rationalized in cultural terms that redeployed the poetics of myth to reproduce Indige-nous Peoples and the hinterland as a colonizable other within postcolonial-ity. I therefore hope to move beyond claims that Indigenous Peoples were "excluded" (Hintzen) from the center of national and political life to demonstrate that it is in fact in relationship to Indigenous Peoples and cultures that Afro-Creole nationalism works and Creole subjectivity becomes consolidated. Ultimately, I seek to demonstrate that sociological class-based and race-based analyses of ethnic antagonism and ethnic nationalism do not address the larger epistemological issues that shape the material and cultural relationships within societies. The nationalism of the first postindependence regime in Guyana worked not solely because of Afro-Creole nationalist identification and an inherited structure of racial inequality, as Hintzen has suggested, but because it was articulated through the colonial poetics of myth. Like race, myth is an inherited structure of colonial power that, at independence, facilitated the emergence of an ethnonationalism that allowed development to be maintained as an uneven element of democracy. Thus, Burnham's redistribution of land and the linking of the Guyana Defense Force to hinterland development reflect not just a desire to redistribute wealth to blacks, but an understanding that legitimacy for that redistribution simultaneously rests upon socioeconomic reorganization and the continued articulation of Afro-Creole nationalism *with* particular elements of colonial discourse. What the regime therefore retained, in its justification of the cooperative and securing of a black patrimony, were the mytho-discursive structures of the myth of El Dorado, which continue to offer a colonialist way of representing the land and its original inhabitants. The extension of their discursive and economic containment within the myth allowed blacks to secure the narrative of inheritance that was most visibly challenged when Hoyte, the PNC leader, lost the 1992 election to Jagan.

This approach to postcolonial discourse in Guyana is shaped by two theoretical elaborations on the concept of nation and nationalism. It is first informed by Homi Bhabha's view of the nation in terms of its textuality.[7] In the introduction to *Nation and Narration*, Bhabha writes that the emergence of the nation as a "form of narrative—textual strategies, metaphoric displacements, sub-texts, and figurative stratagems—has its own history."[8] He continues, "To encounter the nation *as it is written* displays a temporality of culture and social consciousness more in tune with the partial, overdetermined process by which textual meaning is produced through the articulation of difference in language. . . ."[9] Bhabha's work allows me to discuss the nation in terms of strategies of representation that ideologically link Guyanese society through various forms of articulation.[10] The second elaboration is Partha Chaterjee's study of Third World nationalisms, *Nationalist Thought and the Colonial World: A Derivative Discourse?,* in which he finds that post-colonial states borrow from earlier forms of European and American nationalisms. Thus, in spite of the fact that anticolonial resistance is significant in the emergence of protonationalist sentiment, the nationalist form the nation assumes remains "derivative." The textuality of the nation is what we encounter with Burnham's *Co-operative Republic,* whose authors are very much aware of the indebtedness to European political forms, of the inability of starting with a clean slate, so to speak. My focus on this textuality will I hope show not its divorce from material reality but how the former shapes the latter and the lives of the nation's citizens.

The chapter begins by sketching the political and historical context for Burnham's cooperative endeavor in the early 1970s and the production of *Co-operative Republic,* drawing heavily on the work of Hintzen. The next section analyzes *Co-operative Republic* as a literary and cultural product rather than just as evidence of development discourse. This work of cultural nationalism deploys the structuring paradox of El Dorado as the essays extend the "spacial vocabulary of colonialism," to borrow a phrase from Linda Tuhiwai Smith, which continually maps a "centre" and an "outside."[11] The center in this case is Georgetown and its economy, the new republican economy of the Burnham administration, and Creole culture; while the outside remains, complexly so, Dutch and British history, native history and culture, the native body, and the hinterland that the myth of El Dorado first managed. The chapter ends with a discussion of Burnham's legacy for political subjectivity in Guyana by focusing on its consequences for Indigenous Peoples today through an interview I conducted with Jean La Rose, the head of the Amerindian Peoples Association, in 2006. Throughout this chapter, I use the term *Amerindian* to refer to Indigenous Peoples, largely in keeping with the Guyanese documents discussed.

POLITICAL AND HISTORICAL CONTEXT

In 1950, Cheddi Jagan (a self-proclaimed Marxist) started the Peoples Progressive Party (PPP) with Forbes Burnham (a socialist). In 1953, the PPP came to power, but 133 days later Britain suspended the constitution under which it was elected and reinstated an interim colonial government. Britain and the West, including the United States, felt threatened by the Marxist-leaning government, which did not have the support of international actors with vested interests in the Guyanese economy. In the 1950s, the United States and others repeatedly intervened to stem the threat of a Marxist government led by Cheddi Jagan that would be sympathetic to the communist Soviet Union and Cuba. Britain and the United States considered Burnham's Fabian socialism preferable to Jagan's more openly Marxist and communist platform, which had the potential to create another anti-Western state in the hemisphere and further extend Soviet influence in the region.[12] The intervention by the British government, which could be read as imperialist discipline, compounded the problem of sovereignty and self-rule in a country that could not, by itself, even determine its own date of independence. Not only was the ethnic rivalry in the colony then subsumed within a Western state form and political structure that could not adequately resolve it, but this intervention or bullying set the terms and limits of postcolonial democracy as something that could only be guaranteed by undemocratic means. According to Hintzen, the constitution's suspension was the "result of successful efforts by the local middle and upper classes, in an alliance with the colonial elite, to wrest control of the state away from those representing the interests of the lower classes."[13] In 1955, following constitutional suspension, the branding of the Jagans and several others as communists, and their subsequent imprisonment, the leadership struggle between Jagan and Burnham intensified.[14] Burnham left the PPP in 1955, and in 1957, he named his faction of the party the Peoples National Congress, which was more sympathetic to the interests of middle-class economic actors, thereby distancing himself from the more radical Marxist "rhetoric" of the PPP. This, according to Hintzen, made the possibility of an independent Guyana led by the socialist Burnham more palatable to the British government and its allies. It was at the point of the party split, and the formation of a new black-led party, that scholars of the political system in Guyana argue that race became the defining factor in Guyanese politics. Further, in subsequent elections, slogans such as the Indian popular cry, "Apan Jhat" ("Remember our kind/vote for your own"), became political custom.

In the 1961 election, the United States, with the involvement of the Central Intelligence Agency and Great Britain, intervened once again to support a new voting system of "proportion representation" for which Burnham had fought. This essentially functioned to push out Jagan and the support he received from the Indian population. In an effort to force Jagan to accept the system, the PPP faced a mass oppositional campaign from both trade unions and political parties that led to a series of riots and nearly three hundred deaths in early 1962.[15] Jagan was forced to accept the new constitution and the change from the first-past-the-post voting system to that of proportional representation. In the 1964 elections, the PPP was ousted by the PNC, which, lacking a sufficient number of votes on its own, joined with the United Force (UF), a party that the PNC also maneuvered out of power by the end of the decade.[16] The Burnham regime therefore came to power not by a free and truly democratic process but by a series of actions by local and foreign actors designed to install a leader favorable to the long-term strategic, political, and economic interests of First World nations in the region. Thus began, Hintzen argues, a system of political domination by the black-led PNC regime. Through means such as pervasive electoral fraud, the regime lasted until the early 1990s, when the PPP, with Jagan at its head, returned to power. Long overdue, the 1992 election of Jagan could not curb the racial antagonism between blacks and Indo-Guyanese.

Burnham's regime stayed in power largely because of its ability to manipulate labor. In *The Costs of Regime Survival: Racial Mobilization, Elite Domination and Control of the State in Guyana and Trinidad,* Hintzen identifies the means through which the Eric Williams regime in Trinidad and Tobago and Forbes Burnham in Guyana came to power and sustained themselves, largely through appeals to labor. Both countries have a strong history of labor struggle and trade unionism, beginning in the twentieth century. After initial labor resistance by enslaved, indentured, and freed peoples, the local trade unions in Guyana began anticolonial mobilization.[17] The two most significant organizations to emerge in the early twentieth century were the Man Power Citizen's Association (a union of Indian sugar estate field workers), begun by Ayube Edun in the late 1930s, and the British Guiana Labor Union (black urban proletariat), founded in 1919 by Hubert Critchlow.[18] Emerging out of the labor agitation of the period, these two unions represent the first consolidated political challenge by the Indian and black middle class to British colonial governance. According to Chaitram Singh, trade unions in Guyana have long been instrumental to politics. Not only do they precede "mass-based" political organizations, but they were and are key in galvanizing the popular vote and garnering support for the major parties, such as the PPP and PNC. Further, both of Guyana's major political leaders were involved with and headed labor unions, even while both held political office.[19]

Hintzen argues that after labor's initial mobilization against colonial domination, the struggle in both countries shifted in the 1950s, with concessions from Britain that made independence inevitable. He also argues that the initial struggle against colonial domination became a "competition for state control," which necessitated "a new mobilizing 'idiom.'" At this point, Hintzen holds, "Race became the preeminent ingredient in the organization of popular political participation."[20] Despite the difference in the ideological positions of the Burnham and Williams regimes, the former employing a form of Fabian socialism and the latter a capitalist economic policy, the result was the same, according to Hintzen. With both regimes, broader, more socially just development plans failed in the face of methods used to satisfy the "accumulative claims" of the black middle class of both countries.[21] The nationalization programs of Burnham's cooperative socialism led to the weakening of the private sector, which created such problems as food and gas shortages and led to mass migration to the United States, Canada, and the United Kingdom in the late 1970s and the 1980s—one of the "costs" that Hintzen explores.[22]

In Guyana, from 1971 to 1976, Burnham's socialist economic policy sought to bring most areas of the state's economy, including the private sector, under state control through the nationalization of the major industries such as sugar and bauxite.[23] Hintzen writes that the Burnham regime, in order to maintain its economic base and guarantee popular support, "employed ideology . . . to justify and legitimize its program of state ownership and control of the economy in developmental terms."[24] The regime sought to legitimate its programs and mobilize and gain the support of different sectors of the population, from the middle classes to the lower classes. For the middle classes, nationalization under a socialist economic policy, what Hintzen terms the Third World "variant" of "market socialism," meant "public sector expansion," and for the lower classes, particularly lower-class blacks, the regime offered the "cooperative" as an "entrée" into the agricultural sector from which they had previously been excluded.[25] As discussed by Hintzen and others, when blacks exited the plantation system and eventually became situated in civil service jobs, Indians were given land in exchange for forgoing their return passage to India at the end of the indenture period. This initial, officially sponsored land ownership, suggests Hintzen, paved the way for the "upward mobility of many East Indians."[26] Hintzen thus argues that the "implicit intention of the policy was to deliver a larger share of state resources to the country's black population. . . ."[27] In addition to nationalization, the institutions of government were reorganized in the 1970s and led to the eventual adoption of a new constitution, making Burnham the executive president of the country, with the new power to "dissolve and suspend parliament."[28] To secure the regime's power, Burnham's government found new ways to bring even broader areas of society under its control. There was, for example, the creation of the Guyana National Service, which brought not only young blacks and Indo-Guyanese together to defend the country but was also responsible for hinterland development.[29]

The current political problems in Guyana obscure the fact that prior to the 1953 suspension of the constitution and the 1955 PPP split, Burnham and Jagan envisioned a similar political and economic future for the country. However, by the time Burnham went to England in November 1965 to discuss the terms of independence with the British government, the PPP was firmly to the left of his platform, and, to register their protest over the process and at having been manipulated out of political power, Jagan and the PPP did not attend.[30] It thus became Burnham's task to "create" the nation out of these disparate elements, and his socialist program became an ideology of economic egalitarianism designed to foster nationalist sentiment through an economic program. Burnham and the PNC-led government created a nationalism based on economic rationality, which operated through multicultural rhetoric that secured the right to rule of a *particular* racial group. Rather than promote real democracy or class reform, Burnham's policies and their "costs" confirm lawyer Amy Chua's point that most nationalization programs in Third World countries "never sought to eliminate private property or eradicate all economic classes."[31] Instead, like Guyana, they were aimed at curtailing the power of "market-dominant" minorities, in this case the increasing market-dominant and eventual majority Indian population. Burnham turned postcolonial nationalism in Guyana away from its anticolonial and anticapitalist roots. Although in *Stains on My Name, War in My Veins: Guyana and the Politics of Cultural Struggle,* Brackette F. Williams writes that in the 1980s Guyanese were nation building, Burnham had already provided a fundamentally uneven foundation that continues to inform politics today.

DEVELOPMENT AND DISPLACEMENT IN THE COOPERATIVE REPUBLIC

After Guyana was granted its independence from Britain in 1966, the ruling PNC put in place three major development plans: the first would last from 1966 to 1972, the second from 1972 to 1976, and the third from 1978 to 1982. According to Chaitram Singh, the first development plan, which focused on the country's infrastructure, failed. In 1970, Burnham made the country a republic, and the government declared that "cooperative socialism would be its ideology and development strategy."[32] Under this new governing ideology, or modified socialist experiment, the goal of the second plan was to make Guyana independent of foreign economic domination by 1976.[33] However, both plans, Singh writes, caused the erosion of the private sector and the loss of private sector funds, which had a hugely negative impact on the economy. Although the plans were a deliberate attempt by Burnham to limit dependence on Western influence—the same that had brought him to power—they ultimately fostered greater dependence on foreign aid in later years.

Co-operative Republic, Guyana 1970: A Study of Aspects of Our Way of Life was published in 1970 just prior to the launch of the second development plan. With it, Burnham ties the new socialist economic plan to the cultural expression of the country as an independent nation. The intertwined cultural and economic argument in *Co-operative Republic* is firmly focused on the interior of the country as a potential source of national wealth. The flap of the book jacket tells readers that the mission of each author in the text is "to evaluate our heritage and to indicate paths to the future," a future that includes the need to focus on the "*urgent* task of hinterland development."[34] The core mission of the cooperative is therefore identified as the continuation of the work begun during the time of Dutch settlement by identifying new (interior) spaces for development.[35] Cultural nationalism thus comes to be paired with an idea of progress and defense that stems from the early colonial period and can be enacted and achieved in the interior. The book jacket continues, "It is the ruins of Fort Zeelandia which stand on Fort Island today, a reminder of the challenge which faces this new Republic as we reach back beyond the origins of Fort Zeelandia to begin the urgent task of hinterland development."[36] Ironically, it is at Fort Zeelandia that in 1778 the Dutch held a ceremony to formally recognize indigenous chiefs and the "alliances" of groups with them. Further, these alliances are credited with preventing the establishment of Maroon communities in Guyana in the way they arose in Suriname.[37] *Co-operative Republic* sought to fundamentally shift the way in which Guyanese perceived the interior by transforming their relationship to it from waste to possible wealth. As one writer in the volume puts it, "If we are to extend our vision beyond the coast and if we are to utilize the country's potential to its fullest, we must study the resources available in the interior. . . . A knowledge of the land and its resources is therefore a pre-requisite to any programme of development."[38] In order to achieve this, the government had to at least figuratively remove its inhabitants, Amerindians, which it did by simultaneously and symbolically bringing them into the heart of Guyanese culture, as essays by A. J. Seymour and others show. The argument that achieves both the establishment of a new relationship to the interior for Creoles and the displacement of Indigenous Peoples takes place in four main areas, around which the following discussion is organized: labor, culture, history, and the nation's borders.

Labor

In *Co-operative Republic* the discussions that involve labor are designed to first argue for the replacement of foreign capital with local wealth (hence the importance of the interior) and to link middle-class ideology to the labor of lower-class or working Creoles. Bringing together several of Burnham's speeches, the opening essay by Burnham, "A Vision of the Co-operative Republic," reveals the historiographic import of the collection of essays as he strategically begins to tie the new cooperative to the country's past and the nation's future. In doing this, he establishes for the cooperative its first hero, a national hero (Cuffy), around whom expression of this new economic direction and national identity can congeal. He thereby intertwines Guyanese cultural, political, and economic identity and continually inscribes it as a teleology. According to Burnham, Guyanese "are the children of a paternalistic colonial society which taught us to depend on others rather than on ourselves, to regard things foreign as better than our own. . . ." They must, therefore, be "trained again."[39] Burnham's speeches argue for the cooperative republic as the instrument that will transform Creoles into true postcolonials by tying economic progress to cultural decolonization. Burnham states, "Our main theme then, our common goal, is to give the *small man* in Guyana an opportunity to own, control and use for his own and the country's benefit and development all those forms of enterprise from which the Republic of Guyana can grow and prosper."[40] Burnham further distinguishes this attempt at cooperative government and the remaking of the country's economic system from First World economic endeavors, stressing the need for Guyanese to look within, and not seek foreign aid. Otherwise, he claims, "In spite of the interior which we claim to be *penetrating* . . . we are doomed to perpetual poverty and mendicancy."[41]

The interior, therefore, emerges as that which will define the new economy and its independence from foreign capital. The essay reveals one ideological argument of the regime, aimed at the black lower class, that promises to redefine not just its relationship to labor but its access to capital (wealth): a careful and calculated ideological argument that aims to have lower-class blacks accept roles as *producers* of the postcolonial nation's wealth by working in the interior, while seeing this as being in their own best interest. Eusi Kwayana's essay reflects the deployment of middle-class needs and ideology as that which the lower classes must see as beneficial for themselves, hence their strategic rescripting not as workers but as "agents."

In "Economic Relations in Pre-Republican Guyana," Kwayana, then chair of the Guyana Marketing Corporation and coordinating elder of the African Society for Cultural Relations with Independent Africa (ASCRIA), outlines the economic benefit of cooperativism against colonial economic domination, never mentioning the regime's first failed development plan. Largely directed at labor, Kwayana's essay is essential in reassuring the Guyanese of the future of the entire economy and especially the three main industries: rice, sugar, and bauxite. Kwayana addresses the competition for scarce resources in Guyana and the economic legacy of Dutch and British colonial rule. His essay advocates the cooperative system proposed by the Burnham government as a mode of "democratic" land reform that counters the colonial "nature" of ownership, in which labor was akin to slavery.[42] Kwayana points to historian Walter Rodney's view of Indian rice farming as a way of escaping slavery and as a means to "social freedom" that can be a model for the cooperative. Adamant about the need to restructure the entire economic system of the country, he is wary of the fact that the government could still maintain colonial forms of ownership and labor in the sugar and bauxite industries if it did not democratize them.

Kwayana invokes a common condition of subordination and disenfranchisement for blacks and Amerindians under colonial social and economic policy when he discusses the manner in which the Amerindian way of life was altered with the policies of the Dutch governor, Laurens Storm van 's Gravesande, and the way in which blacks were discriminated against in the banking system. He offers Booker Brothers McConnell and Company, Ltd., which still met in England to decide policy in Guyana, as an example of the presumably shared "colonial hangover" of former colonies.[43] According to Kwayana, Burnham's declaration of the cooperative "inspires the disinherited classes to be the active agents of change and development. . . ."[44] Committed to the idea of Guyanese owning their own wealth, Kwayana writes, "Guyana aims at proving to the world that he whom history has called a proletarian, a peasant, an employee with the support and positive alliance of the State . . . can organise and manage economic activity that fits into an overall economic objective. . . ."[45] In other words, they can effect a move from being capital to possessing and controlling it. Kwayana's focus is echoed in *Cooperative Republic* by the Guyanese economist Winston King, who writes that through the formation of cooperatives as part of a socialist government, there can be a transfer in the "fount of economic power . . . from expatriate power blocs . . . to the people of Guyana. . . ."[46] King and Kwayana both address the Burnham government's fear that foreign capital and consumer goods could dominate the country's markets and reveal the understanding that the lower classes need to see their own economic fate in terms of the national economy. Addressing Cold War fears, Kwayana argues that, although those against democracy and black freedom in the United States would see this as "'bolshevism' or as a subtle form of communism," and still others would see it as colonialist, this must be the new direction for the Guyanese economic system.[47] Kwayana's vision for the cooperative would eventually become radically different from what was implemented, leading him to become sharply critical of PNC rule. However, at this moment, similarly to the well-known poet Martin Carter, who also eventually opposed Burnham, he shared a belief in the form of socialist democracy Burnham envisioned. Both men locate the republic's wealth in the labor performed by the worker on potentially colonizable land and for the benefit of the middle classes.

CULTURE

The cultural argument in *Co-operative Republic* emerges around one major aim, and that is to rescript the culture of Indigenous Peoples as a precolonial origin for national culture: in other words, use indigenous culture to decolonize. Although Kwayana is focused on the worker, the essays that deal with culture and aesthetics are decidedly aimed at the middle class and are especially significant for transforming or preparing the interior of the country for development, beyond simply getting Guyanese to see their success as connected to the development of that space. They provide a culturally legitimating argument for the development (read civilizing) of the interior that literally empties it of its inhabitants, thereby representing it as *terra nullius*. While Charles Mills and Brackette Williams, discussed in the introduction to this book, are correct when they argue about the overidentification of Amerindians with the underdevelopment of the interior space, it is precisely that identification that proves problematic for a postcolonial government that hopes to make the land productive, without appearing to use colonial techniques with regard to labor or land acquisition. Therefore, the essays, such as those of poet and cultural and social critic A. J. Seymour and architect Rory Westmaas later discussed, at least symbolically extract Indigenous Peoples from the interior by bringing them into the center of national culture. The construction of the Umana Yana for the Non-Aligned Nations' conference was a significant step toward this, but the essays reveal, apart from the international orientation of that symbol, the local and discursive mechanisms that were deployed within the country. Three points from A. J. Seymour's essay, titled "Cultural Values in the Republic of Guyana," bear mentioning: the incorporation of Amerindian cultures; his suggestions about the origin and direction of postcolonial Guyanese culture; and his views about racial and cultural mixing.

Seymour discusses the cultural influences of all groups entering the region, identifying what he sees as the most significant contribution of each, from food to religious practice. In doing so, he hopes to "draw attention to the distinctive elements in our Guyanese history . . . which by a deliberate act of faith we can take and seek to build into a new national approach and way of live [sic], worthy of our Republican era."[48] "To my mind," Seymour holds, "the Guyanese house of culture rests upon a number of pillars which stand up out of the participating ethnic traditions."[49] For Seymour, the most important pillar in the production of a distinctively Guyanese national culture is Amerindian, which he labels the "distinguished element" in Guyana's "national life" and one that sets it apart from other Caribbean territories.[50] Seymour outlines the government's place in determining and reevaluating the new role of Amerindian culture, writing that in seeking "national identification," the PNC government "has been turning the pages of our Amerindian history, looking for examples of tribal organization in a cooperative basis, and . . . one feels certain that here is a quarry of great value waiting to be mined as we go forward in the future."[51]

Seymour's article seeks to foster the development of national pride by tapping into the cultural reservoir of Amerindian heritage as the single, original element of Guyanese culture, and which therefore plays a significant role in this search for a postcolonial aesthetic. However, the 1969 Rupununi rebellion, which was the impetus for Seymour's focus on Amerindian culture and the more immediate reason for the PNC outreach to Indigenous Peoples, is not mentioned. According to Robert H. Manley, the PNC administration's "strongest pleas for national unity" followed the revolt, which forced Burnham to question "the loyalties of the nation's citizenry, especially those in remote hinterland areas."[52] As I discussed in the introduction to this book, the rebellion put in question Amerindian loyalty as Guyanese citizens, and even the extent to which they considered themselves to be citizens, because they were purportedly aided by Venezuela and frequently crossed the border into Venezuela for work.[53] Amerindians, to the extent that they are not associated with the "coast," represent the limits of postcolonial power and the fragility of national borders; therefore, the cooperative must at least symbolically integrate them. In his essay, Seymour includes a picture of Amerindian rock carvings that predate "discovery" and identifies Rev. W. H. Brett's collection of Amerindian legends as one "source" for "our Guyanese culture."[54] Seymour writes that the government has "adopted" *Timehri* as the name for the main airport, a point to which I return in chapter 5. The adoption, he suggests, has opened the door for the design of textiles, fabrics, and jewelry imprinted with that symbol. He adds, "The way lies clear for some industrial printer to create fabrics where the timehri markings might be used on the cotton, as in the case of the afro prints, so that we in Guyana would have a distinguished textile material, which would certainly attract the attention of tourists."[55] Seymour's emphasis on Amerindian culture, especially the ability to both find a new national origin in Timehri and market that origin to make it productive for the new economy, begins the most significant turn in his argument.

Amerindian culture, "discovered" by imperialists and documented by colonials, is significantly reclaimed toward nation building in Seymour's piece. As part of a national culture, it can be articulated with neocolonial tourist economies—to recall John Crocker's *The Centaur Guide to the Caribbean and EL Dorado*—and other markets against which the cooperative comes into being and with which it must compete. More important, the cultural excess of early narratives can be used to underwrite both the culture and economic currency of the new republic. Amerindian culture therefore becomes the bridge between colonial exploitation of labor and resources, between the loss of El Dorado and the new economy and postcolonial culture that will arise from the transformation and extension of that narrative by identifying a new cultural and material treasure. Bringing Amerindian culture further into the national consciousness as a key element of the new cooperative socialism scripts a new ending for the narrative of loss, as the myth, and the people and land that it designates, can now be brought forward in a modern economy and market-based cultural aesthetic. It further makes Amerindians crucial, not marginal, for the success of cooperative socialism.

Amerindian culture is the central aspect of the larger cultural revolution taking place in the republic that Seymour sees Burnham leading. While he argues that the "small man" must be allowed to participate more fully in his own governance, Seymour affirms the second-class status of that small man in the new economy when he argues for the "need for . . . moral intellectual and artistic leadership" in order to develop a "special national culture in Republican Guyana." Seymour holds that since it is always the elites who lead social change, the government must develop this elite to "educate, symbolise and guide the Guyanese people along the road of greater personal freedom, combined with a gradually rising standard of living imbued with distinctively Guyanese values."[56] Seymour's charge reveals where culture in fact can and should come from for the new nation. Despite the harkening back to Amerindian cultural forms, "culture" as "value" for the nation, Seymour and the other writers of *Co-operative* seem to indicate, must come from the elite. Within the division of (cultural) labor, Amerindians serve as raw material. Culture cannot be either entrusted to or emerge organically from the "small man," from either Amerindian peoples or the working classes, even at his moment of transition to full manhood. Amerindian culture, while it serves as a source for national culture, must be understood as a raw cultural element to be transformed by elites, like Seymour, to fulfill this role. As exemplified by the Umana Yana, Amerindians especially cannot be responsible for which elements of their cultures they contribute to the national identity. Thus, Seymour not only identifies the new cultural source for the cooperative republic but establishes the cultural elite, whose role is as significant as the intelligentsia's to the rise of nationalism in the nineteenth century, as its new "culture bringers," appointed by the state.[57] Further, while the new nation will require labor and the continued maintenance of a peasant class, it is Amerindian culture that is equally significant in maintaining the bourgeois subject.

The final argument of Seymour's that has significance for this chapter is his discussion of cultural mixing. In a section that takes its name from the national motto, Seymour argues that a racially mixed and cross-cultural population is being created in the country as "we move into a vocabulary of shades and distinctions, the precise meanings of which have now been lost as we become One People, One Nation with One Destiny."[58] In other words, cultural and racial mixing is necessary to create the singular people and destiny of the national motto. The motto reflects the multicultural rhetoric of many nations seeking to incorporate and sublimate potentially disruptive differences of race and ethnicity, though not class. Seymour seems to suggest that the different ethnic groups in Guyana should recognize their cultural contributions as those things that allow them to gain entry into a new national culture and at the same time secure their place in it as distinct ethnicities, though emphasis on individuality is secondary to the national will. Amerindian ethnicity (as that which makes them Creole) can thus be represented as productive for Creole nationalism.

Difference, in Seymour's essay and in the larger nationalist platform of the PNC, is reduced to cultural contributions and assigned a value that is symbolical and can be captured within nationalist discourse and by the national economy. The value of these contributions lies in their ability to be articulated with the discourse of a new, national destiny that extends from the economy (and the nationalization of the private sector) to the social and cultural life of the nation. Further, this emphasis on cultural difference to create a national, multicultural identity is directly tied to concerns by the PNC government, about neocolonial economic and cultural domination by Britain and the United States. Paranoia, therefore, about Christmas being a cultural element that brings in foreign goods that should have no place in the new republic, is as much about national culture as it is about the national economy.[59] As for the inescapable acculturation that has taken place, Seymour writes, "The Queen's English becomes the President's English, the national honours will now be awarded by the President, and . . . the small man will become *a real man,* since he will participate in the important decisions of policy affecting his national welfare."[60]

Seymour's writing suggests that crucial to peasant or "the small man's" socialist-inspired restoration of his manhood is the cultural transformation that accompanies this economic vision for the republic. He reveals that the nation's manhood (its cultural and political sovereignty) is dependent upon its cultural integrity, something that is threatened by foreign cultural and economic interests. Not only does his essay reinforce the idea of colonial domination as a psychological, social, and economic castration, but it further suggests that the transformation to a republic, in order to be successful, must manage the superabundance of cultural differences in the country that threatens the national character and *realization* of its manhood.[61] By embracing the cooperative, both in its cultural and economic elements, the "small man," specifically blacks, will in some ways "inherit the earth" through the redistribution of land. Black masculinity, cowed in slavery, will be restored through the mechanisms of the cooperative. Like the patriarchal discourse of many twentieth-century nationalist movements in the Third World, the restoration represents black manhood as that which is always already whole and was only lost under colonialism because of the inability to control the relationship to labor and capital that the cooperative now achieves. The very patriarchal tone of nationalist ideology therefore reflects an additional continuity in the right to rule that can only be attained with male dominance.

Along with Seymour's piece, Rory Westmaas's essay is also indicative of the cultural argument and redefinition of Amerindian presence within the nation. In "Building under Our Sun: An Essay on the Development of a Guyanese Architecture," Westmaas, then chief architect with the Ministry of Works, echoes the main themes of the book as he identifies a distinctive Guyanese architecture and its sources. For Westmaas, "becoming conscious of ourselves as a nation" means architectural modernization on par with the rest of the world.[62] However, the style of these modern buildings must be Guyanese. Westmaas is adamant that, in Guyanese architecture, there is a distinctive style and historical evolution, which goes back to the Moors in Spain and Georgian and Victorian England. He warns against modernist architecture with its "smooth lines" and against modern conveniences such as air conditioners that conflict with the colonial, Demerara windows that are integral to Guyanese architectural style. Westmaas therefore turns to Amerindian architectural style as an example of the direction Guyanese architecture should take, because, he argues, Amerindians let the surroundings, not foreign style, dictate their building of, for example, a hut, "a thing of beautiful simplicity."[63] Westmaas writes, "Ours has been described as a derivative culture—like an old lean-to-shed taking support from. [sic] and at the same time propping up, an older body-house. Let us now dismantle that old structure and using what material is good along with fresh sound scantlings erect a new building *under our sun and on our piece of earth*—the only two things, after all, of which we can be sure."[64] Paradoxically, Westmaas both affirms colonial architectural style and argues that, against its modernization, which reflects a distasteful, new economic imperialism from the West, Amerindian architecture serves a decolonizing function in its reflection of a distinctly Guyanese modernity.

Westmaas's piece offers an example of the fundamental crisis of this new independent government, which literally has to create a cultural base for itself by building the symbolic and rhetorical structures that would anchor Burnham's cultural-nationalist, egalitarian vision. Westmaas's phrase "under our sun and on our piece of earth" is significant because in it we read the legitimizing structures that affect the language of cooperativism. Westmaas's rhetorical and imagistic arrangement reflects the deployment of the signifiers of a new cosmogony that legitimates black rule by doubling and displacing that "sun" of empire. It works through a reinscription of the territory in European religious cosmology that, prior to Columbus's "discovery," held that this land was "uninhabitable" because it fell outside of the then-known world.[65] That cosmology is now historical within the republic, within its resolved borders, and validates the new "descent" narrative for blacks that is historicized by Vere T. Daly.

HISTORY

In *Co-operative Republic*, two essays deal predominantly with Guyanese history in what we can view as an effort to rewrite the nation's history as one that is the product of black slave labor and rebellion: Vere T. Daly's "Historical Background to the Co-operative Republic" and Tommy Payne's "Windows on Guyanese History." Daly, then a lecturer at the Government Teacher's Training College and a historian, wrote the first postcolonial histories of the new Guyana, *The Making of Guyana*, first published in 1967, and his *A Short History of the Guyanese People*, first published in June 1966. In his essay in *Co-operative Republic*, he writes that "the problem in Guyana, and perhaps in every ex-colonial territory, is how to educate a young nation to see virtue in its own people and its own culture and traditions."[66] He continues by citing the reasons for becoming a cooperative republic, specifically the history of exploitation that began with Dutch and British imperialism and continued with the intervention that led to the 1953 suspension of the country's constitution. Crucially, it is in Daly's writing that the nation most clearly emerges as a historical outcome of black labor and black prior arrival. He claims:

> When emancipation took place it could have been said that two ethnic groups regarded Guyana as their *home*—Amerindians and Africans. . . . Portuguese, East Indians and Chinese also came to better their condition and return to their native land. And though Amerindians had no doubt that Guyana was their home, their preference was for the hinterland; so that the Negro alone was left to face up to the competition of the incoming immigrants who came to work on the coastal estates.[67]

Reiterating a narrative typical among black Guyanese, Daly adds that this situation, created and manipulated by the British, resulted in tensions between "Negroes" and other ethnic groups. This moment in Daly's essay has even greater significance when one considers Burnham's endorsement, in a preface to Daly's history, *The Making of Guyana*. In the preceding quotation, Daly discusses emancipation and indenture through the concept of Guyana as a "home." Home, however, seems to provide critical currency for a black narrative of belonging and political rights. Of significance is something that both Daly and Tommy Payne claim: that the foundation of the cooperative in Guyana is not the rice plantations run by Indians, which Kwayana looks to as an example for the cooperative, but rather the villages created by blacks who left the plantations.[68] In his essay, Payne, a government archivist and self-styled historian, confirms this when he says, "The villages had been established on a cooperative basis which challenged the capitalistic structure of an economy controlled by sugar planters."[69] By linking the image of home with blacks in the cooperative ideology of the new nationalism, Daly and Payne secure the image of the republic as a specifically black Guyanese achievement and fulfillment of Dutch vision. Additionally, Daly's discourse of home levels the playing field between blacks and Amerindians by discrediting the latter's discourse of prior rights, which has always been a problem for black nationalism and discussions of political right to rule among both blacks and Indo-Caribbean peoples. For blacks, home, which is clearly identified with the coast and the plantation, becomes a more solid foundation for such arguments than prior occupation because it not only solves the "problem" of Indians but of Amerindians as well. It is this narrative of home that Burnham is securing with the agrarian reform policy directed at blacks, disenfranchised by post-emancipation government land policies. With the cooperative, Burnham can distribute to blacks the land they should possess if the country is truly theirs. In this reasoning, home becomes a discourse of dis/possession and inheritance, and Daly's work demonstrates how the history of Guyana, its narrative of independence, can be interpreted and manipulated at strategic moments to provide legitimacy for a particular group's social and political agenda. It further demonstrates, despite his emphasis on economic equality, the ways in which the regime's financial motives remain racially motivated. Daly's history, to which I turn briefly, clarifies the overidentification of the nation as a black nation and the rescripting of indigeneity for blacks and Indigenous Peoples.

With *The Making of Guyana,* Daly challenges the Christian, religio-historical distortions about Adam and Eve and thereby mobilizes a disavowed version of history. He achieves this by opening his narrative with an account of "early man" and says that the first humans were from Africa. He then suggests that during the Ice Age those who are in fact the forefathers of the Amerindians in Guyana today migrated to South America across an ice bridge.[70] Daly then recounts the origin myths of the Carib Indians in Guyana, which describes them coming down from the sky.[71] I argue that Daly uses the origin myth of the Caribs to establish a descent narrative for blacks in the Guyana by reestablishing their origin myth as a myth of migration. In other words, Indigenous Peoples emerge, like blacks, as migrants. Thus, Daly not only recontextualizes native myths of belonging but provides a way for migration to be read *as* origin, thereby legitimating black belonging. While this historical revision would seem to legitimate Europeans as well, having arrived after the Caribs and before Africans, Daly remedies this by informing students that the Europeans only sought a *temporary* home, or camp, in Guyana. Through this establishment of prior occupation, Daly is then later able to address Indian and Chinese "indenture" as "immigration" (which he admits, in the preface, to having left out of earlier versions of this work) in a chapter titled "Negro Villages and Immigration."[72] Daly's recognition of the importation of Indian and Chinese labor to Guyana, under the British, as "immigration" erases the historical fact of their migration and places them within the rescripting of "prior arrival" in which black slavery can now also be presented. Daly not only rewrites the history of the region but pulls historical facts into what becomes "an evolutionary narrative of historical continuity" for blacks in Guyana.[73] His ability to read Amerindian belonging as originating in migration gives legitimacy to all other migrations and their ability to be read as origin. However, in Daly's narrative black migration emerges as primary because it is the first to be associated with the modern forms of labor that will eventually produce the nation-state. His historical narrative effectively links labor and migration with origin. He writes, "It was the strength of the African, whether working in the fields or in the sugarmills, which laid the foundation of the sugar industry, and Guyanese who are descendants of African slaves should be proud of this fact since it is the sugar industry which has made Guyana."[74] In turning slavery, a state of being "owned," into a moment that allows blacks to lay claim to the region (access to capital), Daly not only relies on the popular claim of "We made this country" but also turns labor and servitude into part of a European goal for the land and thereby revalorizes it. It is this that Burnham's recourse to Dutch, not British, occupation secures when he essentially suggests that the cooperative republic is a completion or fulfillment. It is teleological. Labor (of blacks) is represented as the new ground for belonging (inheritance) because it is identified as it is with European modernity.

Borders

In *Co-operative Republic,* the self-conscious, contradictory negotiation with the colonial state inherited by the Burnham regime is best exemplified with the discussion of the nation's embattled borders around which Burnham tries to foster national integration. Especially in Rudolph Collins's "The Story of the Borders," there is a concerted effort to affirm the hinterland as potential wealth. Collins's essay establishes the terminology for the relationship of the cooperative government to Guyana's land, particularly the borders and the interior, and reveals the reason for Burnham's recourse to Dutch prior occupation. Collins, a senior civil servant, writes about the border disputes between the former British Guiana, the United States of Venezuela, the United States of Brazil, and Suriname during the nineteenth century. He documents the various treaties signed over the past hundred years, which he claims have "resolved the disputes" and upheld Guyana's right to boundaries first set by the German explorer Robert Schomburgk in his 1841 survey commissioned by the British government.[75] Collins cites the "Memorandum on Actual State of the Boundaries of Guiana and Proceedings of Brazilian Authorities on the Frontier" (1841), which reads, "The British Empire therefore acquired Guiana with the same claims to the termini of its boundaries as those of the Dutch before its cession. . . ."[76]

The focus in the essay is the border dispute with Venezuela, which was reopened in 1962 when Venezuela again rejected the "Arbitral Award of 1899" among Brazil, Venezuela, and Guyana, claiming that all lands west of the Essequibo River belonged to it.[77] Venezuela not only says that the boundary established for Britain by Schomburgk is invalid, referring to it as "la pseudo-línea de Schomburgk de 1840," but it also rejects Guyana's claims to the region through Dutch settlement.[78] Further seeking to validate Guyana's claim, Collins argues that the "by-product" of European exploration was the formation of the colonies that now comprise Guyana. He adds, "It was their land, their country and they guarded and defended it from all external encroachments. To know the history of our borders is to be aware of what is rightfully our possession and, *having a stake in such possession,* to guard and defend it. . . ."[79] Collins concludes the essay by asserting that the borders "enclose a geographical entity that has its sanction in the facts of history, in international law and by mutual agreement legitimized over centuries of acceptance."[80] Collins deploys colonialist language to bring the hinterland into the mainstream of Guyana's national consciousness, engaging a language of possession that sees Guyana as an inheritance from the British and the Dutch. While the "our" of Collins's claim is thought to represent the entire country, in cooperative discourse its implied "we" was symbolically represented by only one group in the independence administration's cultural, nationalist rhetoric: blacks.

In this same section of his essay titled "Co-operative Republic, the Framework for Expansion," Collins notes, "The areas that had proved so attractive to the trading capacities of the Dutch and had borne such a rich harvest under the exploitation of the British between the seventeenth and the nineteenth centuries are still there to provide an even greater reward to those of courage and imagination. The Cooperative Republic is the conceptual framework in which the enterprising can reap rich rewards for honest endeavour."[81] Collins not only seeks to have Guyanese identify with the dispute, to see what they have at stake in it, but he also provides a way for them to, rhetorically at least, begin to cultivate a relationship to land that, for many, has little to do with their life on the coast. In so doing, he illustrates the how of Antonio Benítez-Rojo's claim that Guyanese are "repossessing" the interior by revealing the way in which the Burnham administration continued to use forms of colonial domination to justify its style of postcolonial rule. Collins utilizes colonial claim to the disputed areas as proof of Guyana's right. In a clear deployment of the poetics of myth, he distinguishes the contemporary search for wealth in the region from colonial "exploitation" by presenting the cooperative effort as more "honest," arguing that although, like the Dutch and British, Guyanese too seek to harvest wealth from the interior, the benefits will be for all Guyanese, who should think of the region as theirs collectively. Guyanese therefore must now see interior exploitation, under postcolonial rule, as a necessary part of their economic progress, as indistinguishable from it, while Amerindians are still exposed to colonization practiced by the postcolonial regime.

Collins's discussion of the border controversy takes on greater significance when considered alongside D. Graham Burnett's argument in *Masters of All They Surveyed: Exploration, Geography and a British El Dorado*. The significance of first colonial and then postcolonial cartography is reinforced in Burnett's book on Guyana's borders, in which he claims that for Europeans "myths" are what imbued the New World with significance.[82] Burnett examines what he describes as the tension between colonial "boundary making" and "boundary crossing" and the legacy it has created for Guyana in terms of its border disputes.[83] Burnett's is a "revisionist" look at the country's borders, which emphasizes their "arbitrariness and ambivalence."[84] He essentially theorized the boundary dispute as a productive one for the Burnham regime, a "stage of siege" that allowed Burnham to silence his opposition and "consolidate national loyalties" to this territory whose integrity must be defended and maintained.[85] Burnett mentions what he terms the "national call to arms" of the 1970s and 1980s by the Burnham administration: "All Guyana is ours to defend."[86] This is not to collapse what the Burnham regime became versus what it was in 1966 at independence. In this examination of the history of Guyana's borders, Burnett has written that Burnham used the borders and the discourse of protectionism and national integrity to engender national allegiance. Burnham encouraged Guyanese, Burnett writes, to "adopt . . . an imperial perspective on their own nation."[87] Instead of an Amerindian symbol being placed on products, for which Seymour argues, according to Burnett, Burnham used a map of the country, cementing the images of the threatened borders in the national consciousness. According to Burnett, Burnham's attitude to the border was "paranoid." This paranoia about borders under constant threat from Venezuela in its desire to acquire more oil resources, a desire that has greater regional significance under Hugo Chavez's presidency, is echoed in an essay by then–Minister of Energy and Natural Resources H. O. Jack ("Minister Without Portfolio with responsibilities for Youth and Interior Development"). Jack carefully links the border dispute and its evolution to the development of the interior, again providing a motive for Guyanese to identify with the hinterland. He writes, "With our coastlands already crowded, with the need to develop the enormous resources of the Interior so as to maintain and improve the standard of living of our people, faced with the urgent need to establish communities in the Interior, if only to thwart the designs of those who cast envious eyes on our land, the people and Government of Guyana are now embarked on the challenging task of making the Interior lands of their country truly their own."[88]

Jack's and Collins's discussion of "borders" focuses on such key terms as *possession, right,* and *legitimacy.* These are the terms threaded through the language of the cooperative's initiation and they indicate the real function of *Co-operative Republic* and its language of becoming. Ironically, this is not just a narrative of people inheriting a land that they worked for centuries. It employs the legitimating language of imperial adventure and colonial governance. The emphasis on possessing the interior, in this instance, is about securing interior borders and fixing Amerindian movement, both physically and politically, through the discourse of nationhood as it emerges in the creation of the cooperative. The whole of Guyanese history has been a struggle for possession. The push into the interior under the cooperative program allows blacks to finally inhabit a conquering position in that narrative, as what Burnett refers to as a "British El Dorado" becomes Burnham's Creole

El Dorado or patrimony. As a whole, *Co-operative Republic,* particularly the essays by Collins and Jack, shows the articulation of pan-African, Afro-Creole discourse with the language of possession and subordination of land and people that allowed the myth of El Dorado to be effective for imperial and colonial domination. Thus, throughout *Co-operative Republic,* there are two registers of belonging, most clearly seen in Westmaas's, Daly's, and Collins's writings. The first is constituted by the rejection of imperial origin—reflected in the attempt to both establish Amerindian heritage as a precolonial, local origin for Guyanese culture and the claim that the Dutch and British didn't really see the New World as "home." The second, seemingly contradictory register, is most visible in the discussion of the borders in which Dutch and British origin is appropriated because they secure the boundaries of the current nation-state, which did not exist at the time the boundaries were first determined.

In drawing this discussion to a close, I suggest that Burnham's commissioning of these essays in *Co-operative Republic* demonstrates that he fully understood that the rhetorical ground on which a national unity could be fostered was one of a shared vision of economic prosperity. What he also understood was that the ground upon which that vision and economic possibility could occur was both the interior, which needed to be reclaimed and rescripted from within the colonial polity and imagination, and a new singular image of the entire landscape within the new economy and culture of the republic.[89] The interior is the space for the imaginative as well as real economic transformation and creation of a "truly" Guyanese cultural aesthetic as something that must come into being against a colonial economic and cultural system. It is a fertile space with which to secure a postcolonial cultural revolution that is also nationalistic. The Honourable H. O. Jack writes that Guyanese have been a "coastal people," and the interior has been neglected by the sugar planters and, until now, has only been thought of "as the part of the country where *our* Amerindians lived."[90] Jack also informs Guyanese that "it was also a domain of the imagination, where once men had sought in vain for the golden city of El Dorado, where the writer [William Henry] Hudson had created his 'bird girl' heroine Rima and where in more recent times Conan Doyle had sited his 'Lost World.'"[91] He not only tells readers that the interior needs to be physically and imaginatively embraced, but he clearly reveals the Burnham effort to create a new mythology around the interior space that will be materially and culturally productive. In creating a new narrative, one that could emerge from the cooperative itself, Guyanese too can extend the promise of wealth and write their own narrative of "discovery." The land is integral to the transformation of the myth by allowing Guyanese to redraw the literal and figurative map of exploration and conquest. However, bringing the hinterland into the mainstream of the national economy and cultural consciousness is, therefore, still not significant enough to work the kind of change that Burnham is seeking. What is needed above all is echoed most forcefully by Payne, who stresses "the necessary assimilation of the Amerindian into a modern scientific and socio-economic system. . . ."[92] The incorporation places Amerindians in a dialectical relationship with Creoles, making them both inimical to and necessary for Creole humanity, in its yoking with wealth (capital). Their incorporation in this manner brings about the transformation and rewriting of the narrative of the myth of El Dorado and its poetics inside the postcolonial state. The land and its human and cultural surplus are now the real treasures for this regime, on which it can build an economic and cultural base that can sustain a program of economic egalitarianism. The myth and its poetics, which first managed native cultural difference and tied it to imperial wealth, continue to be deployed in the reclamation of the land, through a new imaginative relationship to it, and, most crucially, through Amerindian incorporation and subordination within the new cooperative nationalism.

Ultimately, Amerindian entry into nationalist discourse as "our Amerindians" is essential for the "possession" of the interior. Since Amerindian containment on reservations with porous borders is insufficient, the Amerindian body must be "brought" into the new politico-national consciousness in which their imagined cultural identification with the state can be manipulated: this is in order to seal the narrative of descent and inheritance that blacks at this critical historical moment are inventing for themselves. Consequently, Burnham's policies of interior development worked through a rhetoric of national unity that masks a strategic visibility and invisibility of Amerindians. In the discourse of cooperativism, Amerindians became, figuratively, a part of the national landscape, but their "representation" as a people tied to the hinterland and lacking a discourse of nationalism outside of "prior rights" excludes them from full "participation" in the political and economic center of the country. Amerindian dis/possession, and the reclamation of the interior inside the cooperative nationalist discourse, is an integral part of Burnham's legacy, which ultimately constitutes a patriarchal inheritance for the black middle class. Further, this narrative of possession was preserved in the PNC platform under Burnham's leadership and continues to limit the discourse of today's PNCR (Peoples National Congress Reform).

Burnham's Legacy: The Small Man and the Real Man

Two months after Burnham's death in 1982, his successor and former head of the PNC, the late Desmond Hoyte, gave an address to the nation titled "My First Sixty Days in Office." In his speech, meant to reassure the nation that since Burnham's passing, economic and social stability have continued, he claims that the PNC government is committed to restructuring elements of the electoral system, such as proxy and overseas voting, to prevent further accusations of fraud and unfairness in the election process that plagued the PNC leadership under Burnham. As for the PPP opposition, Hoyte mentions "cordial" meetings with Jagan and the head of the United Force party, both of whom he suggests can work with him in developing the nation on the principles of "justice and equality."[93] He quotes a supporter who said that "with the passing of our Founder-Leader, we have a change of President, not of Government. . . ."[94] With Burnham's death, the nation that Hoyte invokes throughout his speech has in fact been passed on as an inheritance left by the founding father, Burnham, to his party and to the country as a whole. It is a legacy that Burnham created for blacks and one that carries with it a black, ethno-national right to rule the nation. Hoyte, who endorsed Young's *Guyana: The Lost El Dorado* (discussed in chapter 3 of this book), is here securing the historical narrative of Burnham's own legacy enabled by the myth's poetics, through the continued envisioning of Guyana as an El Dorado, as it was in Young's text. Hoyte refers to Guyanese as stewards of Burnham's "legacy" and continues the administration's narrative of progress when he references "the road into the future which [Burnham] pointed out for us."[95] He also continues to link progress to black rule by further instantiating the relationship among development, inheritance, and what he refers to in his speech as the very tangible "sense of nationhood" that Burnham created for Guyanese.

In his eventual position as opposition leader, Hoyte bitterly contested the 1997 elections, which confirmed Janet Jagan as president and did not confirm, for blacks, Burnham's legacy. Upon Janet Jagan's illness in 1998, Bharrat Jagdeo (PPP) became president and has led Guyana to date. The political antagonism and rejection of an Indian leadership reflected the sense of loss for Guyanese black nationalism since Burnham's death, despite the fact that under his rule, Guyana's economy worsened, forcing many blacks and others to leave the country. It was the loss of a black narrative of progress, of an unquestionable right to rule, and the inability to continue to secure the validating elements of pan-Africanist discourse of the 1960s and the discourse of the myth of El Dorado that Burnham had engaged to secure.

Hoyte's "sense of nationhood" is critical for blacks. It is a reflection of Burnham's ability to reenvision the subordinate position of blacks in the New World as one of prior occupation and material right, as blacks identify Guyana, particularly the coast, as their "home," to recall Daly, and as the first to fight for its liberation, to recall the narrative around Cuffy. Slavery holds within it a relationship to the land that can be represented here as one of entitlement because it forever speaks to the place of blacks, though subordinated, as prior arrivants to subsequent groups who seek power. Burnham thus weds the labor of the formerly enslaved to the nation-state as its product or outcome, positioning blacks as the rightful recipients of the colonial discourse of possession still inherent in myth. Essential for the style of Creole belonging, in *Co-operative Republic* we see Burnham building on the racial structure that emerged out of plantation era society in creating the "small man" as a cultural hybrid to inherit the narrative of progress and development bequeathed to the nation by British colonialism. While, however, Burnham's "small man" is, narratively at least, moving up (from labor to civil service; from lower to middle class) and being made to see his self-interest in terms of the self-interest of the middle and upper classes, the Amerindian in Guyana is made into a perpetual small man inside the nation, a position necessary for this teleology of labor to remain viable.

In envisioning what he termed the "small man" under imperialism as the "real man" or subject of the postindependence nation, Burnham continued to engage the ideological value of the myth in order to produce Indigenous Peoples and the interior as an internal other, the necessarily different and uncultivated but potentially assimilable and profitable cultural base against which the liberated, sovereign, and *indigenous* Creole can emerge as both postcolonial and bourgeois. In other words, the "real man," the ideally masculine subject of the nation, represents not only the material achievement of the former colony but a shift in social being that rests on a new structure of power that emerges from a discourse of development that engages the structure of the myth of El Dorado. It is against this Creole subject that the Amerindian, essentially reduced to raw cultural material, emerges to fill the now vacant place of the colonial "small man." The cooperative republic of Guyana, as a cultural, political, and economic entity, achieves the consolidation of the status of blacks as the new indigenous by simultaneously rescripting indigeneity through the ontoepistemic terrain of labor (identified with the plantation labor product: the nation-state) and the first discourse of possession, myth. In its socialist agenda, Burnham's regime represented the state as the historical and material outcome or fulfillment of the labor process (the history of black and Indian labor). We can suggest that while Burnham endorsed socialism, PNC nationalism embraced an idealist (or Hegelian) production of the nation (and Creole subjectivity) as a cultural transcendence, again by marking off the interior limit or temporal-spatial anteriority of both economic and cultural development. The indigenous Creole subject of the postcolonial nation-state is thereby able to materially and discursively secure that patrimony that Aimé Césaire's Henri Christophe, in his borrowing of imperial culture and technologies of power with regard to labor, so feared losing.[96]

The way in which the Forbes Burnham administration envisioned the postcolonial state with regard to the role of Indigenous Peoples shares some similarity with Trinidad. Maximilian Forte's anthropology of the descendants of aboriginal peoples, *Ruins of Absence, Presence of Caribs: Post-colonial Representations of Aboriginality in Trinidad and Tobago,* is a study of the ways in which indigeneity has been configured in colonial and postcolonial Trinidad. Forte's point of departure for the book is what he sees as the dualistic representation of Indigenous Peoples as both absent and present within modern Trinidad. In Forte's work, it is clear that the present-day descendents of Trinidad's aboriginal peoples, the Caribs, share similar concerns as the Indigenous Peoples in Guyana, particularly in terms of cultural self-representation and representation by the state, despite the fact that the Carib community is much smaller than Guyana's indigenous population and doesn't share the same land rights issues. Forte is primarily concerned with the way the state mediates indigenous and ethnic identity, or as he terms it "the political economy of tradition," as it evolved from the colonial to postcolonial period. To that end, he points out that nearing the end of the colonial period, there was a shift in representation of Indigenous Peoples with regard to the state and that today in the co-optation of Amerindian symbols by the state or cultural elites, "the Amerindian thus bestows on the new nation a sense of antiquity and a sense of continuity of occupation of the territory that is Trinidad." He continues, "The new antiquity of a national history that appropriates the Amerindian renders Caribbean states as ancient as any in Europe."[97] In other words, like Guyana, it is not simply the transfer of power from European states that can guarantee the sovereignty of modern day Trinidad but the idea that there has always been a single, historical occupant. Forte thus finds that while the idea of Amerindian "backwardness" was essential in the late colonial and early postcolonial periods for marking the economic and social "progress" of the state, the Amerindian presence also secures the state.

Forte argues that in Trinidad, *Carib* is in fact both a "label" and a "field of signification" that from the colonial period to the present is redeployed by Caribs and non-Caribs and by a range of "actors" and "institutions" across space and time and within the global capitalist economy.[98] Writing on one of the many appropriations of Indigenous Peoples as cultural symbols, he also claims that Caribs serve as an "interethnic bridge . . . where indigeneity subverts the bipolar divide between Africans and East Indians."[99] This framing of the Carib within the modern state is echoed in Guyana, as my analysis of *Co-operative Republic* has shown. That document reveals the constant representation of the indigenous as antemodern and only provisionally modern—a status conferred through symbolic presence inside the most representative space in the nation (Georgetown)—yet essential for Caribbean modernity and national sovereignty. I go further to suggest that what Forte has termed "national indigeneity" (the use or appropriation of indigenous culture by the state) is actually something greater. It is the simultaneous rescripting of indigeneity itself *for* blacks and Indo-Caribbean peoples. Native culture is not simply being appropriated by the state, but it is in fact being represented by the state within the specific epistemic terrain that guarantees both Creole being and right to the state as the completion of the labor process. The valorization of the colonial subject, of the "small man" as the modern national and native subject (the Creole—masculine and middle class), and that dual representation of the native as premodern yet essential for the modern sovereignty of the nation-state turns *native indigeneity* into the edge or marker of difference for *Creole indigeneity* or belonging. Native indigeneity thus comes to mark a condition of otherness, difference, or exteriority with regard to the true subject of the state who is fully capable of being represented within political processes and for whom culture *works*.

There are thus two senses of indigeneity that operate in postcolonial Guyana and the relation to manual labor there, and in the wider Caribbean, that I elaborate. They constitute a historical unconsciousness around which two vastly different expressions of social being are articulated. This comes to the fore in the 2006 interview I conducted with Jean La Rose, the head of the Amerindian Peoples Association (APA) in Guyana and winner of the 2002 Goldman Environmental Award. In that interview, La Rose discussed indigenous American culture, land rights issues, and the relationship with the Guyana government. In that discussion, the profoundly separate relationships of Indigenous Peoples, blacks, and Indo-Caribbean peoples to land, indigeneity, and labor congeals, revealing itself as epistemic with regard to the expression of social subjectivity and political sovereignty. My conversation with La Rose clearly shows that indigenous communities, especially in Guyana, have a relationship to the land that is dually articulated as historical or ancestral and contemporary, having nothing to do with some mythic sense of belonging to the land. It is the former (ancestral) that gets read in colonial and postcolonial discourse not as history but as prehistory or premodern and that the Burnham administration engaged as it extended and adapted its colonial policy toward Amerindians. The historical presence of Indigenous Peoples is never understood as always in fact "active." It is this active relationship (past and present) that La Rose sees as markedly different from that of blacks and Indo-Guyanese, whether they are identified as laborers or simply as coast dwellers. Following is an excerpt from that interview.

JACKSON: You talk specifically about the relationship to the land that you have as an Amerindian which is very important to your culture. What about the relationship that Blacks and East Indians have to the land?

LA ROSE: Well, you'd have to ask a Black and an East Indian. [Laughter] I wouldn't be qualified enough to answer that.

JACKSON: I wanted your opinion on it because it is a different relationship— they are the ones in control of the land and how it is distributed.

LA ROSE: They are in control of the land. Ahm. I don't want to talk about who is in control, I would more want to refer to the majority. The majority. The way I see it, the majority of the East Indians are agricultural farmers. . . . And to some extent a huge area of land is required for that. But the majority of the East Indians and including the Blacks who live on the coast here don't live a similar lifestyle for the hunting and fishing as the Amerindians and so the use of the land is different, would still be different. I know we talk about ancestral lands, and I've heard some of the former slave population talk about a relationship to their ancestral lands as well. Yes, they may have ancestral lands wherever it is, but remember people came and they met us here. We were here. We were driven from the coast. The coast even could be our ancestral lands. But our communities are not seeking—I haven't

heard any community saying "we're looking for Georgetown, we [sic] looking to repossess Georgetown or the rest of it."

LA ROSE: . . . So you know I've heard of people referring to it in the sense of we
were here as well and we were driven further inland. We resisted enslavement and so forth. . . . But I think the relationship—and like I said you have
to ask those people—but I think it's more agricultural space rather than the
other side, than in the same view as we have it.[100]

La Rose articulates a relationship to land and labor that is distinct from Creoles. Despite the fact that Indigenous Peoples were engaged for plantation
work even during slavery and indenture, albeit in small numbers, she foregrounds indigenous resistance to forced labor and engages the history that
placed them outside slave labor under Dutch and British rule, especially when
they were used to capture runaway slaves, most significantly in the Berbice
Slave Rebellion from which Cuffy emerges as the nation's hero.[101]

The distinction among three aspects of the land–labor interface shows La
Rose's multiple interpretations of what it means to labor: (1) Amerindian
forms of culturally determined labor or practices upon ancestral lands; (2)
noncoercive or nonslave plantation labor; and (3) slave labor as that which
blacks performed and Indians later inherited under indenture. In the excerpt
from our interview, for example, La Rose deliberately opposes "hunting and
fishing" to Indian agricultural work, which comes out of colonial plantation
history. Later in the interview, she talks about her own adjustment to the
coast when she moved from the interior to Georgetown for work to underscore the profound difference and anti-indigenousness of a *modern* coastal
life for Amerindians. What La Rose reveals is not only a positioning of Amerindians outside the coastal center of national life, but a concept of indigeneity that exists firmly outside the relationship to labor that blacks and Indians
have with slavery and indenture. The indigeneity of the latter is enacted on
the coast, where their labor and survival were largely determined. The space,
labor, and time of black and Indo-Caribbean presence in Guyana are thus
fundamentally different from that of Indigenous Peoples for whom the coast
represents a *past* history (not present, lived reality). The coast also represents
a space not only of prior arrival but of prior departure or leaving behind
within the time of their *own* history in the region. The interior then is not
just outside the plantation and its modes of labor, but the coast is positioned
against it within and by the native "past." The coast is thus already scripted
within and by native indigeneity. This is one of the ways that we can interpret

La Rose's claim of her inability to "know" of black and Indo-Guyanese relationships to the land despite geographic, familial, or cultural proximities, which fits with another moment in the interview in which La Rose talks about the failure to respect the boundaries of aboriginal lands because of the incapacity of outsiders, specifically the government, to really "see" them. La Rose says of the delineation of the boundaries of native territory by the Ministry of Amerindian Affairs that "they draw a boundary based on what people are seeing," not in terms of the historical and contemporary relationships different groups have to the land.

The inability to "know" or "see" is not only about governmental indifference but represents an ontological difference rooted in practices and labor on the land, one so profound that it cannot even be communicated as history. La Rose can't "know" the relationships of blacks and Indo-Guyanese to the land, and vice versa, because as the relationship of each group evolved through material and cultural practice, they produced separate ways of being, separate ways of knowing that support the production of identity and sociality. Indigeneity, or belonging, for Indigenous Peoples, reflects the *simultaneity* of relation to the land (past and present), while for Creoles it reflects *progress* that comes from modern labor. It is this progress that necessarily produces belonging as a teleological process that can thus be captured by the history of the modern nation, which validates the coast as its core—the space in which the bulk of colonial labor was performed. What is considered "labor" (always already modern or understood within Western time) is marked off from native being upon the land, and it is these two different senses of action or practice upon the land that conflict and that the poetics of myth manages. The rescripting of Creole indigeneity through a teleological relationship to labor reduces past and present Amerindian action on the land and refashions it as a cultural rather than material product or outcome, which can be as profitable for the national economy as the product or outcome of Creole labor. Amerindians, who cannot therefore change their relationship to materiality, to capital, or to history, in the same way Creoles have, remain the small man as Creole indigeneity confronts and challenges the persistent reality of being a settler population that could never, within the terms of native indigeneity, claim political right and sovereignty.

Conclusion

This chapter sought to show that the Burnham regime secured legitimacy not only through race and labor but that the development discourse in Guyana is more broadly shaped by the poetics of El Dorado. While the Burnham administration and the predominantly black PNC tapped into the discourse on nationalism in classical modernism and pan-African nationalist discourse, with both its conservative and more radical anticolonial elements, in order to produce a Creole nationalism, none was sufficient to supply the regime with the legitimating cultural-national rhetoric it needed in a multiracial and multiethnic society. Instead, the liberal-rationalist structures of thought inherent in European nationalism since the eighteenth century were made to articulate with the poetics myth of El Dorado to create an unequal, exploitative system of political and cultural representation that maintains inequalities created by the plantation and that have become fundamentally constitutive of Creole society. Burnham's cooperative plan for republican Guyana developed a program of economic egalitarianism that worked to secure Guyana as a black patrimony and consolidate Creole identity as indigenous within the postcolonial state. Through the economic and ideological apparatus of the cooperative, Burnham sought to bring all Guyanese into a new structure of belonging and participation in the state. He redefined for the nation who its citizens were in both economic and cultural terms as he attempted to consolidate all areas of society, from economics to ethnic diversity, into one narrative that the regime could essentially manipulate and propagandize to engender loyalty to the state. In crafting for the whole of Guyana the language of cooperative nationalism, an extension of Afro-Creole nationalism that retained blacks and the "small man" as its subjects, Burnham incorporated the oppositional discourse of early free peoples and that of early twentieth-century black and Indian laborers who collectively challenged their exploitation to European domination. He absorbed these once oppositional, anticolonial positions into a popular discourse that he then wedded to official nationalism, validated by the system of proportional representation that, in turn, reinscribed the historical and racial fragmentation and social segregation that all the previous popular representations agitated against. Burnham succeeded in giving what amounts to constitutional force to the social injustice of the colonial period.

As propaganda, *Co-operative Republic* offered a historiography of the region centered on its territoriality, the most crucial factor in Burnham's ethno-nationalism. The specific challenge of the regime was to find a way to represent the interior, which to this point had always been outside of plantation society proper, as falling within the terms of the legitimating structures of Creole society, thereby making it unquestionably subject to its exploitation. In this way, the Afro-Creole nationalism of Burnham and the PNC sought to turn a specifically Creole relationship to the land into a condition for a new, indigenous belonging inside the postcolonial state. Burnham ultimately affirmed one mode of being upon the land affected through Western (modern) modes of labor that have always already been elaborated through a linear notion of time, especially with regard to the nation-state. Blacks therefore emerged as, following Marx, those "men" who make history, thereby coming to inhabit a subject position that had previously belonged to the white Western colonial and that is achieved only through difference (racial) or opposition. With the cooperative, Burnham not only created the conditions to legitimize Afro-Creole domination, but he recreated the relation of culture to development embedded in the myth. Thus, under Burnham, indigenous cultural difference (bound to the hinterland) became a productive resource of the state, a relationship that continues to be maintained by subsequent governments.

Unlike his ally Robert Mugabe in then–Northern Rhodesia (Zimbabwe), who would not see independence until 1980, Burnham's nationalization could not strictly rely on the rhetoric of pan-Africanist discourse with its claims of prior "African" ownership of indigenous lands.[102] Directed primarily at the white British minority and at the Indo-Guyanese, Burnham's nationalist discourse sought to validate the claim of black prior rights and inheritance in Guyana by tapping into the mechanisms of power that recreate Indigenous Peoples and cultures as an internal other and reproduce the land as that which can be possessed, inherited, or represented as a patrimony. For this he needed to establish the postcolonial relationship to Indigenous Peoples as a continuation of the colonial one, even while it shifts so that the possession becomes largely cultural rather than physical. It is thus their overidentification with the interior that ultimately became productive for Burnham. When blacks in Guyana inherited the colonial narrative of the myth at independence, one of the ways they could enact it was to usurp the place of Europeans and to establish themselves as the new "culture bringers."[103] By seeking to develop the region and to modernize its inhabitants, in essence to continue the civilizing mission begun by Europeans, they could pull the interior further into the state's domain of influence and at the same time solidify their role as inheritors of not only the land but also the colonial mandate that once governed it. At independence, blacks, therefore, shift from being involuntary settlers to active colonials.

In the following chapter, I argue that despite the different trajectories for Indo-Caribbean social and cultural being in the New World—indenture versus slavery, or *kala pani* trajectories versus black Atlantic ones—Indo-Caribbean modes of being, even where they undermine some of the legitimating elements of Afro-Creole nationalism, still fundamentally depend upon the manner of achieving and consolidating Creole indigeneity and political subjectivity established with Burnham.[104] Thus, Indo-Guyanese nationalism continues to deploy similar criteria for belonging as blacks did. What we are seeing with these discourses is literally the grammar of being that has developed and deployed with those first narratives in which Europeans had to justify their presence in a world that was thought not to have existed.

5

The Baptism of Soil: Indian Belonging in Guyana

I long to fertilize your womb
begetter of many sons—
to *baptize* you with brown soil
staining my hands
in the hour of twilight,
the hour of creation

—ROOPLALL MONAR, from "Darling of the Rising Sun," *Koker*

The East Indian race in British Guiana has not yet begun its history as a race. Its past has been chaos and darkness. Our people *shall* be great and *must* be great in the future. . . . They shall participate in all our industries. . . .

— CLEM SEECHARAN, *Joseph Ruhomon's India*

AMID BARELY RECORDED PROTEST BY INDIGENOUS PEOPLES IN 1997, the Timehri International Airport in Guyana was renamed for the late president Cheddi B. Jagan, with support from the then–Minister of Amerindian Affairs, Vibert DeSouza.[1] DeSouza endorsed the renaming because of what he saw as gains for Amerindians under Peoples Progressive Party (PPP) leadership. As mentioned in chapter 4, Forbes Burnham's administration had chosen the name *Timehri*—also the name of the town in which the airport is located—as part of its attempt to develop an indigenous symbolism for its cooperative based, cultural nationalism. The renaming of the airport that now boasts pictures of Jagan and information about his political life as well as wood carvings by Indigenous Peoples and "The El Dorado Bar" celebrated Jagan's legacy.

An indefatigable advocate for political freedom and labor rights in Guyana, Jagan was also a prolific writer, authoring roughly a dozen books, which include collected speeches. Additionally, his life and commitment to Marxism have been the subject of many works. His political and intellectual struggles led Carole Boyce Davies and Monica Jardine in 2003 to include him in a list with other Caribbean intellectuals, such as Sylvia Wynter, Aimé Césaire, and C. L. R. James, who they claim share the same "intellectual journey."[2] Whether Jagan is the "Grandpa Cheddi" of his wife's—former President Janet Jagan—short story about his life as a boy or the "doctrinaire" Marxist, his achievements and the narratives that circulate about them are crucial both for the nation and especially for the Indo-Guyanese.[3] In spite of Jagan's differences from Burnham and his broad commitment to labor equality, the Timehri renaming points to something fundamental, both about how Jagan is celebrated and more generally about how Indo-Guyanese and the contemporary PPP have articulated their sociopolitical belonging within the broad scripting and deployment of Creole indigeneity by the Burnham regime.

While Jagan has been referred to as a "friend" to Amerindians, there are crucial similarities, especially with regard to politics, in how Indo- and Afro-Creoles relate to Indigenous Peoples.[4] In our 2006 interview, for example, Jean LaRose suggested that the current PPP government, which is continuing with interior development projects in a manner similar to Burnham, only pays lip service to Amerindian needs and essentially buys their votes.[5] In this light, the naming *and* renaming of Timheri should more accurately be read as the recreation of indigenous history as palimpsest, which speaks profoundly to the imbrications of *kala pani,* or "dark waters," and black Atlantic trajectories of modernity and the ways in which one ocean flows over and through another. Here we continue to see the consequences of deploying certain means to produce belonging and right, which require both the "baptism of soil" and the figurative writing over of Amerindian hieroglyphics with modern space and labor. We see the ways in which Indo-Caribbean peoples come to belong to a region whose original inhabitants are now known through their misidentification as "Indian," by both the invocation of British imperialism as a racialized birthright and the strategic linking and delinking of indenture and slavery, among other factors.

The previous chapter argued that Burnham essentially wed economic rationality and progress to the discourse of the myth of El Dorado, the poetics of which forced him to articulate black humanity, manhood, and social progress as a colonialist endeavor with regard to Indigenous Peoples and the interior. This chapter focuses on the ways in which Indo-Caribbean peoples, specifically Indo-Guyanese, articulate belonging in the production of a first-person plural that is dialectically structured both materially and ideologically.

Framed by the tension of what was to be a "temporary" stay and the quotidian relationship to the material world of the colony in which Indians recreated their communities, histories, and futures, this chapter looks at how Indo-Guyanese have remade themselves and articulated national and/or cultural, ethnic belonging through labor. I argue that they have done this in ways that both differ from and affirm black modes of producing Creole belonging as indigenous. The chapter reveals that although not always formally articulated, both labor and myth circulate largely as an ontoepistemic undercurrent in Indo-Caribbean discourse that cements their belonging to the nation in ways similar to blacks. One crucial parallel, for instance, that this work does not take up is the way in which the Indian woman, much like the black woman, serves as a necessary other in the indigenizing processes of Indians: something that is all too conspicuous in Monar's writing. What does preoccupy me, however, is the ways in which Indian collective political belonging or subjectivity, like that of Afro-Creoles, necessitates the continued displacement of Indigenous Peoples.

The discussion begins by addressing the strategic linking and delinking of indenture and slavery in terms of the differences between black Atlantic and *kala pani* trajectories of modernity. The goal is to move beyond the dominant mode of articulating Indian entry into the Caribbean, which continues to position them against blacks and black labor. Instead, I stress the complexity of Indian entry and tease out the significance of its representation as both coerced and volitional. Later, the chapter turns to the complex issue of Indian belonging through a discussion of Indo-Guyanese histories, among other works. These texts illustrate the ways in which the particular juncture of history and diaspora for Indo-Caribbean peoples is the productive tension that governs modes of belonging that are different yet dependent upon Afro-Creole ones. The chapter closes with a discussion of Jagan both in his own words and through imagistic depiction of his life. This section illuminates how his struggle in the opposition and his presidency ultimately secured a mode of political belonging for Indo-Guyanese. This mode reinforced Burnham's ethno-nationalism, precisely by recoding the pasts discussed in the preceding section and establishing "Enmore" as a formative break in modern Guyanese labor history.

KALA PANI MODERNITY

Typically, *kala pani* is the term used to describe the crossing of first the Indian then the Atlantic Ocean by Indians to work on Caribbean plantations.

In different texts it is referred to as the "dark waters of the ocean." Kumar Mahabir, in his introduction to a special issue of the anthropological journal *Man in India,* describes *kala pani* in this way: "Many Indians regarded departing from India with horror and referred to the passage from India to the West Indies as the dreaded *kalapani* or dark waters."[6] Throughout the Caribbean, this passage is affirmed annually by the widely celebrated Indian Arrival Day (May 5 in Guyana). The day marks the first landing of Indians in the Caribbean at the start of the indenture period in 1838. The protracted and successful effort to make Arrival Day a public or national holiday in Guyana, which finally happened in 2004 with the support of President Bharatt Jagdeo and his PPP administration, demonstrated not only an Indo-Guyanese desire to commemorate the event, but what it meant as a reflection and confirmation of their cultural and political right to belong in the Caribbean.[7] From what was supposed to be a temporary stay based on initial five-year contracts of indenture, the indenture period extended to about eighty years. It saw the arrival of nearly half a million Indians—only a quarter of whom were able to return to India—into the Caribbean (the majority to Guyana) and resulted in the addition of a new settler-Creole population that, in Guyana, now outnumbers blacks.[8]

Although the celebration of Indian Arrival Day speaks to the ways in which Indians have established new roots in the Caribbean, it also demonstrates two significant tensions in the shaping of Indian identity in the Caribbean. The first is the tension created by the manner in which their belonging occurs differently from blacks (indenture versus slavery) and the second is how an identity as Caribbean peoples profoundly abuts and comes in conflict with an identity as Indian Diaspora peoples, where culture and practice tie Indo-Caribbean peoples both to the Caribbean and its diasporas and to India and its diasporas (again differently from Afro-Creole ties to an African or Black Diaspora which is not one of nation, but race). Together, these tensions not only reveal a unique relationship to modernity informed by the *kala pani* crossing, but they allow us to speak in fact of a *kala pani* modernity with its own alternative history and discourses that can serve as a framework for reading Indian cultures outside India.

The different economy of signs and material history in which parts of the Indian Diaspora become embedded and reproduce in the constitution of an alternative or "counterculture" of modernity is reflected in the photograph on the next page.[9] It shows two billboard advertisements that appear to be near each other on a street in Georgetown; one for an Indo-Guyanese club and the other for Guyanese rum. The images reflect the transformation of the cultural currency that Indo-Caribbean peoples continually draw from India. In the first, the lucrative Bollywood film industry gestures toward Indian origins (understood as contemporary and secular) and is linked here as a profitable industry to Hollywood and American capital (rather than Guyana's rice or sugar industry). The second billboard proclaims the myth and material reality, including the figurative ships that brought Indians and blacks to the West Indies, embedding them both in labor. Sugar, rice, cotton, and tobacco are all crops that, as suggested by the different ages of the rum (in this case five years), collapse thousands of years into the history of commodities, markets, nations, and modern empires. These signs reflect both the reach into Indian Diaspora and the "myth" that embeds Indo-Creoles in the Caribbean, as Jagan reminds us early in *The West on Trial: My Fight for Guyana's Freedom,* when he writes of "El Dorado to which my grandmothers were lured."[10] The images reveal the way in which the indenture period evolved into a belonging to the Caribbean that granted to Indians the same status as settlers as that granted to blacks by roughly two centuries of black presence and labor on the plantations prior to Indian arrival. However, the invocation of Bollywood gestures

Street signs in Georgetown. Photograph by author.

to a formative feature in that belonging and that was the desire of Indians who first entered the Caribbean *not* to be Creole.

The desire not to be Creole has been documented by several critics. Lee Drummond, for instance, has indicated the role that religion played in the initial distance between Christian blacks and newly arrived Hindu and Muslim Indians.[11] Patricia Mohammed, in her writing on Indian women in Trinidad, notes the religious, economic, and cultural differences that created the gulf between Indians and blacks:

> Certainly neither Indian men nor women attempted at first to become integrated . . . with the new society. Loyalties were first to India, to which they hoped to return some day. . . . Geographical and occupational separation, combined with mutual contempt and misunderstanding, kept the various races apart. . . . Blacks, who had internalised the values of Creole society had contempt for this group of immigrants who spoke "barbarous" languages, dressed differently, and worked for cheaper wages than they did. Indians, on the other hand, regarded the Blacks as untouchables and polluted as they ate the flesh of pigs and cattle and engaged in occupations which they considered ritually impure.[12]

Of particular importance in Mohammed's writing is the loyalty to India that initially prevented Indians from being able to form community with Creoles. That loyalty was based on the promise of return, presumably in a better economic position. In contrast, black loyalty to Africa in the early stages of New World enslavement was informed not by the promise of return. In other words, despite the deception involved in the various indenture schemes, Indians were not forced, nor were they considered slaves, although their actual treatment was often not much different. In his articulation of Guyana as an El Dorado that "lured" Indians, Jagan does not make the comparison between slavery and indenture that he often utilizes. Rather than reference indenture as coercive labor, Jagan presents a narrative of desire. Indians thus claim belonging within the terms inaugurated by Afro-Creoles by engaging two different narratives around indenture: one that links indenture to slavery; and another that reads indenture in terms of some amount of volition or agency on the part of Indians. By gesturing to the latter, Jagan reinforces postcolonial theorist Vijay Mishra's argument about indentured Indians in the nineteenth century.

According to Mishra, when Indians left India under the indenture scheme, they were no longer subaltern. He writes that "for the first time Indian subalterns became historical subjects."[13] For Mishra, Indians become "historical"

through the indenture experience because it was fundamentally modernizing. In an essay on Fijian ethnopolitics, Mishra claims:

> Indenture introduced us to industrialization—steam ships, sugar mills, trains—
> and quickly transformed us from caste-ridden, illiterate rejects to an enlight-
> ened, progressive and a relatively homogenous "race." Laborers we remained,
> and working class in our attitudes as well, but we were all brushed very quickly
> with the capitalist economy. We became a working class that aspired to the con-
> dition of the bourgeoisie.[14]

Mishra reads the volitional element of Indian migration to the region as
according them a modicum of agency, significant enough to distinguish them
from their counterparts on the subcontinent. He goes a step further in making the distinction between the "older diasporas of classic capitalism," where
he locates Indian diasporas produced through indenture, and "the mid- to
late-twentieth-century diasporas of advanced capital to the metropolitan centres of the Empire, the New World and the former settler colonies."[15]

For Mishra, the nation-state plays an essential part in the development of
the "diasporic imaginary" for the later diaspora. In focusing on what he has
determined is the old diaspora, and specifically its incorporation and transformation of Caribbean culture, we see another important difference, which has
a profound effect on Indo-Caribbean identity within diaspora, and as Caribbean peoples and now subjects of the nation-state: the stages of capital development. While Mishra notes that the later diasporas, largely part of the "brain
drain" phenomenon, are bound up with advanced capital, the old diaspora
(again nineteenth- and early twentieth-century indenture) entered the Caribbean at a particular moment in the development of capital that occurred
coterminous with black enslavement. In other words, the Indian diaspora
produced through this initial *kala pani* crossing emerged at a particular
moment with regard to the rise of capital, significantly after the first Industrial Revolution in the eighteenth century. As that diaspora transforms itself
in the Caribbean with Indian peoples becoming historical subjects as "East
Indian" and then national subjects as Indo-Caribbean (a significantly under-
theorized shift), that diaspora is no less a diaspora of modernity in a more
advanced state of capital. It also suggests that Indians are becoming historical subjects through a particular style of documentation (Mishra notes, for
example, the details of the emigration passes) while blacks become so in transitioning off the plantations. The plantation thus becomes a space of *history*

for Indians, and space of *prehistory* for blacks, which they do not enter in the same way: emigration pass versus bill of sale. This critical distinction registers Indo-Caribbean difference from blacks that is reinscribed in the transition from East Indian to Indo-Caribbean. It undergirds Monar's baptism of soil or the way in which Indian belonging is produced through material and cultural relationships developed through the plantation.[16] In that remaking of Indian identity, there are those who see it as being unalterably wedded to India, as an extension of Indian culture, while there are others such as Monar who reject India as an endlessly renewable origin.

For Monar, Indian culture is in the "past," and he rejects the idea of an ethnic "Indianness," arguing that it is "fissiparous."[17] It is tied to India, and for Indians in Guyana, it remains there. In a letter to the editor of the *Stabroek News,* Monar writes that while he does not deny his past, which he identifies by listing the "Indian" music to which he listens, "it would be false to act as an East Indian burdened with the trappings of a past, which to my mind, has no bearing on my conscious awareness as a Guyanese." Monar locates the origins of an Indo-Guyanese culture in the cultural practices of his Indo-Guyanese ancestors indentured on sugar plantations and rice-growing villages. However, for Monar, there is a huge difference between this cultural past and what Indian culture has become in Guyana. More important, he suggests that those who doubt him should turn to Indo-Guyanese elders to help them distinguish between "Indian" culture and Indo-Guyanese culture. In his view, to claim that what is being represented in Guyana is "Indian" culture would put Guyanese Indians in the habit of always mimicking that culture. He ends his letter by adding, "We have been tribalised and Creolised and those who claim kinship with their brothers in India ought to be awakened .... We are Guyanese." For Monar, the appropriation of May 5 marks a rupture from that home society (India) that another letter writer, Babur M. Khan, finds essential to Indian ethnic identity in Guyana; it also marks the moment of origin for a distinctive Indo-Guyanese culture.[18] Monar's letter to the editor claims a definitive space in Guyanese culture for Indians, a space that he elaborates in his poetry.

In Monar's poetry collection *Koker,* the title of which refers to the sluice gates the Dutch established on sugar plantations, we see him shape this space. In the collection, the poem "Babu" evinces what Jeremy Poynting has said of the titular poem; it demonstrates "the cultural tensions between ancestral voices and the difficult commitment to an Indo-Guyanese beginning. . . ."[19] However, "Babu," with its "images of immigrant ships/barrack confinements/cutlasses, decapitated women/dance in the rhythm of seasons/ an enclosed world of canefields," speaks to the remaking of Indian cultural heritage and social and political subjectivity in and through the plantation, in and through their own labor.[20] What Poynting reads as a largely cultural tension, the poems frame as both a physical and metaphysical struggle. They reflect a complex relationship to labor that produces these intangible "meanings" (see also the poem "Meanings" in the same collection) through which material heritage is attached to a new cultural discourse of belonging. Monar himself has tackled the issue of material and spiritual or cultural identity in two collections of short stories, *Estate People* and *Backdam People*. The first collection focuses on Indentured Indians more directly under the thumb of plantation rule in the early days of indenture. In the latter, the *backdam* refers to the "distant" areas of the sugar estates where Indians could work for themselves or congregate without supervision. It calls to mind but differs from the "slave plot" on which enslaved blacks could grow food for both subsistence and for sale, with the hope of amassing enough funds to buy their freedom. The difference between the stories, the first centered around Indian plantation workers and the second (set between the 1930s and 1950s) around Indian sugar estate workers, culture, and the separate spaces Indians were able to work, points to the coercive conditions under which culture is transformed and reinscribes the volitional element of Indian crossing.

The images of water in *Koker* maintain in the collection a tension between flux and change and the potential for cultures and peoples to be endlessly reborn, making it seem as though the khoker, rather than just a device to control water on the land, in fact represents the flow of Atlantic ("dark waters") *onto* the land and the way they reproduce material and cultural selves. As Monar tries to acknowledge what parts of Indian cultures have been preserved while in no way endorsing them as dogmatic and unaltered, the poems achieve this powerful connection to rebirth through labor and the relationship to the land. We see this in lines such as "our ancestors carved these fields," and in the acknowledgment and anxiety over the way in which the gods of history (with its subsumption of Indian modes of being and belonging in the precolonial and colonial British periods) are reenvisioned in the poem "Darling of the Rising Sun" as the "god of the canefields and ricefields."[21] Monar is not unaware of the consequences of such a rebirth, as the poem "Snake Alter" suggests, but what he does here is locate that rebirth in labor, which is the anchor of the aesthetic, and so reproduce the epistemological basis for political and cultural right developed by blacks as a condition of articulation. In Monar's work, however, an alternate possibility with labor emerges, which I discuss elsewhere.[22] What is crucial here is the way in which his work, together with Mishra's discussion of subalterneity, allows us to see that Indo-Caribbean belonging also reflects a transition from myth to market, but it underscores that the tension between claiming an Indian "past" and a Guyanese future is more sharply a transition from and within history and diaspora.

In this transition, Indian culture is expressed either as a break or continuity, given the more contemporary relationship Indians have to a homeland. There is the need to either place the long history and contemporary culture of India in a "historical" role in order to assert national belonging and citizenship rights, or to assert a religious difference (Hindu, for instance) identified with the majority population of a homeland, thereby shifting the Indian conflict of Hindu versus Muslim to, for instance, Hindu or Indo-Caribbean versus blacks, which represents a profoundly active ontoepistemic shift at the core of Indo-Caribbean identity as revealed in their writing of history and themselves as historical subjects.

History and Diaspora

This slippage between history and diaspora that governs the linking and delinking of slavery and indenture prompts a new examination of Indian historiography and the writing of the Indo-Caribbean as historical subject, starting with more contemporary work like Basdeo Mangru's *Indians in Guyana: A Concise History from Their Arrival to the Present*. Such works clearly demonstrate the tension with and borrowing from Afro-Creole material and discursive modes of indigeneity. Mangru's self-declared motive for writing *Indians in Guyana* is to provide additional material for the social studies curriculum on Latin America and South Asia in New York City public schools. The history covers the conditions in the colony immediately after slavery was abolished in the 1830s; the socioeconomic factors that led Indians to come to the colony; conditions for Indians in Guyana; and the "second migration," as Mangru terms it, that Indians have made to New York and Canada. Mangru repeats the colonial logic of indenture when he writes that after emancipation, blacks began to leave the plantation and move into villages ("village movement"). He describes the immigration schemes that brought Indians to the region as an attempt by plantation owners to control labor and wages, something that could no longer happen with former slaves who, he says, were now free to control their labor.[23]

In identifying indentured labor in this manner, Mangru establishes a link between slavery and indenture while at the same time deemphasizing the negative historical representation of the latter by blacks. In comparing indenture and slavery, Mangru highlights the complete subjection of the worker in both institutions to the estate. Later, he describes the movement to end indenture and the campaign to abolish slavery as "similar." Overall, Mangru strives to limit the "blame" for wage control placed on Indians by blacks at the time. He contends that it was the "cheap, reliable" labor provided by Indians that helped to develop the Guyanese agricultural industry and economy into what it is today, adding that the "Victorian virtues of thrift and industry" further helped Indians prosper.[24] He also holds that Indians have introduced a "rich" culture in the Caribbean and that it is this commitment to family and culture that allowed them to "prosper" in the region.[25] Of key importance to Mangru is the degree to which Hindu and Islamic traditions in India were maintained in the overseas colonies in the form of epics such as the *Ramayana* and festivals such as Tadjah. Mangru includes photos of patriarchal family life, both on the cover of the book and inside, in order to stress that despite being removed from the heart of Indian culture, Indians in the colonies maintained cultural and moral values through the family. He emphasizes the continued centrality of religion in social and cultural life in the colonies and continues through to his discussion of Indian life in the diaspora, in New York's "Little Guyana," Richmond Hill (Queens). Mangru is careful to assert Indian religious and cultural loyalty against Creole culture, saying that plantation life ultimately "shielded" Indians from "Creole practices," thereby walking a fine line in his text in emphasizing the similarities between slavery and indenture while deemphasizing the extent to which Indians became creolized. The former comparison allows Indians to claim that Guyana is as much theirs as it is Afro-Creole's—proving loyalty to Guyana and the Caribbean; the latter position asserts, however, a separate cultural identity from blacks that is more authentic and that is linked, after 1947, to an *already* sovereign Indian state—linking them to an Indian Diaspora.

Closer reading of Mangru's work suggests that at least three of the stages of Creole identity that I mapped in chapter 1 in terms of the Afro-Caribbean experience correspond to Indian identity as well: the relocation to the colonies through indenture; the move "off" the plantation, which needs to be seen in light of the fact that the majority of Indians in Guyana today are still identified with agricultural work; and the moment of independence, which for Indians is more complex. In his history, Mangru includes a discussion on race relations in the colony between blacks and Indians. He holds that there was initial tension between the groups because blacks believed that Indians were introduced to the colony to allow planters to control labor and wages. He also suggests that planters exploited black and Indian tension, which heightened in the late 1890s when Indians began moving off the plantations and into towns, competing with blacks for the better-paying skilled jobs they held, among other kinds of work. Mangru writes that blacks called Indians derogatory terms that were eventually replaced by "coolie," a term that still exists today. However, in mentioning the term *coolie*, Mangru is careful to distinguish between "Coolie laborers" and "East Indians." Mangru quotes a writer in the newspaper the *Argosy* whose writings reflect "Indian resentment" about the use of such derogatory terms by blacks. According to the writer, "Coolies are laborers such as work on sugar estates or do odd jobs about town. But take a walk anywhere in the colony and you will find East Indians in positions other than these."[26] In moving off the plantations and out of a situation similar to slavery, "East Indians," Mangru suggests, *stopped* being Coolies at the moment they also risked greater exposure to Afro-Creole culture, which was considered a corrupting cultural force. Mangru seems to suggest that transition off the plantation for Indians was less about social structure than culture and that it had a profound impact on Indian self-conception. In other words, it reflects a changing relationship to culture that does not undercut the economic contributions of Indians as workers.

Both Mangru's work and that of his predecessor, Peter Ruhomon, maintain that Indians in the Caribbean preserved their cultural heritage through assertions that Indians did not want their children educated by blacks and exposed to Creole culture.[27] Therefore, in saying that Indian labor "saved" the colony, they assert Indo-Caribbean rights to leadership based on economic, not cultural contributions. This is very different from what Burnham did with *Co-operative Republic* in linking economic progress with culture. Further, there is an irony in the symbolic and discursive confinement of the "coolie" to the plantation, while the claims that Indians "saved" the colony are wholly dependent on its portability. It is not tied to those Indians who exited the plantation, achieved middle-class status, and gave the colony its first Indo-Caribbean political leaders. "Coolie," ultimately, is an identity placed upon Indians, and neither Mangru nor the *Argosy* writers object to it entirely because it allows them to share subordination with blacks under British rule and therefore assert a claim on the land and the nation's future in a similar manner. However, a primarily economic claim will never be sufficient to erase

the tension the letters reveal between claims that Indo-Caribbean peoples
are either Indian first or Guyanese.

Mangru concludes his history with a set of questions for the New York
City high school teacher and student audience for which he has written it
that reveal a preoccupation with and anxiety about cultural belonging and
historical representation—most specifically, about how Indian national identity is constructed out of a shared history with blacks who are not only prior
arrivants but have a prior claim on the history itself. These questions include
the following: "Was indenture a new form of slavery? . . . Is Richmond Hill
'Little Guyana'?"[28] While Indo-Caribbean historical right is constructed
through assertions like Mangru's that indenture was "like slavery," an opinion widely held in the Caribbean, that association stands in contrast to the
volitional narrative we saw mobilized by Jagan and Mishra. Furthermore,
these assertions must be understood within the larger national and diasporic
Indian cultural context that Mangru reserves for Indo-Caribbean peoples.
Regardless of the similarity of the conditions of Indian indenture to black
enslavement, it is used as a narrative device to shore up belonging through
labor that is oriented toward the national economy and its continued growth.
Further, the comparison to slavery must also be read through the distance
in time and capital between slavery and indenture that factors into survival,
sociality, and identity construction. The title of Mangru's history explicitly
identifies Indo-Guyanese as "Indians," allowing it to circulate in diaspora as
confirmation of a larger Indian diasporic presence, thereby delimiting the
historical and knowledge base for his discussion of blacks and Indians and
the anxiety around what each group is entitled to or can achieve based on
when and how they entered the colony. Mangru avoids mentioning the predominantly black Caribbean diaspora in New York and so does not ally
himself or Indo-Caribbean peoples with it.

Consequently, in New York, in diaspora, Mangru's text must function as
more than a history. It must also be representative of multifaceted loyalties
at once cultural and national: Indo-Caribbean national loyalty, historical loyalty to Guyana (ethno-nationalism), and cultural loyalty to India and, hence,
to the Indian Diaspora. Mangru's text plays a particular kind of "national role"
in an international diasporic arena. It ultimately functions through identifying Indian cultural allegiance as "cultural capital" (Hintzen) that works by
putting India into a teleology of economic progress that secures an Indian
right to power in Guyana by welding Indian history to production and
development—land, rice, and sugar. Mangru reflects the attitude of Peter

Ruhomon that Indian cultural nationalism in Guyana is an extension of *continental* Indian cultural nationalism. Thus, the anxiety of culture and place in Mangru's work must be looked at, briefly, in conjunction with earlier work during the colonial period by Ruhomon.

Originally published in 1947, the year of India's independence from Britain, *Centenary History of the East Indians in British Guiana, 1838–1938* by civil servant and amateur historian Peter Ruhomon was reprinted in 1988 by "The 150th Anniversary Committee of the Arrival of Indians in Guyana (May 5, 1838)." Committee Chairman Yesu Persaud writes in the preface that the reprinting "is done at a time when we are engaged in the search for what is usable in the past to assist us in the task of working together in building our nation."[29] The tone of this history is significantly different from Mangru's or Vere T. Daly's, discussed in the preceding chapter, falling as it does in the category of a native colonial history. While Daly's writing included a preface from then–Prime Minister Forbes Burnham, Ruhomon's is endorsed by the then-governor of the colony. Born in 1880, Ruhomon is part of the class and generation of Indians who first began to move off of the plantations, thereby coming in greater contact and conflict with blacks. He is the brother of Joseph Ruhomon, recognized as the "first" Guyanese Indian intellectual.[30] Peter Ruhomon is part of a generation sent to schools rather than kept in the fields, in spite of the fact that they would be taught by blacks and would be more exposed to Creole cultural influences. He is part of the generation that first poses a problem in Mangru's narrative because it represents a shift away from India and an identity as Indians (first colonial and then national). As a history that chronicles this shift away from the culturally insulated world of the plantation, Ruhomon's history comes directly out of an anxiety over Indian social status, especially because many were uneducated due to the lack of enforcement of the Education Act and few entered the civil service or politics. At the time of the writing, there was a conflict between Indian identity as defined by those who remained on the plantation and those who moved to the towns to be educated.

Placing himself as one in a line of British historians and as a preserver of the Indian experience in the colony, Ruhomon delineates a singular purpose for his history that locks Indian labor and life in the Caribbean into a narrative of progress linking Indo-Caribbean peoples to colonial development and capital accumulation through their initial position as laborers, setting up the basis for belonging through labor. He achieves this by informing readers that "it will be the Author's main purpose to prove by the incontestable evidence of *facts* that Indian immigration has not only been the salvation of the Colony, . . . after the abolition of Negro slavery, . . . but that the Indians, themselves, have proved to be the most valuable assets to the industrial welfare of the Colony, as is evidenced by the development, through their unaided efforts, of the rice and cattle industries."[31] Ruhomon's discussion of the role of Indians in the colony and the results and reasons for their introduction produces an economic claim that anticipates later work, such as Mangru's history. Ruhomon writes extensively of the state of ruin most plantations fell into due to the significant drop in land under cultivation, after blacks left the plantations. He eventually agrees with a local commission report and finds that the "sole" reason the colony was being swept back into its "original, native chaos" was because of the "scarcity of labour."[32] Using British imperial documentation to support his claim, Ruhomon endorses the imperial view that what was encountered in the New World at the time of discovery was not in fact civilization but anachronism and that labor is the path to civilization. In other words, the land is nothing without its transformation through the application of the techniques of modern labor, both coerced and free. This is of course an image that still governs the contemporary relationship to the (native) interior. Ruhomon goes on to cite a commission report that claims that most black workers spent their time in "absolute indolence." "These observations," continues the report, "must be understood to apply principally to the native population, for the immigrants worked more continuously and steadily, although physically inferior to the Creoles."[33]

Like Mangru, Ruhomon uses available colonial sources to tie Indians to (imported, English) cultivation and development as opposed to (native) "chaos," linking them with a teleology of progress from which blacks are excluded. He references other documents to attest that blacks, who function as natives in his narratives, were adverse to hard labor and that Indians were able to provide stable labor for Guyana and other colonies where they were sent to work. The immigrant status of Indians not only secures their cultural difference from blacks but as later arrivants, they effect change on a now stagnant (less productive) native landscape that requires their civilizing labor. Ruhomon entirely devalues blacks' contributions to the sugar industry over Indians', citing a Des Voeux Commission report that claims "'the prospect of making sugar out of the black population had vanished and that from this time forward the remedy was immigration.'"[34] In his repeated assertions that Indians were, in his words, the "salvation of the Colony," Ruhomon's history clearly demonstrates a central fact of ethnic historical writing in the colonial period that has carried over into the postcolonial one.[35] It under-scores that the historical and rights claims of each group must be made against those of other groups and that Guyanese history is a collection of divisive ethno-nationalist claims that for majority groups are embedded in labor.

Both Ruhomom and Mangru use the comparison to slavery as a key strat-egy in asserting the significance of Indians in the colonies, identifying the move off the estates by indentured laborers as a transition into a free state. In other words, the transition off the estates (which can also be seen in light of Monar's distinction between the estate and backdam areas) is as impor-tant for Indo-Guyanese as emancipation was for blacks. Thus it is not the "freedom" of Indian independence in 1947 that liberated Indians in Guyana, but something altogether different. In support of this perspective, Ruhomon cites a discussion of the land settlement schemes Indians entered into after their contracts expired. He quotes Lord Salisbury, identified as the secretary of state for India in 1875, as saying "Indian settlers, who have completed their terms of service to which they agreed . . . will be, in all respects, *free men*. . . ."[36] In a chapter titled "Indians as Colonists," he elaborates on the conditions of Indians postindenture, which, in previous chapters, he stated was an improve-ment from conditions in India. According to Ruhomon, "The Indian is no longer content to remain as a Cinderella in the household of British Guiana but is determined to take his rightful place at the Council Board and help decide the future destiny of the Colony."[37] Ruhomon continues this line of reasoning in a subsequent chapter on "The Rice Industry," arguing that its development, which he notes at the time is second only to the sugar industry in the colony, shows the Indian's "usefulness as a colonist."[38] While blacks in Walter Rodney's work humanized the landscape, Indians in Ruhomon's have made their mark in developing it by serving as colonizers. The latter is more valuable than the former in Ruhomon's narrative because it coincides with ideas of national development and progress. The comparison to slavery is thus not meant to equate Indians with blacks but to suggest that Indians performed as great a labor on the land as when blacks first arrived on a *terra nullius* that they then fundamentally changed with their labor.

Nearing the end of his history, Ruhomon discusses the improvement of the Indian condition in British Guiana over that in India. He writes, "Here in this Colony, the immigrant breathed the air of a new freedom,—thanks to the influence of Western contacts and Western Institutions—and whatever remained in them, of hope and ambition, of courage and manliness. . . ."[39] As further evidence of the better conditions experienced by Indians in the colony, he does not cite Indians, but rather Henry Kirke, a former sheriff "who knew the Indian in his native home in India. . . ."[40] Kirke bears out Ruhomon's contrast between life in India and life in the then-colony. Ruhomon himself adds that after indenture, "possibilities" arose for Indians, possibilities of "amassing a competence and rising to a full consciousness of his manhood and individual worth. . . ."[41] Ruhomon continues, arguing that "from what [Indians] have already achieved in the conquest of the land, . . . the Colony is theirs and 'the fullness thereof.'"[42] For the colonized subject, this history achieves what a history at independence, with a black prime minister, does for blacks: it articulates and secures belonging through a particular relationship to the land, here as colonizers in the name of both Britain and India, and with Burnham, through Daly, as postcolonials. Ruhomon characterizes the "national awakening" among Indo-Caribbean peoples, spurred by visits from Indian delegates, and reflective of "a growing pride in the consciousness of race and the cultural heritage that has been bequeathed to them."[43] Ruhomon's history ultimately serves a legitimating function for Indian culture in the New World. By relying on colonial historical and administrative documents to lend fact to Indo-Caribbean claims, it also secures an Indo-Caribbean cultural right to the land as part of an Indian narrative of progress.

The histories of Indo-Caribbean writers are evidence of a singular tension between history and diaspora that frames Indian modes of belonging and their own evolution into new natives in the Caribbean. Clem Seecharan has written that "wherever Indo-Guyanese live today—in derelict Guyana or in the second diaspora: New York, Toronto, London, etc.—visions of India will not leave them. . . . To Indo-Guyanese, this India of the imagination is real; it instructs, inspires, and sustains them. . . ."[44] In *India and the Shaping of the Indo-Guyanese Imagination, 1890s–1920s,* Seecharan argues that it was an image of India—the India of the nineteenth-century valorization of Hinduism, and particularly its Aryan origins inaugurated by British intellectuals (Orientalism)—that formed the core of Indian "cultural resistance" in Guyana.[45] For Seecharan, it is this image of India that comes to circulate in the diaspora and that inspires those like Joseph Ruhomon and other educated Indians through the early part of the twentieth century, who Seecharan suggests were looking for a way to counter the image of "the menial, ignorant 'coolie.'"[46] This image of an epic, ancient India was so strong, according to Seecharan, that it delayed Indian integration into Guyanese society and the fight there for labor rights through the formation of labor unions.[47]

It instead contributed greatly to postindenture colonization schemes, the ultimate goal of which was to produce an extension of India in Guyana. It led to a view of the struggle for independence in India as a nationalist struggle for all Indians, a perspective that was fostered by Indian nationalists like Nehru.[48] Seecharan writes, "This unambiguous identification with a 'New India' . . . strengthened Indians in the colony psychologically. . . . It also inspired hopes for the future, for the freedom of India, which until the rise of their own leader, Cheddi Jagan, after 1947, Indo-Guyanese, in an instinctive, millennial way, interpreted as coterminous with their own freedom, their dignity—an elemental act of repossession; a catharsis. . . ."[49]

Although much can be said of this image of India and the way in which it alternately led to identification with both the British Empire and Indian nationalist struggle, of importance is the way in which Seecharan connects an idealist India to cultural and psychological formation and resistance, and particularly the way in which for the upper classes, this image of India becomes divorced from labor and from the Indian laboring body as "coolie." Further, Seecharan identifies in Joseph Ruhomon's work a "watershed in the transformation of the Indo-Guyanese psyche" as he and subsequent writers seek to "gnaw away at the deep-rooted construct, 'the coolie.' . . ."[50] It is Seecharan who counters Joseph Ruhomon's negative assessment of Indian achievement in British Guiana ("We have done nothing in the Colony that has redounded to our credit . . ."). He does so by pointing to the fact that "something *was* being achieved," indicating that Indians were laying a foundation for future economy.[51] In Seecharan's work, labor serves to justify Indian belonging, while in Ruhomon's and other earlier work social progress necessarily meant some amount of rejection of an identity in labor, but only after demonstrating the civilizing effect of that very labor.

The previous discussion illustrates that in Indian histories, labor is put to particular ends for representing national identity and right. Madhavi Kale's work reveals this in her exploration of the role that labor has played as an economic, analytic, and ideological category. Kale looks at Indian indentured labor as imperial labor, not labor migration, to reject sequential narratives of indentured migration from India to the British Caribbean. According to Kale, this trajectory obscures the mutually constitutive histories of the British Empire in India, the Caribbean, and Britain.[52] Indian postslavery indenture in the Caribbean, Kale argues, must be understood in a new way. She rejects the predominant causal and linear narratives for indenture that see it as the solution to a labor problem. This is a view put forward not just in imperial documents and has become part of popular historical narrative and research, such as the introduction to a 2008 volume of the anthropology journal dedicated to the Indian Diaspora in the Caribbean, *Man in India*. In his introduction to the journal issue, Kumar Mahabir, for instance, claims that the labor shortage brought about by abolition was a "catalyst" for indenture, despite the efforts of at least one contributor to argue that it was not.[53] There is also the introduction by David Dabydeen and Brinsley Samaroo to their edited volume, *Across the Dark Waters: Ethnicity and Indian Identity in the Caribbean*, in which they cite the "abandonment" of plantations by blacks. In the latter collection, black abandonment of plantations is reiterated as a justification for Indian indenture in the essays (see, for example, Verene A. Shepherd's and Ralph Premdas's chapters) but is never questioned. *Across the Dark Waters* itself is interested in the break that separates being Indian in India from being Indian in the Americas, and the work in the volume is not so much sociological as cultural exploration and preservation. Kale, however, argues that indenture must be understood not as any singular history of a population or nation but as a feature of empire and the manipulation of the category of labor by planters, abolitionists, recruiters, and others for different financial or ideological ends.[54] She writes that "both planter's claims of labor shortage and the archives in which these claims are preserved were synthetic political projects."[55] For Kale, indenture cannot be understood simply as labor migration or the result of "labor shortage," a view that has been produced by its manipulation in colonial narratives and flawed analyses based on those records. She instead argues that the entire basis for indenture and for the antagonism between blacks and Indians, as well as that which allows Indo-Caribbean peoples to invent a new narrative as colonizer or settlers, is just an "argument" reflective of the "technologies of plantation sugar production."[56] "While conditions in Trinidad and British Guiana were crucial to the development of Indian indentured migration to these colonies," Kale writes, "they were not determining, and the relative portability of capital and labor constrained each differently according to extra-local as well as local conditions, discursive as well as material."[57]

Kale's argument and its framing within the sphere of empire is fundamentally different from the way in which labor has been cast by both blacks and Indians as they seek to assert rights, the ways in which labor moves from the power of empire to that of the production of subaltern histories, oriented ultimately by the notions of progress that culminate with the postcolonial nation. It is therefore not an argument that can be accepted if the present foundations for political and cultural right are to continue. However, her claims make clear that what has been refashioned is not just the category of labor but the real and discursive technologies of power through which it was constituted in empire, and this is what is so difficult to overcome. Kale herself acknowledges, especially with her discussion of the 1884 killing of Indians in Trinidad celebrating the Shia Muslim festival of Hosay (Tadjah in Guyana), that Indian identity was in no way reducible to the labor they performed. It is labor (subaltern labor in India–cum–historicized labor in the Caribbean), however, that produced new methods of belonging in the New World that were creolized. When it came to political subjectivity, Indians used black modes of establishing both political and cultural right, such as representing themselves as colonists, as happens in Ruhomon's narratives. However, it is labor that has come to serve as an origin narrative: a narrative of imperial expansion and productivity or power that has been refashioned into one of or for subaltern right. It is Jagan himself who represents both a break from this looking toward India, as Seecharan notes: a break through labor and his focus on the class struggle. In other words, this tension between diaspora and history that, for example, led Joseph Ruhomon to use the term *East Indian* to refer to all Indians in the Caribbean (a concept of race noted here as being carefully and strategically uncoupled from labor) is ultimately resolved in Jagan's figure, which marries idealist visions of India with the material—with labor. The notion of a "spirit of progress" that marked early Indo-Caribbean intellectual idealism inheres in the anticolonial and post-colonial attitude toward labor. In fact, a notion of progress circulates throughout all of these texts. Joseph Ruhomon himself links what it means to be human to "individual and national progress." According to Ruhomon:

> Go wherever you may, from one end of the earth to another, from east to west, from north to south, and evidence is not wanting to show us that the world is deeply impregnated with this spirit. The *car of progress* is ever marching forward. Mankind is growing wiser, better, and more enlightened under the purifying influence of civilization. . . . Humanity is no more to be . . . confined . . . as in the by-gone years, when so many pernicious and dwarfing influences existed to hinder the acquisition of knowledge and individual and national progress.[58]

Later, as he continues to talk about progress in Africa, which he notes flows first from Egypt, he claims:

Darkest Africa is no more darkest Africa since Livingstone and Moffat and Stanley and Baker and others have gone there and scattered broadcast Christianizing and civilizing influences that have paved the way for great moral and social reforms. In that once midnight-dark country full of ignorance and superstition and wickedness of every kind, the golden light of knowledge has broken.[59]

Ruhomon's notion of racial progress is tied to Western influences and the acquisition of wealth and social status. This is made clear by the examples of Indians and blacks who have achieved such status, although blacks are necessarily associated with a spatial past ("darkest Africa") that for Ruhomon marks their greater cultural and racial backwardness. Ruhomon engages the British imperial history of conquest and exploration (Livingston, Moffat, Stanley) that subordinates the non-European world and essentially uses it to map a particular future for Indian culture in the colony. Ruhomon, who never mentions Amerindians in the 1894 pamphlet, presents an idealist view of culture and humanity. Despite his profound challenge to the colonial image of Indians, his intervention is Orientalist. It also subscribes to eighteenth-century Enlightenment ideas of the triumph of reason over bodily irrationality and a very Hegelian notion (although it is not clear if he knew of or read Hegel) of progress, one that is and continues to be the rationale for empire. The later histories of his brother Peter Ruhomon and of Basdeo Mangru therefore reflect a shift from an earlier mode of articulating Indian identity that rejected an identity based in labor, which was not a factor in loyalty to the British empire. The shift, reflected more profoundly by Peter Ruhomon's work, comes about precisely in the 1940s with the rise of anticolonial struggle in the colony, more firmly directed at the empire at home. It is in light of this shift between ideology and labor that I locate Jagan's significance, which I discuss shortly. The shift is the substitution of an ideology of progress and subsequent telos with regard to labor, culminating in national belonging or belonging to the state. For blacks, labor (sugar) and prior arrival confront and shape the articulation of Indo-Caribbean labor (rice and sugar) and Arrival Day.

Indian historian Dipesh Chakrabarty has offered a Marxist critique of history that claims that non-Western histories are in a position of perpetual subalternity compared to European history. Chakrabarty claims that "'Europe' remains the sovereign, theoretical subject of all histories, including the ones we call 'Indian,' 'Chinese,' 'Kenyan,' and so on."[60] Chakrabarty suggests that even new methods of gathering historical material are still biased. The focus, therefore, should not necessarily be on removing Europe or simply privileg-ing other forms of evidence and evidence gathering. A new method should expose the way in which "its reason" inhabits other attempts at writing his-tory and "has been made to look 'obvious' far beyond the ground where it originated."[61] While Joseph Ruhomon's work is not a history, it is engaged in an act of recovery and, along with Peter Ruhomon's and Basdeo Mangru's writings, reflects the way in which Indo-Caribbean identity comes into view and is articulated through the history of empire through a relation to West-ern subjecthood.

All the works discussed here seek to transform Indian identity from frag-ment or break. The form of subjectivity they seek to uncover or recover, however, is based on the particular narrative tools of empire and colonial domination. Part of Indians becoming Creole is not necessarily their cul-tural creolization but this way of thinking about identity that represents an ontological shift structured by different moments of becoming. Indian iden-tity in the New World is born of the challenge posed by diaspora(s) and its relation to empire and the attempts to imagine themselves as historical sub-jects within the break produced by the trip across the *kala pani*. In their arti-cle in *Man in India,* Ellen Bal and Kathinka Sinha-Kerkhoff describe the "only published autobiography of a first generation . . . indentured . . . labourer," which they helped translate, as reflecting an "aesthetics of migra-tion" that captures the "ontological insecurity" of self and community that the voyage represented. They demonstrate how the author, Munshi Rahman Kahn, moves from an Indian identity to a diasporic concept of "self."[62] To a large extent, the development of the term *coolitude* to express Indo-Caribbean identity and processes of creolization also captures this. It must therefore be theorized as a particular counterculture of modernity, to borrow from Paul Gilroy, but one that is framed by and challenged by that narrative. The chal-lenge faced by current scholarship, suggested by Kale's work, is that in dis-cussing Indo-Caribbean history and subjectivity, we still do not have adequate methods. Subaltern studies, for example, is configured around a particular project of historical articulation that is determined by relationships of power that were different for Indians in the Caribbean and that, given Mishra's claim, leads to the question, How in fact are Indians who went through the indenture process subaltern? Does the late twentieth-century currency of the term in application to broader groups of subordinated peoples apply to them, and does it remake them as subaltern? Further, comparisons of inden-ture with slavery continue to complicate a discussion about Indo-Caribbean subjectivity and the emergence of a critical historiography that does not still depend on imperial narrative, as did the nineteenth-century project of Indianization or creolization of the educated classes. Ultimately, when *kala pani* histories confront black Atlantic histories, they change how each must be theorized and understood because of the different, racialized status held by blacks and Indians in the opposition between labor and capital under empire.

Following, I conclude the exploration of Indo-Caribbean historiography with a discussion of Cheddi Jagan, who comes to serve a particular role in the production of Indo-Caribbean identity (according to Seecharan as "their own leader"). His presidency reflects a firm shift from myth and imperial labor to a national identity yet one that profoundly abuts and is informed by imperial history even as it is articulated by a "new" labor, his/story.

Recreating Indian Belonging: Jagan and the Labor Struggle

After roughly thirty years as opposition leader in Guyana, Cheddi Jagan finally gained control of the government with his election as president in 1992. The unfair system of proportional representation that was first engineered by Burnham and the British government to keep Jagan out of office finally ushered him in. On December 15, 1997, Guyana held presidential elections following Jagan's death.[63] The party in power at the time, the PPP, retained its political majority, and, as noted in chapter 4, government control has, to this date, remained in the hands of the PPP. Thus far, however, the Indian-led PPP has not realized the socialist democracy envisioned by Cheddi Jagan. The party is routinely criticized for its control of state media, and in 2002, due to internal pressure, it considered removing all Marxist rhetoric from its constitution. Further, a wave of racial violence against Indo-Guyanese and anti–PPP mobilizations intensified after the 1997 election.

In Georgetown in 2002, the Cheddi Jagan Research Centre opened. The Centre offers memorabilia that include images of Jagan from his well-known labor activism and independence struggle to postage stamps on which he appears with former U.S. President Bill Clinton. These contrasting images of Jagan as both anticapital and pro–United States reflect a profound ambivalence and contradiction in how the nation has sought to remain stable and compete on the global stage, and how Indo-Guyanese and Indo-Caribbean peoples in general have created belonging and established political and cultural rights. It also becomes incredibly problematic when viewed against Peter Ruhomon's earlier mobilization of British imperial history to articulate a discourse of Indian progress and superiority in then British Guiana. More specifically, do we read it as a continuity with imperial narrative, or does Jagan's labor platform represent a significant break in the ability of Indian belonging to draw upon imperial narrative? I explore this first through discussion of an event, mentioned in the introduction for its monumentalization, cemented in the Guyanese imagination as a "massacre" and the place it holds in Jagan's discourse on labor.

On June 16, 1948, five striking sugar estate workers on the Enmore plantation were shot and killed by police who were trying to keep the hundreds of striking, largely Indian workers out of the compound. Under Burnham, a monument was erected to honor the lives lost. In 2009, the Guyana Agricultural and General Workers Union (GAWU) commemorated the sixty-first anniversary of the event. In his speech to commemorate the killing, union president Komal Chand claimed that the reasons this brutal event turned out to be the last of its kind in Guyana's labor history was due in large part to Cheddi Jagan's entrance into the legislature and his advocacy on behalf of labor, and to the 1946 formation of PPP predecessor, the Political Affairs Committee (PAC).[64] Chand's view is in keeping with other Indo-Guyanese narratives, particularly PPP, about the event.[65] The five workers, who eventually became known as the "Enmore Martyrs," had started striking a few months earlier for better working conditions and in support of their union, the Guyana Industrial Workers Union (GIWU), with which the Sugar Producers Association (SPA) would not negotiate. The SPA instead chose to recognize the Man Power Citizen's Association union (MPCA), with which the striking workers did not identify. Occurring nearly ten years after the last violent end of the workers' struggle and, consequently, in the moment of a more solidified independence movement, the Enmore deaths famously became the main impetus behind Jagan's lifelong dedication to labor struggle. In his introduction to a collection of Jagan's speeches, Hon. Moses V. Nagamootoo, then the senior minister of information in Jagan's cabinet, referred to the strike and subsequent deaths as the "roots" of Jagan's efforts on behalf of labor. According to Nagamootoo, the Enmore Martyrs Monument "overshadows and, at the same time, embodies Dr. Jagan's historic mission" in indirect reference to the cover of the collection, which superimposes an image of Jagan's head over the monument.[66] Jagan himself has said that the event led to his "silent pledge" to work for labor rights. In various speeches as president, he repeatedly went back to the event, which, in conjunction with political gains since that time, is now a marker of progress. Speaking in

1993 on the anniversary of the killing, Jagan affirmed that "we are meeting today to pay tribute to our comrades who fell under colonial bullets in 1948. They made the supreme sacrifice so that Guyana and its people could live better lives. . . . " Continuing, he proclaimed, "We must be prepared also to sacrifice because without struggle there can be no progress."[67]

For members of the PPP and particularly Jagan supporters, Enmore clearly marks the beginning of a legacy of political activism. His remembering of Enmore as part of a continuous line of labor struggle allows him to reclaim from Burnham's legacy a monument that works for his own. In his speech, Jagan identifies himself not as having been an activist who is now president, but as an activist president still very much engaged in a continued anticolonial struggle that may require further bodily sacrifice. It is this kind of language that in the 1950s and 1960s led to U.S. fear of his potential Marxist-communist bent. However, in contrast to the way in which Jagan and his supporters have represented the Enmore event, black historians Maurice St. Pierre and Vere T. Daly see it differently. St. Pierre, who devotes three short paragraphs to Enmore in his *Anatomy of Resistance: Anti-colonialism in Guyana 1823–1966,* recognizes what the event meant for Jagan's career and labels it an "important shift in political activity" in terms of organizing.[68] Vere T. Daly, in his *A Short History of the Guyanese People,* makes no mention of Enmore. Instead, it is the fight of enslaved peoples that he sees as the "first steps to freedom" for Guyanese people. In contrast, in Chand's speech at the sixty-first anniversary of the event, as well as in Jai Narine Singh's *Guyana: Democracy Betrayed* and Jagan's speeches and writing, Enmore emerges as a symbol of the largely and singularly Indian commitment to worker's freedom, especially after the 1955 PPP split and Burnham's subsequent identification not only with oppressive governmentality but on the other side of Jagan's commitment to labor reform. It also emerges, with this commitment, as the first strike for the larger political struggle that led to independence. The 1948 event represents a before-and-after in Guyanese politics and society. When Jagan says at the 1993 anniversary that "we honour Cuffy, because he and others fought against slavery. We honour others who fought against indentureship, a different form of slavery," we see the emergence of a break in the line of continuity, where antislavery and anti-indenture agitations constitute one type of struggle at a given historical moment, and Enmore in the mid-twentieth century constitutes another.[69] Through Jagan's speeches and the images of him at the center, Enmore is literally recreated by subsequent political struggles, by Jagan's efforts on behalf of labor, and through the act of remembering. Simultaneously, it marks the recreation of Indo-Guyanese subjectivity and resolution of the earlier ambiguity surrounding origins in the New World: between volition and coercion and history and diaspora.

Staunch Marxist that he was, Jagan framed his commitment to social justice and workers' rights as a struggle against alienation, saying to workers in a speech to the Guyana Public Service Union (GPSU) that "they must share what they produce."[70] For Jagan, a reconciliation of labor and capital, which as president he saw being affected by his administration, is key in achieving the disalienation of the Guyanese worker. In numerous speeches, Jagan sought to reassure workers of the "historic" alliance between them and government.[71] Conversely, government commitment to and effort on behalf of labor reflected the PPP's legitimacy.[72] According to Jagan, "This country has suffered because the Labour Movement and the Political Movement became divided and if we do not correct that we are going to continue suffering in the future. Foreign domination takes different forms today from the ones in the colonial era."[73] On the one hand, Jagan appealed to foreign capital and, on the other, he sought to limit its potential for neocolonial domination. Jagan, for instance, repeatedly expresses fear of returning to being "Bookers Guyana."[74]

While I draw from other speeches, the collection *Rooting for Labour* is unique in capturing Jagan's language with regard to labor and his mobilization of memory and remembering as a key discursive strategy in discussing labor and in representing his PPP as the "working-class party" in government.[75] For example, according to Jagan, the "new beginnings" in the title of his speech to the GPSU, are "rooted in our working class past."[76] In his 1993 address at the Enmore monument, Jagan says, "So, as we remember our Comrades it is good that we remember from where we started and to where we have come."[77] In that speech, he calls for a new social "ethic" and says that "I don't live in the past but we must never forget the past."[78] He also claims to "remember" what others do not. In his speech in *Rooting for Labour* titled "The New Beginning and the Way Forward," Jagan makes other references to the past, at one point saying that although he doesn't want to dwell on it, it must be put in "perspective."[79]

Jagan actively worked to produce an image of himself as the labor president, and the subordination of the past to memory is key. The Jagan Centre, in its photographic depiction of his political life in Guyana, emphasizes this commitment with numerous photos of him at the head of labor protests. Despite Jagan's reference to himself as a "dialectician" concerned not only with the economic situation, the center and his speeches establish a clear line of progress charting his evolution from activist to president to gains in workers' rights since Enmore. The "past" and its ability to be subjected to a specific process of memory and recreation by Jagan not only gives his government credibility but boosts his credentials as well. The past becomes central as a measure of progress that legitimates his PPP in its commitment to labor. While he continuously stresses the need to "overcome the vestiges of the past," Jagan himself keeps the past current.[80] Jagan's nation building is fundamentally different from Burnham's in that the former hopes it will cohere around social justice and the images produced in the worker's struggle, not abstract cultural images. In this regard, in a speech on the Guyana Prize, a literary competition, Jagan identifies the role of the artist in "rebuilding our society" as one that is less about imagination than about communication.[81] For Jagan, literature is reduced to the use value of education, communication among Guyanese, and the ability to "reflect itself in the daily lives of actual people."[82] The new "global human order" that Jagan sought was less about the imagination and more about gains for the working classes and the curtailment of global capital in the realignment of democracy with human needs.[83]

Despite his emphasis on labor, Jagan has (un)wittingly created a legacy for Indians in Guyana in which their struggle and sacrifice are connected to the future of the nation. His links with the Indian independence struggle (via Nehru) and black struggle in Africa, including his evocation of the anticolonial cry UHURU ("Freedom"), are central in his evocation of a "nexus between Cuffy in 1763, 1946, 1966 and October 5, 1992."[84] As noted earlier, 1946 marks the formation of the organization that has been identified as the PPP predecessor, the PAC. Cuffy has new meaning in Jagan's election, not in independence in 1966 under Burnham. The anticolonial struggle, represented by Cuffy, becomes allied with the labor struggle and specifically with Jagan's labor commitment, which is solidified by Enmore and the ability to keep the event current. Jagan has always claimed to be above racial and ethnic division, something reiterated in his speech marking the anniversary of the arrival of Chinese to Guyana. In this speech he affirms the good of "permissible ethnic expressions and activities," which presumably do not engage in the kind of historical rewriting with which he charges the Burnham administration.[85] However, labor is already racialized, and the continuing evocation of a particular past by Jagan and by others becomes a specific Indian narrative of progress that embraces the same labor teleology that blacks had under Burnham, even where its modes of articulation are different. In Jagan's *Selected*

Speeches, Amerindians are excluded from this timeline and are discussed only in terms of the already established Amerindian Task Force and the Amerindian Development Fund that his office planned to create.[86] Ultimately, Jagan represents progress and futurity in Guyana in the transformation in the labor relationship. Change in that relationship, effected by government, is essential to neocolonial struggle and is the link between past anticolonial efforts and the present.

Although black belonging is predicated on prior arrival, forced labor on plantations, and the creation of an imagistic nationalism of new origins (Burnham), through Jagan, Indian belonging is produced through the change in labor relations and gains for workers. Both are based on labor but in different ways, and both necessarily position Amerindians outside labor and the future it guarantees. While Mishra and Kale suggest that indenture propelled Indians into history, specifically imperial history, that history is also the history of their alienation. Through Jagan, the labor struggle reflects a challenge to alienation and the reproduction of Indian identity in anticolonial labor history, not imperial labor history. Jagan's is the supreme effort to remake indenture not as that which curtailed black labor rights—rights that they had only just begun to acquire with emancipation—but as that which propels all "workers" to take greater control over their own labor power. It is literally the baptism of soil, where labor struggle represents the "hour of creation" (Monar) of a new humanity and the transformation of "East Indians" as a *race* embedded in imperial labor to Indo-Caribbeans as indigenous and postcolonial. Jagan ultimately does not undo the narrative of Indian salvation of the colony, precisely because his narrative of remembering the past in order to move forward continues to mobilize it. However, in this instance, the colony is not so much being saved from financial ruin, as it is in the narratives of indenture that predominate, but from neocolonial domination. The racialization of identity, especially concerning labor, occurs because of this conflict between imperial history and labor and newly freed black labor. El Dorado, as that which captivated and enticed Indians, is transformed via labor into something solid or tangible, as the product of labor struggle. While Jagan and Burnham are quite apart in their political and labor philosophy, both reveal the way in which subaltern settler populations come to belong through recourse to labor and, initially for both, Marxist discourse. More pointedly, Marxism offered the affirmation of certain subjects. As Chakrabarty reminds us, "The category 'capital' . . . contains within itself the legal subject of Enlightenment thought."[87] The transformations from the derogatory *coolie* and East Indian to Indo-Caribbean reflect both the transformations of Indian culture in the Caribbean and more significant, the transformation of Indian relationships to labor. A politics and poetics around labor for Afro- and Indo-Creoles provides a mode of history and subjectivity that achieves the rescripting of indigeneity, in spite of differences in how indenture and postindenture, slavery, and emancipation are narrated. Therefore, those who challenge not only labor inequality but the current discourse in which the production of identities through labor are articulated as profoundly Western and anti-indigenous will always be positioned on the outside of both postcolonial history and humanity in citizenship.

CONCLUSION

Despite early attachments to India, indentured Indians were not considered truly or purely Indian. South Asian novelist Amitav Ghosh has argued that because Indian culture is "constructed around the proliferation of differences (albeit within certain parameters)" it is possible to say that "anybody anywhere who has even the most tenuous links with India is Indian; potentially a player within the culture. The mother country simply does not have the cultural means to cut him off."[88] His claim, however, has not rung true and does not address the creolization of Indian culture. In other words, what Ghosh refers to as "difference" within a culture is not the same as creolization. Thus, when Ghosh defines Indian Diasporic belonging by arguing that "to be different in a world of differences is irrevocably to belong," he is optimistic, but he misses the very complex way in which Indians outside of India belong not necessarily to India but to its diaspora. They are part of the diaspora through culture, and as I sought to demonstrate with this chapter, a *difference* as historical subjects that is not shared by other Indians. This difference led Indians to make claims for belonging and rights in the New World that both drew upon imperial discourse, as we saw with the discussion of Peter Ruhomon, and that represented a significant shift—though not a break—from those modes of being continuous with empire, as we saw with Monar and Jagan. However, in the most glaring ways, postcolonial nationalism inherited the system of inequality at the core of European nationalism that it had defined itself against.

Forbes Burnham relied upon economic egalitarianism and a socialist program to create a cooperative nationalism distinguishable from the more radical Marxist ideology of Cheddi Jagan and Cuban communism. It was a brand of postcolonial nationalism that could strategically be allied with socialist ideas and still preserve the inequality that allowed the middle and upper classes to remain the economic base for the regime.[89] Further, a defining character of this particular "style" of imagining the postcolonial nation was Burnham's ability to draw on concepts of territorial nationalism within European nationalism in order to give occupation (during slavery) the status of historical and cultural right in independent Guyana. Jagan's "style," in contrast, relies on labor struggle as the new basis for a shared nationalism, but it is still one that cannot identify all as workers and one that fundamentally engages in the rewriting of history for specific groups. It is possible that the narrative could have been different with Jagan in power, especially with Jagan's leftist ideology and continued emphasis on anticolonial politics.[90] However, by the time Jagan regained power, political discourse in the country was already a continued negotiation of this politico-discursive legacy, bound as it was to the discourse of myth and history in the region. Thus, while Jagan's presidency signaled a potential shift in the discourse and execution of ethnic nationalism in Guyana, his presidency instead reflected a consolidation of Indo-Creole belonging as indigenous despite his differences from Burnham. Thus, Burnham's politico-discursive legacy remains the singular mode for articulating national identity and historical subjectivity for Guyanese in an economic language closely bound to historical right. It is a language that Indo-Guyanese necessarily confront and engage, in seeking to assert their place in Guyanese history and politics; thus Indo-Guyanese belonging has both been modeled upon and departs from modes of Creole belonging established by blacks. The problems Indo-Caribbean peoples faced in securing political freedom, material success, and belonging are a direct result of the plantation mode of production and the ways in which it produced colonial societies and diasporic populations.

Conclusion:
Beyond Caliban, or the "Third Space" of Labor and Indigeneity

> And, although Shakespeare was great, we cannot merely
> continue to act out the part of Caliban.
>
> —SPIVAK, *A Critique of Postcolonial Reason*

THIS BOOK BEGAN BY HIGHLIGHTING A DISARTICULATION BETWEEN the modes of being and belonging of Indigenous Peoples and Creoles in the Caribbean that congeal around labor. Its principal argument was that the ways in which Creoles indigenized, or came to belong to the Caribbean, particularly after emancipation and during the anti- and postcolonial periods, have led to the material and discursive displacement of the region's Indigenous Peoples. Thus, the aim has been to demonstrate that while the political map of the modern Caribbean continuously shifts as power changes hands, the socioeconomic map has long been established between the discursive formations of European empiricism and capitalist social and material processes, between myth and nation, and between "interior" and "coast." Within these formations, subaltern (a mostly corrupted descriptor of postcolonial criticism) settler groups, largely blacks and Indo-Caribbean peoples, have simultaneously resisted colonialism, become indigenous, and with lasting results for social being in the region, deployed a new understanding of indigeneity that can support modern belonging and the institution of themselves as new natives.

Creole Indigeneity took as its principal object Guyana's social and political history as well as its real and cultural geography to show how contemporary Creole identity can express a particular ontological need: of the urgency of transforming exile into the substance of belonging. This need has been reinscribed or repeated in Caribbean discourse as a governing and inescapable logic—the flaw and epistemic condition of our uneven postcoloniality—and it has been satisfied through Creoles' ability to transform the labor of enslaved peoples into what I referred to in chapter 1 as the "new time of belonging" for new native identities within the postcolonial state.

Guyana's difference as a non-island space makes visible the way in which Creole social and political subjectivity reflects a dual difference and deferring: a difference from the colonizer and a deferring of the existence of Indigenous Peoples. In the organization of Guyana's postcolonial geography, with which this book began, we can see the structure of a difference that intimately informs Creole subjectivity or the constitution of an "I" or ego. This "I" in its dependence on European philosophical and social history has a limited ability to extend full humanity to all, as Achille Mbembe remarks: "We should first remind ourselves that, as a general rule, the experience of the Other, or the *problem of the "I" of others and of human beings we perceive as foreign to us,* has almost always posed virtually insurmountable difficulties to the Western philosophical and political tradition."[1] Having engaged this tradition in the quest for political sovereignty and transparency, the "I" of Creole being that represents the political, economic, and ontoepistemic shift from subaltern settler to a new indigeneity for blacks and Indians, is necessarily structured in, and hence limited by, modern labor and the Hegelian notion of history as progress: maintaining an antithesis or outside that has been sociohistorically produced. This "new" indigeneity ties Creoles to material accumulation derived from coastal plantation labor, while indigenous identity is associated with deprivation as Indigenous Peoples emerge as the material and ontologically necessary other of Creoles materially, discursively, and temporally. Thus, Creoles have essentially effected a material rerouting and rescripting of indigeneity *in* labor and continue to reproduce colonial modes of social being that are tied to the local political economy.

Creole Indigeneity's emphasis on material labor—in conjunction with the pre-plantation discursive economy of myth (chapter 3)—as the axis and aporia of Creole and indigenous identity is not meant to suggest that Indigenous Peoples do not mobilize around labor for their own rights claims (such as the indigenous struggle in Bolivia today), nor to ignore modes of belonging that hinge upon formal connection between Indigenous Peoples and Creoles, such as those evinced by the Garifuna of Belize and the black Caribs of St. Vincent, Dominica, and Honduras. These points of connection between Indigenous Peoples and settler groups not only structure people's lives and provide alternative models of social and political belonging, but they are garnering increasing attention in the academy.[2] The links between nonindigenous and

indigenous cultures are an important redress to the continued disarticulations that force Indigenous Peoples and the descendents of enslaved and
indentured peoples to argue for sovereignty in vastly different terms, recently
exemplified in the United States by Cherokee revocation of citizenship status
to descendants of slaves owned by the Cherokee.[3]

However, with this book, I have sought to demonstrate that Creole modes
of belonging, especially those of blacks and Indians in the Caribbean, require
Indigenous Peoples to remain subaltern with regard to postcolonial history.
It is then against this position of subalternity that the Creole subject comes
into being as both native *and* historical within the postcolonial state, which
as a patrimony secures the teleology of labor that undergirds Creole being.
Even as, for example, Haitian blacks continue to constitute a racialized, laboring underclass throughout the hemisphere and elsewhere, Indigenous Peoples
are forced to remain productive but are policed by others with a new genesis
in "limbo."[4] Their displacement is a key feature of postcolonial epistemology
and is essential for the Creole subject's ability to articulate belonging as both
a national with rights to the land and a subject of a cultural discourse meant
to reflect and ensure those rights. It is not just, as some have argued, that creolization "elides" Indigenous Peoples; they are in fact *central* to the creation
of Afro-Creole social and political subjectivity (chapters 1 and 4) and, by
extension, Indo-Creole subjectivity in which these majority groups seek an
identity as natives as they secure political power (chapter 5).

Creole Indigeneity demonstrated how this mode of being and becoming
for Creoles rested on the reification or doubling of the labor on the land by
enslaved peoples and the way in which this process was Hegelian or "Calibanesque." It did so by elaborating the ways in which the master–slave
dialectic is reproduced for both political subjectivity (the small man versus
the real man) and social and cultural being (peasant versus native). In its
instituting through Caliban's indigenizing function, the dialectic comes to
shape our politics and discourse, as we saw with the Burnham regime, and
in the elision of indigenous culture in the literature, history, and theoretical
production of the region. An exegetical approach to Caliban in chapter 2,
as cultural figure and critical subject, revealed how what was once colonial
textual illegibility becomes a founding moment in the establishment of Creole poetics. The linguistic labor of Caliban's speech and the discursively
rendered physical labor he performed for early modern subjectivity are critical in the establishment of Creole subjectivity as part of a generalized practice of belonging. Caliban, as an appropriated literary figure, thus serves an

ontological and ideological function essential for Creole being, and more specifically, the writing of that being or subjectivity in the ideology of the dominant class that controls his representation in discourse. This *writing* and yoking of the materialist and discursive traditions establishes the new historical role of Indigenous Peoples. No longer confined to the prehistory of Western metaphysics and historiography, Indigenous Peoples move into the place formerly designated for blacks, the beginning of Caribbean history. There they function as crucial markers of material progress and as the necessary *other* for the postcolonial enactment of Creole subjectivity as a negative dialectic of being. This feature of Caribbean discourse—a result of the Hegelian paradox of being—is the basis for postemancipation forms of social and political discourse, cultural identity, and interaction, and it serves as the model for subsequent groups as they establish belonging *as* social and political legitimacy. The question that lingers is, If the Calibanesque mode remains dominant, where can we go and how do we find new answers for Wilson Harris's question, "What is man?"

Unfortunately, much of the recent work that presents opposed critical practices for articulating black subjectivity (chapter 2) reflects the methodological loggerhead or crisis that plagues black diaspora studies. These positions, either in their endorsement or rejection of the model put forward in Paul Gilroy's black Atlantic formulation (a crucial axis in black critical epistemologies), reinscribe the same conditions of possibility for literary discourse that exist in social and cultural discourse: labor and displacement. Thus, playing Caliban, to rephrase Spivak, continues to require relationships to capital and sociality that check indigenous freedom and well-being.[5] Creole subjectivity hinges upon a relationship to labor that excludes Indigenous Peoples and thereby prevents them from realizing their subjectivity as actualized by the state and modes of sovereignty that are not colonially derived. Ian Griffith Williams's poem "Revise 29:01" clearly revealed how the modes of sovereignty of Indigenous Peoples that hinge on prior right are, paradoxically, negotiated through a colonially derived legal system with consequences that are, at least for Williams, not only absurd but fundamentally impinge on native identity and rights: "I have to be registered to be an Amerindian."

BEYOND CALIBAN

In my introduction, I located this project in a trajectory of criticism by Caribbean scholars. As I conclude, I suggest that this trajectory is indicative of a significant and overdue shift in Caribbean studies: the move beyond Caliban, or beyond the metaphysics of modern labor. What is at stake in the ability to stop acting out Caliban's role is both indigenous sovereignty and land rights, as well as a rejection of being in terms of capitalism and its continued requirement of master/slave modes of being that cannot account for Amerindian epistemologies.[6] These modes, as I've demonstrated, tie the displacement of the narrative and political position of "prior arrival" to the solidification of black and other Creole modes of settler belonging in the New World. The work that I discuss here indicates that not all ways of being or belonging in the Caribbean are or must be instituted in this way. Indeed, Elizabeth DeLoughrey's turn to Kamau Brathwaite in *Routes and Roots: Navigating Caribbean and Pacific Island Literatures* explores alternative possibilities that still need to be writ large. DeLoughrey's is the first study to not only look comparatively at indigeneity in the Caribbean and Pacific Islands but to focus specifically on the marginalization of the indigenous Caribbean in the region's literature. DeLoughrey's work represents an important intervention in understanding indigeneity and mapping its relationship to literary aesthetics. It marks a significant departure from earlier modes of addressing indigenous presence in Caribbean literature. In her work, the sea, rather than the land, becomes important for establishing a more fluid methodology. She engages Brathwaite's notion of tidalectics and those Oceanic tropes that she claims "resist the teleology of a Hegelian dialectical synthesis." Similarly to Jodi Byrd, DeLoughrey is concerned with how "postcolonial and diaspora studies have tended to displace indigenous discourses. . . ."[7] She articulates her project in the following manner:

> Drawing upon land/sea cartography, tidalectics foreground historical trajectories of dispersal and destabilize island isolation by highlighting waves of immigrant landfalls into the Caribbean. This dynamic model is an important counter-narrative to discourses of filial rootedness and narrow visions of ethnic nationalism. . . . The shift in focus from terrestrial history to the transoceanic spaces that enabled African, Asian, European and indigenous crossings to the islands complicates genealogical roots and destabilizes the colonial architecture that literally constructed the region as European. In this body of literature, water is associated with fluidity, flux, creolization, and originary routes.[8]

For DeLoughrey, the ship precedes the plantation, and consequently, she argues, "Caribbean theories of plantation creolization may be fruitfully positioned in a tidalectic engagement with transoceanic diaspora."[9] In her discussion of John Hearne's work, she finds that his envisioning of the sea as "waste" in *The Sure Salvation* places the nonlaboring bodies in the slave holds of ships in opposition to practices of labor on the land. She claims that blacks arriving on ships were "not yet rooted," which is connected to "a moment of possibility rather than completion."[10] DeLoughrey thus argues for a repository of Caribbean culture that is unconnected with labor and its models of creolization.

DeLoughrey does find, however, that in the novels she examines, Caribbean writers *are* "invested in recuperating indigeneity for creole cultural nationalism" and that "the discourse of nativisim in the Caribbean is inextricably tied to nation-building and the attempt to naturalize a people's relationship with the land."[11] In other words, Creole writers use Indigenous Peoples to "root"; to create a local "past" for the "forging of a sovereign, creolized future."[12] Significantly, however, DeLoughrey reads these efforts as vested with ambiguity and sea movement. She writes that "the impetus to establish a genealogy of belonging to the land (through the folk) in Caribbean discourse must be read alongside Glissant's reminder that the forced cultivation of the plantation system created a lacuna where 'nature and culture have not formed a dialectical whole that informs people's consciousness.'"[13] There is a disconnection between the land and the cultures that reinscribe it. DeLoughrey's work represents a crucial methodological intervention that suggests that through a new, critical approach to Caribbean literature, a new possibility of relation between literature and society can emerge, one in which the "lacuna" or gap becomes productive.

Another significant difference to current social and political modes of organization is posed by the grassroots Red Thread Women's Development Organization in Guyana, founded in 1986 by women as a broad-based, multicultural group that also rejects the "narrow focus on coastal relations that privileges African and Indian Guyanese while obscuring the lives of hinterland and Indigenous communities."[14] Growing out of Walter Rodney's Working People's Alliance (WPA), Red Thread's challenge to ethnopolitics, violence, racism, and poverty in Guyana is firmly rooted in labor. However, in their modes of resistance to such politics and their consequences, the group offers a view of labor that does not, as D. Alissa Trotz indicates, reinforce modes of being in labor that replicate binaristic colonial oppositions. Red Thread, in other words, refuses to organize around social identities based on Calibanesque notions of labor and instead offers alternative social and political forms. With Red Thread, we therefore see mobilization around labor that does not rely on the dominant narrative of labor and hence holds out the promise of modes of social being that are more inclusive. Red Thread's activism and DeLoughrey's elaboration of tidalectics as a theoretical method offer alternative political and critical or discursive practices. They are glimpses of a non-Hegelian way of enacting and reading other modes of being and autoinscription. They locate for us a method and "third space" in the contradictions around indigenous sovereignty that Kevin Bruyneel draws attention to in *The Third Space of Sovereignty: The Postcolonial Politics of U.S.-Indigenous Relations*.

Bruyneel's book centers on how the "inherent sovereignty" of Indigenous Peoples confronts the "spacial" and "temporal" ways of interpreting that sovereignty within the U.S. political system, producing what he refers to as a "third space of sovereignty." This is both a metaphor and critical apparatus constituted through and meant to reflect the ways in which indigenous sovereignty is "neither simply inside nor outside the American political system. . . ."[15] Bruyneel's deployment of a "third space" is crucial for thinking about these relationships and interventions in political struggle. His work also points to the need for a comprehensive study in the Caribbean of the political rights of Indigenous Peoples, as well as their own ways of rerooting in the region, something which my own work does not offer. What Creole Indigeneity does contribute in its emphasis on ontology and epistemology is a look at the imbrications of political (as seen in policies like the Amerindian Act and propaganda such as *Co-operative Republic*), cultural, and historical discourses.

The move beyond Caliban can thus be understood, after Bruyneel's and DeLoughrey's interventions, as a move into that third space—not of politics but ontoepistemology, where how we live and how we articulate this to ourselves in more fluid ways. With these works, we see the rejection of modernist aesthetics in the Caribbean. Native discourse, often reduced to the function of a muse for Creole speech, disrupts dominant representations and undermines the poetics of Creole labor. Following, I briefly discuss the role labor plays in Caribbean literary subjectivity and representations of Indigenous Peoples before moving to Basil Rodrigues's writing. Having framed the introduction of this book with my visit to Rodrigues, I return to his work in its conclusion to suggest that it, in particular, begins to illuminate a mode of indigenizing that does not require cultural and material negation or displacement.

Indigenous Peoples in Caribbean Literature

Depictions of Caribbean subjects vary widely from the more realistic fiction of C. L. R. James and Zee Edgell, for example, to the modernist work of Wilson Harris, producing different foci yet all formally invested in undoing particular structures—historical, linguistic, temporal, narrative—as they write and voice the Caribbean subject. Much of the literature from the 1950s through the 1980s charts the rise of national consciousness in the region, which grew out of the labor agitation in the preceding decades, prompting Kenneth Ramchand to claim that the rise of nationalism and the rise of literature in the Caribbean are coextensive.

Despite the wide variety of literature published in the 1950s, the idea that the labor experience undergirds this fiction has persisted. In the edited collection *A History of Literature in the Caribbean*, Downing Thompson Jr. and Hena Maes-Jelinek offer an overview of the novel in the English-speaking Caribbean. In spite of the latter's caution not to overdetermine any one aspect or element of West Indian fiction, two things emerge as definitive from their separate essays: the role of the peasant and the impulse toward an integrative aesthetic or identifiable culture. In his essay on the early rise of the novel, Thompson turns to George Lamming and his well-known statement about the emergence of truly West Indian themes or subjects. Lamming has forcefully argued that what defines Caribbean literature is in fact the broad representation of peoples and classes (the common people, the peasantry, the petit bourgeoisie, the middle and upper classes). This is possible because, according to Ramchand, the "social consciousness of writers" is not a "class consciousness."[16] In his turn to Lamming, Thompson quotes one of his most famous descriptions of the Caribbean writer:

> The West Indian novelist did not look out across the sea to another source. He looked *in* and *down* at what had traditionally been ignored. For the first time the West Indian peasant became other than a cheap source of labour. He became, through the novelist's eye, a living existence, living in silence and joy and fear, involved in riot and carnival. It is the West Indian Novel that has restored the West Indian peasant to his true and original status of personality.[17]

Put differently, the rise of the novel, impossible without the growth of an educated elite, saw the centering of the Caribbean subject in a figurative landscape meant to reflect it. The simultaneous exploration of the subject (presumably either whole or fractured behind the mask of colonialism) hinged on representations of the folk and of the peasant, particularly the black Creole peasant. According to Maes-Jelinek, the novel "tends to be oriented toward the folk and the community. . . ."[18] She goes further to argue that "Caribbean consciousness" in the novel is "shaped by a common experience of transplantation, slavery, and indentured labor . . ." and that "all West Indians descend from forced or voluntary migrations, throughout their history, first to the Caribbean and, after World War II, to Britain and North America."[19] Maes-Jelinek identifies a "common experience" of displacement and labor as central to the conditions of production and content of the West Indian novel, conditions that, as we have seen in earlier chapters, play an important part in producing political rights. I center on Lamming's position on the peasant, which we also see in Ramchand's historiography of the West Indian novel in 1970, where he suggests that the novel does not represent specific class consciousness or interests, but the "whole society."[20] In this regard, Lamming's quotation reveals the crucial connection in Caribbean aestheticism between culture and labor on two levels: first the labor of the peasant to the culture of the peasant ("riot and carnival"); and second, the labor of the peasant to the culture or class (location) of the writer. Lamming's prepositional arrangement is revealing: where *in* must refer not just to West Indian society but specifically to the class interests of the writer, and *down* signals the class location of the peasant at odds with that of the writer, even in syntax. Despite Ramchand's claim that the consciousness of the writer is not one of class, Lamming not only suggests that representations of the peasant are indeed instrumental to the formation of an indigenous literary aesthetic in the Caribbean, but the implication is that there is a poetics of labor that defines Caribbean literature as the epistemic condition for its production of Creole subjectivity. Thus, reinscriptions of the peasant in Caribbean literature are instrumental for middle-class Creole subjectivity. In contrast, Indigenous Peoples who have not been so thoroughly identified with labor as the basis for literary subjectivity have been less well represented in the literature.

In *The West Indian Novel and Its Background*, Ramchand includes one short chapter on Indigenous Peoples. He observes that the limited and often stereotyped representation of Indigenous Peoples in Caribbean fiction reflects their larger social and cultural marginalization in the region. According to Ramchand, who does not gesture at the possibility of an Amerindian literature in the region, "The aboriginal Indian seldom appears, and is not a centre of social or political interest either in verse, in drama, or in fiction by writers from the West Indies."[21] At the time Ramchand's work was published, the only writer seriously invested in depicting native characters in fiction was Guyanese writer Wilson Harris who, Ramchand wrote, "discovers relevance in the Indians. . . ."[22] According to Ramchand, Indigenous Peoples are central to Harris's exploration of self and origin in the exploration of the Caribbean psyche. It is precisely because Harris is not invested in social realism, Ramchand claims, that "he is able to use as symbols not only the topical African presence but the socially 'irrelevant' Indians."[23] Harris, in his own essay on the Amerindian presence in the Caribbean, has said that realism is a "dead end."[24] Harris thus tries to advance a new architecture of signs in order to represent the native presence in the region, suggesting that tools for understanding or apprehending it in language might not exist.[25]

In an earlier work, I have discussed Harris's use of the native woman to house an integrated Creole psychic subject that reflects all ethnic groups and historical trajectories in the Caribbean.[26] Here, I point to Harris's rejection of realism and plantation-based narrative veracity, as signaled by Ramchand, as useful for representing Creole psyche as a *native* self beneath the layers of symbolism and history. What emerges in Harris's work is not necessarily a departure from the metaphysics of modern labor (read again the departure from realism) but a borrowing and depiction of indigenous culture in order to chart a movement away from realism. In other words, the modernist rejection of realism frames the representation of an indigenous literary presence, thus making it subject to an aesthetic move that may not have been significant in Indigenous Peoples' own literary articulations of subjectivity but undergirds Creole ones. While Harris's work represents a difference, it also suggests that the difference in representation between the peasant and the native is also indicative of the tension between realism and (post)modernism, which is also reflective of the attempt to change the dependence of subjectivity on labor. Thus the native emerges as part of this effort, rather than in his or her own terms and conditions of speech. Conventional literary techniques for encoding the subject are still heavily dependent upon class and location, and few Indigenous Peoples narrate their own existence in this way. Thus Indigenous Peoples serve and continue to serve as national symbols, obdurate muses, and self-effacing ventriloquists, where plantation logic underwrites postcolonial cultural and social organization.[27]

Some of the more well-known texts in Caribbean fiction that involve representations of Indigenous Peoples are Herbert George de Lisser's *Arawak Girl*, Beryl Gilroy's *Inkle and Yarico*, Wilson Harris's oeuvre, and Pauline Melville's *The Ventriloquist's Tale*. Lisser's early work rehearses the Carib/Arawak divide in retelling the story of Columbus's fourth and final voyage to the New World. He clearly values European aesthetics even as he writes of the New World native rejection of Columbus. Notably, Lisser deliberately depicts Indigenous Peoples as the "present" owners of the land at the time of Columbus, something that both points to what's to come with colonization and simultaneously suggests that there can be other, equally legitimate owners; ownership is not a permanent state.[28] Beryl Gilroy is also concerned with that early period as she inverts the relationship of connoisseurship in eighteenth-century works that revise the myth, so that the European is the collected object rather than the native.[29] The work that comes closest to dealing with the rerooting or creolization of Indigenous Peoples in the Caribbean is Pauline Melville's, which positions itself as a critique of structuralism and the influence of Lévi-Strauss. The novel offers a commentary on European anthropological and literary tradition as well as tries to deal with the cultural and other forms of uprooting faced by a native and Scottish-descended family, the Mckinnons. This is represented, for example, when one of the main characters, Chofy, takes up with a white woman in Georgetown, representing a larger erosion of the native cultural self. At the outset of the novel, the native narrator announces himself and "vanishes" in what can be read as a comment on the third-person structure in writing but also on the practice of writing as representation and of reading as understanding and deciphering.

Although Melville's book represents a significant change in how Indigenous Peoples are represented, its critical reception is still in terms of the dominant categories of modernism, postmodernism, and so on. As such, questions emerge not only about the literary traditions in which indigenous characters are depicted but about our approaches to writing by Indigenous Peoples, especially those who have experienced their own processes of creolization. To what extent do we see them in terms of this opposition between realism and (post)modernism? How do we read indigenous literature not in terms of the dominant categories and oppositions that support the Creole? How instead can we view them with an eye to that third space or mode of articulation that does not force indigenous culture to be corralled off from indigenous sovereignty? It is with these questions in mind that I turn to Basil Rodrigues's work.

The "Third Space":
Basil Rodrigues's Indigenous Aesthetic

Basil Rodrigues is a Lokono/Arawak educator, community organizer, song-writer, and poet from Guyana. For nearly all of his adult life, Rodrigues has worked to educate various groups of Amerindian peoples in formal English and to revive, preserve, and transmit native culture and history. In 2006, I traveled to his home in Santa Rosa on the Moruca reservation. In our conversation and in his biography, which bears the title by which is he affection-ately known, *Uncle Basil,* Rodrigues has spoken of his early youth in Waini, his move to Moruca, his time teaching and training to be an educator in the south Rupununi, and finally his retirement and return to Moruca. Here I discuss Uncle Basil and his work through two filters. The first is the inter-view and conversation that I conducted on my visit with him, and the sec-ond is the 1998 biography written by Justin Greene-Roesel, then a graduate student doing fieldwork who spent a year in Guyana and eventually tran-scribed Rodrigues's life story. The biography includes photographs and some of Rodrigues's songs and poems, accompanied by Greene-Roesel's anno-tated explanations. The matter of framing is essential to my discussion here because it involves Rodrigues's own construction of his life; the first repre-sentation is shaped by Greene-Roesel's fieldwork, and the second by my ques-tions and responses. Further, many of Rodrigues's songs were performed publicly to highlight Amerindian heritage in Georgetown, providing an ini-tial context of national culture for some of his songwriting. Rodrigues's fram-ing raises questions about access; cultural, ethnic, and geographic privilege; disciplinary methodology; ethnography; and the complex issue of represen-tation, of speaking for and about.

In the introduction, Greene-Roesel describes the biography as essen-tially an historical and ethnographic project. "The process of making and becoming text," writes Greene-Roesel, "is especially important since very little ethnographic work exists on Amerindians in Guyana, and particularly on the Arawaks and Waraos of the coast. . . . Through Basil's life and work, *Uncle Basil* offers an ethnographic sketch of a village and several communi-ties in the space of almost three quarters of a century."[30] Greene-Roesel's introductory narrative seems to reflect some of Rodrigues's own anxiety about the futurity of Amerindian culture, when Greene-Roesel writes:

> Basil's re-invention of a modern Amerindian cultural life stands particularly
> against the prejudice and processes of acculturation that indigenous peoples

have for centuries endured. The songs and poems acknowledge change in Amerindian communities, but while exalting the traditions of the past, they portray Amerindians as the definers of their own futures.[31]

And later, "Basil Rodrigues' life history . . . narrates the post-modern processes of self-definition of an individual and several communities struggling with cultural change."[32] Greene-Roesel's introduction highlights something of the academic approach to indigenous studies. Regardless of Rodrigues's own articulation of his life and the processes of acculturation and creolization faced by Amerindians, such as in the poems "Arrow and Bow" and "Lament of a Hunter," Greene-Roesel's self-conscious framing of it as the production of "text" that has formerly been missing, one which can "add to the 'storybooks' (history books)" leads to an approach to Amerindian culture as that which must be preserved because it is a culture that can only survive through textuality.[33] It is an implicit recognition and positioning of native culture as having been defined as a culture of the past, and yet is postmodern through change. Time then becomes the central factor in what we recognize as Amerindian culture, and ethnography is both the means of identifying what the culture was and is and its gateway to futurity, modern legibility, and textuality.

Greene-Roesel's juxtaposition of Rodrigues's creative work to his narrative about his life, and his own commentary as constituting a cohesive ethnographic object, highlights the relationship between textuality and ethnography as well as the difficulty of writing about a people or culture that is always-already the function of a relationship to Western time as it organizes disciplines, texts, and interpretive strategies. It calls attention to the difficulty of both textualizing and "reading" Amerindian narratives because of the very different and peculiar experience of Amerindian subalternity.

In Rodrigues's narrative, poems, and songs about his life and Amerindian life, several themes emerge, including the loss of language and culture, change, and nature. In describing life for Arawaks, Wapishanas, and others, Rodrigues talks, for example, about the informal, noncapitalist, or barter systems that existed among peoples and that have eroded, he says, as more money has entered relations of exchange. He discusses community and compares the rapid deterioration of it and of community structures of authority for those living near the coast with those living further in the interior. Following, I focus on themes of change or movement and labor that appear throughout the biography, but I pay particular attention to their appearances in the form of a poem or song. I frame this section as an informal engagement with Elizabeth DeLoughrey's exploration of globalization, creolization, indigeneity, and of what she terms "urban indigeneity" when she notes the consequences of creolization for Native Americans as being ontological (anxiety) and material.[34] DeLoughrey rejects the essentialist positioning of the native as outside of what is considered modern, something that Greene-Roesel unwittingly does and that I want to dislodge as a frame for reading Rodrigues's discussion of change.

In Rodrigues's narrative and work, the issues of cultural change and loss he presents are not typical. He was born in the Waini area and spent nearly all of his life in the interior, largely between the Rupununi and the coastal reservation of Moruca. He and his family lived in Georgetown only for a brief period of time while he was completing teacher training. The cultural change that Rodrigues witnesses with Amerindians is not singly based, measured, or experienced as erosion because of coastal influence, but it is also understood through the cultural preservation he witnesses by Indigenous Peoples, such as the Wai Wai, who live further south. Further, cultural loss is not limited to those things that are native, that is, languages and practices, but things that have become native. Many of the Indigenous Peoples in the interior who were exposed to Portuguese and Spanish priests, for example, have over time come to speak Spanish and have absorbed some Spanish and Portuguese culture, which is slowly being lost with greater influence from the coast. Thus what is changing in the late twentieth and early twenty-first centuries for indigenous cultures is already the result of a creolization process that involves relations of exchange outside the plantation.

In chapter 4, I discussed Jean LaRose, who represents the small number of Amerindians who have professional lives in Georgetown. Rodrigues's experience offers an alternative way of viewing the shift in native relationships with land, culture, and internal change both in terms of and as distinct from globalization. One of the most striking things about his experience that has surfaced in the biography, our interview, and in his creative writings is the concrete way in which he experienced the change from living near water in Moruca, to which one travels by boat, to living on the Rupununi savannah. He talks about how difficult it was to adjust to having to walk everywhere rather than take a boat. In our interview he refers to the trip to the Rupununi as "going into this strange land."[35] In the biography, he says of the journey to Sand Creek, "I am accustomed to paddling around, not to walking 50 miles in one day and night, which I had to do."[36] That experience is so significant for Rodrigues that he notes the change in his song "Back to My Canoe," about his decision to return to Moruca. Greene-Roesel, possibly in conversation with Rodrigues, writes that the song contains a nostalgic reflection on childhood experiences and refers to the "exhaustion" of the work in Rupununi; a desire for a more peaceful life and a call to Arawaks and other Amerindians who have retained their culture "to rest a while"; and to "return to the values, the sharing and unity of traditional Amerindian culture; in a metaphorical sense, to return to their canoes."[37]

Chorus:
I am going back to my canoe
Back to my canoe, where the Moruca waters flow. . . .
The rivers beckon me
to float so silently
as I used to do
With my paddle by my side
On my canoe as I ride
Gliding with the tide.
What a pretty sight
to see the birds in flight
and canoes up and down
The rippling waters near
Making shadows look unreal
In the setting sun.[38]

On its face, the final part of the song seems to be a simple description of a phenomenon, the river at sunset. What is noteworthy, however, is the power Rodrigues ascribes to the river. In other songs, Rodrigues openly uses apostrophe. Here, however, the speaker's movement at the beginning shifts and becomes secondary to the river's movement and its ability to transform what is real. Shadows, already ephemeral, become even more so with the river's current. In marking this as a return, Rodrigues is undoubtedly chronicling a loss, as Greene-Roesel indicates, and a desire to "return" to older cultural values. However, it is not just a loss of childhood, youth, or culture; it is the loss of an experience of culture and place conditioned by the river, an experience of the body in relation to nature that is determined by the rivers and is altered by living in the savannah. Part of Rodrigues's experience of himself as Arawakan is this relationship to nature, which changes when he lives with the Wapishana. This shift in Rodrigues's understanding of himself is and must be seen as just as important as that between other forms of material change caused by more globalizing forces. Attempts to frame native culture in terms of loss due to external globalization miss the internal patterns of movement, change, and globalizing that also condition what it means to be native, and they speak more profoundly to the ongoing processes of indigeneity in which Indigenous Peoples are involved. While the forces that shape the move from coast to interior are global, the movement itself is understood or interpreted in specific cultural and ontological terms. Further, the desire to return to one mode of native life is marked here as a desire to return to the past, but it is the past of Rodrigues's life only, not of Amerindian life in general. It is not a past, in other words, with regard to Western culture.

Rodrigues is often ambiguous about the role of Western culture. In many of his pieces, he writes of its intrusion, which in one poem is clearly referred to as a "new light" that "threatens my traditional way." Throughout, change causes him to be, as the piece's title indicates, a "merry Indian no more."[39] This sense of happiness denoting a prior experience of *being* Indian is complex, and I want to read it through Rodrigues's preoccupation with Amerindian pasts in two other pieces, "Sun Mountain" and "I Shar Toon." The first work appears in the biography, after the narrative section about his years at Shea Rock, where he conducted his own school. According to Greene-Roesel, "Sun Mountain" is a song for children that has to do with nostalgia, "freedom," and a relationship to nature that coastal Amerindians do not share.[40] The chorus and the body of the song work in two different ways. In an excerpt from the chorus, Rodrigues uses apostrophe to address the mountain: "Sun Mountain, Sun Mountain/What mystery do you hide from us?/Sun Mountain, Sun Mountain,/Your suns and daughter you should trust."[41]

The remainder of the short song, performed at Amirang, the National Conference of Indigenous Peoples in 1994, talks about those people, the "Savannah natives" and their "panoramic view." The song belies a greater working through of the connection to the past than nostalgia. It is a negotiation of the contemporary relationship to native pasts and/or as history, which the poem "I Shar Toon" makes more clear. Greene-Roesel writes that "I Shar Toon" reflects his preoccupation with the "need for Amerindian cultural and historical continuity."[42] More important for this study is the dimension of the preoccupation with the past and, precisely, the "inquiry into the origins of the village Aishalton, its heritage and the motivations of its ancestors," as Greene-Roesel writes.[43]

Aishalton is the blessed place
Where my life began
What fun in hunting, fishing
Returning, fish in hand.
I wonder now who first came here
Way back in that bygone year?
Who first drove his post to ground
In this graceful land which mountains surround?
Who first came to build his home
And make these ancient names be known?
But lo! We glean our answers without fail
From this our ancient grandfather's tale.
The cavemen from westward came
To a fertile valley and abundant game.
What a land they saw, what a glorious land!
Source of life for me and for my band.
We shall build our homes and lay our graves
And carve our legacy into the rocks and caves.[44]

Both "Sun Mountain" and "I Shar Toon" speak to something that is more often considered a Creole phenomenon: the question of origins. This question comes from Rodrigues, who is obviously more creolized with regard to coastal and other native cultures; however, the creolization has worked differently and the question speaks for many native groups as it removes native history from an abstract, calcified past or absolute origin to a living thing. In "Sun Mountain," Rodrigues endows the mountain with some "secret" that its children and descendants wish to discover, and of which they wish to be worthy. In that poem it is the land that serves as origin, though not in an organic or simplistic way. Throughout his work, Rodrigues chronicles that exchange between human and Earth that transforms landscapes and produces life-sustaining food: "We shall build our home and lay our graves." "I Shar Toon," however, transforms the secret of Sun Mountain and in answer to the speaker's question, "I wonder now who first came here/Way back in that bygone year?," there is a narrative response, "Grandfather's tale." Both offer two different approaches to native histories and origins. In the first, a dialectical or reciprocal relationship to nature holds an inviolable truth about origin, precisely because it can't be known; in the second, migration precedes nature's role in defining the culture, and it is this that produces layers of narratives (grandfather's tale; "Carve our legacy into the rocks and caves"; and Rodrigues's poem) that re-embed native histories.

Rather than produce a version of native histories that are akin to myth, as is often the case, and as I demonstrated with the myth of El Dorado in chapter 3, Rodrigues offers a history that is actively engaged with, shaped, and reshaped by the "question" asked by successive generations and how they choose to answer it. Even when myth is a factor, as it is when he describes building a house on land that, according to myth, is haunted, the myth itself is questioned for its current relevance and in that instance disregarded. The answers and questions modernize native histories within the terms of creolized native culture, not Western culture.

In our interview and throughout the biography, Rodrigues talks frequently of the erosion of native cultures and the need to preserve them. For example, he mentions the younger generation preferring the more Creole-identified musical style reggae and other increasingly global cultural products to native traditions. He says he is almost "ashamed" of being native in part because of the profound condition of poverty or lack of material things that it implies, as well as the notion of cultural backwardness or lack of sophistication.[45] This, however, is juxtaposed with other moments when Amerindians choose progress over tradition. At one point in Rodrigues's narrative, for example, he talks about a challenge faced when the *toshao* of a village did not want him to teach craft work. According to Rodrigues, the village got rid of its toshao and kept him, the teacher. This and other moments speak directly to Amerindian modes of creolization and progress with regard to the West and coastal colonialism but that are not necessarily singularly determined by either. What I am trying to highlight here are the processes of creolization and cultural accretion that occur. As I noted earlier, one of the cultural losses Rodrigues mentions is not just the loss of Arawak language but of Spanish, which the older generation spoke due to the influence of the Catholic Church. In contrast, the Wapishana, for example, have had the Bible translated into their language. This creolization is best understood through the poem, "By Candlelight."

I wake at dawn and grope around,
patting for a light,
for the box of matches
left there last night.
With a shake and a scratch
A grumbling flame explodes

and my faithful *jumbie lamp*
springs to life.
As if on guard, the *hanaqua*
calls to wake the other birds
And soon the air becomes alive
with varied melodies.
Sleeping shadows expose themselves
to my flickering sentinel
and I begin my studies
by candlelight.[46]

The light in the other poems that represents Western cultural knowledge is not positioned here as something exterior to Rodgrigues as a native person, hence the claim about his ambiguous relationship to the dominant "Western" Creole culture. It is one that is now fundamentally part of his existence, and it changes and renews every dawn of self and culture. This is not a simple contrast of native culture as backwardness or darkness (shadow) to Western culture, but an expression of creolization that is reflected in the complex issue of identity. Following is his response to a question in our interview about how he identifies himself in which he privileges national identity over ethnic/racial identity:

> As Guyanese first. Yes, I think that I like to be first as Guyanese, because we must be recognized as a nation, as a people. We are getting so much trouble through race and all that in Guyana. Next as an Amerindian. Not necessarily an Arawak, but as an Amerindian because we have one culture. Although it varies a little bit here and there. But all Amerindians in Guyana eat Cassava, live on Cassava. So that's one thing that they do. They suffer under the same conditions here as in Mabaruma, as in Rupununi in that they are discriminated against. They are discriminated against by the Indians, by the Blacks, and by the government still.[47]

About his writing, however, Rodrigues says that especially because there are fewer of them, he would prefer to be known as Amerindian/Arawak. Rodrigues's claim of a national identity foregrounds the common condition of subordination of Indigenous Peoples and also a common culture connected to something that has to be harvested (labor) and the product of which is the maintenance of Amerindian cultural life.

Rodrigues contemporizes native histories, and he does something with native labor that is crucial for how we understand its role for Creoles and Indigenous Peoples in narrative. Throughout the narrative about his life, Rodrigues talks about the kinds of labor that he and other Amerindians performed, from carpentry, to working in mines, to bleeding balata trees in the production of latex and rubber, to teaching. He talks, for instance, of trying to do mine work, except that most workers were "negro" and instead he was tasked with doing their laundry.[48] In our interview, he discussed labor that is often not seen in Georgetown. In the song "Karaudarnau," also preoccupied with origins, he refers to the balata men, who are the entire subject of the poem "Balata Worker." This poem chronicles the seasonal labor of balata workers, who leave their homes for months at a time to tap trees for their sap. In chronicling the balata workers' job, Rodrigues emphasizes two things: the cyclical and seasonal nature of the work, and the preparation for the trip. The end product of the balata workers' "labour of climbing and cutting/As long as the balata milk is flowing" is not the money received for it. As the poem says, "For the Christmas festivities/He spends all his hard earned money/As the new year rolls around/He departs to find another balata campground."[49] The money is dissolved in the cycle of the work, the cycle of the poem's rhyme scheme, a cycle that goes into sustaining Amerindian customs, life, and celebrations. In the poem, Rodrigues is distanced from this kind of work, which speaks to another distance of Amerindians to other forms of coastal labor. It is not that they do not perform it, but the labor is first conditioned by their marginalization to plantation work and by the way in which that labor, and the racial/ethnic social organization it has produced, continues to generate a rather ethnicized relation to work. This is reflected above by the unwillingness to see Rodrigues's Amerindian body as a laboring one with regard to mining.

According to Greene-Roesel, since balata "bleeding" is no longer common, the poem "is designed to record and preserve the lifestyles and labours of those Amerindians and others who relied on the balata trade to supplement their livelihood. It particularly describes the cycles of labour performed in the trade and the impact of the balata industry on the physical geography of the region" as well as the "movements and the animation of families, labours and locations by the cycle of rains."[50] This relationship to work, however, still persists with the mining industry, and as Rodrigues notes in our interview, it is still very common for men to leave for months at a time to look for work in the mines. Although, however, labor is a part of native life, it is not uniformly modern. All of the labor, balata or mine work, is contrasted with hunting and fishing as ways of living upon the land and doing that type of subsistence labor. What emerges is a difference between how Amerindians experience labor and the way labor is represented as part of an aesthetic—as outside the teleological relationship to labor that influences dominant Creole aesthetics. Their work is not any less in the service of the production of a Creole-native subject, but it is one that fundamentally still depends upon labor as immediate sustenance, as opposed to labor that must be converted into money or wealth, or more specifically labor that ultimately represents alienation through commodity fetishism. Ironically, native youth may in fact be moving to a more "normative" Creole identity through material desire.

In our interview, Rodrigues describes how he came to write poetry and songs after being captivated in the late 1940s and early 1950s by the Hank Williams music he heard on a gramophone. He said that he "fell in love listening to this man playing these Western songs" and this, in combination with the "loneliness" he experienced when he went to Shia, in the Rupununi, led him to writing.[51] He spoke about the role of Catholicism, the Spanish-speaking elders, and the fact that he did not pass the Arawakan language, Lokono, or Spanish along to his children. He can speak Wapishana better than Lokono. Further, it is from his experiences traveling in Guyana that he considers himself Guyanese first, even as he works to have Amerindian culture recognized nationally, and despite the fact that he says independence meant little to Indigenous Peoples when it happened. Throughout the interview and in his biography, Rodrigues describes an Amerindian life that is creolized. In other words, he is Creole, but his process of creolization is distinct and results in a differently produced modern Amerindian subjectivity. There is thus a fundamental gap between Rodrigues's experience and articulation of creolization and the Créolistes' proclamation of Creole identity as a reflection of experience. When Rodrigues talks, for example, of the Harrapo, a Venezuelan dance, or mentions the influence of Brazilian rhythms in native dance, he is presenting us with an image of native culture in relation to borders and national cultures that are in turn creolized by native culture. Rodrigues's image of creolization is not based on negation; it is not antinationalist, nor is it consolidated by the moment of independence. It is also not configured through modern plantation labor, although these "peripheral economies" of mining, in terms of location and the time in which they were developed, have some relation to them. The reservation, as a space that incorporates and negotiates with coastal governmentality and multiple national cultures, must be understood in Guyana at least as an alternative to plantation-based epistemologies and organizations of labor.

The alternative to Creole identity that Rodrigues presents, despite concerns about the loss of culture, is one that instead of subverting difference in fact has a tense relationship to it. Labor is also configured pre- ("who first drove his post to ground") and postcolonization. Native identity in the interior is not shaped across time by that teleological relationship to labor that produces the nation-state as a patrimony and produces the Creole as citizen-subject. Rodrigues does not aestheticize Amerindians as peasants, not because they aren't or because being a peasant represents a certain kind ideological investment, but because their effective relationship to labor is not capable of being represented within those terms in so far as the peasant can be understood through the nation-state. Amerindians are typically associated with peripheral economies (peripheral both monetarily and within the historical development of the country) and surplus labor. They are thus culturally and materially outside what is Creole. However, while Rodrigues does not represent them as peasants, his work is also not antirealist or postrealist, or even conventionally romantic. His writing as someone who is Guyanese and native must be read through the uncomfortable yoking of these identities and the way in which that writing, consequently, not only disrupts the dominant epistemology but reflects a relationship among textuality, culture, and society that rejects articulations of creoleness with modern power. Finally, his work suggests that there is a choice that remains for critical scholarship: Do we continue to read Indigenous Peoples as functioning within the dialectic, and thus see them as we have enslaved blacks and those fighting for independence, as holding the most promising or productive position with regard to labor—that is, as the bondsman who in laboring for the lord has the potential to liberate "himself"? Or, can we identify and accept the ways in which indigenous identity, in spite of its creolization, is located outside the master-slave dialectic and may be, ultimately, beyond Caliban?

In and through the figures of the peasant and the native in the bulk of Caribbean literature, a mode of being is deployed that continues to reinscribe the paradoxes and binarisms that structure Caribbean discourse as a negotiation between the local and the global, the abstract and the real. Caribbean subjectivity is still determined by a consolidating dialectical operation that requires continued objectification, as did European Enlightenment and colonial metaphysics. Caliban was both anticolonial and nationalist, and Caribbean (post)modernity must find a way to extend the oppositions of the former while subverting the latter. I am not suggesting that to be truly postmodern the Caribbean must move beyond labor, but rather to truly exit modernity it must reject the metaphysics of labor deployed in the opposition of the "Creole" self to the "native" other. Further, where politics and aesthetics meet, the state's role in the consolidation of Creole identity as tied fundamentally to the state's role in disseminating capital must be undone. We must reject the way Caribbean social and political thought continue to establish Indigenous Peoples as an object or other: an other with which the Caribbean subject must reconcile, yet one that must always remain on the margins of Creole being as a possibility for the becoming and instituting of Creoles as human, sovereign, and native within modernity.

Acknowledgments

This has been a long and difficult work, and I think that I can say, without too much confusion, that the person who finished this book is not the one who began it. Both thank the following people for reading portions of the manuscript: Koritha Mitchell, M. Jimmie Killingsworth, Nandini Bhattacharya, Christopher M. Sutch (under duress), Charles Rowell, Paul Christensen, and Anne Morey. I thank Robert Griffin for his diligence and guidance in helping me draft a proposal. Yael Ben-zvi faithfully read a first draft of the entire manuscript, sometimes aloud to Yael Ronen, and gave me great feedback. I thank her for her friendship, encouragement, and wisdom.

At Texas A&M University, several graduate research assistants between 2006 and 2010 were instrumental in helping me collect and organize research: Yeonsik Jung, Crystal Boson, De'Jhan Burns, Courtney Stoker, Matthew Davis. The Glasscock Center for the Humanities has supported this project on numerous occasions with Stipendiary Fellowships. Without these fellowships and an award from the Program to Enhance Scholarly and Creative Activities (PESCA), the research would not have been completed. In Guyana, I thank for their help with research the amazing staff at the library of the University of Guyana and Jeanne Whishurt of the Amerindian Research Unit. I owe an enormous debt of gratitude to Basil Rodrigues and his family for allowing me to conduct interviews and giving me a place to sleep when I had none. I thank Jean La Rose, Miranda La Rose, and Francis Farrier for taking time out of busy schedules to allow me to interview them. I thank my wonderful aunt Grace Ann Parris and her sons Ashton and Odel for putting me up, helping me get around, assisting with last-minute permissions, and for a night at the Sea Wall.

Portions of this work were presented at the Modern Language Association, the American Studies Association, the Caribbean Studies Association, and at A&M through the Glasscock Faculty Colloquium. I owe a debt of gratitude to my mentors in graduate school: Sylvia Wynter, for long talks at her home and profoundly shaping my intellectual path; Mary Pratt and Paula Moya, for their work, for always supporting me and showing me how to do so for others; John Rickford, for that little piece of Guyana at Stanford; and the incomparable Arnold Rampersad. Without Shireen K. Lewis and the wonderful women of SisterMentors, I would not have finished the dissertation. I thank the fabulous intellectual community of MTLers at Stanford: Yael Ben-zvi, Maria Ruth Flores, Bakirathi Mani, Lisa Arellano, Mishuana Goeman, Helle Rytkønen, Raul Coronado, Kyla Tompkins, Ebony Coletu, Evelyn Alsultany, Lisa Thompson, Tim'm West, and especially Nicole Fleetwood and Celine Shimizu for their advice and help always. None of us would have made it through without the support of Monica Moore and Jan Hafner.

Although they may not remember precisely when, Sandra Paquet and Carole Boyce Davies provided words of support at crucial moments: Sandra by giving me the courage to finish the dissertation and Carole the courage to finish the book. I also thank Cheryl Wall and Judylyn Ryan, who, when I was an undergraduate, both suggested English rather than accounting. At A&M, I thank Anne Morey and Claudia Nelson for mentorship. I thank Anitra Grisales for editing an early draft of the manuscript. At the University of Minnesota Press, Jason Weidemann has been terrific, as has his assistant Danielle Kasprzak. Without Jason I would never have attended the conference of the Native American and Indigenous Studies Association (NAISA), where I always needed to be. The First Peoples Manuscript Development workshop with Mishuana was wonderfully helpful in the last month of revisions—Mark Rifkin, you are the bomb! Elizabeth DeLoughrey and Jodi Byrd helped tremendously to make this manuscript what it is. I owe them a debt of gratitude.

For seventeen years, Karina L. Cespedes Cortes has been a wonderful friend, from helping me stretch *colones* by sharing boiled cassava and macaroni in Costa Rica to coming all the way to Guyana with me, helping with interviews and sleeping on the floor in Moruca. I thank my writing partner at A&M, Zulema Valdez. For friendship and guidance along the way, I thank Gina Dorcely. My most heartfelt thanks go to Scott Trafton, who taught me how to P.L.O.A.P and so much more. The brilliant and hard-working Faedra Carpenter was there every week, every day, every time I needed her, from coffee shops to long-distance calls. My family has always been supportive. I thank my dad for research help, my aunts, my cousins, and friends—especially Seimond, Nicole, RayeAnn, and Tonia—my beautiful brother Shevon; and most important, my mom for carrying me all these years.

Along this journey, the racism, sexism, and misogyny that are so widespread in this world have at times overtaken me, as has the loss of six aunts and uncles. When I could not get up, when I could not find my voice, the unyielding friendship, dignity, and support of several people helped me through. I thank Nandini Bhattacharya, Kimberly Nichele Brown, and Paul Parrish for helping me get on my feet again. I am forever in debt to Giovanna Del Negro and Harry Berger for helping me to find, near the end of this process, what I searched for in vain for a decade—unrelenting joy. Finally, for Robert Carley, who took my hand junior year at Rutgers to keep it warm and never once let it go, I run out of words.

Notes

PREFACE

1. For a study of Indian music, see: Manuel, *East Indian Music in the West Indies*. I use "East Indian" here to capture the popular way in which Indians were referred to in Guyana in the 1970s and even today.

2. *Buck* is a pejorative term for Indigenous Peoples that has its origins with the Dutch. Very little is known of my great-great-grandmother other than that she was half Amerindian and came from the interior.

INTRODUCTION

1. I have encountered two spellings: *Moruka* and *Moruca*. The first appears in Rodrigues's biography. I use the latter, which appears in newsletters of the Amerindian Peoples Association.

2. The figure of 6,000 years comes from Wilson, *The Indigenous People of the Caribbean*. Newer work such as Mann's *1491* suggests that much of the dating of the indigenous presence in the Americas is flawed.

3. See: Fujikane and Okamura, eds., *Asian Settler Colonialism*.

4. Lawrence and Dua, "Decolonizing Antiracism," 134.

5. Byrd used the term in her Native American and Indigenous Studies Association (NAISA) presentation, "The Masques of Empire."

6. This was reportedly said by Chief Guarionex in November 1511. http://www.indigenouspeople.net/taino.htm.

7. Lawrence and Dua, "Decolonizing Antiracism," 130.

8. Huhndorf, *Going Native*; Deloria, *Playing Indian*.

9. Kwayana, *Next Witness*.

10. This figure is from the 2002 census and is the most current according to the Guyana Bureau of Statistics. Stacey-Ann Williams, in conversation, estimates that the figure is today between 10 and 15 percent, thus making the votes of Indigenous Peoples essential for winning any election under proportional representation (NAISA conference, May 2011).

11. The Umana Yana served as a VIP lounge and recreation spot during the conference.

12. Prime Minister Hinds is one of the few black members at the upper levels of the Jagdeo administration, and he exists in a very tenuous position.

13. Jones, *Towards Further Amerindian Integration and Development,* 54. In the 1970s, Guyana established a Ministry of Information and Culture that is now the Ministry of Culture, Youth, and Sport. Jones's document refers to the former only as the Ministry of Information.

14. Cuffy has an alternate spelling of *Coffy.* Both spellings appear in the historical literature of the region.

15. See work by Daly.

16. Buckley, "East Indians Flee Race Violence in British Guiana Mining Area." The attacks were part of a pattern of recriminatory violence among blacks and Indians, supposedly backed by the PPP and PNC (Peoples National Congress), leading up to independence.

17. In 1969, Martin Carter, then minister of information, referred to the Cuffy rebellion as "the first serious attempt to make a qualitative change in the then existing economic and social relationships . . . ," with the founding of the Co-operative Republic on February 23, 1970, being the most definitive. See Carter, *Republic of Guyana.* See also Burnham, "A Vision of the Co-operative Republic," 9.

18. Burnham, "The Small Man a Real Man in the Co-operative Republic, Guyana," 4.

19. For a discussion of the violence, and specifically its repercussions for women in Guyana, see Trotz, "Between Despair and Hope."

20. This was reported to me by then-CARICOM employee Andrea Watson-James in July 1999 while on a trip to Barbados.

21. Indian Arrival Day is not an official holiday in all Caribbean countries. Arrival in Guyana occurred on May 5, 1838.

22. *Anatomy of Resistance* is one of the few texts to deal significantly with Amerindian rebellion and really foreground their efforts in identifying a broad tradition of resistance in the country.

23. Pateman, "The Settler Contract," 39–40.

24. Mills, *The Racial Contract,* 42.

25. Ibid., 50.

26. Ibid., 50–51, author emphasis.

27. Williams, *Stains on My Name, War in My Veins,* 139.

28. Menezes, *British Policy,* 255.

29. Wallerstein, *The Modern World-System I.*

30. Kambel and MacKay, *The Rights of Indigenous Peoples and Maroons in Suriname,* 11.

31. Benítez-Rojo, *The Repeating Island,* 5.

32. Ibid., 8.

33. See Jackson, "Subjection and Resistance in the Transformation of Guyana's Mytho-Colonial Landscape."

34. This was the subject of a panel on Guyana at the Caribbean Studies Association's 2009 conference that I organized with Nalini Persram (York University): "Guyana: History, Theory-Specificity, Difference."

35. Miller, *The French Atlantic Triangle,* 22.

36. The Carib peoples of Dominica are also referred to as Callingo and Karifuna.

37. See Maximilian Forte's "Extinction."

38. See Castanha's recent book on the Jíbaro of Puerto Rico, *The Myth of Indigenous Caribbean Extinction*. See also research on the indigenous presence in the Netherland Antilles. For excellent work on the indigenous presence throughout the Caribbean today, see Maximilian Forte, *Indigenous Resurgence in the Contemporary Caribbean*.

39. Moberg, "Continuity under Colonial Rule." For discussion of British attempts to use Maya labor in Belize, see Bolland, *Colonialism and Resistance in Belize*.

40. Kambel and MacKay, *The Rights of Indigenous Peoples and Maroons in Suriname*, 16. Previous references to the number of these communities in Suriname and French Guiana are taken from this study.

41. See Tully, "The Struggles of Indigenous Peoples for and of Freedom."

42. See Spivak, "Righting Wrongs."

43. Niezen, *The Origins of Indigenism*, 9.

44. Ibid., 3.

45. See Anaya's *Indigenous Peoples in International Law*. For an in-depth discussion of the historical and contemporary relationship of Indigenous Peoples and the law, also see the following: Lâm, *Indigenous Peoples and Self-Determination*; Nelson, *A Finger in the Wound*; Brysk, *From Tribal Village to Global Village*; Ivison, Patton, and Sanders, *Political Theory and the Rights of Indigenous Peoples*.

46. See Schildt, *The Balance between Indigenous Land Claims and Individual Private Property Rights in Latin America*.

47. According to Ronald Niezen, the ILO is one of the first international groups to support the rights of Indigenous Peoples. What is significant about this for my study is that, as Niezen points out, the ILO's initial interest was in the rights of indigenous *workers* (36).

48. UNFII, "The Declaration on the Rights of Indigenous Peoples," 5.

49. See "Amerindians Divided."

50. The Amerindian Act of 1976 was preceded by three previous ordinances in 1902, 1910, and 1951. The 1951 ordinance is also sometimes referred to as an act. For a brief summary of its history, see "About Laws Relating to Amerindians: History of the Amerindian Act."

51. Menezes, "The Controversial Question of Protection and Jurisdiction Re the Amerindians of Guyana," 13.

52. Menezes, *British Policy*, 259.

53. British Information Services, "British Guiana," 9.

54. Ministry of Information and Culture, "A Brief Outline of the Progress of Integration in Guyana," 6.

55. Marilyn E. Lashey has done comparative work on British colonial policies with regard to Indigenous Peoples in several former colonies. Her work reveals the different strategies, from *terra nullius* to an adaption of indigenous systems that the British employed. Although Lashey doesn't talk about Guyana, it is important to look at how policies evolved there as compared with other colonial contexts. Lashey, "Globalization in Australia, Canada, Fiji, and New Zealand." Also see the following for such a comparative focus: Young, *Third World in the First*.

56. See Davson, "How the Warraus Came," n.p.

57. Ministry of Information and Culture, "Brief Outline," 5.

58. Green et al., "Aboriginal Indian Committee-Interim Report," n.p. The report also updates work of the various agencies and commissions concerned with the protection of Indigenous Peoples, including the Aboriginal Indian Protection Ordinance of 1911. The

final version was published in 1948. The 1959 document by the British Information Service also refers to the British Guiana and British Honduras Settlement Commission of 1948 as one source or context for the provisions of the 1951 policy, but I do not consider that work here.

59. For discussion of the Dutch policy, see Menezes, "The Controversial Question." There is some confusion on the point of who controlled the appointing of Toshaos. According to the Ministry of Information and Culture, Amerindians could vote them in since 1955, but in discussing the revised Amerindian Act, the Ministry of Amerindian Affairs claims that while it could previously appoint them, Toshaos can now be voted in.

60. Bulkan and Bulkan, "'These Forests Have Always Been Ours,'" 143.

61. See Hanbury-Tenison, "Guyana."

62. Ibid., 3.

63. Jeanette Forte, *Amerindian Concerns*.

64. Ibid., 12.

65. Ibid., 8.

66. From Laws of Guyana:

> Power of Chief Officer to exempt Amerindians from the act. {6 of 1976]
>
> 44. (1) The Chief Officer may, where he thinks it desirable so to do, grant a certificate to any Amerindian exempting such Amerindian from the provisions of this Act, and thereupon such Amerindian shall, while such certificate remains in force, for the purposes of any of the provisions of any Act or regulations relating to Amerindians, be deemed not to be an Amerindian.
>
> (2) Any such certificate as aforesaid may, with the consent of the Amerindian, be revoked by the Chief Officer where he considers it desirable so to do.

67. Bulkan and Bulkan reinforce this in their essay when they write that "Amerindians did not provide direct labor power to the plantation economy" ("'These Forests Have Always Been Ours,'" 146).

68. Williams, "Revise 29:01," *Wa-Wii-Wa*, 15.

69. This book's unconventional capitalization of *Indigenous Peoples* throughout, except in quoted material, is meant as a gesture of affirmation of Indigenous Peoples' desire to control their own modes of identification within the Guyanese state.

70. Amerindian Peoples Association, "Amerindian Act Update," 3.

71. Menezes, *British Policy*, 22.

72. Michael Swan also documents this in *The Marches of El Dorado*.

73. Menezes, *British Policy*, 24.

74. Mentore, *Of Passionate Curves and Desirable Cadences*, 11.

75. Ibid., 13–14.

76. "Prior rights" is the name given to Amerindian claims to land that rely on "historical and ancestral occupation." It is based on the idea that they are the first inhabitants of the region and as such should have innate political rights greater than what they have been accorded.

77. Forte, "Extinction."

78. An important exception that significantly includes Indigenous Peoples in its discussion of ethnicity in the Caribbean is the following: Reddock, *Ethnic Minorities in Caribbean Society*.

79. Pitman, *The Development of the British West Indies, 1700–1763,* 61. Pitman notes that in the French territories there were more enslaved Indians, but his work does not discuss them. Further, a narrative of extinction also attaches to Indigenous Peoples of the Francophone Caribbean.

80. See the following, for instance: Ashcroft, Griffiths, and Tiffin, *The Empire Writes Back,* 116.

81. Quoted in Retamar, *Caliban and Other Essays,* 4.

82. In his essay "Extinction," Forte explores this erasure of Indigenous Peoples from the historical record. The reference to it as a "paper genocide" is the phrase of another writer cited in Forte's essay.

83. In *There Ain't No Black in the Union Jack,* Gilroy has talked about this confusion of ethnicity and race (34), and in her work, *Toward a Global Idea of Race,* Denise Ferreira da Silva also addresses the racialization of cultural difference or the misreading of culture as race.

84. Other examples include the following: Joan Dayan, "Playing Caliban: Césaire's Tempest." In the opening lines of her essay, Dayan writes, "After the Amerindians (Carib, Arawak, Taino, and Siboney), the original inhabitants of the Caribbean, were annihilated, and nothing remained but a blankness waiting to be filled by African slaves, a name would remain. The name alone would stand for all that had been destroyed: 'Cannibal'" (125). A. James Arnold has written, "In the Creole idiom of Martinique a *Zindien* designates a member of the local East Indian merchant class, there being no surviving indigenous West Indians (Caribs) in the area" ("Césaire and Shakespeare: Two Tempests," 245, author emphasis).

85. Salinger Ferrante, "Telling Our History," 27.

86. James, *The Black Jacobins,* 391.

87. Ibid., 405. David Scott also quotes the same passage from James's appendix to *The Black Jacobins.* See Scott, *Conscripts of Modernity,* 125–26.

88. Walter Rodney, *A History of the Guyanese Working People, 1881–1905.* Rodney is speaking of a much later time period, and hence of Creoles, while James is speaking mainly of Africans.

89. For a consideration of sexuality and settler colonial nationalism, see Morgensen, "Settler Homonationalism."

90. Burnham's and other leaders' interest in socialism attempted to redress the economic wrongs of colonial society, but, as the problem of racism in Cuba demonstrates, socialism has inherited the biases of the capitalist system and still functions to maintain black subordination.

91. Fanon, *The Wretched of the Earth,* 233.

92. This project is tentatively titled "Working People: Labor and Subjectivity in the Caribbean."

93. Means, "Black Hills Speech."

94. She discusses this in the following and with regard to how biological race works: Wynter, "Beyond Miranda's Meanings," 111, 117.

95. Waswo, "The History That Literature Makes," 545.

96. This reference is from Hintzen's *The Costs of Regime Survival.*

97. See Seth, *Europe's Indians.*

98. Charles Rowell used this term to describe enslaved peoples during a conversation. I use it provisionally here to talk about blacks and Indians.

1. Creole Indigeneity

1. Burton, *Afro-Creole,* 14. Burton's phrasing, "commonly allowed," points significantly to the coercive elements of plantation economy against and within which Creole identity emerges.

2. Creolization is often spelled the British way, *creolisation.* I retain the latter spelling in this chapter when discussing texts in which it appears.

3. Allen, "Creole," 52.

4. Ibid., 53.

5. Allen cites Wynter, "Creole Criticism."

6. Allen, "Creole," 55.

7. Wynter, "Jonkonnu in Jamaica," 36, 39. Wynter's is a complex argument that makes a distinction between plantation identity as leading to the "superstructure of civilization in the Caribbean" and slave plot identity and nonproperty relationships to labor as leading to "the roots of culture" or a second level of society that she elsewhere (see Scott, "The Re-enchantment of Humanism") suggests is the ground for a new humanism (37). She also seems to share the position of Rodney and others about the relationship between nature and labor when she claims that "the African presence . . . 'rehumanized nature'" (36, author emphasis). In "Jonkonnu," Wynter cites Karl Polanyi, who has argued about "the reduction of Men to labour and of Nature to Land under the impulsion of the market economy . . ." (35, author emphasis). She writes that enslaved blacks in the New World "represented both *labour* and *capital*" (36, author emphasis). Although she emphasizes this, she is most interested in showing how it changed the relationship of blacks to nature and its relevance thus for "folk culture" like the dance: "The folklore of the Jamaican sprang out of the slave's attempt to grapple with a new Nature . . ." (36). In "Jonkonnu" she writes that the slave plot made the slave "part slave" and "part peasant," which was one of the "crucial factors in the indigenization process" (35). Wynter's distinction between labor on the plantation and labor for the self serves as a check on the primacy of theories that see Caribbean culture and agency as primarily deriving from the plantation. Further, it does suggest the importance of the difference between notions of "home" that I have discussed and private property either for individuals or industry (here I refer to post-independence nationalization schemes). However, in making the distinction between the locus of labor and hence the forms of production and agency that occur, Wynter's argument does not move us away from labor. More important, Indigenous Peoples are again represented as having escaped "forced labor" and consequently not being "part peasant" and outside of this particular cultural indigenization. Because the work concerns itself with Jamaica, Wynter is forced to repeat the "fact" that "the Arawak Indians died out" (36). Wynter's work endorses rather than critiques this very problematic articulation of the role of labor and the marginalization of native peoples necessary for the Afro-Creole indigenous processes. Further, while slave plot identity could ultimately lead to a nonteleological relationship to labor, it is not the one that emerges from slavery and indenture and becomes writ large.

8. Ibid., 35, author emphasis.

9. Ibid., 41; emphasis added.

10. See Shepherd and Richards, "Introduction."

11. See Warner-Lewis's *Central Africa in the Caribbean.*

12. As quoted in the introduction to Allen, *Questioning Creole,* xi–xii.

13. Put differently, Goveia's work suggests that creolization is undercut by and achieved upon the subordination of blackness, which while it may not be a formal cultural rejection is at the very least an unconscious one, or, after Fanon, an internalized self-hatred. See Goveia, "The Social Framework," and Fanon, *Black Skin, White Masks.*

14. Gregg, "'Yuh Know Bout Coo-Coo?'" 148.

15. See Hintzen, "Race and Creole Ethnicity," 99. See also Rahier, "Blackness as a Process of Creolization."

16. Williams, "A Class Act," 434.

17. Ibid., 432, emphasis added.

18. Khan, Aisha, "Mixing Matters," 54.

19. Niezen, *The Origins of Indigenism,* 203.

20. Brathwaite, Edward Kamau, "Timehri," 35.

21. Ibid., 38.

22. Ibid., 35.

23. Ibid., 42, author emphasis.

24. Ibid., 43.

25. Harris, "Creoleness," 238.

26. Brathwaite, "Timehri," 44, emphasis added.

27. Burton, *Afro-Creole,* 13.

28. Benítez-Rojo charts the emergence of the Creole in the Hispanophone Caribbean, which occurs at a different point than in the Francophone or Anglophone Caribbean and which, he points out, was not in every case produced by the plantation because it was not fully developed in every society. See in *The Repeating Island,* "From the Plantation to the Plantation."

29. See Burton's chapter in *Afro-Creole,* "From African to Afro-Creole: The Making of Jamaican Slave Culture, 1655–1838."

30. Gonzalez, *Puerto Rico,* 10.

31. Rodney, *A History of the Guyanese Working People,* 3.

32. Gramsci, for example, writes that "man" is "the process of his actions." *Prison Notebooks,* 351.

33. Lukács, *The Ontology of Social Being,* 23.

34. Ibid., 20.

35. Ibid., 103. He writes that labor "necessarily changes the nature of the men performing it."

36. Munasinghe, *Callaloo or Tossed Salad?,* 41, author emphasis; quoting Bolland.

37. For such a use of "home," see Daly's *A Short History.*

38. Lukács, *The Ontology of Social Being,* 4.

39. Foucault, "Labour, Life, Language," 254, 259.

40. Midgett, "West Indian Version," 339.

41. Silva, *Toward a Global Idea of Race,* xx.

42. Ibid., xxiv, author emphasis.

43. Ibid., xv, xvi.

44. Ibid., 174, author emphasis.

45. Deloria, *God Is Red,* 58.

46. Wynter, "The Ceremony Must Be Found," 50.

47. Wynter, "Columbus and the Poetics of the *Propter Nos,*" 253.

48. Ibid.

49. Lamming, *The Pleasures of Exile*, 34.

50. Ibid., 35, 33; emphasis added.

51. Ibid., 30. Lamming writes that he was asked a question by this seventeen-year-old girl who did not understand herself as a colonized person.

52. Watler is the author of the novel *sea Lotto* and other work. I spoke with him when he came for a reading in College Station, Texas.

53. Hall, "Cultural Identity and Diaspora," 116–19.

54. I am referring to three of Césaire's works, *A Tempest, The Tragedy of King Christophe,* and *Notebook of a Return to the Native Land*. The most overt reference is to the latter. In *Modernism and Negritude,* A. James Arnold has said, according to Jennifer Wilks, that the land is "concrete and metaphorical." In "Writing Home," Wilks argues that the Caribbean landscape in *Notebook* can be read as a staging ground for "modernist encounters" rather than as opposed to or antimodern.

55. See: http://tequilasovereign.blogspot.com/ and http://settlercolonialstudies.org/.

56. See the following: Goldstein, "Where the Nation Takes Place"; Saldaña-Portillo, "'How Many Mexicans [Is] a Horse Worth?'"

57. Wolfe, *Settler Colonialism and the Transformation of Anthropology,* 1–2.

58. Farred, "The Unsettler," 794.

59. Ibid., 796–98.

60. Ibid., 796–97.

61. Fanon, *The Wretched of the Earth,* 36.

62. Mamdani, "Beyond Settler and Native," 660–61.

63. Ibid., 657.

64. Ibid., 652.

65. Ibid., 659.

66. Stasiulis and Yuval-Davis, "Introduction," 22.

67. Winn, *Americas,* 49. Sylvia Wynter has repeatedly said that there were no "indios" in the Americas before Columbus came. See also: Field, "Who Are the Indians?"; Spivak, "Imperialism and Sexual Difference." For want of space, in this study I do not consider the huge debate about the use of the terms *Native American, First Peoples, Indian,* and others to describe native peoples, nor do I deal with nineteenth-century American nativist discourse.

68. Premdas, *Ethnic Identity in the Caribbean,* 22.

69. centrelink.org and kacike.

70. Forte, *Ruins of Absence,* 220.

71. Ibid., 26, 28.

72. Ibid., 37.

73. Forte, "Extinction."

74. Polanco notes that following independence in the nineteenth century, Hispanic nations tried to extend *repartimiento.*

75. The reference here is multiple. It is first to Fanon, who has observed in *Black Skin, White Masks,* which he says concerns West Indians, not Africans, that every ontology is made unavailable in a colonized society. He has also noted instances in which Africans would rather pass as West Indian natives (blacks). In Césaire's *Discourse on Colonialism* he writes of "thingification" under colonialism, and this is in part how I interpret what Fanon says. Additionally, when Bernabé, Chamoiseau, and Confiant delimit Creole identity in *In Praise of Creoleness* (121), they proceed from this point of negation by defining the Creole in terms of what it is not.

76. See 56, 107, 120, 263 for Deloria's thesis that Western cultures have essentially chosen time (Christian historical time) over space. In what can be read as an implicit critique of Hegel, he claims that this history is problematic because Christianity is "divorced from space and made an exclusive agent of time" and necessarily rejects native religions, which, he claims, are special (120). Throughout, I make reference to Deloria's space/time frame rather than employ Denise Ferreira da Silva's universality and historicity. The concept of historicity is embedded in Deloria's concept of time, and my analysis is grounded in a concept of space (liminal)—real and discursive.

77. Williams, *Capitalism and Slavery.*

78. Césaire, *The Tragedy of King Christophe,* 19.

79. Forbes, *Black Africans and Native Americans,* 69, author emphasis. He refers to Indigenous Peoples as Americans in his text.

80. Ibid., 72. Forbes notes briefly that at times in present-day Brazil, native peoples are still sometimes referred to as blacks.

81. Ibid., 73

82. Las Casas, *In Defense of the Indians.* See also work by Sylvia Wynter in *Jamaica Journal* on Las Casas.

83. Frantz Fanon, Sylvia Wynter, and Paget Henry all make the argument about blacks serving as the "zero" sum of humanity. See for example: Fanon, *Black Skin, White Masks,* 129.

84. See Mentore's "Guyanese Amerindian Epistemology."

85. Greene-Roesel, *Uncle Basil,* 99.

86. See the chapter entitled "The Religious Challenge" in *God Is Red.*

87. Rohrer, "Attacking Trust." See also Kauanui, "Colonialism in Equality."

88. Gilroy, *There Ain't No Black in the Union Jack,* 18.

89. *Wa-Wii-Wa,* 4. This issue of the Amerindian Peoples Association (APA) newsletter includes a summary of an application for land rights made by six Amerindian villages. The term appears there.

90. Wynter, "1492: A New World View," 8. 1492 is commonly viewed from a "dissident" perspective, which is Harjo's. According to Wynter, it does not matter who (present or past) subordinates Indigenous Peoples, "rather, as Susan Shown Harjo (1991) argues, for the native peoples of [sic] Americas what needs to be brought to an end is the entire history of these past five hundred years" (6, author emphasis).

2. Labor for Being

1. Joseph, *Caliban in Exile,* 2, 114.

2. Eagleton, *The Function of Criticism.*

3. Césaire, *A Tempest,* 60–61.

4. Nixon, "Caribbean and African Appropriations of 'The Tempest,'" 564–65.

5. Shakespeare, *The Tempest,* 121.

6. Césaire, *A Tempest.*

7. Nixon, "Caribbean and African Appropriations of 'The Tempest,'" 558.

8. Ibid., 566, emphasis added.

9. Lamming, *The Pleasures of Exile,* 118.

10. Nixon, "Caribbean and African Appropriations," 568.

11. Ibid., 569.

12. Shakespeare's island is not in the New World, despite a reference to "Bermudas" in the text and the close friendship of Shakespeare to Montaigne's English translator.

13. Almquist, "Not Quite the Gabbling of a 'Thing Most Brutish,'" 595–96.

14. Ibid., 594. The reference to the mountain occurs on page 47 of the play. In her essay, "Playing Caliban: Césaire's Tempest," Joan Dayan also refers to Caliban as a "force" that "lies in ambiguity" (126).

15. Almquist, "Not Quite the Gabbling," author emphasis.

16. Hulme, *Colonial Encounters,* 108. In academic work on the mixture of Old and New World references in Shakespeare's play, there has been no substantive discussion by literary critics of the scientific idea that Africa and the New World were in fact joined at one point.

17. Almquist, "Not Quite the Gabbling," 595, emphasis added. In his essay, "Césaire and Shakespeare: Two Tempests," A. James Arnold also refers to Césaire's "Africanization" of Caliban, which he says is "reinforced by his affirmation of indigenous cultural values and . . . his insistence on the necessity of seizing his freedom" (240). Benítez-Rojo's work offers an unexplored approach to thinking about Shakespeare's island, which could be read as that ubiquitous "repeating" island that is without place and constituted or located through the power dynamics among those who inhabit it.

18. Byrd, *Colonialisms.*

19. Almquist, "Not Quite the Gabbling," 590. I don't agree fully with the idea of Africanization, this being Césaire's third play and the one that comes, as many scholars have noted, after the sociocultural (*The Tragedy of King Christophe*) and the political (*A Season in the Congo*) failure of liberated African and New World African-derived states, in the figures of Henri Christophe and Lumumba, respectively.

20. Byrd, *Colonialisms,* 38.

21. Hulme, *Colonial Encounters,* 109.

22. Byrd, *Colonialisms,* 43–44.

23. Ibid., 41.

24. Almquist refers to the native as a "subconscious presence," which may be true for the Francophone Caribbean. However, regionally, I would argue that engagement with native peoples is not subconscious but rather constructed historicity. For her claim about representations of the native in the work of Wilson Harris, see Byrd, *Colonialisms,* 73.

25. He ignores the internal movement of Indigenous Peoples and their own displacement under colonial rule and before blacks.

26. See Silva, *Toward a Global Idea of Race,* xxxvii.

27. Deloria, *God Is Red,* 58.

28. Shakespeare, *The Tempest,* 116. Peter Hulme also suggests that he is native and only his mother is not. See *Colonial Encounters,* 113, 114. According to the *Oxford English Dictionary, litter* as a verb refers to animals and means to "bring forth (young)."

29. In her discussion of black subjectivity, Michelle Wright makes a somewhat similar point when she claims that Césaire, Fanon, and others demonstrate with their work that "the Black cannot only become a subject, he can be a subject *within* Western civilization— or, . . . the nation" (*Becoming Black,* 10). Wright notes that for anticolonialists it was "crucial to show that the Black individual deserved to be a full citizen within the Western nation and/or that the Black collective deserved to be recognized as a nation" (10).

30. Shakespeare, *The Tempest,* 202, emphasis added. For more on race, see Hall, *Things of Darkness.*

31. The quoted material is from Eric Cheyfitz's *The Poetics of Imperialism,* xii. Dayan notes in "Playing Caliban" that "Caliban will merge Carib and African" (127).

32. Shakespeare, *The Tempest*, 146.

33. If we follow Wynter's discussion of Jonkunnu ("Jonkunnu in Jamaica"), the dance is about allowing for these altered gods to remain, although transformed.

34. I refer here indirectly to the final pages of Chinua Achebe's *Things Fall Apart*, when the clan system through which the protagonist has understood himself and his culture is renamed by the colonizer as the "tribe."

35. Byrd, *Colonialisms*, 73.

36. Ibid.

37. In "Beyond Miranda's Meanings," Wynter collapses native and black labor when she writes that Caliban represents both African and Arawak forced labor. Roberto Retamar, in *Caliban and Other Essays*, seems to embrace Caliban as a figure who can represent all racialized labor, large peasant classes of native peoples, marginalized Blacks in Latin America, and the largely "white," organic intellectual.

38. Walcott, "The Muse of History," 4. Another relevant and fascinating adaptation beyond the scope of this project is Lemuel Johnson's *Highlife for Caliban*, for which Sylvia Wynter provides the afterword.

39. Dayan notably writes that "to reconstitute a self through language is not always a luxury of leisure." See "Playing Caliban," 139.

40. Ibid., 140.

41. Ibid., 132.

42. Ibid.

43. Ibid.

44. Ibid., 137.

45. Arnold, "Césaire and Shakespeare," 243.

46. Ibid., 245.

47. Further, he claims that Afro-Caribbean philosophy has been unable to root out the "anti-African bias" of European philosophical thinking.

48. Henry, *Caliban's Reason*, 4.

49. Ibid., 7.

50. Ibid., 4, 5.

51. Ibid., 8. In his essay, "Philosophy and the Caribbean Intellectual Tradition," Henry lists Caribbean and other philosophers who have left out Africa, in order to claim that the invisibility of Africa is a "systematically reproduced outcome" (14).

52. Henry, "Philosophy and the Caribbean Intellectual Tradition," 26–28.

53. Henry, *Caliban's Reason*, 11.

54. Ibid., 15.

55. Ibid., 24.

56. Lamming, *The Pleasures of Exile*, 13, emphasis added.

57. Henry, *Caliban's Reason*, 25.

58. Ibid., 32.

59. Ibid., 48.

60. Ibid., 48–49.

61. Ibid., 57.

62. Ibid., 55.

63. Ibid., 71.

64. Hulme, *Colonial Encounters*, 119.

65. Henry, *Caliban's Reason*, 70.

66. Ibid., 87. Henry writes that natives and Africans could not leave a written record and it was instead oral (72).

67. Ibid., 75, 79.

68. Ibid., 93.

69. Ibid., 111. See also chapter 6, Fanon, *Black Skin, White Masks.*

70. Gramsci, *The Prison Notebooks.*

71. In his chapter on Sylvia Wynter, Henry writes that for Derek Walcott, "history is anything but the primary medium of self-creation or redefinition" (121). If we combine the racial contract argument with Wynter's rethinking of the color line, then we can argue that this is where the new line is enacted in postcolonial government. This can be used to reread Walter Rodney, whose emphasis on labor forces him to leave Indigenous Peoples out.

72. Scott, "The Re-enchantment of Humanism," 136, author emphasis. Wynter is here drawing upon Foucault.

73. Fanon, *Black Skin, White Masks,* 109.

74. See DeLoughrey, *Routes and Roots,* 2, 6.

75. Edwards, "The Uses of Diaspora," 63.

76. Fox, *Being and Blackness in Latin America,* 28.

77. Ibid., 27.

78. Ibid., 32.

79. Wright, *Becoming Black,* 3.

80. Ibid., 5.

81. Ibid., 26.

82. Ibid., 39.

83. Buck-Morss, "Hegel and Haiti." Buck-Morss uses this paradox, as she calls it herself, to argue that what have been considered discrete historical and academic traditions should be pulled into a single framework.

84. Wright, *Becoming Black,* 17–18.

85. Although she does not discuss it here, Wright's claims about women and the nation have been anticipated in many texts, including *Between Woman and Nation,* edited by Caren Kaplan, Norma Alarcón, and Minoo Moallem. For a discussion in Wright of how black writers used the materialist dialectic to produce black subjectivity as a response to idealist dialectical methods (Hegel and Gobineau), see her chapter 2, "The Trope of Masking." For the failure of the materialist dialectic, see her chapter 3, "Some Women Disappear," specifically 126.

86. Hegel, *The Philosophy of History,* 91, 93 95, 96, 99, author emphasis. While I do not have time to consider it here, Madureira's work makes an argument about Hegel's notion of the spirit and the master–slave dialectic with regard to Toussaint's figure. He argues that in anticolonalist writing Toussaint not only embodies the Spirit but interrupts the dialectic. See Madureira, *Cannibal Modernities,* 147–50.

87. Hegel, *The Philosophy of History,* 36.

88. Ibid., 9, 16, 17.

89. Ibid., 39.

90. Ibid., 40–41, author emphasis.

91. Ibid., 81, 82.

92. Wright, *Becoming Black,* 43.

93. Williams, *Capitalism and Slavery.*

94. Susan Buck-Morss also notes that the rejection of Eric Williams's thesis by "official Marxism" was racist, but she mentions Williams only briefly and to suggest that Marxists transformed an already idealized dialectic of masters and slaves into that of the struggle between classes. For her mention of Williams, see Buck-Morss, "Hegel and Haiti," 50. My own argument is squarely focused on the notion of primitive accumulation in Marxism in order to make a point about Caliban, labor, and subjectivity.

95. According to the *Encyclopedia of Marxism,* "Since capital is both a pre-condition and outcome of capitalism, a period of *primitive accumulation* marks the beginning of capitalism; this may involve outright theft and plunder, and . . . the *creation* of a class of people who no longer own any means of production—a proletariat."

96. This claim finds support in Susan Buck-Morss's argument that Hegel read Adam Smith and "understands the position of the master in both political and economic terms" ("Hegel and Haiti," 857).

97. For an example of recent scholarship that rethinks the Marx–Hegel relationship, though again without a consideration of race, see Norman Levine's *Divergent Paths.*

98. Wright, *Becoming Black,* 66.

99. Vera Palmer's presentation on "Verses Versus: Native Poetry and Settler Colonialism."

100. Wright, *Becoming Black,* 34.

101. Hegel, "Independence and Dependence of Self-Consciousness," 118–19.

102. Buck-Morss, "Hegel and Haiti," 850.

103. Ibid., 844, author emphasis.

104. Theories of fluidity are still concerned with particular configurations of diaspora.

105. For a discussion about Cherokee rejection of Lumbee claims to be fully indigenous and deserving of government funding, see Hochberg, "Lumbees' Tribal Recognition Depends on Senate."

106. In his essay, "The Uses of Diaspora," Brent Hayes Edwards cites Du Bois's *The World and Africa* (1947), and Du Bois's use of the term for all blacks (46).

107. Rosser, "Figuring Caribbeanness," 481.

3. "God's Golden City"

1. For more on the exhibiting of Indigenous Peoples by Columbus see the article by Vilches, "Columbus's Gift," as well as Carpentier's historical novel, *The Harp and the Shadow.*

2. Galeano, "Myths as Collective Metaphors."

3. Glissant, *Caribbean Discourse,* 71. Glissant uses the rhizome to describe Caribbean culture following its definition by Deleuze and Guattari, and its workings can be productively thought with Benítez-Rojo's description of the plantation as a polyrhythmic and uniquely Caribbean sociocultural machine. See Glissants, *Poetics of Relation;* Benítez-Rojo, *The Repeating Island;* and Deleuze and Guattari, *A Thousand Plateaus.*

4. Waswo, "The History That Literature Makes," 541.

5. Ibid., 541.

6. Ibid., 542.

7. Ibid.

8. Barthes, *Mythologies,* 110.

9. Ibid., 118.

10. Ibid., 121, author emphasis.

11. Ibid., 131, 129.

12. Loss here refers to texts like Naipaul's *The Loss of El Dorado* and Young's *Guyana*.

13. Walter Ralegh is often also spelled *Raleigh*. I defer to the first throughout except where authors deliberately use the latter.

14. http://www.silvertorch.com/guysongs.html. Linguist John Rickford first pointed out the song to me. There is another well-known song with reference to the myth: "My Guyana, El Dorado."

15. Henwood, "Profiteering in the Hemisphere."

16. Hardt and Negri, *Empire*, 11.

17. Obama, *Dreams from My Father*, x.

18. Wynter, "Columbus and the Poetics of the *Propter Nos.*" Wynter writes, "In the old logic the torrid zone had had to be as uninhabitable as land in the Western Hemisphere to be nonexistent. Within the logic of our behavior-orienting ideology and conceptual classificatory schema, the analogues of the torrid zone/Western hemisphere—i.e., the *niggers,* the *non-whites,* the *natives*—have to be both perceived as, and socio-institutionally produced to be in a large part *poor* and *jobless, homeless, relatively lowly skilled,* and *underdeveloped.* The classificatory schema based on the binary opposition of the *genetically redeemed* and the (supposedly) *genetically condemned* (Dubois's [sic] *Color Line*) encodes the criterion of our contemporary model of *Man,* just as the binary opposition of the *habitable/uninhabitable* and of the *celestial/terrestrial* had encoded that of the feudal-Christian model" (274–75, author emphasis).

19. Glissant, *Caribbean Discourse,* 64.

20. See Trouillot, *Silencing the Past,* and Certeau, *The Writing of History.*

21. Dash, *The Other America.* For the specific reference to "remythification," see 24.

22. For Dash's reference to Manifest Destiny, see 10.

23. Ibid., 25.

24. Holt et al., dir., *The Magnificent Voyage of Christopher Columbus;* Ralegh, *The Discoverie of the Large, Rich, and Bewtiful Empyre of Guiana,* 123, author emphasis. This is Neil L. Whitehead's transcription of *The Discoverie.* The quotation is taken from Ralegh's opening dedication. In addition to a new transcription of Ralegh's text, Whitehead offers a reading of it as both literature and ethnography.

25. For a summary of treatments of the myth in Caribbean literature, see Maes-Jelinek's "The Myth of El Dorado in the Caribbean Novel."

26. Bernabé et al., *In Praise of Creoleness,* 80, emphasis added.

27. Ibid., 75.

28. For this first poetics of the *propter nos* that Wynter revisits in the discussion of Bernabe et al., see Wynter's "Columbus and the Poetics of the Propter Nos."

29. Bernabé et al., *In Praise of Creoleness,* 121.

30. Wynter, "'A Different Kind of Creature,'" 147, author emphasis.

31. For her specific use of "radical alterity," see Ibid., 148.

32. Ibid., 144.

33. Ibid., 143.

34. Cesaire, "Calling the Magician," 120–21. For more of James's recourse to Neitzsche's use of myths, see the chapter titled "Miraculous Weapons" in A. James Arnold's *Modernism and Negritude.*

35. Ainsa, "From the Golden Age to El Dorado," 44.

36. Ainsa revisits the topic in a later article, "The Myth, Marvel, and Adventure of El Dorado."

37. Ainsa, "From the Golden Age to El Dorado," 38.

38. Ibid., 22.

39. Ibid., 24.

40. I am very loosely working with Marx's concept of alienation.

41. Ainsa, "From the Golden Age to El Dorado," 42.

42. See Columbus, "The First Voyage of Columbus," in *The Four Voyages of Columbus*, 2–12.

43. Arnold, *Modernism and Negritude,* 55.

44. Vidal, *The Legend of El Dorado,* i. Throughout history, the term *El Dorado* has been invariably used to refer both to a man and to a city of gold. For more on the myth in Latin American literature, see Lewis, *The Miraculous Lie.*

45. The Chibcha people, who were either replaced by the Muisca (spelled *Muysca* by Ainsa) or are simply alternately referred to *as* the Muisca, for which there are multiple spellings in the historical and contemporary records, are thought to be the people who performed the ceremony at the lake. According to Hemming, historian Demetrio Ramos Pérez has argued that the story is "entirely" linked to the Muisca people. Other historians disagree. Of note, however, is that water rituals were only one aspect of the Chibcha's religion. Hemming, *The Search for El Dorado,* 97.

46. Ibid., 101.

47. Gaffron, *El Dorado, Land of Gold,* 42.

48. Vidal, *The Legend of El Dorado,* n.p. The quotation appears on the publication page and therefore has no page number reference. "For my father who told me stories and showed me the road to El Dorado."

49. Ibid., i, emphasis added.

50. Ibid.

51. In 1844, J. A. Van Huevel published *El Dorado,* in which he sought to vindicate Sir Walter Ralegh by arguing that he did not embellish his accounts of El Dorado and Guyana.

52. Some of the other treasures were auctioned at Sotheby's and some placed in museums.

53. Gaffron, *El Dorado, Land of Gold,* 12. Gaffron's text is part of the series "Great Mysteries: Opposing Viewpoints."

54. Ibid., 15.

55. Hemming, *The Search for El Dorado,* 193.

56. Ibid., 10–11.

57. According to Hemming, these men are all considered, along with Benalcázar, the main sources for the myth. Castellanos did warn that he had no actual proof of the existence of an El Dorado (Hemming, *The Search for El Dorado,* 101).

58. Hemming, *The Search for El Dorado,* 102. According to Hemming, Simón plagiarized Castellanos's version, turning the latter's verse into prose, connecting the account of the gold dust ceremony with sacrifice to lakes, and locating the ceremony at Lake Guatavita. He also wrote that the chief's unfaithful wife threw herself in the lake because of her husband's "scorn." Here we get a sense of the sensationalizing of the myth, which made it more palatable as it was rewritten in terms of the ideologies and literary aesthetics of the Western world at the time.

59. Gaffron, *El Dorado, Land of Gold,* 49.

60. *Loss* here plays on titles about the loss of or the lost El Dorado in the region and on the fact that apart from museum items, no treasure was found. In *The Loss of El*

Dorado, Naipual tries to restore Trinidad to the history of the search for El Dorado. His work is about Ralegh's visit to Trinidad in 1595, at the beginning of his search, and of his return in 1617. Although Naipaul holds that El Dorado is a "Spanish delusion," he writes Trinidad back into the history of this myth of the South American mainland. He is interested in restoring Trinidad's significance to the myth and restoring its loss from European history. What needs to be further discussed is the idea that the myth gives historical significance to some places and not others.

61. Ralegh, *The Discoverie,* 121. Concerning Ralegh's banishment, in his *The Golden Antilles,* Timothy Severin writes that Ralegh married Queen Elizabeth's "maid of honor" and therefore lost her favor and was banished from the court (25). Ralegh, he adds, hoped that finding El Dorado would (1) "do for Elizabeth what it had done for Philip" and (2) restore him to glory (26). Prior to his expulsion from the English court, Ralegh had been the Captain of the Queen's Guard. After his first exploration of America, he spent thirteen years in the tower accused of treason. He was released by James I, Queen Elizabeth's successor, in order to return to his exploration of South America. Upon his return to England, he was imprisoned and beheaded for disobeying the king's orders against provoking the Spanish in the "New World."

62. Crocker, *The Centaur Guide to the Caribbean and El Dorado,* xi, xii. Crocker's work contains sources similar to Swan.

63. Ibid., xv–xviii.

64. Hollett, *Passage from India to El Dorado,* 7, emphasis added. Hollett's sources include Vere T. Daly's work, but not historical sources by Indo-Guyanese such as Peter Ruhumon's history of Indians in Guyana. He also uses Swan in addition to Annual Reports on the Colonies and Bookers' records and shipping registers.

65. Bookers is now Booker Group plc.

66. Hollett, *Passage from India to El Dorado,* 14, emphasis added.

67. Ibid., 7.

68. See Kempadoo, *Sun, Sex, and Gold.*

69. Crocker, *The Centaur Guide to the Caribbean and El Dorado,* 374.

70. Severin, *The Golden Antilles,* 334. These tourists did not head to Guyana but to more palatable vacation destinations, such as those that Crocker writes about. Unlike much of the Caribbean and West Indies, Guyana's tourist industry (largely based on ecotourism) has not been its largest source of revenue.

71. Ibid., 333.

72. U.S. and British intervention in Guyanese politics is well documented. See work by Hintzen, Manley, and Thomas.

73. Crocker, *The Centaur Guide to the Caribbean and El Dorado,* 334.

74. I italicize *you* and *we* here to signal the fact that Young's own subjectivity is shifting. Young's book was published posthumously. He died in 1996.

75. Young, *Guyana, The Lost El Dorado,* 303.

76. Ibid., 165, 183, 204. He also worked on the Mabura-Kurupukari Road.

77. Ibid., 286.

78. Jack, "The Thrust into the Hinterland," 209, emphasis added. The essay also mentions a proposed Guyana Development Corporation that would handle all development plans in the interior.

79. Ethnic strife and labor disputes took the lives of at least one hundred black and Indian Guyanese in 1964.

80. Young, *Guyana, The Lost El Dorado,* 7–8.

81. Wynter, "1492," 14.

82. The words are as follows: "Through sunshine and shadow, From darkness to noon, Over mountains that reach, From the sky to the moon, A man with a dream that, He'll never let go, Keeps searching to find El Dorado" (Gaffron, *El Dorado, Land of Gold,* 106). Gaffron also juxtaposes these works from the movie, which have nothing to do with the original El Dorado, with a picture of a gold mask, which she calls "a piece of the treasure of El Dorado (Ibid.). In 2000, Walt Disney released its own film titled *The Road to El Dorado.*

83. Waswo, "The History That Literature Makes," 544.

84. This is a point at which to launch a new critique of histories on the region that take the plantation as the genesis of race relations in the Caribbean. They necessarily ignore a huge historical and ontological problem.

85. Benítez-Rojo, *The Repeating Island,* 4.

86. Braithwaite, "Gold," n.p.

87. In his preface to Joycelynne Lonke's essays on the art and politics of Caribbean literature, *In the Shadow of El Dorado,* and the "epistemology of the modern search" for El Dorado, Hillary Beckles has written, "The fact of the matter is that such a place will forever have many eldorados [sic] simply because no square deal can ever be struck between the power of the landscape and the many limitations resident within the mindscape. Ancient travelers—the first Caribbean folk—have their own; the Europeans envisioned a separate and elusive 'other'; now the children of Africa and Asia are in search" (n.p.). The essay is not specifically on El Dorado but generally involves the idea that this literature is generated by the struggle for identity that the conquest of the Americas initiated.

88. According to Hemming, since the sixteenth century, the world's overall population has steadily risen, but the native, lowland population has declined by 95 percent (23).

89. Waswo, "The History That Literature Makes," 546.

90. See Neil L. Whitehead's discussion of the veracity of aspects of native culture that Ralegh's El Dorado includes.

91. Benítez-Rojo, *The Repeating Island,* 189.

92. See Chatterjee's *Nationalist Thought and the Colonial World.*

93. Hemming, *The Search for El Dorado.* Brett's work is often considered a "primary source" for material on Indigenous Peoples in Guyana, but it must still be looked at as a text by someone brought to the region to do missionary work with Indigenous Peoples. His writings about them reflect his religious bias. (The date for the work is most likely 1880, but even in the text itself it is unclear.)

4. FROM MYTH TO MARKET

1. This look within was undertaken not only by Guyana alone but also by other newly independent countries in the region. Further, it was anticipated by the region's artists and cultural thinkers. Selwyn Cudjoe points out in his introduction to Harris's *History, Fable, and Myth in the Caribbean and Guianas* the growing number of Caribbean artists, historians, and the like who turned inward, of which Harris, of course, is one.

2. Ministry of Information and Culture, "A Brief Outline of the Progress of Integration in Guyana," 9.

3. Ibid., 12.

4. See Hintzen, "Reproducing Domination Identity and Legitimacy Constructs in the West Indies."

5. Ibid., 47, 49.

6. Ibid., 67, emphasis added.

7. Timothy Brenan writes, "The 'nation' is precisely what Foucault has called a 'discursive formation'—not simply an allegory or imaginative vision but a gestative political structure which the Third World artist is consciously building or suffering the lack of" (Brenan, "The National Longing for Form," 46–47). While I do not wholly agree with his labeling of "the" Third World artist's project, I do find his use of Foucault important.

8. Bhabha, "Introduction," 2.

9. Ibid., author emphasis.

10. In a later essay in the volume, Bhabha argues that "this cultural construction of nationness" is in fact "a form of social and textual affiliation. . . ." Bhabha, "DissemiNation," 292.

11. Smith, *Decolonizing Methodologies,* 53. Smith uses the term with regard to the nineteenth century.

12. For more on Fabian socialism, its origins in Guyana and Burnham's platforms, see Hintzen, *The Cost of Regime Survival.*

13. Ibid., 46.

14. The commission that investigated the constitutional suspension noted, according to Singh, that the PPP was essentially two factions, one communist and the other socialist or democratic (Singh, *Guyana,* 25).

15. See Colonial Office, *Report of a Commission of Inquiry into Disturbances in British Guiana in February 1962,* 51.

16. Founded in 1960 by Peter D'Aguiar and initially supported by Portuguese and Indian businessmen, the United Force, still in existence, was also made up of Chinese and a cross-section of the upper class. It was one of the parties, along with Burnham's PNC, that participated in the campaign to oust the PPP. For more on the change in the voting system that essentially changed the rules for how a majority in government could be determined, see Jagan's *The West on Trial.*

17. Although this section primarily engages Hintzen's work, much of the factual material is taken from several sources.

18. For Guyana, Critchlow is often regarded as the "father of trade unionism" (Singh, *Guyana,* 14). There are many more influential unions and organizations, secular and religious, like the League of Colored Peoples, the British Guiana East Indian Association, the Trades Union Council, and the Council of Churches, to name a few. However, it is generally agreed by Hintzen and most scholars that the Man Power Citizens Association (MPCA) and British Guiana Labour Union (BGLU) were the most significant. For more, see Singh, *Guyana,* and Jagan, *The West on Trial.*

19. Singh, *Guyana,* 90.

20. Hintzen, *The Costs of Regime Survival,* 39.

21. Ibid.

22. See Singh, *Guyana,* specifically "The Economy under Cooperative Socialism," 23.

23. Burnham, "To Build a New World," 67. For more, see Hintzen, *The Costs of Regime Survival,* specifically "Elite Support and Control of the State: Race, Ideology and Clientelism." Hintzen gives 1971 as the start of the nationalization plan, a full year earlier than the 1972 date normally given for the start of the government's second development plan.

24. Hintzen, *The Costs of Regime Survival,* 163.

25. Ibid., 157.

26. Ibid., 24.

27. Ibid., 158.

28. Burnham, "To Build a New World," 97.

29. Ibid., 92. The majority of Guyanese in civil service jobs at that time were blacks.

30. For Jagan's position on independence, see "Labor and Independence" in *The West on Trial*.

31. Chua, *World on Fire*, 132.

32. Singh, *Guyana*, 104.

33. Ibid.

34. Emphasis added.

35. The linking of the current project to the Dutch effort is extremely significant. Part of Venezuela's claim to Guyana's land relies on a disavowal of any real claim by the Dutch. The basis for Venezuela's claim is the boundaries set by the British, by Richard Schomburgk, which it holds are false. Guyana, in countering, finds its initial justification for its claim over the territory to the Dutch. For more, see Jackson, "Guyana, Cuba, Venezuela and the 'Routes' to Cultural Reconciliation between Latin America and the Caribbean."

36. A major claim of *Co-operative Republic* is that the Dutch erection of the fort on Fort Island (before Zeelandia) "changed the course of Guyanese history" because it led to the transfer of the capital of the colony to Fort Island and to the eventual settlement of Demerara by the Dutch. This settlement is what Guyana claims, in its boundary dispute, constitutes colonial and therefore postcolonial right, prior to even the British, who obtained the land from the Dutch.

37. See Menezes, "The Controversial Question of Protection and Jurisdiction Re the Amerindians in Guyana."

38. Poonai, "Wilderness and Wildlife in Guyana," 162.

39. Burnham, "A Vision of the Co-operative Republic," 17–18.

40. Ibid., 19, emphasis added. In another speech on the formation of the cooperative, Burnham reiterates this idea. See Burnham, "The Power of Cooperative Ownership."

41. Burnham, "A Vision of the Co-operative Republic," 13–14, emphasis added.

42. Kwayana, "Economic Relations in Pre-Republican Guyana," 26.

43. Ibid., 23. In her work, Mary Noel Menezes represents Gravesande as continuing "friendly" Dutch politics with regard to Amerindians, but it was also under him that Dutch colonial government was reorganized. The move to Gravesande here is therefore complex because it potentially undermines the continuities established earlier between Dutch rule and black rule.

44. Ibid., 33.

45. Ibid., 36.

46. King, "Planning in the New Society," 44.

47. Kwayana, "Economic Relations in Pre-Republican Guyana," 36.

48. Seymour, "Cultural Values in the Republic of Guyana," 87.

49. Ibid., 80.

50. Ibid.

51. Ibid., 82. Seymour holds that there are six stages of cultural evolution and that Guyana is now in the sixth, which is characterized, roughly, by putting back culture. According to Seymour, these are stages initially proposed by anthropologist Margaret Mead.

52. Manley, *Guyana Emergent*, 45.

53. For details on the rebellion, see Ibid. After the rebellion, Burnham created a 10-mile buffer zone along the border with Venezuela to dissuade Amerindian travel across the border.

54. Seymour, "Cultural Values in the Republic of Guyana," 80.

55. Ibid., 82.

56. Ibid., 92. The idea that national culture must come from the elite is reinforced when Seymour writes of the "problem" in Haiti with Voodoo that he sees as a "threat" that obviously comes from the bottom up. He writes, "Despite the continued threat of the Haitian religious possession of spirits, the darker reaches of obeah practices were quickly overlaid by the Christian religion but with the fading of the influences of the Christian faith, obeah which has survived like pools of standing water . . . tend to make a sporadic reappearance in certain isolated spots" (86).

57. Here I deliberately play on Waswo's writing that in epic history culture is thought to come from the "West." By sanctioning the Western educated elite, Seymour unwittingly demonstrates how the idea still persists. Further, it adds validity to my argument later in the chapter that the interior was the last undeveloped space onto which Burnham could shift the colonial narrative of progress, using the myth of El Dorado and the containment of Amerindians.

58. Seymour, "Cultural Values in the Republic of Guyana," 90.

59. There was an ongoing attempt to "decolonise Christmas" by banning some imported items typically associated with the celebration.

60. Seymour, "Cultural Values in the Republic of Guyana," 91, emphasis added.

61. While much more can be said about masculinity and nationalism, I note the echo by Burnham in PNC nationalist discourse of the idea that colonialism, especially slavery, emasculates black men, something that affected the black psyche then, and now. It is a perspective shared by African peoples and is most profoundly expressed in literature, in Chinua Achebe's character Okonkwo in *Things Fall Apart*.

62. Westmaas, "Building under Our Sun," 155.

63. Ibid., 148.

64. Ibid., 158, emphasis added.

65. See Wynter, "Columbus and the Poetics of the *Propter Nos*."

66. Daly, "Historical Background to the Co-operative Republic," 221.

67. Ibid., 216, emphasis added. Daly and others in the PNC, while they rely on European settlement and boundary delineation, are careful not to represent Guyana as a "home" for them in the way that it is for blacks now.

68. While it is true that early villages were run in a cooperative manner, Daly does not go further back in history to cooperative examples from different groups in the region. Instead, he chooses black villages in a narrative that is compatible with black rule.

69. Payne, "Windows on Guyanese History," 233.

70. Daly, *A Short History*, 1–8.

71. Daly establishes the Amerindians as the first inhabitants of the region and retells the "legend" of the coming of one of the larger groups, the Caribs; how they descended from the moon on clouds, a moon Daly takes to be Asia and the clouds the ice bridge that presumably connected Asia and South America at one time (*The Making of Guyana*, 3).

72. Daly, *The Making of Guyana*, 141–51.

73. Bhabha, "Introduction," 3.

74. Daly, *The Making of Guyana*, 48.

75. For more on the border dispute, see Jackson, "Guyana, Cuba, Venezuela." Of note is a reference in Whitehead to Robert Schomburgk, who edited an 1848 edition of Ralegh's *The Discoverie* that he claims "awakened past recollections. . . ." As quoted in Whitehead, "*The Discoverie* as Enchanted Text," 8. The significance of Schomburgk as both the surveyor who gave Guyana its contemporary boundaries and Ralegh's editor further indicates the links among imperial power, imagination, and the textual construction of the nation state by postcolonials.

76. Collins, "The Story of Our Borders," 261.

77. For Venezuela's position, see Fernández, *La Historia y el Derecho en la Reclamación Venezolana de la Guayana Esequiba*. Surinam renewed its claim to Guyana in 2002 by seeking to have a new map of its territory approved, one that includes the New River Triangle of Guyana. See "Suriname to Be Told Guyana's Boundaries Have Not Changed." See also "Guyana to Approach Suriname on Border Talks."

78. Ministerio de Relaciones Exteriores, *Informe que los expertos venezolanos para la cuestión de límites con Guayana Británica presentan al Gobierno Nacional*, 8.

79. Collins, "The Story of Our Borders," 260.

80. Ibid., 282.

81. Ibid., 260.

82. Burnett, *Masters of All They Surveyed*, 14.

83. Ibid., 256.

84. Ibid., 260.

85. Ibid., 259. Burnett does not cite Manley's discussion of Guyana's borders despite parallels.

86. Ibid.

87. Ibid., 258.

88. Jack, "The Thrust into the Hinterland," 208.

89. The following serve as examples: As a then-practicing solicitor, N. O. Poonai argues in his essay "Wilderness and Wildlife in Guyana" that "the resources of the interior, as well as the coast, must be made to contribute to our economic advancement. . . . Thus would be built a broader and deeper national consciousness, embracing a greater Guyana than the coast-dwellers have known in the past" (193). Confirming the importance of the hinterland for Guyana's future, Tommy Payne cites a Ministry of Information booklet from 1969 that holds that "the co-operative effort is the only method for interior development which will fully utilize our human resources. . . . The Co-operative method provides a rapid and profitable means of *re-settling* population in the interior. . ." (250, emphasis added).

90. Jack, "The Thrust into the Hinterland," 197, emphasis added.

91. Ibid., 97.

92. Payne, "Windows on Guayanese History," 248. The "chief instrument" for achieving this, as H. O. Jack informs us, is through education, the key component of the cooperative plan (205).

93. Hoyte, "My First Sixty Days in Office," 8.

94. Ibid., 2.

95. Ibid., 1.

96. Césaire, *The Tragedy of King Christophe*.

97. Forte, *Ruins of Absence*, 142.

98. Ibid., 217.

99. Ibid., 141.

100. Jean La Rose, in discussion with the author, December 2006, Georgetown, Guyana.

101. Reference to native involvement in the slave rebellion can be found in Menezes, *British Policy,* 47.

102. In *World on Fire,* Amy Chua discusses the anti-white minority rhetoric employed by Mugabe, a longtime supporter of Burnham, to gain the popular black vote. Mugabe included in his platform a claim to African soil by blacks as the original inhabitants. For more, see Chua, specifically "Backlash against Markets: Ethnically Targeted Seizures and Nationalizations." Mugabe's visits to Guyana are documented and represent concrete proof of the link between Afro-Creole discourse in the Caribbean with pan-Africanist discourse on the African continent.

103. See Waswo, "The History That Literature Makes," and work by Wynter.

104. Percy Hintzen holds that "an 'East Indian' government is incompatible with the conceptualizations of an Afro-Creole nation" and he argues that East Indians would have to "redefine the nation symbolically *as* East Indian" to resist challenges on ethnic grounds (Hinzen, "Reproducing Domination Identity and Legitimacy Constructs in the West Indies," 67). Although his argument says they are "incompatible," I maintain that the substitution of one ethnic concept for the nation with another is still being done through the terms set by Burnham.

5. The Baptism of Soil

1. See Nagamootoo, "Remembering Cheddi Jagan," for the full text by DeSouza and others.

2. Davies and Jardine, "Imperial Geographies and Caribbean Nationalism," 156.

3. See Janet Jagan, *When Grandpa Cheddi Was a Boy and Other Stories.* Clem Seecharan has referred to Jagan's "doctrinaire Marxism" as his "Achilles heel." The reference is made in the abstract of a scheduled seminar by Seecharan, "Tripping on His Own Banana Peel: Cheddi Jagan's 'Struggle' for Guyana's Freedom, 1946–1966," at the Institute of Commonwealth Studies in England on December 3, 2008.

4. Vibert DeSouza has referred to Jagan in this manner.

5. Following is a short section of my interview with Jean La Rose in which she discusses this:

> LA ROSE: Yes. And it's exactly what you're saying; it's symbolic. It's symbolic rather than really trying to understand. I mean look how our people were during the last elections. They were used because some people don't know better, some of the people in our community—
>
> JACKSON: How were they used?
>
> LA ROSE: They were used by dangling money in front of them, right? And shamefully the government did it.
>
> JACKSON: So they would go into communities and promise to do things—
>
> LA ROSE: Just before elections revolving loans popped up. Just before elections, generators popped up. Just before elections, tractors popped up. Just before elections, you name it.

For some of these government projects, which include building roads, see: Guyana Information News Agency, *Hinterland Highlights.*

6. Mahabir, "Introduction," 2, author emphasis. This term is spelled in two different ways: *kala pani* and *kalapani.* I use the former throughout except when quoting Mahabir.

7. According to a *Stabroek News* article, the parliamentary committee that reviews public holidays says that one reason arrival day was selected as a national holiday is the

fact that Indians are a majority and have made a "significant contribution" to the economic development of Guyana.

8. In different texts, the indenture period in the Caribbean is given either as 1838–1917 or 1838–1920. As far as I can determine, the earlier date refers to the last set of arrivals from India under the indenture scheme, and the later date refers to the actual end of indenture itself or the cessation of all contracts. Additionally, the estimate of the number of Indians arriving in the colonies varies from just under a half-million to just over a half-million people. Under this indenture scheme, Indians were sent not only to the Caribbean but to Fiji, South Africa, Sri Lanka, Mauritius, and Malaya. In his introduction to a collection of speeches by Jagan, John Gaffar LaGuerre refers to indentured Indians as "birds of passage" (*Cheddi Jagan Selected Speeches,* 7).

9. I borrow the term *counterculture* from Paul Gilroy in *The Black Atlantic.*

10. Jagan, *The West on Trial,* 24.

11. Drummond, "The Cultural Continuum," 196.

12. Mohammed, "The 'Creolisation' of Indian Women in Trinidad," 133, author emphasis.

13. Mishra, "The Diasporic Imaginary," 429.

14. Mishra, "The Feudal Postcolonial," 336.

15. Mishra, "The Diasporic Imaginary," 421.

16. This reference is to the chapter's epigraph: Monar, *Koker,* 22–23, emphasis added.

17. Monar, "We Are Not Indians, We Are Guyanese."

18. In an untitled letter, Lin-Jay Harry-Voglezon replies to Ravi Dev's letter "Indian Arrival Day's Should Be a National Holiday." Harry-Voglezon argues that the day would be anti-African and goes on to "remind" Dev of some key historical facts that undermine his argument, not only about the holiday, but also about "Indianness." Harry-Voglezon, Letter.

19. Poynting, "Introduction," n.p.

20. Monar, *Koker,* 15.

21. Ibid., 22–23. Poynting claims that in the collection, "the third source of meanings is sought in local traditions of spiritual resistance to what Monar sees as the ossifications of brahminical Hinduism, a resistance expressed in the mixing of the South Indian traditions of *bhakti* and the proletarian and sometimes anti-brahminical ideology of the estate worker" (Poynting, "Introduction," n.p.).

22. See Jackson, "The Baptism of Soil: Rooplall Monar and the Aesthetics of the *Kala Pani* Modern."

23. Mangru, *Indians in Guyana,* 11.

24. Ibid., 95.

25. Ibid., 88.

26. Ibid., 67.

27. Mangru has written that "many parents preferred to allow their children to 'grow up in ignorance' than to be converted to Christianity or taught by Black teachers" (*Indians in Guyana,* 52).

28. Ibid., 97.

29. Persaud, "Preface," n.p.

30. For a fascinating discussion of Joseph Ruhomon and more of his own writing, see Seecharan's *Joseph Ruhomon's India.*

31. Ruhomon, *Centenary History of the East Indians of British Guiana. 1888–1938,* 5, emphasis added.

32. Ibid., 17, 13.
33. Ibid., 15.
34. Ibid., 45.
35. Ibid., 60.
36. Ibid., 154, emphasis added.
37. Ibid., 174.
38. Ibid., 175.
39. Ibid., 284.
40. Ibid.
41. Ibid., 285–86.
42. Ibid., 286.
43. Ibid., 288.
44. Seecharan, *India and the Shaping of the Indo-Guyanese Imagination,* 60.
45. Ibid., 10, 13.
46. Ibid., 27.
47. Ibid., 56.
48. Ibid., 59.
49. Ibid., 54.
50. See Seecharan, *Joseph Ruhomon's India,* 5. The epigraph to this chapter is from 68.
51. Seecharan, *India and the Shaping of the Indo-Guyanese Imagination,* 23. It is from Seecharan that this Ruhomon quotation is taken, with Seecharan's emphasis. The second quoted portion is Seecharan himself with his own emphasis. Seecharan counters Ruhomon's negativity with this view of Indian efforts from the work of Tyran Ramnarine.
52. Kale, *Fragments of Empire,* 10. Kale is ultimately concerned with how labor categories became formulated. I do not rely on her work for my analysis of Rodney's use of the phrase "working people" to describe Guyanese in his *History of the Guyanese Working People, 1881–1905.*
53. For a criticism of the labor shortage thesis in that volume, though not on the order of Kale's, see SookDeo, "Involuntary Globalization."
54. Kale, *Fragments of Empire,* 3–4, 156.
55. Ibid., 8.
56. Ibid., 5, 60.
57. Ibid., 6.
58. Seecharan, *Joseph Ruhomon's India,* 49, emphasis added. This line is from a speech of Ruhomon's quoted in Seecharan.
59. Ibid., 50–51.
60. Chakrabarty, "Postcoloniality and the Artifice of History," 1.
61. Ibid., 20. Chakrabarty continues, "The idea is to write into the history of modernity the ambivalences, contradictions, the use of force, and the tragedies and the ironies that attend it" (241). While the "ambivalences" Chakrabarty refers to here may seem similar to Glissant's "ruptures," they are not. An idea of history as "rupture" still posits a whole as an outside and we must ask the following: What generates these ruptures? Are they constituted against a continuous Western history that lies uninterrogated and intact, and that presents its continuity as intrinsic and not open to investigation? The emphasis on ruptures still allows Europe an integrity that exists as a problem for Caribbean historical writing. This is one way in which even new historical methods for the Caribbean continue to subscribe to Western "reason."

62. See Bal and Sinha-Kerkhoff, "Migrations and Shifting (Communal) Identifications," 43–44.

63. In the interim, Samuel Hinds, then prime minister under Jagan, served as president.

64. Chand, "Address on Enmore Martyrs Day 2009."

65. J. Singh emphasizes his own role, rather than Jagan's. Singh, *Guyana*.

66. Ibid., 3.

67. Jagan, *Rooting for Labour*, 13. The speech is titled "Social Development for Economic Growth through Unity. Enmore Martyrs Made the Supreme Sacrifice."

68. St. Pierre, *Anatomy of Resistance*, 67.

69. Jagan, *Rooting for Labour*, 13.

70. Ibid., 29.

71. Ibid., 30.

72. Jagan's exact language: "This democratically elected government, born out of struggle and unity, has unpretentious working class credentials" (*Rooting for Labour*, 20).

73. Jagan, *Rooting for Labour*, 30, author emphasis.

74. Ibid., 8.

75. Ibid., 21.

76. Ibid., 22.

77. Ibid., 15.

78. Ibid., 20.

79. Ibid., 23.

80. Ibid., 30.

81. Jagan, *Selected Speeches*, 25.

82. Ibid.

83. See Jagan, "A New Global Human Order."

84. Jagan, *Selected Speeches*, 88.

85. Ibid., 53.

86. Ibid., 93.

87. Chakrabarty, "Postcoloniality and the Artifice of History," 225. For the initial reference, see chapter 7 of his *Rethinking Working Class History*.

88. Ghosh, "The Diaspora in Indian Culture," 78.

89. The role of middle class capital in maintaining the economic base of the regime is noted by Hintzen. See *The Costs of Regime Survival*.

90. For more on Jagan's position, see his book, *The West on Trial*.

CONCLUSION

1. Mbembe, *On the Postcolony*, 2, emphasis added.

2. There is a growing body of work on the Garifuna in the Caribbean. For a U.S. example, there is the Miles and Holland's edited collection, *Crossing Waters, Crossing Worlds*. Mark Anderson's book looks at the imbrications of blackness and indigeneity among Garifuna in Belize. See *Black and Indigenous Garifuna Activism and Consumer Culture in Honduras*.

3. See Morris, "Cherokee Tribe Faces Decision on Freedmen." For more on the history of Cherokee rights claims, see Denson's *Demanding the Cherokee Nation*.

4. For the reference to Haiti, see Kaussen, "Slaves, *Viejos*, and the *Internationale*."

5. Spivak, *A Critique of Postcolonial Reason*, 37. Spivak goes on to offer, via a reading of Hegel on the *Gita*, a possible "deconstruction" of this problematic.

6. For a discussion of Amerindian epistemology as an alternative to current racial hierarchies, see Mentore's "Guyanese Amerindian Epistemology."

7. DeLoughrey, *Routes and Roots,* 51, 45.

8. Ibid., 51.

9. Ibid., 83, 65.

10. Ibid., 93.

11. Ibid., 240.

12. Ibid., 230.

13. Ibid., 66. This desire is obvious in Harris's novels.

14. Trotz, "Red Thread," 74.

15. Bruyneel, *The Third Space of Sovereignty,* xvii.

16. Ramchand, *The West Indian Novel and Its Background,* 4.

17. The passage is quoted by J. Downing Thompson Jr. in "The Novel Before 1950," 116. I quote from the original: Lamming, *The Pleasures of Exile,* 39, emphasis added. Ramchand also quotes the same passage. Gordon Rohlehr has disagreed with Lamming on this point, saying that his image of the peasant is reductive and, further, that the writer can only represent what the peasant has already accomplished. See Rohlehr, "The Folk in Caribbean Literature."

18. Maes-Jelinek, "The Novel from 1950–1970," 128.

19. Ibid., 127, 165.

20. Ramchand, *The West Indian Novel and Its Background,* 4.

21. Ibid., 164.

22. Ibid., 165.

23. Ibid., 173.

24. Harris, "The Amerindian Legacy," 171.

25. Harris calls for a "new anthropology," despite positively viewing Lévi-Strauss's work.

26. I have argued this point elsewhere in an essay on Harris's *Palace of the Peacock.* See Jackson, "Race, Sex, and Historical Tension."

27. I loosely reference Wilson Harris's *The Palace of the Peacock* and Pauline Melville's *The Ventriloquist's Tale.*

28. Lisser, *Arawak Girl,* 12.

29. This is my reading of Gilroy's work that I develop from Nandini Bhattacharya's discussion of other versions of the Inkle and Yarico tale in "Family Jewels."

30. Greene-Roesel, *Uncle Basil,* vi.

31. Ibid., iii.

32. Ibid., iv.

33. Ibid.

34. See DeLoughrey's chapter in *Routes and Roots,* "Adrift and Unmoored: Globalization and Urban Indigeneity."

35. Jackson, Interview with Basil Rodrigues, December 2006.

36. Greene-Roesel, *Uncle Basil,* 40–41.

37. Ibid., 134–35, fn. 32.

38. Ibid., 97.

39. Ibid., 100–101.

40. Ibid., 130.

41. Ibid., 76.

42. Ibid., 133.

43. Ibid.
44. Ibid., 86.
45. Jackson, Interview with Basil Rodrigues.
46. Greene-Roesel, *Uncle Basil,* 55, author emphasis.
47. Ibid., 24.
48. Ibid., 29–30.
49. Ibid., 56–57.
50. Ibid., 127.
51. Jackson, Interview with Basil Rodrigues.

Bibliography

Achebe, Chinua. [1959] 1991. *Things Fall Apart*. New York: Fawcett Crest.

Ainsa, Fernando. 1986. "From the Golden Age to El Dorado: (Metamorphosis of a Myth)." Translated by Jeanne Ferguson. *Diogenes* 34 (133): 20–46.

———. 1993. "The Myth, Marvel, and Adventure of El Dorado: Semantic Mutations of a Legend." *Diogenes* 41.4 (164): 13–26.

Allen, Carolyn. 2002. "Creole: The Problem of Definition." In *Questioning Creole: Creolisation Discourses in Caribbean Culture, in Honour of Kamau Brathwaite*, edited by V. A. a. G. L. R. Shepherd, 47–63. Kingston, Jamaica: Ian Randle.

Almquist, Steve. 2006. "Not Quite the Gabbling of a 'Thing Most Brutish': Caliban's Kiswahili in Aimé Césaire's *A Tempest*." *Callaloo* 29 (2): 587–607.

"Amerindians Divided over LCDS, Minister Joins Protest." 2010. *Kaieteur News Online*, April 10. http://www.kaieteurnewsonline.com/2010/04/10/amerindians-divided-over-lcds-minister-joins-protest/.

Amerindian Peoples Association. 1999. "About Laws Relating to Amerindians: History of the Amerindian Act." *Wa-Wii-Wa: Amerindian Peoples Association Newsletter* 1 (May): 9–11.

Amerindian Peoples Association. 2003. "Amerindian Act Update." *Wa-Wii-Wa: Amerindian Peoples Association Newsletter* 3.

Anaya, S. James. [1996] 2004. *Indigenous Peoples in International Law*. Oxford, UK: Oxford University Press.

Anderson, Benedict. 1983. *Imagined Communities*. New York: Verso.

Anderson, Mark. *Black and Indigenous Garifuna Activism and Consumer Culture in Honduras*. Minneapolis: University of Minnesota Press, 2009.

Anonymous. 1998. "The Highest Courts of Many Commonwealth Countries Have Recognized the Concept of Aboriginal Title." *Stabroek News*, December 25.

Appiah, Kwame Anthony. 1991. "Is the Post- in Postmodernism the Post- in Postcolonial?" *Critical Inquiry* 17 (2): 336–57.

Arnold, A. James. 1978. "Césaire and Shakespeare: Two Tempests." *Comparative Literature* 30 (3): 236–48.

———. 1981. *Modernism and Negritude: The Poetry and Poetics of Aimé Césaire*. Cambridge, Mass.: Harvard University Press.

Ashcroft, Bill, Gareth Griffiths, and Helen Tiffin. 1989. *The Empire Writes Back: Theory and Practice in Postcolonial Literatures.* London: Routledge.

Atkinson, James. 1998. "Government Should Work with Existing Amerindian Organizations." *Stabroek News,* December 23.

Bal, Ellen, and Kathinka Sinha-Kerkhoff. 2008. "Migrations and Shifting (Communal) Identifications: Munshi Raman Khan (1874–1972)." *Man in India* 88 (1): 43–55.

Barthes, Roland. [1957] 1972. *Mythologies.* Translated by A. Lavers. New York: Noonday.

Beckles, Hilary. 1980. *Sea of Lentils.* Translated by J. Maraniss. Amherst: University of Massachusetts Press.

———. 1996. *The Repeating Island: The Caribbean and the Postmodern Perspective.* Durham, N.C.: Duke University Press.

———. 1998. "Centering Woman: The Political Economy of Gender in West African and Caribbean Slavery." In *Caribbean Portraits: Essays on Gender Ideologies and Identities,* edited by C. Barrow. Kingston, Jamaica: Ian Randle.

Bernabé, Jean, Patrick Chamoiseau, and Raphaël Confiant. [1989] 1990. *In Praise of Creoleness.* Baltimore: Johns Hopkins University Press.

Bhabha, Homi K. 1990. "DissemiNation: Time, Narrative, and the Margins of the Modern Nation." In *Nation and Narration,* edited by H. K. Bhabha, 291–322. London and New York: Routledge.

———. 1990. "Introduction." In *Nation and Narration,* edited by H. K. Bhabha, 1–7. New York: Routledge.

———. 1994. "The Other Question: Stereotype, Discrimination and the Discourse of Colonialism." *The Location of Culture,* 66–84. New York: Routledge.

Bhattacharya, Nandini. 2001. "Family Jewels: George Colman's Inkle and Yarico and Connoisseurship." *Eighteenth-Century Studies* 34 (2): 207–26.

Bolland, O. Nigel. [1998] 2003. *Colonialism and Resistance in Belize: Essays in Historical Sociology.* Jamaica: University of the West Indies Press.

Boucher, Phillip P. 1992. *Cannibal Encounters: Europeans and Island Caribs, 1492–1763.* Baltimore: Johns Hopkins University Press.

Braithwaite, L. E. 1996. "Gold." In *New World: Guyana Independence Issue,* edited by G. Lamming and M. Carter. Georgetown, Guyana: New World Group.

Brathwaite, Edward Kamau. 1970. "Timehri." *Savacou* 2: 35–44.

Brenan, Timothy. 1990. "The National Longing for Form." In *Nation and Narration,* edited by H. K. Bhabha, 44–70. London and New York: Routledge.

Brett, William Henry. 1880. *Legends and Myths of the Aboriginal Indians of British Guiana.* London: W. W. Gardner.

British Information Services. 1959. *British Guiana.* England.

Bruyneel, Kevin. 2007. *The Third Space of Sovereignty: The Postcolonial Politics of U.S.-Indigenous Relations.* Minneapolis: University of Minnesota Press.

Brysk, Alison. 2000. *From Tribal Village to Global Village: Indian Rights and International Relations in Latin America.* Stanford, Calif.: Stanford University Press.

Buckley, Thomas. 1964. "East Indians Flee Race Violence in British Guiana Mining Area." *New York Times,* May 27, 14.

Buck-Morss, Susan. 2000. "Hegel and Haiti." *Critical Inquiry* 26 (4): 821–65.

Bulkan, Janette, and Arif Bulkan. 2006. "'These Forests Have Always Been Ours': Official and Amerindian Discourses on Guyana's Forest Estate." In *Indigenous*

Resurgence in the Contemporary Caribbean: Amerindian Survival and Revival, edited by M. C. Forte, 135–54. New York: Peter Lang.

Burnett, D. Graham. 2000. *Masters of All They Surveyed: Exploration, Geography, and a British El Dorado*. Chicago: University of Chicago Press.

Burnham, Forbes. 1966. "Foreword." *A Short History of the Guyanese People*. Kitty, Guyana.

Burnham, LFS. 1969. "The Power of Cooperative Ownership." Speech by the Prime Minister delivered at the Georgetown Regional Conference of the People's National Congress, August 24, 3–11.

———. 1970. *The Small Man a Real Man in the Co-operative Republic, Guyana: Speeches by the Prime Minister, Mr. Forbes Burnham, in the National Assembly on the Republic Motion*. Edited by Ministry of Information. Georgetown: Guyana Lithograph.

———. 1970. "A Vision of the Co-operative Republic." *Co-Operative Republic, Guyana 1970: A Study of Aspects of Our Way of Life*, edited by L. Searwar, 9–19. Georgetown: Government of Guyana.

———. 1976. *Review: A Pictorial Review of Prime Minister Forbes Burnham's Visits to China, Cuba, and Romania in Commemoration of the Fifty-Third Birthday Anniversary of Guyana's Prime Minister, Feb. 20, 1976*. Georgetown, Guyana: Office of the Prime Minister.

———. 1981. *To Build a New World: Speeches by Comrade LFS Burnham, O. E, S. C., Prime Minister of the Co-operative Republic of Guyana, at the Sixth Conference of Non-Aligned Countries in Havana, Cuba on Tuesday 4th September, 1979*. Georgetown, Guyana: Ministry of Information, Publications Division.

Burton, Richard D. E. 1997. *Afro-Creole: Power, Opposition, and Play in the Caribbean*. Ithaca, N.Y.: Cornell University Press.

Byrd, Jodi Ann. 2002. "Colonialisms: Natives and Arrivants at the Limits of Postcolonial Theory." Dissertation, University of Iowa, Ames, Department of English.

———. 2011. "The Masques of Empire: Torture, Internment, and the Apotheosis of Settler Colonial Commonwealth." Native American and Indigenous Studies Association Conference, May 19–21, Sacramento, Calif..

"Capitalism: Historical Development." *Encyclopedia of Marxism*. Marxists Internet Archive. http://www.marxists.org/glossary/terms/c/a.htm.

Carpentier, Alejo. 1990. *The Harp and the Shadow*. San Francisco: Mercury House.

Carter, Marina. 1996. *Voices from Indenture: Experiences of Indian Migrants in the British Empire*. London: Leicester University Press.

Carter, Martin. 1969. *Republic of Guyana: Broadcast Statement by the Minister of Information Mr. Martin Carter*, August 1. Georgetown: Guyana Lithographic.

Carver, T., ed. 1997. *Marx: Later Political Writings*. New York: Cambridge University Press.

Castanha, Tony. 2011. *The Myth of Indigenous Caribbean Extinction: Continuity and Reclamation in Borikén (Puerto Rico)*. New York: Palgrave Macmillan.

Certeau, Michel de. 1986. *Heterologies*. Volume 17, *Theory and History of Literature*. Minneapolis: University of Minnesota Press.

Césaire, Aimé. [1955] 1972. *Discourse on Colonialism*. New York: Monthly Review Press.

———. [1969] 1970. *The Tragedy of King Christophe; A Play*. Translated by R. Manheim. New York: Grove.

———. 1983. "Birds." In *Aimé Césaire: The Collected Poetry,* edited by C. E. a. A. Smith, 275. Berkeley: University of California Press.

———. 1983. "Notebook of a Return to the Native Land." In *Aimé Césaire: The Collected Poetry,* edited by C. E. a. A. Smith, 32–85. Berkeley: University of California Press.

———. 1996. "Calling the Magician: A Few Words for a Caribbean Civilization." In *Refusal of the Shadow: Surrealism and the Caribbean,* edited by M. Richardson, 199–122. London: Verso.

———. [1969] 2002. *A Tempest: Based on Shakespeare's The Tempest, Adaptation for a Black Theatre.* Translated by R. Miller. New York: TCG Translations.

Chakrabarty, Dipesh. 1989. *Rethinking Working-Class History: Bengal, 1890–1940.* Princeton, N.J.: Princeton University Press.

———. 1992. "Postcoloniality and the Artifice of History: Who Speaks for 'Indian' Pasts?" *Representations* 37: 1–26.

Chand, Komal. 2009. "Address on Enmore Martyrs Day 2009." June 16. http://gawu.net.

Chatterjee, Partha. 1986. *Nationalist Thought and the Colonial World: A Derivative Discourse.* London: Zed.

Cheyfitz, Eric. 1991. *The Poetics of Imperialism: Translation and Colonization from "The Tempest" to "Tarzan."* New York: Oxford University Press.

Chippendale, Neil. 2002. *Sir Walter Raleigh and the Search for El Dorado.* Philadelphia: Chelsea House.

Chua, Amy. 2003. *World on Fire: How Exporting Free Market Democracy Breeds Ethnic Hatred and Global Instability.* New York: Doubleday.

Collins, Rudolph. 1970. "The Story of Our Borders." In *Co-Operative Republic, Guyana 1970: A Study of Aspects of Our Way of Life,* edited by L. Searwar, 257–84. Georgetown: Government of Guyana.

Colonial Office. 1962. *Report of a Commission of Inquiry into Disturbances in British Guiana in February 1962.* London: Her Majesty's Stationery Office.

Columbus, Christopher. 1960. *The Journal of Christopher Columbus.* Translated by C. Jane. New York: Clarkson N. Potter.

Crocker, John. 1968. *The Centaur Guide to the Caribbean and El Dorado.* Fontwell, Sussex, UK: Centaur.

Crocker, John. 1968. *The Centaur Guide to Bermuda, the Bahamas, Hispaniola, Puerto Rico and the Virgin Islands.* Fontwell, Sussex, UK: Centaur.

Dabydeen, David, and Brinsley Samaroo. 1996. *Across the Dark Waters: Ethnicity and Indian Identity in the Caribbean.* London: Macmillan Caribbean.

Daly, Vere T. 1970. "Historical Background to the Co-operative Republic." In *Co-Operative Republic, Guyana 1970: A Study of Aspects of Our Way of Life,* edited by L. Searwear, 211–25. Georgetown: Government of Guyana.

———. [1967] 1974. *The Making of Guyana.* London: Macmillan Education.

———. [1966] 1975. *A Short History of the Guyanese People.* London: Macmillan Education.

Dash, J. Michael. 1998. *The Other America: Caribbean Literature in a New World Context.* Charlottesville: University Press of Virginia.

Davies, Carole Boyce. 1994. *Black Women, Writing, and Identity: Migrations of the Subject.* New York: Routledge.

Davies, Carole Boyce, and Monica Jardine. 2003. "Imperial Geographies and Caribbean

Nationalism: At the Border between 'A Dying Colonialism' and U.S. Hegemony." *CR: The New Centennial Review* 3 (3): 151–74.

Davson, Victor. 1972. *How the Warraus Came.* Georgetown, Guyana: Ministry of Education.

Dayan, Joan. 1992. "Playing Caliban: Césaire's *Tempest*." *Arizona Quarterly* 48 (4): 125–45.

Deleuze, Gilles, and Félix Guattari. 1987. *A Thousand Plateaus: Capitalism and Schizophrenia.* Minneapolis: University of Minnesota Press.

Deloria, Philip J. 1998. *Playing Indian.* New Haven, Conn.: Yale University Press.

Deloria, Vine Jr. [1973] 2003. *God Is Red: A Native View of Religion.* Golden, Colo.: Fulcrum.

DeLoughrey, Elizabeth. 2007. *Routes and Roots: Navigating Caribbean and Pacific Island Literatures.* Honolulu: University of Hawai'i Press.

Denson, Andrew. 2004. *Demanding the Cherokee Nation: Indian Autonomy and American Culture, 1830–1900.* Lincoln: University of Nebraska Press.

Dev, Ravi. 1998. "One People, One Nation." *Stabroek News,* June 1.

Drummond, Lee. 1998. "The Cultural Continuum: A Theory of Intersystems." In *Blackness in Latin America and the Caribbean: Social Dynamics and Cultural Transformations,* edited by J. a. A. T. Norman Whitten. Volume II, 189–214. Bloomington: Indiana University Press.

Eagleton, Terry. 1984. *The Function of Criticism: From the Spectator to Post-Structuralism.* London: Verso.

Edwards, Brent Hayes. 2001. "The Uses of Diaspora." *Social Text* 19 (1): 45–73.

———. 2003. *The Practice of Diaspora: Literature, Translation and the Rise of Black Internationalism.* Cambridge, Mass.: Harvard University Press.

Emmer, P. C., ed. 1999. *General History of the Caribbean.* Volume II: *New Societies: The Caribbean in the Long Sixteenth Century.* London: Unesco Publishing; Basingstoke: Macmillan Education.

Fanon, Frantz. 1963. *The Wretched of the Earth: Presence Africaine.* New York: Grove Press.

———. [1967] 1998. *Black Skin, White Masks.* Translated by C. L. Markmann. New York: Grove Weidenfeld.

Farred, Grant. 2008. "The Unsettler." *South Atlantic Quarterly* 107 (4): 791–808.

Fernández, Antonio de Pedro. 1969. *La Historia y el Derecho en la Reclamación Venezolana de la Guayana Esequiba.* Caracas and Madrid: Editorial Mediterráneo

Field, Les. 1994. "Who Are the Indians? Reconceptualizing Indigenous Identity, Resistance and the Role of Social Science in Latin America." *Latin American Research Review* 29 (3): 227–38.

Fischlin, Daniel, and Martha Nandorfy, eds. 2002. *Eduardo Galeano: Through the Looking Glass.* New York: Black Rose Books.

Forbes, Jack D. 1988. *Black Africans and Native Americans: Color, Race, and Caste in the Evolution of Red-Black Peoples.* New York: Blackwell.

Forte, Jeanette. 1994. *Amerindian Concerns: A Compilation from the Written Submissions Received by the Amerindian Research Unit from Amerindian Village Councils in Preparation for the National Conference of Amerindian Representatives.* Turkeyen: University of Guyana, Amerindian Research Unit.

Forte, Maximilian C. 2004–2005. "Extinction: The Historical Trope of Anti-indigeneity in the Caribbean." *Issues in Caribbean Amerindian Studies* 6 (4): 1–24.

———. 2005. *Ruins of Absence, Presence of Caribs: (Post)colonial Representations of Abo-riginality in Trinidad and Tobago.* Gainesville: University Press of Florida.

Forte, Maximilian C., ed. 2006. *Indigenous Resurgence in the Contemporary Caribbean: Amerindian Survival and Revival.* New York: Peter Lang.

Foucault, Michel. [1966] 1994. "Labour, life, language." *The Order of Things: An Archae-ology of the Human Sciences,* 250–302. New York: Vintage Books.

Fox, Patricia D. 2006. *Being and Blackness in Latin America: Uprootedness and Improv-isation.* Gainesville: University Press of Florida.

Fujikane, Candace, and Jonathan Y. Okamura, eds. 2008. *Asian Settler Colonialism: From Local Governance to the Habits of Everyday Life in Hawai'i.* Honolulu: University of Hawai'i Press.

Gaffron, Norma. 1990. *El Dorado, Land of Gold: Opposing Viewpoints.* San Diego, Calif.: Greenhaven.

Galeano, Eduardo. 2006. "Myths as Collective Metaphors." *MR Zine.* http://mrzine .monthlyreview.org/2006/galeano240906.html.

Gampat, Ramesh. 1998. In Guyana Politics Dictates Economics. *Stabroek News,* Octo-ber 30.

Gellner, Ernest. 1983. *Nations and Nationalism.* Ithaca, N.Y.: Cornell University Press.

Ghosh, Amitav. 1989. "The Diaspora in Indian Culture." *Public Culture* 2 (1): 73–78.

Gilroy, Paul. [1987] 1991. *There Ain't No Black in the Union Jack: The Cultural Politics of Race and Nation.* Chicago: University of Chicago Press.

———. 1993. *The Black Atlantic: Modernity and Double Consciousness.* Cambridge, Mass.: Harvard University Press.

Glissant, Edouard. 1989. *Caribbean Discourse: Selected Essays.* Charlottesville: Univer-sity of Virginia Press.

———. 1997. *Poetics of Relation.* Ann Arbor: University of Michigan Press.

Goldstein, Alyosha. "Where the Nation Takes Place: Proprietary Regimes, Antistatism, and U.S. Settler Colonialism." *South Atlantic Quarterly* 107 (4): 833–61.

Gomes, Ralph. 1998. "Race, Class, and Politics in Guyana: The Role of the Power Elites." In *Blackness in Latin America in the Caribbean: Social Dynamics and Cultural Transformations,* edited by J. a. A. T. Norman Whitten. Volume II, 146–59. Blooming-ton: Indiana University Press.

González, José Luis. [1980] 1993. *Puerto Rico: The Four Storeyed Country.* Translated by G. Guinness. Princeton, N.J.: Markus Wiener.

Goveia, Elsa. 1970. "The Social Framework." *Savacou* 2: 7–15.

Gramsci, Antonio. 1971. *The Prison Notebooks.* New York: International Publishers.

Granger, McDonald. 2004. "Talk of Motherlands Is Divisive, ARC Is the Answer." *Stabroek News,* April 3.

Green F. Ray H. et al. [1945] 1946. "Aboriginal Indian Committee-Interim Report." Georgetown, Demerara: Department of Lands and Mines.

Greene-Roesel, Justin. 1998. *Uncle Basil: An Arawak Biography.* Georgetown, Guyana: Hamburgh Register.

Gregg, Veronica. 2002. "'Yuh Know Bout Coo-Coo? Where Yuh Know Bout Coo-Coo?': Language and Representation, Creolisation and Confusion in 'Indian Cui-sine.'" In *Questioning Creole: Creolisation Discourses in Caribbean Culture, in Honour of Kamau Brathwaite,* edited by V. A. a. G. L. R. Sheperd, 148–68. Kingston, Jamaica: Ian Randle.

Guyana Bureau of Statistics. "Chapter II: Population Composition." 2002 Census, 27–29. http://www.statisticsguyana.gov.gy/pubs/Chapter2_Population_Composition.pdf.

Guyana Information News Agency (GINA). 2011. *Hinterland Highlights,* May 1–4. http://www.gina.gov.gy/Hinterland%20Highlights-%20Vol%201.pdf.

"Guyana to Approach Suriname on Border Talks—Insanally." 2004. *Stabroek News,* January 9.

Hackett, M. L. 1998. "The Conference on Race and Discrimination Was a Success." *Stabroek News,* December 25.

Hall, Kim. 1996. *Things of Darkness: Economies of Race and Gender in Early Modern England.* Ithaca, N.Y.: Cornell University Press.

Hall, Stuart. 1996. "Cultural Identity and Diaspora." In *Contemporary Postcolonial Theory: A Reader,* edited by P. Mongia, 110–21. London: Arnold.

Hanbury-Tenison, Robin. 1985. *Guyana: Indian Lands in Guyanan-Venezuelan Border Dispute Communication to the United Nations Information Pack/Guy/Lands/Jun/1985.* London.

Hardt, Michael, and Antonio Negri. 2001. *Empire.* Cambridge, Mass.: Harvard University Press.

Harris, Wilson. 1968. *The Palace of the Peacock.* London: Faber and Faber. Original edition 1960.

———. 1995. *History, Fable, and Myth in the Caribbean and Guianas.* Edited by Selwyn Reginald Cudjoe. Calaloux.

———. 1999. "The Amerindian Legacy." In *Selected Essays of Wilson Harris: The Unfinished Genesis of the Imagination,* edited by A. J. M. Bundy, 167–76. New York: Routledge.

———. 1999. "Creoleness: the Crossroads of a Civilization?" In *Selected Essays of Wilson Harris: The Unfinished Genesis of the Imagination,* edited by A. J. M. Bundy, 237–47. New York: Routledge.

———. 1999. "History, Fable and Myth in the Caribbean and Guianas." In *Selected Essays of Wilson Harris: The Unfinished Genesis of the Imagination,* edited by A. J. M. Bundy, 152–66. New York: Routledge.

———. 1999. "Profiles of Myth and the New World." In *Selected Essays of Wilson Harris: The Unfinished Genesis of the Imagination,* edited by A. J. M. Bundy, 201–11. New York: Routledge.

Harry-Voglezon, Lin-Jay. 1998. Letter to the Editor. *Stabroek News,* June 2.

Hawley-Bryant, W. n.d. *Song of Guyana's Children.* http://www.silvertorch.com/guysongs.htm.

Hegel, G. W. F. [1807] 1977. "A. Independence and Dependence of Self-Consciousness: Lordship and Bondage." In *Phenomenology of Spirit,* 111–18. Oxford, UK: Oxford University Press.

———. 1991. *The Philosophy of History.* Translated by J. Sibree. New York: Prometheus.

Hemming, John. 1978. *The Search for El Dorado.* London: Michael Joseph.

Henry, Paget. 1998. "Philosophy and the Caribbean Intellectual Tradition." *Small Axe* 4: 3–28.

———. 2000. *Caliban's Reason: Introducing Afro-Caribbean Philosophy.* New York: Routledge.

Henwood, Doug. 2000. "Profiteering in the Hemisphere." *North American Congress on Latin America Report on the Americas* 34 (3): 49–59.

Higman, B. W. 1999. *Writing West Indian Histories.* London: Macmillan Education.

———. 2011. *A Concise History of the Caribbean.* Cambridge, UK: Cambridge University Press.

Hintzen, Percy. 1989. *The Costs of Regime Survival: Racial Mobilization, Elite Domination and the Control of the State in Guyana and Trinidad.* Cambridge, UK: Cambridge University Press.

———. 1997. "Reproducing Domination Identity and Legitimacy Constructs in the West Indies." *Social Identities* 3 (1): 47–76.

———. 1998. "Democracy on Trial: The December 1997 Elections in Guyana and Its Aftermath." *Caribbean Studies Newsletter* 25: 13–16.

———. 2002. "Race and Creole Ethnicity in the Caribbean." *Questioning Creole: Creolisation Discourses in Caribbean Culture, in Honour of Kamau Brathwaite,* edited by V. A. a. G. L. R. Sheperd, 92–110. Kingston, Jamaica: Ian Randle.

Hochberg, Adam. 2007. "Lumbees' Tribal Recognition Depends on Senate." *All Things Considered.* National Public Radio, July 18.

Hollett, David. 1999. *Passage from India to El Dorado: Guyana and the Great Migration.* Madison, N.J.: Farleigh Dickinson University Press.

Holt, Sarah, Steve Audette, Daniel McCabe, and Zvi Dor-Ner, dirs. 2007. *The Magnificent Voyage of Christopher Columbus.* Boston: WGBH.

Hoyte, Desmond. 1985. *My First Sixty Days in Office: Address to the Nation by His Excellency, Cde H. D. Hoyte, S. C. President of the Co-operative Republic.* Georgetown, Guyana: Office of the President.

Huhndorf, Shari M. *Going Native: Indians in the American Cultural Imagination.* Ithaca, N.Y.: Cornell University Press, 2001.

Hulme, Peter. 1987. *Colonial Encounters: Europe and the Native Caribbean, 1492–1797.* London: Methuen.

Huntley, Eric L. 1994. *The Life and Times of Cheddi Jagan.* London: Bogle-L'Ouverture Press.

Ivison, Duncan, Paul Patton, and Will Sanders, eds. 2000. *Political Theory and the Rights of Indigenous Peoples.* Cambridge, UK: Cambridge University Press.

Jack, H. O. 1970. "The Thrust into the Hinterland." In *Co-Operative Republic, Guyana 1970: A Study of Aspects of Our Way of Life,* edited by L. Searwar, 197–209. Georgetown: Government of Guyana.

Jackson, Shona N. 2004. "The Recalcitrant Muse: Race, Sex and Historical Tension in the Search for the West Indian (Trans) Subject." *Caribbean Quarterly* 50 (3):47–62.

———. 2005. "Subjection and Resistance in the Transformation of Guyana's Mytho-Colonial Landscape." In *Caribbean Literature and the Environment: Between Nature and Culture,* edited by Elizabeth DeLoughrey, Renée K. Gosson, and George B. Handley, 85–98. Charlottesville: University of Virginia Press.

———. 2006. "Guyana, Cuba, Venezuela and the 'Routes' to Cultural Reconciliation between Latin America and the Caribbean." *Small Axe* 19 (February): 28–58.

———. 2006. "Race, Sex, and Historical Tension in the Search for the Transcendental Creole Subject." In *Changing Currents: Transnational Caribbean Literary and Cultural Criticism,* edited by E. A. W. a. M. B. Rahming, 195–219. Trenton, N.J.: Africa World Press.

———. 2010. "The Baptism of Soil: Rooplall Monar and the Aesthetics of the Kala Pani Modern." *Journal of Caribbean Literatures* 6 (3): 9–22.

Jagan, Cheddi. 1993. *Rooting for Labour: Selected Address of President Jagan as He Speaks Out for the Working Class*. Guyana: Guyana National Printers.

———. 1995. *Cheddi Jagan Selected Speeches, 1992–1994*. Edited by D. Dabydeen. London: Hansib Publishing.

———. [1980] 1997. *The West on Trial: My Fight for Guyana's Freedom*. Antigua: Hansib Caribbean.

———. [1999] 2001. *A New Global Human Order*. Milton, Ontario, Canada: Harpy.

Jagan, Janet. 1993. *When Grandpa Cheddi Was a Boy and Other Stories*. Leeds, UK: Peepal Tree Press.

James, C.L.R. [1963] 1989. *The Black Jacobins: Toussaint L'Ouverture and the San Domingo Revolution*. 2nd ed. New York: Vintage Books.

Jane, Cecil, ed. 1988. *The Four Voyages of Columbus: A History in Eight Documents, Including Five by Christopher Columbus, in the Original Spanish, with English Translations*. New York: Dover.

Johnson, Lemuel. [1973] 1995. *Highlife for Caliban*. Trenton, N.J.: Africa World Press.

Jones, Wayne. 1981. *Towards Further Amerindian Integration and Development: The Persuasive Approach*. Ministry of Information.

Joseph, Margaret Paul. 1992. *Caliban in Exile: The Outsider in Caribbean Fiction*. Volume 43: *Contributions to the Study of World Literature*. Westport, Conn.: Greenwood.

Kale, Madhavi. 1998. *Fragments of Empire: Capital, Slavery, and Indian Indentured Labor Migration to the British Caribbean*. Philadelphia: University of Pennsylvania Press.

Kambel, Ellen-Rose, and Fergus MacKay. 1999. *The Rights of Indigenous Peoples and Maroons in Suriname*. Copenhagen, Denmark: International Work Group for Indigenous Affairs/The Forest Peoples Programme.

Kaplan, Caren, Norma Alarcón, and Minoo Moallem, eds. 1999. *Between Woman and Nation: Nationalisms, Transnational Feminisms, and the State*. Durham, N.C.: Duke University Press.

Kauanui, J. Kēhaulani. 2008. "Colonialism in Equality: Hawaiian Sovereignty and the Question of U.S. Civil Rights." *South Atlantic Quarterly* 107 (4): 635–50.

Kaussen, Valerie. 2004. "Slaves, *Viejos*, and the *Internationale*: Modernity and Global Contact in Jacques Roumain's *Gouverneurs de la Rosée*." *Research in African Literatures* 35 (4): 121–41.

Kemala, Kempadoo, ed. 1999. *Sun, Sex, and Gold: Tourism and Sex Work in the Caribbean*. Lanham, Md.: Rowman & Littlefield.

Kersting, M. L. 1998. "No True Racism in Guyana." *Stabroek News*, December 24.

Khan, Aisha. 2007. "Mixing Matters: Callaloo Nation Revisited." *Callaloo* 30 (1): 51–67.

Khan, Babur M. 1998. "Ethnicity Is Breaking Loose from the Confines of the Nation-State." *Stabroek News*, December 24.

King, Winston. 1970. "Planning in the New Society." In *Co-Operative Republic, Guyana 1970: A Study of Aspects of Our Way of Life,* edited by L. Searwar, 39–48. Georgetown: Government of Guyana.

Knight, Franklin. [1978] 1990. *The Caribbean: The Genesis of a Fragmented Nationalism*. Oxford, UK: Oxford University Press.

Kwayana, Eusi [Sydney King]. 1970. "Economic Relations in Pre-Republican Guyana." *In Co-Operative Republic, Guyana 1970: A Study of Aspects of Our Way of Life,* edited by L. Searwar, 21–36. Georgetown: Government of Guyana.

———. 1999. *Next Witness: An Appeal to World Opinion: Commentary on the Commission of Inquiry into Disturbances in British Guiana in February 1962.* Georgetown, Guyana: n.p.

LaGuerre, John Gaffar. 1995. "Introduction." In *Cheddi Jagan Selected Speeches, 1992–1994,* edited by D. Daybdeen, 7–15. London: Hansib Publishing.

Lâm, Maivân Clech. 2000. *Indigenous Peoples and Self-Determination.* New York: Transnational.

Lamming, George. [1983] 1991. *In the Castle of My Skin.* Ann Arbor: University of Michigan Press.

———. [1960]1992. *The Pleasures of Exile.* Ann Arbor: University of Michigan Press.

Las Casas, Bartolomé de. [1548–1550] 1974. *In Defense of the Indians: The Defense of the Most Reverend Lord, Don Fray Bartolomé de Las Casas, of the Order of Preachers, Late Bishop of Chiapa, Against the Persecutors and Slanderers of the Peoples of the New World Discovered Across the Seas.* Edited by S. Poole. DeKalb: Northern Illinois University Press.

Lashey, Marilyn E. 2011. "Globalization in Australia, Canada, Fiji, and New Zealand." Panel: Other and Otherness: Indigeneity and Multiculturalism. Native American and Indigenous Studies Association, May 19–21, Sacramento, Calif.

Lawrence, Bonita, and Enakshi Dua. 2005. "Decolonizing Antiracism." *Social Justice* 32 (4): 120–43.

Lenin, V. I. 1899 [1974]. *The Development of Capitalism in Russia.* Moscow: Progress Publishers.

Levine, Norman. 2006. *Divergent Paths: Hegel in Marxism and Engelsism.* Lanham, Md.: Lexington Books.

Lewis, Bart L. 2003.*The Miraculous Lie: Lope de Aguirre and the Search for El Dorado in the Latin American Historical Novel.* Lanham, Md.: Lexington Books.

Lewis, Gordon K. 1983. *Main Currents in Caribbean Thought: The Historical Evolution of Caribbean Society in Its Ideological Aspects, 1492–1900.* Baltimore: Johns Hopkins University Press.

Lisser, Herbert George de. 1968. *The Arawak Girl.* Kingston, Jamaica: Pioneer.

Loncke, Joycelynne. 1994. *In the Shadow of El Dorado: A Collection of Essays on Caribbean Themes in Literature.* Trinidad and Tobago: Port of Spain: J. Loncke.

Lukács, Georg. 1980. *The Ontology of Social Being 3. Labour.* Translated by D. Fernbach. London: Merlin.

Madureira, Luís. 2005. *Cannibal Modernities: Postcoloniality and the Avant-Garde in Caribbean and Brazilian Literature.* Charlottesville: University of Virginia Press.

Maes-Jelinek, Hena. 2001. "The Novel from 1950–1970." In *A History of Literature in the Caribbean,* edited by A. J. Arnold. Volume II, 127–48. Philadelphia: John Benjamins.

Mahabir, Kumar. 2008. "Introduction: An Overview of Indian Diaspora in the Caribbean." *Man in India* 88 (1): 1–4.

Mamdani, Mahmood. 2001. "Beyond Settler and Native as Political Identities: Overcoming the Political Legacy of Colonialism." *Comparative Studies in Society and History* 43(4): 651–64.

Mangru, Basdeo. 1999. *Indians in Guyana: A Concise History from Their Arrival to the Present.* Chicago: Adams Press.

Manley, Robert H. 1982. *Guyana Emergent: The Post-independence Struggle for Nondependent Development.* Boston: Schenkman.

Mann, Charles C. [2005] 2006. *1491: New Revelations of the Americas before Columbus.* New York: Vintage Books.

Manuel, Peter. 2000. *East Indian Music in the West Indies: Tân-singing, Chutney, and the Making of Indo-Caribbean Culture.* Philadelphia: Temple University Press.

Marx, Karl. 1974. "The British Rule in India." *On Colonialism,* 35–41. Moscow: Progress Publishers.

Mbembe, Achille. 2001. *On the Postcolony.* Berkeley: University of California Press.

Means, Russell. 1980. "Black Hills Speech." http://www.blackhawkproductions.com/russelmeans.html.

Melville, Pauline. 1997. *The Ventriloquist's Tale.* New York: Bloomsbury.

Menezes, Mary Noel. 1977. *British Policy towards the Amerindians in British Guiana, 1803–1873.* Oxford, UK: Clarendon Press.

———. 1992. "The Controversial Question of Protection and Jurisdiction Re the Amerindians in Guyana." *SWI forum voor Kunst, cultuur en Wetenschap* 9 (1&2): 7–24.

Mentore, George. 2005. *Of Passionate Curves and Desirable Cadences: Themes on Waiwai Social Being.* Lincoln: University of Nebraska Press.

———. 2007. "Guyanese Amerindian Epistemology: The Gift from a Pacifist Insurgence." *Race and Class* 49 (2): 57–70.

Midgett, Douglas. 1998. "West Indian Version: Literature, History, and Identity [Grenada]." *Blackness in Latin America and the Caribbean.* Volume II, 337–64. Bloomington: Indiana University Press.

Mignolo, Walter. 2000. *Local Histories/Global Designs.* Princeton, N.J.: Princeton University Press.

———. 2008. "The Geopolitics of Knowledge and the Colonial Difference." *Coloniality at Large: Latin America and the Postcolonial Debate.* Durham, N.C.: Duke University Press.

Miles, Tiya, and Sharon P. Holland, eds. 2006. *Crossing Waters, Crossing Worlds: The African Diaspora in Indian Country.* Durham, N.C.: Duke University Press.

Miller, Christopher L. 2008. *The French Atlantic Triangle: Literature and Culture of the Slave Trade.* Durham, N.C.: Duke University Press.

Mills, Charles W. 1997. *The Racial Contract.* Ithaca, N.Y.: Cornell University Press.

Ministerio de Relaciones Exteriores. 1967. *Informe que los expertos venezolanos para la cuestión de límites con Guayana Británica presentan al Gobierno Nacional.* República de Venezuela: Caracas.

Ministry of Amerindian Affairs. 2005. *The New Amerindian Act: What Will It Do for Amerindians?* Georgetown, Guyana: Guyana Government Information Agency (GINA).

Ministry of Information and Culture. 1970. *A Brief Outline of the Progress of Integration in Guyana.* Georgetown, Guyana. Ministry of Information and Culture.

Ministry of Legal Affairs. 1976. "Chapter 29:01, Amerindian Act." *Laws of Guyana,* 3–40.

Mishra, Vijay. 1996. "The Diasporic Imaginary: Theorizing the Indian Diaspora." *Textual Practice* 10 (3): 421–47.

———. 2001. "The Feudal Post-colonial: The Fiji Crisis." In *Diaspora: Theories, Histories, Texts,* edited by M. Paranjape, 319–40.

Moberg, Mark. 1992. "Continuity under Colonial Rule: The *Alcalde* System and the Garifuna in Belize, 1858–1969." *Ethnohistory* 39 (1): 1–19.

Mohammed, Patricia. 2002. The 'Creolisation' of Indian Women in Trinidad." In *Questioning Creole: Creolisation Discourses in Caribbean Culture, in Honour of Kamau Brathwaite,* edited by V. A. a. G. L. R. Shepherd, 130–47. Kingston, Jamaica: Ian Randle.

Monar, Rooplall. 1987. *Backdam People.* Leeds, UK: Peepal Tree Press.

———. 1987. *Koker.* Leeds, UK: Peepal Tree Press.

———. 1994. *Estate People.* Lacytown, Guyana: Roraima.

———. 1998. "We Are Not Indians, We Are Guyanese." *Stabroek News,* October 30.

Monroe, James. 1823. *Monroe Doctrine.* New Haven, Conn.: Yale Law School, Lillian Goldman Law Library. http://avalon.law.yale.edu/19th_century/monroe.asp.

Morgensen, Scott Lauria. "Settler Homonationalism: Theorizing Settler Colonialism within Queer Modernities." *GLQ : A Journal of Lesbian and Gay Studies* 16: 1–2.

Morris, Frank. 2007. "Cherokee Tribe Faces Decision on Freedmen." National Public Radio, February 21.

Moses, Nagamootoo. 1999. "Remembering Cheddi Jagan: He Planted a Tree of Memories." Cheddi Jagan Research Centre. http://jagan.org/remembering13.htm.

Munasinghe, Viranjini. 2001. *Callaloo or Tossed Salad? East Indians and the Cultural Politics of Identity in Trinidad.* Ithaca, N.Y.: Cornell University Press.

Naipaul, V. S. 1973. *The Loss of El Dorado: A Colonial History.* Harmondsworth, UK: Penguin.

Nelson, Diane M. 1999. *A Finger in the Wound: Body Politics in Quincentennial Guatemala.* Berkeley: University of California Press.

Niezen, Ronald. 2003. *The Origins of Indigenism: Human Rights and the Politics of Identity.* Berkeley: University of California Press.

Nixon, Rob. 1987. "Caribbean and African Appropriations of 'The Tempest.'" *Critical Inquiry* 13 (3): 557–78.

Obama, Barack. 2007. *Dreams from My Father: A Story of Race and Inheritance.* New York: Crown. Original edition 1995.

Omi, Michael, and Howard Winant. 1994. *Racial Formation in the United States: From the 1960s to the 1990s.* New York: Routledge.

Oxford English Dictionary. 1989. 2nd ed. Oxford, UK: Oxford University Press. http://dictionary.oed.com.

Palmer, Vera. 2011. "Verses Versus: Native Poetry and Settler Colonialism." Native American and Indigenous Studies Association Conference, May 18–21, Sacramento, Calif.

Paquet, Sandra Pouchet. 1991. "Foreword." In *the Castle of My Skin,* ix–xxxiii. Ann Arbor: University of Michigan Press.

Pateman, Carole. 2007. "The Settler Contract." *Contract and Domination,* 35–78. Cambridge, UK: Polity Press.

Patterson, Orlando. 1991. *Freedom: Freedom in the Making of Western Culture,* vol. 1. New York: Basic Books.

Payne, Tommy. 1970. "Windows on Guyanese History." In *Co-Operative Republic, Guyana 1970: A Study of Aspects of Our Way of Life,* edited by L. Searwar, 227–54. Georgetown: Government of Guyana.

Persaud, Yesu. 1988. "Preface to Second Printing." *Centenary History of the East Indians of British Guiana, 1888–1938.* Georgetown, Guyana: East Indians 150th Anniversary Committee.

Pitman, Frank Wesley. 1917. *The Development of the British West Indies, 1700–1763.* New Haven, Conn.: Yale University Press.

Polanco, Hector Diaz. 1997. *Indigenous Peoples in Latin America: The Quest for Self-Determination.* Translated by L. Rayas. Boulder, Colo.: Westview.

Poonai, N. O. 1970. "Wilderness and Wildlife in Guyana: An Ecological Study of the Flora and Fauna." In *Co-Operative Republic, Guyana 1970: A Study of Aspects of Our Way of Life*, edited by L. Searwear, 161–94. Georgetown: Government of Guyana.

Poynting, Jeremy. 1987. "Introduction." *Khoker.* Leeds, UK: Peepal Tree.

Pratt, Mary L. 1991. "Arts of the Contact Zone." *Profession* 91: 33–40.

Premdas, Ralph. 1995. *Ethnic Identity in the Caribbean: Decentering a Myth.* Toronto, Ontario, Canada: University of Toronto Press.

Price-Mars, Jean. [1928] 1983. *So Spoke the Uncle.* Washington, D.C.: Three Continents Press.

Rahier, Jean. 1999. "Blackness as a Process of Creolization: The Afro-Esmeraldian *Décimas* (Ecuador)." In *The African Diaspora: African Origins and New World Identities*, edited by I. Okpewho, Carole Boyce Davies, and Ali A. Mazrui, 290–314. Bloomington: Indiana University Press.

Ralegh, Sir Walter. 1997. *The Discoverie of the Large, Rich, and Bewtiful Empyre of Guiana.* Translated by N. L. Whitehead. Norman: University of Oklahoma Press.

Ramchand, Kenneth. 1970. *The West Indian Novel and Its Background.* New York: Barnes & Noble.

Reddock, Rhoda, ed. 1996. *Ethnic Minorities in Caribbean Societies.* St. Augustine, Trinidad: ISER, University of the West Indies.

Retamar, Roberto Fernández. 1889. *Caliban and Other Essays.* Translated by E. Barker. Minneapolis: University of Minnesota Press.

Rivière, Peter, ed. 2006. *The Guiana Travels of Robert Schomburgk 1835–1844.* Volume II: *The Boundary Survey.* London: Ashgate: Hakluyt Society.

Rodney, Walter. 1981. *A History of the Guyanese Working People, 1881–1905.* Baltimore: Johns Hopkins University Press.

Rohlehr, Gordon. [1972] 1978. "The Folk in Caribbean Literature." In *Critics on Caribbean Literature: Readings in Literary Criticism*, edited by E. Baugh, 24–26. New York: St. Martin's.

Rohrer, Judy. 2010. "Attacking Trust: Hawai'i as a Crossroads and Kamehameha Schools in the Crosshairs." *American Quarterly* 62 (3): 437–55.

Roosevelt, Theodore. 1905. *Theodore Roosevelt's Corollary to the Monroe Doctrine.* http://www.ourdocuments.gov/doc.php?flash=true&doc=56.

Rosser, Miriam 1998. "Figuring Caribbeanness: Identity, Home, Nation, Woman, 1972–1999." *Centennial Review* 42: 475–510.

Ruhomon, Peter. [1947] 1988. *Centenary History of the East Indians of British Guiana, 1888–1938.* Georgetown, Guyana: East Indians 150th Anniversary Committee.

Saldaña-Portillo, María Josefina. 2008. "'How Many Mexicans [Is] a Horse Worth?': The League of United Latin American Citizens, Desegregation Cases, and Chicano Historiography." *South Atlantic Quarterly* 107 (4): 809–31.

Salinger Ferrante, Allyson. 2008. "Telling Our History: The CSA Presidents' Archive." *Caribbean Studies Association Newsletter* 35 (2): 23–31.

Sarnecki, Judith Holland. 2000. "Mastering the Masters: Aimé Césaire's Creolization of Shakespeare's *The Tempest.*" *French Review* 74 (2): 276–86.

Saunders, Andrew. 1972. "Amerindians in Guyana: A Minority Group in a Multi-Ethnic Society." *Caribbean Studies.* 12 (2): 31–51.

Schildt, Janine. 2009. *The Balance between Indigenous Land Claims and Individual Private Property Rights in Latin America: A Challenge for the Human Rights Jurisdiction of the Inter-American Court of Human Rights*. Berlin: Hertie School of Governance.

Scott, David. 2000. "The Re-Enchantment of Humanism: An Interview with Sylvia Wynter." *Small Axe* 8: 119–207.

———. 2004. *Conscripts of Modernity: The Tragedy of Colonial Enlightenment*. Durham, N.C.: Duke University Press.

Seecharan, Clem. 1993. *India and the Shaping of the Indo-Guyanese Imagination 1890s–1920s*. Leeds, UK: Peepal Tree Press.

Seecharan, Clem, ed. 2001. *Joseph Ruhomon's India: The Progress of Her People at Home and Abroad, and How Those in British Guiana May Improve Themselves*. Kingston, Jamaica: University of the West Indies Press.

Selvon, Samuel. [1952] 1979. *A Brighter Sun*. Washington, D.C.: Three Continents Press.

Seth, Vanita. 2010. *Europe's Indians: Producing Racial Difference, 1500–1900*. Durham, N.C.: Duke University Press.

Severin, Timothy. 1970. *The Golden Antilles*. New York: Knopf.

Seymour, A. J. 1970. "Cultural Values in the Republic of Guyana." *Co-Operative Republic, Guyana 1970: A Study of Aspects of Our Way of Life*, edited by L. Searwear, 79–92. Georgetown: Government of Guyana.

Shakespeare, William. 1994. *The Tempest*. Edited by S. Orgel. New York: Oxford University Press.

Shannon, Magdaline. 1996. *Jean Price-Mars, the Haitian Elite and the American Occupation, 1915–1935*. New York: St. Martin's.

Shepherd, Verene A., and Glen L. Richards. 2002. "Introduction." In *Questioning Creole: Creolisation Discourses in Caribbean Culture; In Honour of Kamau Brathwaite*, edited by V. A. a. G. L. R. Shepherd, xi–xxvii. Kingston, Jamaica: Ian Randle.

Silva, Denise Ferreira da. 2007. *Toward a Global Idea of Race*. Minneapolis: University of Minnesota Press.

Singh, Chaitram. 1988. *Guyana: Politics in a Plantation Society*. New York: Praeger.

Singh, Jai Narine. 1996. *Guyana: Democracy Betrayed, A Political History 1948–1993*. Kingston, Jamaica: Kingston Publishers.

Smith, Anthony D. 1983. *State and Nation in the Third World: The Western State and African Nationalism*. Brighton, Sussex, UK: Wheatsheaf.

Smith, Linda Tuhiwai. 1999. *Decolonizing Methodologies: Research and Indigenous Peoples*. London: Zed.

Smith, Raymond T. 1962. *British Guiana*. London: Oxford University Press.

SookDeo, Neil A. 2008. "Involuntary Globalization: How Britain Revived Indenture and Made It Largely Brown and East Indian (Trinidad 1806–1921)." *Man in India* 88 (1): 5–27.

Spivak, Gayatri. 1986. "Imperialism and Sexual Difference." *Oxford Literary Review* 8 (1–2): 225–40.

———. 1988. "Can the Subaltern Speak?" *Marxism and the Interpretation of Culture*, edited by C. a. L. G. Nelson, 271–313. Urbana: University of Illinois Press.

———. 1999. *A Critique of Postcolonial Reason: Toward a History of the Vanishing Present*. Cambridge, Mass.: Harvard University Press.

Spivak, Gayatri Chakravorty. 2004. "Righting Wrongs." *South Atlantic Quarterly* 103 (2/3): 523–58.

Springfield, Consuelo López, ed. 1997. *Daughters of Caliban: Caribbean Women in the Twentieth Century*. Bloomington: Indiana University Press.

St. Pierre, Maurice. 1999. *Anatomy of Resistance: Anti-colonialism in Guyana, 1823–1966*. London: Macmillan Education.

Stasiulis, Daiva, and Nira Yuval-Davis. 1995. "Introduction: Beyond Dichotomies—Gender, Race, Ethnicity and Class in Settler Societies." In *Unsettling Settler Societies: Articulations of Gender, Race, Ethnicity, and Class*, edited by D. a. N. Y.-D. Stasiulis, 1–38. London: Sage.

Sued-Badillo, Jalil, ed. 2004. *General History of the Caribbean*. Volume I: *Autochthonous Societies*. London: Unesco Publishing; Basingstoke: Macmillan Education.

Swan, Michael. 1958. *The Marches of El Dorado: British Guiana, Brazil, Venezuela*. Boston: Beacon Press.

Thomas, Clive Y. 1984. *The Rise of the Authoritarian State in Peripheral Societies*. New York: Monthly Review Press.

Thompson, J. Downing Jr. 2001. "The Novel before 1950." In *A History of Literature in the Caribbean*, edited by A. J. Arnold. Volume II, 115–26. Philadelphia: John Benjamins.

Topa, Wahinkpe, D. T. (Four Arrows/Donald Trent Jacobs). 2006. "Prologue: Red Road, Red Lake—Red Flag!" In *Unlearning the Language of Conquest: Scholars Expose Anti-Indianism in America: Deceptions That Influence War and Peace, Civil Liberties, Public Education, Religion and Spirituality, Democratic Ideals, the Environment, Law, Literature, Film, and Happiness*, 1–17. Austin: University of Texas Press.

Trotz, Alissa D. 2004. "Between Despair and Hope: Women and Violence in Contemporary Guyana." *Small Axe* 15: 1–20.

———. 2007. "Red Thread: The Politics of Hope in Guyana." *Race and Class* 49 (2): 71–130.

Trouillot, Michel-Rolph. 1995. *Silencing the Past: Power and the Production of History*. Boston: Beacon Press.

Tully, James. 2000. "The Struggles of Indigenous Peoples for and of Freedom." *Political Theory and the Rights of Indigenous Peoples*, 36–59. Cambridge, UK: Cambridge University Press.

United Nations Permanent Forum on Indigenous Issues [UNPFII]. 2007. *The Declaration on the Rights of Indigenous Peoples*. http://daccess-dds-ny.un.org/doc/UNDOC/LTD/G06/125/71/PDF/G0612571.pdf?OpenElement.

Van Huevel, J. A. 1844. *El Dorado*. New York: J. Winchester.

Vidal, Beatriz, and Nancy Van Laan. 1991. *The Legend of El Dorado: A Latin American Tale*. New York: Knopf.

Vilches, Elvira. 2004. "Columbus's Gift: Representations of Grace and Wealth and the Enterprise of the Indies." *Modern Language Notes* 119: 201–25.

Wainwright, Joel, and Joe Bryan. 2009. "Cartography, Territory, Property: Postcolonial Reflections on Indigenous Counter-Mapping in Nicaragua and Belize." *Cultural Geographies* 16 (2): 153–78.

Walcott, Derek. 1974. "The Muse of History." In *"Is Massa Day Dead?": Black Moods in the Caribbean*, edited by O. Coombs, 1–28. New York: Anchor Books.

Wallerstein, Immanuel. 1976. *The Modern World-System I: Capitalist Agriculture and the Origins of the European World-Economy in the Sixteenth Century*. New York: Academic Press.

Warner-Lewis, Maureen. 2003. *Central Africa in the Caribbean: Transcending Time, Transforming Cultures.* Kingston, Jamaica: University of the West Indies Press.

Waswo, Richard. 1987. "The History That Literature Makes." *New Literary History* (Spring): 541–64.

Watler, John Alexander. [2003] 2004. *$ea Lotto.* Belmopan, Belize: Print Belize.

W *a-Wii-Wa: Amerindian Peoples Association Newsletter.* 2002. December 7.

Westmaas, Rory. 1970. "Building under Our Sun: An Essay on the Development of a Guyanese Architecture." In *Co-Operative Republic, Guyana 1970: A Study of Aspects of Our Way of Life,* edited by L. Searwear, 129–58. Georgetown: Government of Guyana.

Whitehead, Neil L. 1997. "The Discoverie as Enchanted Text." In *The Discoverie of the Large, Rich, and Bewtiful Empyre of Guiana,* 8–59. Norman: University of Oklahoma Press.

Wilks, Jennifer M. 2005. "Writing Home: Comparative Black Modernism and Form in Jean Toomer and Aimé Césaire." *Modern Fiction Studies* 51 (4): 801–823.

Williams, Brackette F. 1989. "A Class Act: Anthropology and the Race to Nation across Ethnic Terrain." *Annual Review of Anthropology* 18: 401–44.

———. 1991. *Stains on My Name, War in My Veins: Guyana and the Politics of Cultural Struggle.* Durham, N.C.: Duke University Press.

Williams, Eric. [1970] 1984. *From Columbus to Castro: The History of the Caribbean, 1492–1969.* New York: Vintage Books.

———. [1944] 1994. *Capitalism and Slavery.* Chapel Hill: The University of North Carolina Press.

Williams, Ian Griffith. 2002. "Revise 29:01." *Wa-Wii-Wa: Amerindian Peoples Association Newsletter.* December 7: 15–16.

Williams, Raymond. 1975. *The Country and the City.* London: Oxford University Press.

Williams, Robert A. Jr. 1990. *The American Indian in Western Legal Thought: The Discourses of Conquest.* New York: Oxford University Press.

Wilson, Samuel M., ed. 1997. *The Indigenous People of the Caribbean.* Gainesville: University Press of Florida.

Winn, Peter. 1992. *Americas: The Changing Face of Latin America and the Caribbean.* New York: Pantheon.

Wolfe, Patrick. 1999. *Settler Colonialism and the Transformation of Anthropology: The Politics and Poetics of an Ethnographic Event.* London: Cassell.

Wright, Michelle. 2004. *Becoming Black: Creating Identity in the African Diaspora.* Durham, N.C.: Duke University Press.

Wynter, Sylvia. 1970. "Jonkunnu in Jamaica: Towards the Interpretation of Folk Dance as a Cultural Process." *Jamaica Journal* 4 (2): 34–48.

———. 1972. "Creole Criticism—A Critique." *New World Quarterly* 5, no. 4: 12–36.

———. 1984. "The Ceremony Must Be Found: After Humanism." *Boundary 2* 12 (3): 19–70.

———. 1991. "Columbus and the Poetics of the *Propter Nos*." *Annals of Scholarship* 8 (2): 251 86.

———. 1995. "1492: A New World View." In *Race, Discourse and the Origin of the Americas: A New World View,* edited by V. L. H. a. R. Nettleford, 5–57. Washington, D.C.: Smithsonian Institute Press.

———. 1995. "'The Pope Must Have Been Drunk, The King of Castile a Madman': Culture as Actuality, and the Caribbean Rethinking Modernity." In *The Reordering of*

Culture: Latin America, the Caribbean and Canada, edited by A. Ruprecht, 17–42. Ottowa, Ontario, Canada: Carleton University Press.

———. 1997. "'A Different Kind of Creature': Caribbean Literature, The Cyclops Factor and the Second Poetics of the *Propter Nos." Annals of Scholarship* 12 (1&2): 153–72.

———. 2000. "Beyond Miranda's Meanings: Unsilencing the Demonic Ground of Caliban's Woman." In *The Black Feminist Reader,* edited by J. J. a. T. D. Sharpley-Whiting, 87–127. Malden, Mass.: Blackwell.

Young, Elspeth. 1995. *Third World in the First: Development and Indigenous Peoples.* New York: Routledge.

Young, Mathew French. 1998. *Guyana, The Lost El Dorado: A Report on My Work and Life Experiences in Guyana, 1925–1980.* Leeds, UK: Peepal Tree Press.

Index

Shona N. Jackson is associate professor of English at Texas A&M University. She works across the fields of Caribbean, black diaspora, indigenous, postcolonial, and transnational American studies.